*Fictions of Certitude*

# Fictions of Certitude

Science, Faith, and

the Search for Meaning,

1840–1920

JOHN S. HALLER JR.

THE UNIVERSITY OF ALABAMA PRESS

TUSCALOOSA

The University of Alabama Press
Tuscaloosa, Alabama 35487-0380
uapress.ua.edu

Typeface: Scala Pro, Adobe Caslon Pro

Cover image: Photography by (*clockwise from top left*) Artem Kniaz, Peter
Bucks, Luigi Boccardo, Adrienguh, and Tanner Mardis via Unsplash.com

Cover design: David Nees

Cataloging-in-Publication data is available from the Library of Congress.
ISBN: 978-0-8173-2053-9
E-ISBN: 978-0-8173-9286-4

In an intellectual age there can be no active interest which puts aside all hope of a vision of the harmony of truth.

—Alfred North Whitehead, *Science in the Modern World*, 1926

# Contents

# Acknowledgments

Those to whom I am indebted include Beth Motherwell, senior acquisitions editor for the natural sciences, with whom I initially corresponded; Claire Lewis Evans, who replaced Beth upon her retirement; project editor Kelly Finefrock-Creed; copyeditor Lisa Williams; and Daniel Waterman, editor in chief of the University of Alabama Press. These five individuals I wish to acknowledge for their unstinting commitment to my project, for their choice of outstanding readers, and for shepherding the manuscript through the necessary stages of production. To each I remain deeply appreciative. A special note of appreciation extends to the two anonymous readers of the manuscript. Each in his or her inimitable way provided me with excellent comments, criticism, and suggestions that opened my eyes to much-needed clarifications, revisions, and deeper analysis. To them I owe a special thanks. Others to whom I am indebted include colleagues David Wilson, Don Rice, Howard Allen, David Werlich, and John Dotson, all members of the Retired Old Men Eating Out (ROMEO) Club, where we discuss the university's problems absent our presence, and our individual projects, which range from photography to politics, history, and making music for local retirement homes and outdoor markets. Still others who have assisted me are the librarians and staff at Southern Illinois University Carbondale's Morris Library and its Special Collections Research Center, and JSTOR and Google Books, without which my research productivity would have been much curtailed.

As always, I am grateful to my wife, Robin, who offered inspiration, encouragement, criticism, and substantial assistance, including the reading of numerous drafts and indexing the finished manuscript. Those errors of fact or interpretation that remain are mine alone, and for them I take full responsibility.

*Fictions of Certitude*

# Introduction

IN HIS AUTOBIOGRAPHY, HISTORIAN HENRY Adams, the great-grandson of President John Adams, and grandson of John Quincy Adams, recounted that his Harvard education left him unprepared for the world his generation inherited, filled as that world was with uncertainty and any hard-and-fast assurance that his species had a special purpose in the universe. So pointed was his mockery of the generation's optimists, with their belief in a benevolent God and a world of infinite progression, that he concluded he "really did not care whether truth was, or was not, true [and did] not even care that it should be proved true, unless the process were new and amusing."[1] Adams resigned himself to what he perceived was the ever-quickening pace of change in a world of uncertainty and the bleakness of a vast and incomprehensible universe in which individual purpose had all but disappeared into the ether.

This book concerns the search for certitude among a select group of nineteenth-century American and European intellectuals whose reconstituted vision of the world raised the prospect of knowing too little to believe in God with the same intensity as the unconditioned faith of their forefathers. To explain this quest, the book examines the moral and judgmental efforts by nine members of the educated class (Auguste Comte, John Henry Newman, Herbert Spencer, Alfred Russel Wallace, Thomas Henry Huxley, John Fiske, William James, Lester Frank Ward, and Paul Carus), eight of whom claimed to be guardians of their culture outside the corpus of revealed religion. As guides bound by the collective wisdom of the past and hopeful of the power of the secular mind, they sought to devise an explanation whereby the structure of society as well as the habits and conduct of human beings could be shaped for the better. For these sons of Prometheus, their hopes grew dim when, minus confidence in the *sola scriptura* which answered to the *why*, they witnessed the imperfect ushering in of a world whose secularized sciences offered to explain only the *how* of things.

As a historian, I chose the individuals in this study based on two principal factors. The first was my intent to identify several European intellectuals who embraced the possibility of change without the baneful consequences predicted by Edmund Burke, and whose ideas, with the exception of John Henry Newman, were derivative of science in the broadest sense in that they appealed to human reason rather than to divinely appointed authority. My second purpose was to identify a small number

of American counterparts whose cosmic theories stood on scientific, utilitarian, and rationalistic grounds, and whose liberal thinking sought to
secure a social environment free of dogma and irrational restraints on individual rights. Those chosen were believers in a covenant-driven nation
whose "American God" arrived prepackaged in what John Dewey called
A Common Faith formulated out of a combination of liberal republican
political ideologies, commonsense moral reasoning, and providential
destiny.[2]

In reading the published works and papers of these nine intellectuals,
we learn they belonged to an age whose own world was passing, and another, hardly yet distinguishable but endowed with unprecedented gifts
and insights, was rising to take its place. It this new world the divinities
of science and technology were reshaping patterns of life that had for centuries been patched together with furtive theological stitching. The myriad of discoveries that occurred in the century, including Faraday's elec-
tromagnetic induction, Joule's law of conservation of energy, Pasteur's
germ theory, religion's fascination with the higher criticism, Darwin's
and Wallace's theory of evolution by natural selection, and Planck's work
on quantum theory, had shaken society of its most deep-seated beliefs
and authority. While noted members of this educated class such as John
Henry Newman and William James admitted to having more faith than
skepticism, others like Lester Ward confessed to being destitute of faith
and troubled by skepticism.[3]

Belief is a humbling prospect that demands answers if not dutiful explanations. If beliefs are acquired through culture, family, schools, and a
host of other experiences, are the words "I know," "I believe," "I am sure,"
and "I am confident" simply the outcome of living in that culture? Does
belief rely on propositions that lie outside the test of verification? Does
belief open or close dialogue? Is doubt an indispensable component of
belief? Is belief without doubt of equal value to belief with doubt? Is there
an ethical or moral imperative for belief to require evidence? Can belief
be genuine without being objectively certain? Depending on the answers
to these questions, one is left with the prospect of believing propositions
with or without evidence, making an intellectual commitment incommensurate with the evidence, suspending judgment entirely, or remaining without faith.[4]

In his The Ethics of Belief (1877), mathematician William K. Clifford argued that every unjustified belief, regardless of its triviality, was an endangerment to society because of the mind's propensity to favor more of
the same. To guard the purity of belief, he urged patient investigation and

testing. Nothing should be taken for granted or given a pass on insufficient evidence. Like Locke before him, Clifford insisted that one's degree of commitment ought not to exceed the evidence. All knowledge, whether scientific, philosophical, or religious, was discernible in a concise and exhaustive manner through natural laws rather than from unquantifiable a priori or intuitive thought. Those on the other side of this equation believed that the vital issues of life and being existed outside the scope of rational science. The most-complete knowledge came from a unitary or universal science consisting of sense, reason, and wisdom. The laws governing the natural and spiritual worlds were one, and in either realm the laws were equally and effectually operative. There were two discrete realms, one material, the other spiritual, with the human as the connecting link. On one side was the supersensible realm; the other belonged to the sensible. The transition from one to the other was a matter not of distance but of vision.[5]

The popular tagline "crisis of faith" commonly refers to the beginnings of doubt among the late nineteenth-century British and American middle class regarding what was written in the book of Genesis. Over time, this "crisis" became its own article of faith, although, on reflection, it seemed heavily overdrawn in its simplicity. Initially attributed to theories in the physical sciences, especially geology, it reflected a multitude of secularizing tendencies manifesting themselves within the wider culture. However, Helmstadter and Lightman's *Victorian Faith in Crisis: Essays on Continuity and Change in Nineteenth-Century Religious Belief* (1990) raised the question of whether there really *was* a crisis of faith and, if so, was it what we thought it to be?[6]

Christianity's flawed credibility in the light of the higher criticism was one of several trials that shattered the century's paradigmatic sense of self and society. Using a branch of literary analysis that investigated the origin of ancient texts by purely historical-critical methods, the higher criticism played a major role in undermining scripture's relevance in the modern world. Applied initially by a group of German biblical scholars centered in Tübingen, and later reinforced by Strauss's *Life of Jesus Critically Examined* (1845) and Renan's *Life of Jesus* (1863), it relegated Christianity's pious writings to human origin with a high probability for error. Advances in anthropological and archaeological studies, along with geological findings, and philology with its emphasis on the comparison of the historical states of different languages and literature, cast suspicion on Christianity's long-held explanations for Creation, the Deluge, the Messiah, and the Resurrection. With this scholarship came skepticism, agnosticism, and the equally strong dose of materialism that deflected working- and middle-class families from organized religion.

This paradigmatic change was in stark contrast to the preceding age, where, as Episcopal theologian Henry S. Nash explained, Christian religion had made man at home in the universe by "bringing the heart of God within the heart of man," and where faith provided the answers to life's enigmatic questions by unfolding a spiritual path that brought conviction to those who doubted, and righteousness to those whose actions lacked rational justification.[7] Grounded in church authority and revelation, religion became a sanctuary from the punishing temptations of the secular world, whose materialism and scientific-rationalist interpretations of life and the universe left a sense of unfulfillment with more questions than answers.[8]

In nineteenth-century England, religious doubt weighed heavily among all classes as they came of age. In his *Victorian Doubt: Literary and Cultural Discourses* (1990), Lance St. John Butler distinguished between belief and doubt, pointing out as had Tennyson in his *In Memoriam* ("There lives more faith in honest doubt, / Believe me, than in half the creeds") and Oscar Wilde in *The Picture of Dorian Gray* ("Skepticism is the beginning of Faith") that ever since the higher criticism coming from Germany, and Huxley's use of the term *agnostic*, belief was no longer the norm, and disbelief a variation. Doubt was not itself a denial of faith, but rather a more complex human response to God's absence in the world. Butler referred to Leslie Stephen's *Agnostic's Apology* (1876) and Arthur Balfour's *Defence of Philosophic Doubt* (1879) as examples of the consequences of scientific discovery versus unquestioned belief in God and immortality. Nearly every Victorian had to make accommodations.[9]

Similarly, Timothy Larsen, author of *Crisis of Doubt: Honest Faith in Nineteenth-Century England* (2006), argued that the focus on doubt distorted the Victorian attitude toward faith, which all social classes valued. He depicted doubt or disenchantment as the natural outcome of intellectual inquiry, a response that typically precipitated some form of intellectual reflection and response. This, he insisted, differed from the so-called crisis of faith popularized by Susan Budd's *Varieties of Unbelief* (1977) and A. N. Wilson's *God's Funeral* (1999).[10] In his examination of seven case studies of Victorian working-class intellectuals, Larsen found faith and doubt to be legitimate outcomes of intellectual inquiry, with many doubters eventually "reconverting" to their original beliefs.[11] As John Henry Newman noted, "Ten thousand difficulties do not make one doubt, as I understand the subject; difficulty and doubt are incommensurate."[12]

Any discussion of the relationship between science and religion prior to the mid-nineteenth century requires numerous clarifications regarding content, methods, assumptions, and potentially disputed boundaries.[13] The word *science* is a modern term without an ancient equivalency, a factor that strongly challenges any genealogical relationship to Aristotle's "speculative sciences": metaphysics, mathematics, and natural philosophy. Not until the mid-nineteenth century did the conditions that generated the connection between the study of nature and notions of God undergo a transformation away from God's purposes, intentions, and messages to man.[14] The fact that the term was not coined until 1833, by William Whewell, the Cambridge mathematician and philosopher, and not actually adopted for another several decades, suggests that the birth of science came with the emergence of professional bodies like the British Association for the Advancement of Science and other similar organizations that removed the control of admission away from the clergy and into the hands of narrow groups of disciplinary specialists.[15]

Until then, science's many champions pursued what was more correctly labeled *natural philosophy* or *natural history*. This fact cannot be ignored when attempting to explain the historical relationship, much less the supposed warfare, between science and religion, for, if true, it upends the histories of John Draper and Andrew Dickson White, whose notions of a conflict collapse for lack of discrete spheres of beliefs and practices. Natural history and natural philosophy entailed far different understandings of nature and were motivated by sets of beliefs substantively different from what came to be understood as science in the modern world. "This was particularly so in England," explained Peter Harrison in the *Journal of Religion*, "where up until the mid-nineteenth century natural history was internally ordered according to the theological principle of design."[16] Science and religion were not independent entities competing for the world's stage but inextricably connected in their common pursuits.

Many of those who studied the natural world in the early nineteenth century did so by relying on deductive methodologies of the German School of *Naturphilosophie*, or nature philosophy, most notably the writings of Goethe and Lorenz Oken, who built belief on the prospect of the immutability of species. Each species was a product of the Creator's thought. Its *systema naturae* was no artificial human creation, but a reflection of the distinct thoughts of the Creator. The confidence extended toward science and its community of natural philosophers was one of cautious optimism, a belief that science worked as an integral part of humanity's moral purposes to sustain conviction. Natural philosophers were ready expositors of the harmony existing between science and religion. Even those among them who took a distinctly secular route to certitude and practiced their science separate from religion understood that their methods worked parallel with religion and under the same designing hand of the Creator. True science, even when left to its own devices and unguided by religious truths, found a path back to religion, the glory of creation, and the benevolence of the Creator.

The inclusion of science in the search for certitude had the effect of freeing religion from biblical literalism as the sole manifestation of the Bible's transcendent truths. The combined science/religion approach neutralized the staking of certitude on scripture alone, the fear of punishment, or the hope of reward in the afterlife. It opened the door to a combination of utilitarianism, the model of Jesus's life, and the presumption of a teleology implanted in the natural world that justified faith from Design. Depending on its relative weight in the equation, science either subordinated faith to the certainty of science or was itself subordinated to the certainty of religion.

The rapidity with which Robert Chambers's *Vestiges of the Natural History of Creation* (1844), Herbert Spencer's *Social Statics* (1851), and even Charles Darwin's *Origin of Species* (1859) assimilated into Victorian culture was evidence of how quickly the intellectual world welcomed evolution as a new and innovative method for understanding the modern world. God's Word and God's Works were deemed to be twin facets of the same truth. Such a relationship was manifested in William Paley's *Natural Theology* (1802), which emphasized the argument of design. The same harmony between science and faith mediated by natural theology applied to the *Bridgewater Treatises on the Power of Wisdom and Goodness of God as Manifested in the Creation* (1833–1836) as well.[17]

Unlike those evolutionary and Lamarckian theorists who preceded him, Darwin introduced a purely naturalistic account of development, separating science from religion—not by attacking it, but by ignoring its relevance. Concepts such as geological change and species variation turned from arguments of harmonious and divinely ordained change for each species of plant and animal, to one of impermanence and chance variability, neither of which was tied to religion or the argument of Design. Essentially religion had become immaterial to Darwin's assumptions and implications. The quest for certainty, unity, or at least some level of cosmic comfort, which had been on the front burner of Western philosophy since the Greeks, and through which the Western mind transmitted its central myths, fell before the randomness of a chance universe.[18]

While Darwin's inductive method considered the varieties of species to be the products of chance, time, and circumstance, most of his contemporaries shied away from its stark dysteleology, choosing instead some form of design that varied from the preconceived and providential God of Asa Gray, the Spiritualism and Higher Intelligence of Alfred Russel Wallace, the agnosticism of Herbert Spencer, the law-bound cosmos of Thomas Henry Huxley, and the pragmatic and novel universe of William James. Despite Darwin's law-bound system of matter in motion, his contemporaries looked to a middle ground that would preserve some semblance of order and predictability.

From the safety of Down House in rural Kent, Darwin watched converts won and lost as alliances were packaged and politicized around the terms "Darwinist," "Darwinism," and "Social Darwinism." Though he took a deeply personal interest in those who supported or criticized his theory, he chose to insulate himself from the public side of controversy while corresponding with his strongest disciples and sharing with them his concerns for those who failed to make clear their endorsement of his theory.[19] A tactician who remained behind the scenes, he knew how to use his friends for his own purposes, negotiating the reception of the *Origin* and its theory of natural selection within the currents of scientific acceptability then taking place. His home became a beehive of international correspondence concerning the application of his theory and the machinery that catapulted evolutionary ideas into the marketplace of ideas. With friends like Joseph Hooker at the Royal Botanic Gardens at Kew, Asa Gray at Harvard, and geologist Charles Lyell, he orchestrated a virtual transformation in Victorian thinking, albeit within limits.

Darwin chose to live his professional life in relative seclusion, but his thoughts and written words were continually examined and became topics of intense scrutiny. His work, though not itself a matter of metaphysics, opened minds to new and developing philosophical tendencies, making less plausible the claims of natural theology, including arguments from Design and man's uniqueness. As explained by philosopher John Passmore, Darwin "helped to extend scientific procedures into fields where they had seemed to be quite inapplicable and to bridge that gulf between man and animal which had once been assumed to be unbridgeable."[20]

Taking a backward glance into Darwin's life and times, one cannot escape observing an enormous amount of rummaging into his writings by scholars looking for signs of ambivalence or hesitation that might suggest some modicum of religious belief, however slight. Keith Thomson's

*The Young Charles Darwin* (2009) and E. Manier's *The Young Darwin and His Cultural Circle* (1978) limited their narratives to the years leading up to the 1859 publication of the *Origin*, showing his indebtedness to others. Included among Darwin's circle of friends was the strong Comtean positivistic outlook, the importance of which applied to the use of hypotheses on the role of prediction in scientific theories.[21] Neal Gillespie concluded in his *Charles Darwin and the Problem of Creation* (1979) that while interest in the *Origin* was as "a harbinger of a new positive biology," it was also "one of the last theoretical works of science to be significantly dependent on theology for the force of any part of its argument."[22] Similarly, James R. Moore in his *The Post-Darwinian Controversies* (1979) made clear that there was a deep affinity between the norms of science and Protestant thought. In his study of twenty-eight Christian authors, Moore explained that Darwin's theory of evolution by natural selection was formed around a cosmology with debts to the doctrines of creation and providence, and was therefore consistent with traditional ideas of theism.[23] Finally, Daniel C. Dennett's *Darwin's Dangerous Idea: Evolution and the Meanings of Life* (1997) explained how the idea of evolution by natural selection unified the realm of life, meaning, and purpose in the realms of space and time, cause and effect, mechanism and physical law. It was a mindless and uncaring process that, like some "universal acid," eventually transformed all aspects of life.[24]

Darwin's legacy is weighted with religious implications and context, and his tendency to substitute words in each new edition of the *Origin* only added fuel to the fire. Evidence suggests a steady drift in Darwin from youthful orthodoxy, much of it built upon Paley's *Natural Theology*,[25] to the beginnings of doubt while at Cambridge,[26] to deism evidenced during his five-year voyage on the H.M.S. *Beagle*, to reticent agnosticism and materialistic atheism in his later years.[27] In writing to Asa Gray in 1860, he expressed his personal sense of bewilderment with nature. Though he may have wanted a beneficent God to govern the world, he could find no comfort in what he saw in nature. "I feel most deeply that the whole subject is too profound for the human intellect. A dog might as well speculate on the mind of Newton. Let each man hope and believe what he can." One suspects that his public face was more positive than what science informed him and what, in his heart, he had concluded. Still, Darwin's rejection of the Christian God did not include rejection of some minimal theistic belief, if only to suggest a hypothetical intelligent First Cause—a position he ultimately abandoned as unprovable and therefore untrustworthy as a final judgment.[28]

Restrained from metaphysical speculation and cautious in temperament, Darwin avoided discussion of "Final Cause," "Providence," "Higher Intelligence," and "Design." Equally significant, he avoided any application of his theory to humankind until his *Descent of Man* in 1871. Nevertheless, his scientific hypothesis lent itself to philosophical interpretations that Spencer and others extended to competing forms of moral and social philosophy, including economic and political thought. In effect, the human organism's happiness became an inseparable aspect of life as it evolved in both differentiated and integrated ways. Attention now formed around the inheritance of acquired characteristics and the importance of understanding the natural consequences of one's behavior.

All claims to Darwin's ultimate position remained tentative due to his refusal to take any public stand other than his confession to Gray that he remained "in a hopeless muddle"[29] and his admission to being an agnostic ("The mystery of the beginning of all things is insoluble by us; and I for one must be content to remain an agnostic").[30] His acolytes, however, found in his revisions to the *Origin* signs of a progressive tendency in the evolutionary process. And if not specific, Darwin's lack of certainty opened the door for this interpretation. Darwin rejected the traditional conception of a providential God and the argument from Design, but his reluctance to pronounce any final judgment led others to find positions somewhere between lukewarm theism and a reticent agnosticism.

The same prescientific mythology that dominated so much of traditional Christianity migrated into evolutionary theory with promises of inevitable material and spiritual progress for its believers. Science had "spoken," and a new scientific religiosity revealed a world coming together in optimistic belief. To understand God was to understand evolution, which meant progress and happiness.[31] The fact that Darwin's *Origin* was endorsed in both secular and religious teleologies challenges the depiction of evolutionary theory as a symbol of the separation of science and religion. To be sure, Darwin put traditional natural theology to the sword, but he opened nature to a cosmological revolution from individuals who simply replaced biblical revelations with evolution's values, purposes, and novelties.[32] What Darwinists like Gray[33] chose to accept, and what Wallace and even Huxley identified as "pure Darwinism,"[34] involved meanings that worked at cross-purposes to Darwin's intent. Even though Darwin differed from them, he refused to break with his entourage of supporters, settling for less-than-expected accommodation for no other reason than to retain their support. The *Origin* proved to be more disruptive than anticipated among evolution's proponents who showed their admiration for

Darwin, albeit without committing to the consequences of his mechanism of natural selection.[35]

Darwin's strongest supporters contributed multiple levels of understanding. This included Alfred Wallace, who distinguished between man's physical and mental evolution; Benjamin Kidd and Arabella Buckley, who gave evolution a spiritualist and non-Christian overtone; Asa Gray, Lyman Abbott, George Henslow, Henry Ward Beecher, Joseph Cook, and Charles Kingsley, for whom evolution explained God's method in creation; and Josiah Royce at Harvard, James Edwin Creighton, and Frank Thilly at Cornell, Henry Drummond, John Fiske, Teilhard de Chardin, Alfred North Whitehead, Henry Bergson, Conway Lloyd Morgan, and Samuel Alexander, whose idealistic interpretations envisaged an emergent evolution. They also included George John Romanes, who transformed evolution into a "tenuous theism,"[36] and St. George Jackson Mivart, a transcendental Catholic Tory, who maintained that "the prevalence of this theory [of evolution] need harm no one, for it is, without any doubt, perfectly consistent with the strictest and most orthodox Christian theology."[37]

On balance, Darwin seemed more comfortable with those who gave evolution a cosmic or spiritual motif than those avowed or militant atheists like Edward Aveling, Robert G. Ingersoll, Carl Vogt, and the Prussian naturalist Ernst Haeckel, who approached the topic as radical freethinkers. Clearly, the relationship between the godlessness of Darwin's theory of natural selection and those seeking to soften it by suggesting some form of directive agency was overplayed by parties on both sides, especially those intent on blunting the growing acceptance of reductionist thinking as the rightful heir to the a priori claims of religion. Nevertheless, the age was one of many compromises, as individuals insisted on being more than the outcome of a chance universe.[38] As explained by D. H. Meyer, the Victorians "were perhaps the last generation among English-speaking intellectuals able to believe that man was capable of understanding his universe, just as they were the first generation collectively to suspect that he never would."[39]

In his *Free Religion: An American Faith* (1947), Stow Persons referred to the late nineteenth century as "an age of restatements," meaning that matters of faith, belief, and certitude, where the clergy once claimed exclusive ownership, were now in the hands of secular experts using the tools of the emerging social sciences to interpret the world and humanity's place in it.[40] It is wrong, therefore, to presume a war between science and religion. Instead, there was the recontextualization of faith, belief, and doubt in ways that were much more nuanced than originally thought possible. That the term *God* was replaced with Spencer's "Unknown," Ward's "telesis," and Wallace's "Higher Intelligence" suggests that a new secular language had been introduced to explain the denominational issues surrounding determinism and free will, faith and good works, the structure of the universe, man's place in the universe, and the meaning of progress. The combination of old and new terminology exposed telltale signs that science and religion were by no means in irrevocable conflict.

Besides the presumed challenges coming from the sciences, the once sturdy optimism that had been a hallmark of the early Victorians crumbled when elected and appointed leaders of the modern state failed to produce the benefits they had promised. Classical economics and its corollary belief in the natural depravity of the "vicious poor" were moral truths preached from the pulpits and taught in the schools. Sadly, in the harshness of religion's social conscience, many mainline denominations lost large segments of the laboring classes from their pews, leaving ministers with the dubious luxury of speaking to a singularly homogeneous group of middle- and upper-middle-class believers. Accused of being mercenaries for capitalism and willing participants in the social crisis, the clergy had little in common with the plight of the laborer, and even less with the poor.

With the dwarfing of the individual in the new industrial state came the stripping away of individual autonomy, substituting in its stead the routine of factory life, faceless oligarchies, and an industrial world experiencing multiple depressions, territorial expansion, concentrated economic power, labor disputes and lockouts, race prejudice, and maldistribution of wealth. A broad sense of alienation enveloped this period before the painful realization that industrial democracy was far different from the agrarian was acknowledged. Now economic leadership lay in the hands of a class of plutocrats capable of buying and selling influence in ways that permanently affected the body politic and its moral leadership. The emergence of industrial society brought in its wake a new working class and early signs of industrial strife—disturbing changes that questioned time-honored values.

The economic individualism, political localism, and broad sectarian diversity that once marked the nation's democratic experiment weakened perceptibly during this period, leaving large pockets of disenfranchised workers struggling in their impotence to understand the nature of their plight, and its solution. Henry George, whom John Dewey described as "one of the world's great philosophers," awakened society to the inequities that overshadowed the working classes with his introduction of the single-tax theory and its consequences.[41] Acknowledging the issues and loathing the injustices, George and his proponents became trumpeters of reform, fighting for what they thought was common sense and common decency. Setting out to broaden democracy, they warned that without substantive reform, the nation might sink under the weight of its long-standing problems.

Other events impacted as well on the quest for certitude. The Columbian Exposition of 1893 in Chicago, a large trade fair celebrating the four hundredth anniversary of the discovery of the New World, represented both a celebration of the West's current dominance and a bellwether challenge marking the survival of the fittest as the test of future greatness. Presented as a utopian depiction of Western civilization, the Exposition contrasted the material triumphs of the Western world against portrayals of North African villages, camel rides, bazaars, and spectacles of primitive cultures complete with native peoples. The Exposition was not just a representation of Western material achievements; it stood on the notion of the Caucasian's ascendency over the savage, half-civilized, and bankrupt civilizations of the Old World. Mimicking this solipsism two decades later, Henry Adams remarked, "[American] Society offered the profile of a long, straggling caravan stretching loosely toward the prairies, its few scores of leaders far in advance and its millions of immigrants, negroes [sic], and Indians far in the rear, somewhere in archaic time."[42]

Concurrent with the Exposition was the World's Parliament of Religions, whose Christian delegates heard emotionally charged critiques against their negative view of the human race and the myriad of cloaked prejudices that accompanied their foreign missions. Besides being the first global gathering of its kind in the modern world, the parliament shifted the marginally understood history and culture of Asia into the forefront of global thinking with its focus on science, evolution, industrialization, colonialism, imperialism, comparative religions, and racism. Those Asian delegates who had been educated in missionary schools and acquainted with the inclinations of the West's bigotry and condescension had no qualms providing graphic descriptions of Western society's weaknesses. As Brahman layman B. B. Nagarkar of Bombay observed, the delegates from the West "with their conqueror's pride . . . cannot bring themselves to practice the humility which they preach."[43] Similar remarks came from Vivekananda, the representative of Jainism and admirer of Emerson, who criticized Christian missionaries for building churches instead of distributing food to famine-starved populations. "How much more effective would Christian missionaries be if they taught religion instead of dogmas, and love of truth instead of blind faith?"[44]

The parliament meant different things to different people—then and now. Many denominations refused to send delegates, for fear of corrupting their own religious principles. For those who did attend, most chose to see it as one of the most extraordinary events of the post-Enlightenment and of international significance for generations to come, in that it laid the foundation for a unifying global paradigm. By contrast, religious historians Sydney Ahlstrom, Edwin Gaustad, Martin Marty, and Sidney Mead preferred to interpret the parliament and its congresses as laying the groundwork for a pluralistic approach to religion, rather than one of unity. On the other hand, Protestant missionaries viewed the parliament as an interesting but momentary event that would soon be forgotten. Then again, Paul Carter claimed the parliament acted as an incentive for comparative religious studies and signaled the finale to a century of schisms, while Rick Fields's *How the Swans Came to the Lake* (1980) and Carl T. Jackson's *The Oriental Religions and American Thought* (1981) suggested that the parliament offered the first opportunity for Asians to speak publicly and in their own words. Before returning to their native countries, many embarked on speaking tours, where they continued to reinforce the message that their religions were not only in step with modernity but fully tailored to the West's vision of evolution as the mechanism for human progress.[45]

Of the 216 addresses given at the parliament, 41 were by Asian delegates, including Hindus, Buddhists, Confucians, Zoroastrians, Jains, and Shintos, along with Asian Christians and Theosophists. The sessions of the Psychical Science Congress, along with the Theosophical Congress, elevated the public's understanding of Spiritualism, psychical research, and the progressive nature of Theosophy with its advocacy of reform as a natural outcome of progressive evolutionary forces. The sessions included discussion of telepathy, clairvoyance, and other psychical abilities. It seemed to many attendees that the age of blind belief and obedience was drawing to a close. Dogma no longer sufficed to nourish the soul.[46] Thus began a discourse suggesting that Buddhism, rather than Christianity, best suited the needs of the emerging scientific world. While Christianity continued to struggle with existential challenges resulting from the higher criticism and the unintended consequences of natural selection, Buddhism encountered the world with a sophisticated set of beliefs that minimized the tensions arising from the creeping effects of Western hegemony. As noted by David L. McMahan, "perhaps no major tradition attempted to adopt scientific discourse more vigorously than Buddhism."[47]

All things considered, the parliament turned out to be "a great surprise to the world," a spectacle of dramatic proportions bringing the most powerful religions into the same tent while smaller religions entered if not on a level of equality, then at least one of forbearance.[48] Unfortunately, the world was not yet ready for the ideals expressed among the assembled delegates, a situation caused in no small measure by Pius X's encyclical *Pascendi Dominici Gregis* (1907) which condemned *modernism*, meaning the movement that reduced revealed truths (Trinity, Incarnation, Redemption, Holy Eucharist, etc.) to a natural dimension. To ensure the demise of this "synthesis of all heresies," Pius X required an oath from all Catholic clergy and teachers in theological seminaries opposing any union of Catholicism and Rationalism.[49]

No longer able to square the unfolding of new discoveries with the broken pieces of Christian dogma, the scientific, literary, and philosophical thinkers of the day turned their personal anguish into an ethical undertaking to discover a substitute set of standards applicable to the secular world.

Chapter 1 introduces the philosophy of positivism, a term that Auguste Comte coined and popularized. At its core was a vision of linear progress and the eventual triumph of science over the delusional promises offered by theology and metaphysics. Despite considerable digressions and bizarre behavior that distracted him from his task, Comte laid out the rules and conditions for the pursuit of knowledge essential for humanity's future. Having borne witness to the final days of the ancien régime, he was arguably the first philosopher of science in the modern sense of the term. He not only influenced the work of Marx, Mill, Martineau, and Spencer but through his disciples presaged much of the religious and secular humanism of the nineteenth and twentieth centuries.

Comte's positivism became one of the key buttresses of Social Darwinism and the restoration of certainty amidst the strains affecting the political, social, and moral issues of the period. A key contributor in the development of sociology as a discipline, he replaced intuitionist knowledge of a providential God with a psychological, practical, and ameliorative alternative, namely, a Religion of Humanity—a secular church that was political, utopian, conservative, and temporal. Convinced that Christianity had lost its moral compass, Comte substituted empirical facts and materialistic principles for theological fictions.[50]

With his goal of creating a society that could endure change and stability through a proper explanation of the past and scientific analysis and predictability of the future, Comte set forth his science of "social physics" (later renamed "sociology"), which began with the premise that "every theory must be based upon observed facts [and] that facts cannot be observed without the guidance of some theory." To this he added the admonition that all phenomena were subject to natural laws and that the business of science was "to analyze accurately the circumstances of phenomena, and to connect them by the natural relations of succession and resemblance."[51]

Representing an exaggerated organicism in American political thought, Comtean sociology became the intellectual cornerstone for the subsequent work of Lester Frank Ward, Albion Small, Edward Alsworth Ross, Herbert Croly, and others seeking to reconstruct American public life along the lines of progressivism.[52]

Chapter 2 examines the life and writings of theologian, poet, and priest John Henry Newman, whose place in Roman Catholicism was best demonstrated by his beatification by Pope Benedict XVI on September 19, 2010. A self-absorbed but sensitive recluse, he exhibited an artist's imagination for the coherence and beauty of the universe by leading a diffident band of High Anglican reformers to discover a "middle way" between freethinking and the moral authority of the Anglican Church. Knowledge of God came not from reason alone, but reason aided by grace. Even natural religion, as distinct from revealed religion, required some level of revelation. One of the few intellectuals not disposed to scholasticism and Thomism, Newman was a singularly independent thinker whose approach to spiritual truth through intuition made him more mystic than skeptic.

Religion demanded more than an assent to its truths; it required certitude that came by way of inference, rather than by rational or logical propositions. The accumulation of probabilities, each independent of the other but arising out of circumstances peculiar to the case under review, enabled the individual to become certain of that which was conditional. "Without certitude in religious faith there may be much decency of profession and of observance, but there can be no habit of prayer, no directness of devotion, no intercourse with the unseen, no generosity of self-sacrifice."[53] Certitude was reachable only to the degree that the individual surrendered the right to analyze his or her faith. Essentially, faith occurred to those willing to relinquish the keys protecting their private conscience to the authority of the apostolic chair. The very freedoms that gave Newman his reputation within the Oxford Movement and the Roman Church were silenced with his elevation to the rank of cardinal, abdicating reason for a conclave of priests.

Chapter 3 explores the unshakable social conscience of Herbert Spencer, an English philosopher, sociologist, and classical liberal theorist who for a time enjoyed a reputation that rivaled Darwin's. His unification theory applied evolutionary theory to the fields of biology, philosophy, psychology, and sociology, giving currency to a universal or cosmic movement from the simple to the complex, from the less to the more coherent, from the homogeneous to the heterogeneous, from the indefinite to the definite, from the confused to the ordered.

A dogmatist, he did not hesitate to look on inductive reasoning as the great unifier of natural phenomena, explaining the universe and its laws with a degree of conviction that rivaled the most orthodox believer. Scientific knowledge, constructed from a combination of empirical facts and the certainty of sensory perceptions, embraced a cosmological worldview that connected the myriads of individual facts and observations to a singular overarching law. His erudite and staggering accumulation of data transformed him into a conservative pundit set on maintaining the status quo. His public philosophy, a careful linking of the disciplines with his philosophical speculations and predictions of the future, nurtured the importance of organisms to continually adjust to their environment.

Spencer pursued his interests devoid of any sentiment for the human spirit. "He seems to have no feeling for the traditional, social, and personal elements that enter so largely into art and literature and therefore no sense of the need of culture and sympathy in passing judgment upon them," observed Charles H. Cooley.[54] He not only lacked but purposely avoided having direct and authentic understanding of the phenomena he considered understandable by analogy or by his singularly speculative impulses. Lamarckism was the jumping-off point for both Comte and Spencer, who not only accepted a unilinear concept of social evolution but predicted a sequence of social and intellectual progress through distinct stages. The inheritance of acquired characteristics fit nicely into their intellectual framework.[55]

Chapter 4 recounts the life and contributions of Alfred Russel Wallace, a self-educated genius who began a hobby of collecting plants while working as a surveyor for his brother. During the seven years he spent surveying the districts of England and Wales required by the Commutation of Tithes Act of 1836 and the General Enclosure Act of the commons, he learned the laws pertaining to public and private property and the degree to which the lives of his fellow Englishmen had been affected by the injustices that forced many off the common land into towns and cities to seek their living.

After spending eight years in the Malay Archipelago, Wallace shared with Darwin his views on the mechanism of evolution, establishing joint ownership of the theory of natural selection. Like Darwin, he had observed variations within the same species and distinctive traits inherited by their offspring. Like Darwin, too, he remembered Malthus's essay on population and the concept of survival of the fittest. A spiritualist, he believed that the human brain and mind evolved differently from the lower species, and he spent much of his life attempting to reconcile natural selection with the existence of a higher being. As a formidable controversialist, his writings included a variety of topics—from vaccination and socialism to man's place in the universe. There was a persistent interdependency of Wallace's social issues with those that were scientific. Unsatisfied with the scientist's emphasis on the "how," he chose to ask the philosopher's "why," a choice that gave him entrée into the role of volition and the coherence he saw in the purpose behind the world's existence.

Wallace reasoned that a teleological process coexisted with natural selection, meaning that certain changes in the human species were conditioned by a supposed spiritualist substratum that directed conscious and unconscious life outside of natural selection. Included in this world of spirit were laws of gravitation, electricity, cohesion, chemical force and radiant force, all working towards a "grand, consistent whole."[56]

Wallace avoided allegiance to doctrinal and ecclesiastical artifices as irrelevant to the existence of a Higher Intelligence. Not all theists were spiritualists, but Wallace most certainly included Spiritualism in his worldview. His was not a discourse framed in theology; rather, it was a form of metaphysical and scientific discourse that linked nature and God in an interplay of purposes.[57]

Chapter 5 introduces the brilliant biologist and expositor Thomas Henry Huxley, whose defense of Darwin's theory of evolution indelibly stamped him as "Darwin's bulldog." Notwithstanding the title, Huxley conveyed to audiences very little that explained Darwin's naturalistic, nondirectional, and nonprogressive perspective. While his evolutionary message to popular audiences spoke glowingly of Darwin and his theory, he deliberately chose to avoid discussing the particulars of natural selection. By the same token, he refused to countenance the a priori wisdom of religious orthodoxy, considering its authority unreasonable and in conflict with freethinking. Instead, he joined a network of highly collaborative positivists, scientific naturalists, theological liberals, Protestant nonconformists, and secular intellectuals to oppose the authoritarian politics of the Anglican Church.

Huxley's aversion to existing "isms" (i.e., naturalism, idealism, Spiritualism, positivism, and materialism) led him to identify himself as an agnostic on those matters that reason and experience could not prove. If all that can be known is phenomena, then the argument that matter underlay the data of sensation was without a rational basis. So too was the argument for God's existence. The term *agnostic* represented his recognition of the limits of human thought. While Huxley considered agnosticism an admission of ignorance about ultimate things, he nonetheless placed trust in "the constancy of the order of nature," a condition that stood apart from Darwin's theory of natural selection.[58]

Chapter 6 recounts the life of John Fiske. As the popularizer of Spencer's ideas in the United States, he articulated a philosophy that satisfied the nation's desire to learn how best to align itself with the providential laws and purposes of evolutionary theory. A religious radical in his youth who mellowed over time as he acquired the gravitas of a Protestant intellectual, Fiske built a career inside and outside the academic world by helping Americans understand and accommodate to the intellectual changes of the century.

Fiske enlarged the Christian conception of God from an anthropomorphic being to an infinitely eternal force "incapable of being conceived by the human mind; a being of whom the cosmos is but a phenomenal manifestation."[59] His understanding of evolutionary theory was very much influenced by Wallace, who spoke of man's mental powers as having originated in a second stage of evolution that operated in a manner fundamentally different from the utilitarian struggle for existence. Like Spencer and Wallace, Fiske affirmed a superior force behind evolution that provided both unity and direction. He also offered an extension to their ideas without following Spencer into the Unknown or Wallace into the speculative world of Spiritualism.

Fiske was a behemoth of a man who enjoyed good health, preferred to work in a cold room, and drank several quarts of beer a day while smoking a pipe. He was a good-natured, genial man who was at ease in all sorts of speculations. Although his *Outlines of Cosmic Philosophy* won him recognition abroad, his adaptation of evolutionary theory to American history won him the greatest acclaim at home.

Chapter 7 introduces the life of William James, a philosopher whose writings reflected a change in the tempo of intellectual life following the Civil War, marking an end to the somnambulant world of Emerson's "American Scholar." James attended the Lawrence Scientific School at Harvard, then Harvard Medical School, where he earned his medical degree in 1869, although he never practiced medicine. Instead, he chose to teach physiology and psychology during the heyday of Charles Eliot's presidency.

Having set out on a course of scientific education, James eventually allowed his father's eccentric view of science to intercede in his own vision, taking him far from a purely scientific view of chemistry, anatomy, physiology, and medicine. He learned much from Eliot's chemistry and the physiological topics of Edouard Brown-Séquard and Oliver Wendell Holmes. But his discussions with colleagues in the Metaphysical Club trumped his scientific training. In *The Divided Self of William James*, author Richard Gale portrays James as a deeply troubled soul seeking a combined Promethean pragmatism and an anti-Promethean mysticism, a person whose contradictions included his views on belief, will, freedom, and truth.[60] Others, like James O. Pawelski, present an "Integration Thesis" arguing that James "made real progress in his struggle to integrate the pragmatic and mystical sides of his psyche."[61]

Suffering from private fears and a level of despair and despondency sometimes compared to Kafka's and Kierkegaard's, James eventually overcame his impediments. His "will to belief" became a fixed point from which he celebrated the fullest expression of human power. Surprised and disappointed by many of his scientific colleagues for their refusal to even countenance the possibility of paranormal phenomena, a position not too different from that experienced by Alfred Russel Wallace, he remained open to the chance possibility of there being genuine evidence of spirit communications and mind transmissions across distances.

As a philosopher, James preferred empiricism over rationalism, freedom of the will over determinism, mysticism over the born-again experience, and pluralism over monism. It is important to remember, too, that James was a scientist before he became a philosopher. Nevertheless, he called out the scientist who dogmatized on the basis of "laws." Interestingly, he maintained a strong attraction to mystics and mysticism, more so than any other aspect of religion and religious experience due to his own personal crisis (as well as his father's) and the noetic qualities he so admired in mystical states of consciousness.

Chapter 8 introduces Lester Frank Ward, the philosopher, paleobotanist, and sociologist whose scope of interests placed him among an elite group of scholars. Ward viewed society as a "compound organism" whose actions exhibited the combined individual forces of its members. The challenge was whether humans could control those forces using "teleological foresight" in harmonizing the myriad of individual forces to bring the greatest advantage to the whole. He attacked the defenders of laissez-faire, defining such let-alone policies as doing positive harm to the body politic. Instead, he found in legislation a form of invention "to control the forces of a state as to secure the greatest benefits to its people."[62]

Included among the impediments to moving forward in a progressive direction was the unorganized nature of knowledge, which made it underutilized, and the lack of a broad-based educational system. For these impediments to be removed, society needed to embrace the importance of a scientific education for all its citizens, a force at least as strong as the forces that favored religious education. Such education would accelerate the rate of social advancement in the same manner that the artificial development of domesticated animals proved better than relying on natural selection. The application of foresight and intelligence ensured the securing of advantages that natural selection alone might not realize. Ward applied the terms *anthropo-teleology* or *telesis* to explain the exercise of intelligent foresight in seizing upon the laws of nature and directing them to particular ends.[63]

*Dynamic sociology*, a term that Ward preferred to *positivism*, pointed to progress that was artificial, meaning different from that which resulted from natural selection. A truly telic leader, he saw himself as part of an organic relationship—a relationship that corresponded to the love for God that was the essence of religion—where individual interests corresponded with larger ethical and moral codes inclusive of all classes, races, and sexes. Having spent much of his life in government service, he knew the state to be capable of acting beyond that of a policeman protecting private property and maintaining peace among contending factions.

Ward was no wallflower when it came to the cause of intellectual freedom, the defense of ideals, and building a more functional democracy for the common man. Strong in his convictions, he continued to believe that government could become a positive force in the betterment of society. As a student of Comte, he advocated social change using education to transmit the power of applied sociology to the working classes.[64] "Applied sociology," he explained, "differs from other applied sciences in embracing all men instead of a few. . . . whatever may be the differences in their faculties, all men have an equal right to the exercise and enjoyment of the faculties that they have."[65]

Chapter 9 recounts the life of Paul Carus, the free-thinking German American writer and editor in chief of the Open Court Publishing Company, whose journals the *Open Court* (1887–1936) and the *Monist* (1890–1936) brought together scholars from philosophy, science, mathematics, and religion to discuss the important issues of the day. As editor, Carus had the enviable position of advancing any number of issues, including a serious discussion of the relation of religious faith to scientific rationalism, skepticism, pragmatic theory, Darwinism, Buddhism, progressive evolution, and the 1893 World's Parliament of Religions. Among the many contributors to his journals were John Dewey, Lloyd Morgan, Lester Ward, Charles S. Peirce, Bertrand Russell, Max Müller, Pierre Janet, Booker T. Washington, Elizabeth Cady Stanton, Ernst Haeckel, Alfred Binet, Ernst Mach, and David Hilbert.

Author of seventy-five books on history, politics, philosophy, religion, logic, mathematics, anthropology, and science, and more than 1,500 articles, Carus saw his role as an advocate for the philosophy of *entheism*, which he described as the "Religion of Science." True science and religion could never be in conflict. The fact that conflict existed between the two suggested the need for religion to undertake a "thorough and honest search for the truth with the assistance of the scientific methods of inquiry."[66] Finally, the chapter addresses Carus's *The Gospel of Buddha*, and the perception drawn by many European and American intellectuals that Buddhism offered a friendlier relationship than Christianity with science and evolutionary theory.

Chapter 10 concludes with a summary of the religious and secular philosophies discussed in the book as well as identifies others that were not part of the study, including America's fascination with idealistic philosophies. It offers a brief overview of the Plato Club and American Akadêmê in Jacksonville, Illinois; the Hegelians in St. Louis; and the Concord School of Philosophy, whose annual lectures provided constructive new approaches to Transcendentalism, Hegelianism, Platonism, Gnosticism, and Christian mysticism. The chapter also recounts the early years of Theosophy and the contributions of Helena Blavatsky and Henry Steel Olcott's efforts to create a scientific Buddhism and ends where the book began, speculating on humanity's continued quest for certitude.

# 1

## Positivism
### Auguste Comte

*Positivists may be the enemies of theology, but the friends of religion.*
—Thomas McPherson, "Positivism and Religion," 1954

AUGUSTE COMTE (1798–1857), THE BRILLIANT and eccentric thinker generally recognized as the founder of positivism and high priest of the Religion of Humanity, started a philosophical movement that enjoyed wide diffusion through the second half of the nineteenth century and into the twentieth. Reputedly the first modern philosopher of science, he is credited with placing the study of society on a positive foundation comparable to the natural sciences by invoking the exclusive use of empirical methods (as distinct from theological and metaphysical) in the search of laws governing society. His most significant works include *Early Writings* (1820–1829), which offered insight into the influence of Henri de Saint-Simon, for whom he worked from 1817 to 1824; and a six-volume *Course of Positive Philosophy* (1830–1842), which proposed a systematic roadmap for his philosophy of science. Works of lesser importance included a four-volume *System of Positive Polity, or Treatise on Sociology, Instituting the Religion of Humanity* (1851–1854) explaining the transformation of positivism into a Religion of Humanity; *The Catechism of Positive Religion* (1852), celebrating the lives of historical heroes; *Appeal to Conservatives* (1855) criticizing the antisocial characteristics of the working classes while urging the use of religion as a tool for moral guidance; and *Subjective Synthesis* (1856), regarded as having effectively accomplished the all-embracing harmony of thought, sentiment, and action.[1]

Overall, Comte's influence was enormous, leaving broad swaths of his ideas to ferment among the rationalist and humanitarian movements of the nineteenth century. Tracing the past to forecast the future, he constructed a grandiose philosophy that formulated a law of progress around the unity of all natural and historical processes. His social and political philosophy became the basis for a pro-state and pro-business style of liberalism whose disciples included editor and political philosopher Thaddeus B. Wakeman, author and utopian socialist Edward Bellamy, progressive editor and political philosopher Herbert Croly, and sociologists

Lester Frank Ward, Albion Small, and Edward Alsworth Ross. Moved by the desire to reconstitute society on a more rational and scientific basis, Comte seized on information discovered by observation and induction to arrive at his law of three stages and the classification of the sciences. For Comte and later sociologists, history represented the progressive development of the sciences, of human reasoning, and of the human ability to understand and direct institutions for the betterment of society. And yet, while leading humanity toward a scientific worldview, he embraced a new secular religion with prayers, dogma, rites, temples, and saints—all obeisant to the Great Being of Humanity.[2]

## EARLY YEARS

Born of Catholic parents in the French city of Montpellier, Comte grew up in a household whose father, a royalist-leaning civil servant, admired above all else the need for order. The youthful Comte excelled at the lycée in his native town and, drawn to the study of mathematics, demonstrated his brilliance by ranking fourth at the prestigious École Polytechnique in Paris, a government-supported scientific school created by the Convention but reorganized by Napoleon as a training school for military officers. From Napoleon to the reestablished Bourbon monarchy, to Napoleon's return and the subsequent post-Waterloo period, the École devolved into a camp of disgruntled students and faculty making demands on its administrators to reclaim the school's original scientific mission. Dedicated to the school's future, Comte grew increasingly distant from his parents' world and dreamed of a more republican form of government.

Until he was expelled as a ringleader among the protesters at the École in 1816, the ideas of the Enlightenment, particularly Baron d'Holbach's philosophy of common sense (bon sens) as distinct from supernatural ideas, provided Comte with a framework for his rebelliousness. Following protests in 1816 and the school's closing a year later by Louis XVIII, he supported himself as a tutor and examiner, hoping for the institution's eventual restoration. At one point he even contemplated migrating to America to organize a New World rendition of the École; when the project collapsed, he chose to remain in Paris, where he eked out a living giving private lessons.[3]

In 1817 Comte met the aristocrat and utopian social theorist Henri de Saint-Simon (1760–1825), who lent his support to the American Revolution by taking part in the siege of Yorktown. In 1789 he endorsed the ideals of the French Revolution and faced imprisonment during the Reign of Terror. Advocating a form of technocratic socialism managed by a leadership of faceless industrialists and social scientists, Saint-Simon vowed to create a productive society free of the miseries suffered by the working classes. Linking industrialization and science to social improvement, he imagined a society based on the scientific and efficient production of useful things, the role of the producer, the absence of privilege, full employment, the value of meritocracy, and the importance of civil peace to the health and vigor of the state. As a prerequisite for his brand of socialism, he encouraged a strictly scientific understanding of society, thus laying the foundation for numerous nineteenth- and early twentieth-century philosophies, including positivism, socialism, Marxism, the Social Gospel, progressivism, and Veblenism.[4]

Much like Joseph de Maistre's *Considérations sur la France* (1796), and in contrast to the natural state of moral chaos depicted in Thomas Hobbes's *Leviathan* (1651), Saint-Simon insisted on a place and function for religion, believing that every great society required a common body of ethics, norms, and beliefs to guide activities. Unlike Marx, he believed that religion made positive contributions apart from being simply an instrument of control. Nevertheless, he considered religion relative, recognizing that beliefs changed over time. Thus, to the utilitarian, the value of any religion depended on its functional contributions to the society it served. In this regard, Catholicism had forfeited its functionality by failing to change. Frozen in time, it lost both its legitimacy and its future.[5]

Drawn to this creative genius, Comte became Saint-Simon's secretary, and as the political and social ferment of the time played into their hands, they brought attention to a set of ideas grounded in science and connected to the world of politics. During these formative years, Comte extracted critical elements of Saint-Simon's thought to meet his own personal goal of developing an infallible system of truth that would bring a moral and spiritual regeneration to the West. Instead of fighting traditional religion, he came to appreciate its importance, including its priestly class, as a means of managing society. He also learned to respect the organic aspects of history, including the importance of industry in the growth of nations and in their geopolitical relations.[6] Identified as one of Saint-Simon's more knowledgeable disciples, he acquired a heightened status among those looking to reformulate society. From 1819 until their breakup in 1824 when Saint-Simon incorporated one of Comte's pamphlets as his own work and without reference, Comte had found common cause with his mentor. The differences that separated the two, however, grew significantly during their association, due principally to the disparity in their ages, Saint-Simon's desire for immediate reform, and Comte's more theoretical and scientific approach.

Adrift on his own after their separation, Comte sold subscriptions to a series of public lectures to introduce his theory of *positivism*, a naturalistic science of society that explained humanity's past and offered a blueprint for its future course. Hoping to appeal to intellectuals who, in the wake of the French Revolution, were searching for a new direction in the midst of growing class, religious, and national differences, he linked his philosophy with the practical goal of identifying the building blocks for a more humane world. Convinced that existing institutions had outlived their usefulness, he proposed a theory whose propositions underscored the importance of change while accounting for the role and function of prior institutions, including religion. His blueprint consisted of a combination of science, laws, and a belief in the unlimited capacity for societal improvement.

Comte's positivist philosophy began with the assertion that knowledge was relative; it was impossible to know the essential nature and ultimate causes of phenomena, only their relations to other facts. Nevertheless, certitude was possible if founded on positive truths that promoted logical harmony and unity of minds—a process that built modestly from phenomena constituting the world and not from any absolute. Positivism affirmed that the only reality is the data of experience to which he appealed for verification. Conceiving individual facts as building blocks to more general facts, he used this progressively verified data to extend knowledge. Once initial relations were identified, it allowed the extension of knowledge to operate by deduction. In other words, *a posteriori* knowledge opened the door for *a priori* knowledge. Positivism enabled one to formulate inductively the fundamental principles that constituted the order of nature. This claim was certainly not original with Comte but drawn from the works of Francis Bacon, Newton, Hume, and present as well in Descartes's *Discours de la method* (1637). Their interests, however, differed from Comte's, who chose to do without metaphysical explanations altogether, relying entirely on external and sensorially verifiable observations. In stressing the empirical origin of observed facts, he repudiated all forms of introspection or intuitive discovery.[7]

The idea of progress was very much in evidence in Comte's lectures. Tracing the development of the principal branches of science, he explained how each had emerged out of supernatural beliefs before attaining empirical status. By setting the sciences to work, he considered it possible to understand the natural laws and use them to achieve a more enlightened society. The purpose of science was to understand the natural world and make modifications to human behavior consistent with the evidence learned from its study. Through observation, experimentation, and comparison, scientists could understand human development, the nature of social dynamics, and the limits of social change. His *social physics* (a term borrowed from the statistician Adolphe Quetelet), later renamed *sociology*, promised to change the dynamics of intellectual discourse. It was to be the culmination of the positive sciences, a reflection of a disciplinary approach to the study of human society comparable to the scientist's examination of the physical world. Based on wisdom inductively gleaned from the sciences and then deducing from them universal laws, principles, and doctrines, he laid the groundwork for a preferred social order. The discovery of the laws of order and organization were its first steps.[8]

To the extent that mankind understood how the sciences influenced the intellect, it was possible to rectify human defects to ensure continuous moral improvement. Essentially this meant using positivism to extend the tools of the sciences to social phenomena. Comte identified this as the "Positive Synthesis," which, dismissive of both materialism and Spiritualism, remained the *only* philosophy capable of rendering materialism unimportant and, at the same time, avoiding the machinations of the Catholic Church.[9]

Following the success of his lectures, Comte published a six-volume *Course of Positive Philosophy*, which appeared incrementally from 1830 through 1842. In the first five volumes, he set out to explain the progress made in each of the sciences as they emerged from their entanglement in ancient philosophy. In the sixth and final volume, he introduced the science of sociology, which, although imperfect, explained the natural progress of intelligence and social organization. By extending his positive method to the study of social organization, he hoped to show that "interposing a common moral authority between the working classes and the leaders of society, will offer the only regular basis of a pacific and equitable reconciliation of their chief conflicts, nearly abandoned in the present day to the savage discipline of a purely material antagonism."[10]

Many eminent scholars subscribed to Comte's lectures, including the social theorist Charles Fourier, German philosopher Alexander von Humboldt, mathematician and physician François Broussais, physiologist Alfred Binet, psychiatrist Jean-Étienne Esquirol, and physicist Louis Poinsot. However, having no position or steady source of income and without portfolio in the world of letters and science, he remained isolated in the backwaters of the academic world. Thus, his ambition to spread the benefits of his positive synthesis faced a serious setback, and his efforts to win a position at the École, or elsewhere, failed to materialize, except for a minor position here and there as a tutor or examiner.[11]

## LAW OF THREE STAGES

Comte explained history as the progressive advancement of human intelligence through a series of stages or states ("a slow accumulation, gradual but continuous"), each reaching its fullest development before moving to the next.[12] Historical change involved the unfolding of discrete events that formed a pattern wherein each individual and each generation played a role. This *unfolding*—a metaphor of life's phases—implied that the development of the individual mind recapitulated the mind of the race. In other words, the ontogeny or development of the individual organism recapitulated the intermediate forms of the human race in its transition from the theological to the metaphysical, and then to the scientific or positive. Each stage evolved in close succession with the one immediately preceding it, with the highest order of social organization coming at the end of the process. Of the three stages, the first was provisional, the second transitional, and the third definitive. The difference between the first two stages and the last was the substitution of the relative (positive) for intuitive (absolute) knowledge.[13]

The ascendancy from theological to metaphysical, and finally to the positive, reinforced the significance of the orderliness of the universe, including human development. During the first two stages, human society was incapable of making scientific use of all the available information. Not until the French Revolution and the collapse of the old political order did mankind acquire sufficient capacity to understand the full measure of available data. The facts, when revealed, far surpassed the complex combination of laws derived from deduction and intuition. The new accumulation of empirically organized data pointed to a wholly new and orderly course of development.[14]

The theological phase, with its divine right of kings and theologico-military form of social organization, enabled belief in a deity whose priests, at prescient moments, explained the purpose of life, including a supernatural world of rewards and punishments. According to Comte, humanity invented its gods to explain the world and manage the conditions that made it possible to build a society and claim a purpose beyond mere gratification. These gods began as tribal fetishes before evolving into astral deities and eventually into a single god with priests, rituals, discipline, and order. As the most ancient form of speculative thought, the theological phase held to the belief that a Divine Will controlled, directed, and sustained all existence. In this stage, the human mind acknowledged the preeminence and purposefulness of the Divine Will over the origin, nature, and purpose of all matter. This common faith gave coherence and stability to the community. Essentially, God was a made-up concept reflective of man's mental state and invented to satisfy his temporary needs.[15]

The metaphysical stage moved beyond belief in a supernatural anthropomorphic deity to a nonanthropomorphic or denatured "force." While the theological stage provided humankind with divinely direct (absolute) knowledge, the metaphysical stage offered a modified form of the former, replacing the supernatural with abstract principles still capable of producing the first and final cause of all phenomena. The anthropomorphic deity in the former became an abstraction in the latter. It was also a period of transition when humanity abandoned its responsibilities and the state entered a period of decay. Otherwise, little had differed in the passage from the theological to the metaphysical stage. Of the two, only the latter demonstrated the linkage of facts with laws rather than to some supernatural causation.

The final stage of positivism was much more sophisticated than its two predecessors. Coincident with the end of Catholic hegemony and the rise of libertarian thinking and laissez-faire economics, it rested on a rational system based no longer on speculation but on an indisputable scientific foundation. Here, the mind ceased searching for causation and focused instead on discovering the laws governing society. Drawing on the works of Bacon, Descartes, and Galileo, who had constructed systems of general ideas, man now required all true knowledge to depend upon observed facts.[16] This level of understanding, which ignored insoluble questions concerning origin and purpose, regarded all phenomena as subject to natural laws. Slow in its advance and requiring numerous intermediate steps, positivism affirmed the existence of natural laws proven by experiment, not Divine Will. With this accomplished, the human mind stood alone to interpret the cosmos. Though not every society moved through the stages at the same time or at the same speed, European civilization had advanced to the point where, in the natural sequence of things, its people and institutions were poised to replace egoism with altruism—a time of moral regeneration directed by spiritual philosophers and managed by industrial and financial technocrats.[17]

## The Sciences

Comte's classification of the sciences, arguably the most enduring of his contributions, examined the six fundamental sciences—mathematics, astronomy, physics, chemistry, biology, and sociology—whose building blocks ranged from simple (mathematics) to complex (sociology).[18] Beginning with mathematics, all phenomena were reducible to the attributes of number, extension, and movement, thus forming the logical basis for the sciences and the jumping-off point for all subsequent study. As the most ancient of the sciences and also the most general, simple, and perfect, mathematics had for its object "the indirect measurement of magnitudes [determined] according to the precise relations which exist between them." Limited by human intelligence, however, it depended upon other forms of inquiry to provide clarity.[19]

As a true order and not an artificial unity, each of the sciences rested on the authenticity of those that preceded it. The subordination of chemistry to biology, for example, constituted a natural transition from the inorganic to the organic side of philosophy. The facts from each of the fundamental sciences emerged in the historical order that nature offered them and through which the mind passed from one stage to another. Much like the eighteenth century's idealized "Chain of Being," it organized the whole of existence from the lowest form of inanimate existence to the most complex living organism.[20] "The succession of social states exactly corresponds, in a scientific sense, with the gradation of organisms in biology," Comte explained, "and the social series, once clearly established, must be as real and as useful as the animal series."[21]

In addition to his organization of the sciences, Comte identified two classes of laws: abstract and concrete. Provided that abstract laws were sufficiently understood, there was no problem combining them. Given mankind's "feeble powers of deduction," however, there could be no progress to the final science (i.e., sociology) until a sufficient quantity of data concerning the world and individual life had been accumulated. Thus, social philosophy must be preceded by natural philosophy, which is to say, the study of inorganic and organic nature. This was the *scala intellectus*, or ladder of understanding, by which thoughts passed from abstract to concrete truths.[22]

Sociology exhibited greater complexity than its predecessor sciences in that it coordinated all of the sciences into a coherent system of knowledge as it looked beyond the individual to the greater society. It was the proof that all phenomena were regulated by natural laws. Observing human activity in the context of the broader span of human development, it discerned from masses of unconnected data information that yielded the laws of social life. This meant separating the abstract history of humanity from concrete observations of single human experiences. As the new grand science, it also could forecast how progress materialized. It read the future not by introspection but by tracing the social laws at hand and interpreting their effects on future events. In doing so, sociology held an honored place as a truly universal, dynamic, and final science surpassing all others—the "Queen of the Sciences."[23]

The fundamentals for understanding sociology required the tripartite tools of observation, experimentation, and comparison. Observation did not imply an unguided act, but one connected to theory, however tentative or imprecise. Observations without such connections were of little value. Experimentation was part of natural phenomena, but instances of revolution and disturbances in human affairs (e.g., disease) made it sometimes challenging to address. Still, such instances were important in giving clues to the body politic. Finally, there was the tool of comparison, a central element in all forms of inquiry that gave clues to social relations and their contextual nature across different and often competing societies. The *comparative method* proved indispensable in testing different theories as sociology moved boldly to comprehend the ascendency of the human race. Its emergence remained the central outcome of Comte's three phases of societal development. As he explained: "From science comes prediction; from prediction comes action."[24]

As the summative science, sociology enabled humankind to transform the environment into a governable world that was neither arbitrary nor fortuitous in its behavior. It allowed ameliorative actions to take the place of chaos. By understanding the laws of social interaction, society's new technocrats had the tools to bring order to human affairs, utilizing their understanding of the laws of development to reimagine and reorganize society for collective purposes. Having experienced the disequilibrium produced by revolution and other forms of social distress and uncertainty, Comte realized that change was seldom accomplished without individual and social tensions of some sort. Nevertheless, as the determinants of social progress were better understood, it became possible to achieve progress by the suppression or neutralization of those forces that contributed to destructive disequilibria. The strength of sociology lay in its ability to strip away metaphysical illusions and show the individual regarded intellectually, socially, and morally. Sociology replaced the intuitive knowledge

(absolute) of the past with positive knowledge conceived as an approximation toward a reality that, while never fully realizable, provided observations and generalizations sufficient for belief.[25]

## HUMANITY

Comte's use of the term *Humanity* requires special attention since, in
common with Rousseau, Turgot, Condorcet, Pascal, Leibniz, and Saint-
Simon, it not only implied the "human species," "one people," "family," and "social unit" but was also reminiscent of Swedenborg's Grand
Human, that is, the highest potential of human nature. Humanity represented a social organism whose attributes of growth and continuity
formed the basis of human destiny. The individual was real only in the
context of the social-man. Humanity served as a unifying element based
on the assumption that the individual mind did not diverge radically from
the race. The affective, intellectual, and volitional aspects of human life
formed a unity of character. Like Pascal, Comte regarded the succession
of individual human beings through the course of time as "one man, always living and incessantly learning." Once the idea of continuous progress became real in the human mind, it manifested a tendency of moving
Humanity toward ends substantively different from the past.[26]

Built on the needs and propensities of this larger unit, Humanity resembled a Hobbesian organism held together by bone and muscle. Utilizing this approach, the family, tribe, and nation became the elemen-
tal units of sociological study and the subject of social scientists whose
knowledge of societal interaction allowed them to control Humanity's
egoistic tendencies through the scientific application of order, morality,
duty, and obligation. As described by Mabel V. Wilson, Comte's idea of
Humanity was "human nature writ large." Its unifying principles consisted of language and religion, the latter assuming the more critical
function, binding the social system in common cause against elements
destructive of its purpose. Social scientists became society's technicians,
who, by directing scientific knowledge and spiritual power, had the ability to establish a temporal world with the good of Humanity as its end.[27]

But Comte went further, declaring that Humanity also included the
dead, whose aggregate deeds formed an integral part of the social fabric. The "past" was a significant determinant of history, synonymous with
the aggregate social heritage known as civilization, with the brain serving as the bridge between the living and the dead.[28] To be clear, not all

individuals were included in the term. Humanity formed only from the lives of individuals who were conscious of their social function, not passive creatures with little to offer the whole. Only those lives convergent with the purposes of Humanity transcended their individual selves to become the embodiment of a unified consciousness. In such instances, explained British jurist and historian Frederic Harrison, the individual lived "only by Humanity, in Humanity and through Humanity."[29]

The catalyst for this addition to Comte's concept of Humanity was the French writer and poet Clotilde de Vaux, with whom he fell madly in love. At the time he was forty-six and she twenty-nine, living off a small income from the publication of a novelette titled *Lucie*. Their relationship was short-lived, due to her death from tuberculosis, but it proved to be a life-changing experience for him. Because of her, Comte proceeded to transform positivism into a secular religion, marking an important new direction in his philosophy. Her emotional impact was that of a muse who helped him understand the spiritual dimension of Humanity. She became an object of contemplation and a source for the creeds, beliefs, and sentiments that formed his Religion of Humanity and its affiliation with the "great dead" who had honored Humanity with their service. Here was a nontranscendental religion celebrating the cooperative human spirit utilizing both the living and the dead as participating members. While this turn in thinking lost Comte many of his advocates, it would be wrong to dismiss those who supported this new approach as simply eccentrics out of touch with reality.[30]

Comte built his Religion of Humanity on the assumption that the time for traditional religion with its language of godliness and sin had passed but that people continued to need some form of a spiritual authority. Unlike Marx and Nietzsche, he recognized that loss of faith in God carried too many unintended consequences for society to ignore. Accordingly, he placed morality in the hands of highly trained state philosophers whose sentiments of compassionate altruism operated within the scope of liberty, emotion, and imagination. Thus, while Comte's Humanity became the object of contemplation, it remained concrete, finite, and knowable. The goal of the new religion was to cultivate a spirit of universal brotherhood through the pursuit of a common good and love of fellow man—a goal that drew upon the imaginative capacities of the family and particularly the role of women.[31]

The spiritual reformulation of European polity represented the final and most controversial phase of Comte's positivism. Advocating communities of beliefs and habits based upon a uniform system of education, he hoped to organize society in a more durable manner than what the Catholic Church had achieved during the Middle Ages—the earliest attempt at a unified system in the West. This explains Comte's love/hate relationship with Catholicism, whose political failure he attributed to the "imperfection of its doctrines and the resistance of the social medium in which it worked." Catholicism's medieval efforts proved premature, something Comte intended to rectify based on the scientific demonstration of ethical truth through cultivation of the higher sympathies and the realization in *social love*.[32]

The grand contribution of Catholicism had been its moral power, which began independent of the state but eventually fused over the course of time, and where it remained amidst numerous political fluctuations. As a moral power, its priests served as society's educators, providing a comprehensive and socially binding worldview. And with their use of sacraments, which the Church dispensed incrementally into each person's life, its priests were empowered to enter the daily lives of individuals to punish, instruct, and correct their moral errors. By subordinating private needs to general purposes, the Church imposed its morality across individual, domestic, and social spheres.[33]

All this changed in the fourteenth century with the relaxation of Catholicism's sacerdotal emphasis and the growth of heretical tendencies, the most significant being the appeal to free inquiry characterized by the rise of Protestantism. "The scholars who supported the authority of kings against the popes, and the national Churches which resisted the decisions of Rome," Comte explained, "could not but claim for themselves a right of inquiry . . . [until], by mental and social necessity, it brought on the destruction of the Catholic discipline first, then of the hierarchy, and, finally, of the dogma." With its belief in free inquiry, Protestantism encouraged insurrectionary tendencies and destructive heresies, impairing the domestic and social structure. It laid the groundwork for an antitheological spirit that spread among freethinking scholars who supported the emancipation of the mind and the sanctioning of a spirit of individualism.[34]

The spiritual decay of Catholicism resulted in efforts by kings to overthrow the temporal power of the popes, causing a further decline in the Church's intellectual and moral authority. With the loss of Catholic polity, papal power denigrated into Italian power, leaving the clergy to embrace the political biases of their respective nation-states. This explained the rapidity with which Protestantism took hold and sanctioned the forfeiture of Catholic polity to competing temporal powers.

Comte confessed to having lost all belief at an early age, but he was not
so much an opponent of God or religion as he was concerned with the
vacuum left when religion lost its influence over society. Divorced from
its doctrinal components, his positivist Religion of Humanity continued
its control over education and public opinion, ensuring domestic peace by
stressing altruism over egoism. Its version of immortality hinged on the
inclusion of past leaders into the corporate memory. Positivism's strength
would come from its authoritarian tenets, and, as Catholicism declined as
an institution and its churches emptied of members, Comte hoped that
positivism would avail itself of the Church's many cathedrals, where, as
Christianity's successor, it would formulate a new synthesis founded on
love of Humanity.[35]

Supported by a cadre of disciples who tithed themselves as a way of
supporting his cause, Comte dispensed his wisdom to all who would listen. His *System of Positive Polity* (1851–1854) divided nations into decen-
tralized units called *cités, républiques, patries,* and *sociétés civiles,* controlled
by a hierarchical class structure with financial centralization in the hands
of a few bankers.[36] Unlike the Saint-Simonians, who concentrated power
in the scientific, intellectual, and industrial classes, Comte separated the
functions of those who wielded spiritual control from those with practical
powers managing the state.[37]

Comte regarded the period between 1830 and 1848 as a natural pause
following the French Revolution before the creation of the Republic in
1848–1850 when he predicted positivism would succeed in reconciling order with progress. Here was the official beginning of the social mission
of positivism, which, working in concert with republicanism, would protect free thought, halt political encroachment by the upper classes, and re-
sist the "retrograde instincts" of Catholicism. To accompany this change,
he founded *Société Positiviste* in 1845, a journal that became home to his
teachings in the years that followed.[38]

Accepting the fact that there could not be a religion without a *cultus,*
Comte invented elaborate festivals, nine sacraments, and the posthu-
mous adoration of renowned men and women. Borrowing from Catholicism, with its priests, popes, angels, and saints, he proposed to main-
tain Humanity's continuity through the worship of its heroes—living and
dead. Society remained unified through a secular religiosity and a science of morals founded on the sympathetic instinct of *altruism.* The new
secular Religion of Humanity elevated and purified human feelings, enlarged and enlightened thoughts, and ennobled the individual with collective feelings. Social scientists, the new "priests" of Humanity, aligned
the functions of reason, imagination, and feeling in accordance with

universal morality. They gave an aesthetic form to positivism, ensuring that it would be intelligible to all the classes.[39]

In Comte's new society, bankers, merchants, and industrial leaders would eventually hold the reins of political power, but not before accepting their social responsibilities. As yet, they were "too debased in thought and feeling for an office of such importance." Left to themselves, they would only abuse their power. Eventually, however, he intended for them to assume leadership in the modern positivist society with their power "consecrated in Positive religion" and their functions under constant check by the combined forces of the working classes, scientists, and women, who together ensured "the victory of Social feeling over Self-love."[40] Knowing that he could not rely on the upper classes, because of their "baseless metaphysical theories" and "aristocratic self-seeking," he looked for support among women and the working classes.[41]

To further counteract the destructive tendencies of the wealthy classes, Comte looked to the Society of Jesus, which served as the papacy's enforcers of orthodoxy. Though he disliked the society for its efforts to shore up monarchy, he admired its fight against agnosticism and atheism. For that reason, he modeled his nondenominational enlightened priesthood on the Jesuit order, hoping it would eventually lend its influence on the purposes of the new secular state. As enforcers for the propagation of positivism, it could ensure the transition from Catholicism to positivism.[42]

Comte admired the Church's adoration of the Virgin Mary, since it affected so many Catholics, especially women. The worship of Mary, begun centuries earlier in Spain and Italy, represented the earliest personification of Humanity. Building on this historical reality, he assigned to women the raising of children until the age of fourteen, when scientific instruction would begin. Women had no power within the government and held no property, but he preserved their right of inheritance along with the indissoluble nature of marriage. As the highest representation of the human species, they offset the male intellect with tendencies of social feeling. Morally pure, they supplied a counterbalance to society's destructive tendencies. Together with the working classes, these "priestesses of Humanity" constituted the moral force behind positivism, personifying the principle of Love "upon which the unity of [mankind's] nature depends." Given that the object of positivist philosophy was Humanity, the "worship of Woman, begun in private, and afterwards publicly celebrated," laid the groundwork for his Religion of Humanity.[43]

In *The Catechism of Positive Religion* (1858), which consisted of thirteen conversations between a woman and a priest, Comte introduced the idea of a *sociocracy* that would put into practice the ideas of positivism, that is, "man thinking under the inspiration of woman, the object being to bring about a concurrence of synthesis with sympathy, in order to regularize the joint action of the two sexes." With the motto of "Live for others" and a formula consisting of "Love as our principle; Order as our basis; and Progress as our end," he prepared a positivist library of 150 volumes of poetry (30), science (30), history (60), and synthesis (30) intended to provide guidance.[44]

Comte also introduced a *Calendar of Great Men* (and women) that divided the year into thirteen months of 28 days each.[45] The degrees of distinction among the men and women listed included what George Sarton identified as "the gods first, then the heroes, then the whole bulk." The gods, one for each month, included Moses, Homer, Aristotle, Archimedes, Caesar, St. Paul, Charlemagne, Dante, Gutenberg, Shakespeare, Descartes, Frederick II, and Bichat. This he followed with fifty-two heroes (e.g., Buddha, Confucius, Alexander, Plato, Virgil, St. Augustine, Bacon, Hume, Gall, and Columbus), including six Americans.[46] Comte even replaced the "sign of the cross" with a gesture touching the principal organs of the body.[47]

## CRITICS AND DISCIPLES

Societies dedicated to Comte's positivism organized in numerous cities, including London, where the philosopher and political economist John Stuart Mill discovered much that was worthwhile in Comte, including the science of sociology.[48] A dedicated positivist, he argued in his *Utilitarianism* (1861) for moving people from individual self-interest to a more generalized focus on Humanity.[49] Though he demurred to Comte's anti-Protestantism, women's natural inferiority, the exclusion of psychology from the sciences, and the Religion of Humanity, he shared the same rigorous empiricism and high regard for scientific knowledge. Under the influence of the utilitarian school of Jeremy Bentham, Mill insisted that all knowledge, including universal statements, depended on the test of experience. And unlike the intuitionists, he decried the accusation that the dependence on experience for all knowledge ended in a denial of morality. Such was not the case. A confirmed empiricist, he accepted utility (i.e., greatest happiness) as the foundation of morals and helped to mold the thinking of Great Britain's liberal tradition between 1860 and the First World War, allowing extensive freedom of opinion and action to individuals—the less government, the better for society.[50]

Comte received significant English exposure from Mill's endorsement, but from none so much as the abridged edition of *Course* published by Harriet Martineau. Her translation, a condensed version published in two volumes in 1853, introduced Comte's epistemology as well as his theory of history and classification of the sciences to a whole new generation of readers. By reducing the original six volumes to eight hundred pages, she made Comte's genius known across the English-speaking world. Comte was so impressed with her translation that he recommended it over his own original.[51]

For Comte's English critics, however, his Religion of Humanity came as a source of irony, in that it represented a substitution of one religion for another. Thomas Henry Huxley remarked that Comte's religion was "Catholicism *minus* Christianity." This was not the replacement of religion, but a religion to which sociological science had been added. Given the use of priests, liturgy, saints, catechism, and even a calendar, positivism had become a "judicious imitation" of Catholicism.[52]

According to historian Charles D. Cashdollar, Comte's works were read by a handful of Congregational, Presbyterian, and German Reformed ministers who served as presidents and board members on several hundred private colleges and universities in the United States. To them, Comte's positivism represented an existential threat to the nation's moral fiber. Together and individually, they charted Protestantism's response.[53] Among them were Samuel Harris, Noah Porter, and George P. Fisher of Yale; Henry Boynton Smith of Union Seminary; Lyman Atwater, Charles Hodge, and Charles Shields of Princeton;[54] and James McCosh of Queen's College, Belfast, and later president of the College of New Jersey (Princeton).[55] Utilizing the Ely Lectures sponsored by Union Seminary, McCosh offered a series of talks titled "Christianity and Positivism" to build his case against this foreign influence. Along with Darwin's theory of natural selection and the higher criticism, McCosh considered positivism one of the principal sources of atheism.[56]

On the other hand, Unitarianism, a theologically moderate Christian movement that housed the liberal side of Congregationalism, became home to many of Comte's iconoclasts. Styling themselves as *theists*, they barely fit under the umbrella of Christianity, discarding much of the historical baggage that had once defined Christianity's authenticity, namely, the belief in miracles, the inerrancy of scripture, and the divinity of Jesus. Combined with Darwinism, the higher criticism, and Eastern thought, positivism provided an optional set of building blocks that more than compensated for the questions left unanswered by Protestant and Catholic orthodoxy. Exemplary of this, Octavius Brooks Frothingham, founder of the Independent Liberal Church (1859) and member of the Free Religious Association (1867), helped to reshape the nineteenth century's view of science, history, and social philosophy by shifting attention away from orthodoxy to a more positive and secular view of humanity and of societal change. In place of Comte's Religion of Humanity, he spoke of an Unknowable Power. "The soul," explained Frothingham, "must be content to find a home as wide as infinite thought, as warm as eternal love; but never see the fashioner of it, never to find the soft bosom of the mother in whose breast it can nestle."[57] Salvation, however defined, came by way of altruism working in harmony for a common purpose.

According to Cashdollar, the Unitarians never fully adopted European positivism but were selective, "borrowing those segments which suited their needs and often modifying their original composition in the process."[58] Frothingham's own affirmation of positivism had limits when it came to Comte's Religion of Humanity, which, like Huxley, he described as "the Roman Church over again without its theology." Using the scientific method for social analysis was one thing, but substituting science as the dominant force in social thought was too great an intellectual jump to make, particularly if it removed religion and religious intent entirely from the equation.[59] Others of similar mind included Felix Adler, who founded the Society of Ethical Culture in 1876; David G. Croly, editor of the *New York World*; and Henry Ward Beecher, whose blend of liberal Protestantism and evolutionism borrowed liberally from Comtean positivism.[60]

Positivism, a conception of the cosmos resulting from the systematic study of the exact sciences where the individual was not so much its central figure as a social atom, joined philosophy (i.e., intellectual faculties) with polity (i.e., social sympathies) to form the two principal functions of the social organism. It generalized the individual and systematized social life using information verified by sensory experience, logic, and mathematics. As the sole source of authoritative and authentic knowledge, it rejected all forms of intuitive knowledge and metaphysical abstractions. Emphasizing that knowledge derived solely from sense experience, the positivists denied not just the validity of theological and metaphysical speculations, but the relevance of a personal god. In doing so, it became a secular scientific ideology whose influence profoundly affected all aspects of social evolution.

Comte's writings contained an ingrained pragmatism motivated by the concern for resolving society's social, political, and moral problems. As a system builder, he devised a blueprint for society that encompassed both the capitalist and the proletariat in peaceful coexistence. Together with Saint-Simon, Fourier, Joseph de Maistre, and Chateaubriand, he offered a religious, utopian, and romantic alternative to the existing social structure. Comte used postrevolutionary tremors to construct a comforting and progressive view of the emerging industrial society, a transition to modernity grounded in a dynamic belief in the law of progress. But, as historian George Sarton points out, in Comte's search for a philosophy of the sciences, "the prophet in him had killed the man of science."[61]

## SELECTED WRITINGS

*Cours de philosophie positive* (1835)
*Discours sur l'esprit positif* (1844)
*The Positive Philosophy of Auguste Comte* (H. Martineau, trans., 1853)
*A General View of Positivism* (J. H. Bridges, trans., 1865)
*The Catechism of Positive Religion* (R. Congrev, trans., 1891)
*Comte: Early Political Writings* (H. S. Jones, trans., 1998)

# 2

## Assent
### John Henry Newman

*Faith is illuminative, not operative; it does not force obedience, though it increases responsibility; it heightens guilt, but it does not prevent sin. The will is the source of action, not an influence, though divine, which Baptism has implanted, and which the devil has only not eradicated.*

—John Henry Newman, *The Religious State of Catholic Countries*, 1849

T HE SECULARIZATION OF EDUCATION, MARRIAGE, and divorce in late nineteenth-century England were vivid reminders of a once hierarchical and landed society crumbling amid the separation of church and state, which, until then, had partnered in governing society.[1] Lamenting the demise of what he once perceived as humanity's divinely established order, John Henry Newman (1801–1890) packaged most of what he found unacceptable into the shibboleth he called "liberalism"—the same existential threat to which Edmund Burke had voiced alarm. He defined liberalism as that principle "according to which truth and falsehood are a matter of free opinion." Intent on destroying liberalism in all its pretentious guises, especially the siren appeal of private judgment and distrust of Revelation, he threw himself with a vengeance against what he considered to be one of Satan's greatest temptations. Returning to dogma that more than any other authority had governed religion for centuries, he found in it a bittersweet solution to those desperate for answers to life's contradictions.[2]

Newman's academic career began at Oxford at a time when it was the intellectual center of the English-speaking world, a place where the constellation of faith, science, and law shone brightest. It was there, too, that the Oxford Movement had its beginnings, a revival of an ancient Catholic spirit separate from Rome, with its guiding principles derived from a combination of revelation and Church doctrines. Challenging it was the Reformation, with its emphasis on religious liberty, private judgment, and the enlightened free mind. Having experienced an intimate spiritual relationship with his God as a young man, Newman felt bound by conscience to obey that inner moment between God and his soul. This inner experience preceded anything that derived from the human will and therefore had preeminent claim to that which his conscience bore witness. It was this fidelity that gave him the ability to believe "that there is a God in heaven" and "that the Catholic Church is His oracle and minister on earth." This did not mean that other religions lacked a road to redemption, since all roads eventually converged on the Mother Church. Challenges would prove different for each, but there was no reason why an individual could not move "by an infallible succession from the rejection of atheism to theism and from theism to Christianity, and from Christianity to Evangelical religion, and from there to Catholicity."[3]

The author of forty books and a compendium of correspondence, Newman holds a monumental place within Roman Catholicism. More books have been written about him in modern times than any other English theologian. What made him attractive to his contemporaries as well as later generations stemmed from what he said about the nature and origin of Christian doctrine, his deviation from scholasticism and Thomism, his idea of the university, and his philosophy of assent. In each of these areas, the force and beauty of his rhetoric reflected a gift that charmed critics and proponents alike. He always had a philosophy to expound, points to make, principles to explain. Most of Newman's best work was produced out of controversy. Like Huxley, who once described Newman as "the slipperiest sophist I have ever met with," he thrived on debate—whether papal infallibility, the reasonableness of assent, or belief in miracles.[4] Like Emerson, he had an ear and an eye for the beauty of the word, its sound, and its vision. This seemed always on his mind as he took up his pen. Structure was preeminent; each poem, each essay, each tract or sermon came with a plan, a balance, a proportion. An enchanter in the pulpit, his thinking powers became lessons of style and argument, seizing advantages where they could be found and securing the high ground wherever possible. Nevertheless, his high rhetorical style made it sometimes difficult to understand with clarity what he was saying, creating epistemological obstacles for those otherwise enamored with his words. His mind, formed within the context of his society and the period, was incurably romantic. In his Catholicism and his deference to dogma, his life as an Oxford don and celibate clergyman, an English gentleman, and a member of a highly privileged class, he lived as few could ever imagine.[5]

## EARLY YEARS

The oldest of six children, John Henry Newman was nurtured in an upper middle-class banking family of Dutch and Huguenot descent in an environment of modified Calvinism. A shy boy sent at age seven to Great

Ealing School, where the father of English biologist Thomas Henry Huxley taught mathematics, he took little part in school activities, preferring to spend his hours reading translations of the *Arabian Nights*, Augustine's *Confessions*, Isaac Newton's *Daniel and the Apocalypse*, Thomas Paine's *Tracts against the Old Testament*, David Hume's *Essays*, and the writings of Voltaire. He also took delight in reading the Bible, though he had no formal religious convictions until age fifteen, when he recounted: "A great change of thought took place in me. I fell under the influences of a definite Creed, and received into my intellect impressions of dogma, which, through God's mercy, have never been effaced or obscured."[6] Assisted by classics teacher Walter Mayers of Pembroke College, who offered his library on the English Calvinist tradition to his young protégé, Newman found conversion after reading the works of William Romaine, an evangelical divine whose *The Life of Faith* (1763), *The Walk of Faith* (1771), and *The Triumph of Faith* (1795) stood as testament to the author's disregard for the formalism of the Anglican Church.

Reflecting on his experience years later, Newman could not remember the particular book or topic that had affected him, though he was convinced something had changed his perspective on life. "I received it at once, and believed that the inward conversion of which I was conscious (and of which I still am more certain than that I have hands and feet) would last into the next life, and that I was elected to eternal glory." With conversion behind him, he considered himself predestined to salvation, a concept he later rejected as a "detestable doctrine" because the justified "are conscious of their state of justification, and that the regenerate cannot fall away." Shortly after conversion, Newman decided to lead a single and celibate life.[7]

As with many of the conversions recounted in William James's *Varieties of Religious Experience*, Newman witnessed the darkness of having little or no hope without God in the world and concluded that an authority was essential to deliver humanity from its plight. The Church, he reasoned, "has it in charge to rescue human nature from its misery, but not simply by restoring it on its own level, but by lifting it up to a higher level than its own. She recognizes in it real moral excellence though degraded, but she cannot set it free from earth except by exalting it towards heaven."[8] Thus did Newman feel drawn into the Anglican Church. Like Augustine, conversion was not a matter of understanding but of submission, the acceptance of an authority that guaranteed the truth behind the mysteries of life. With conversion came peace and contentment of mind.[9] He retained this feeling until he was twenty-one, when it gradually "faded away." Until then, as an evangelical Calvinist, he held many if not all the anti-Catholic beliefs that circulated in his day, including the doctrine of justification by faith alone. Having read Joseph Milner's *Church History* (1809), he was convinced that the pope was the Antichrist predicted by Daniel, St. Paul, and St. John.[10]

In 1817 Newman attended Trinity College, Oxford, impressing tutors with his mathematical abilities. Exhausted by the time of the exams, he barely earned his BA degree, graduating with third-class honors in 1821. Intent, however, on remaining at Oxford, he prepared to read for a fellowship at Oriel College, known then as the university's intellectual centerpiece. While there, he took private students and was elected a fellow, after which he turned from studying for the bar to taking up religious orders. In 1824 he was made a deacon in Christ Church Cathedral, where he preached his first sermon, followed by appointment as curate at St. Clements's, where he fulfilled his pastoral duties and was ordained. Following ordination he was appointed vice principal and tutor of Alban Hall, where, in his spare hours, he wrote articles for the *Encyclopedia Metropolitana*.[11]

With the support and guidance of Richard Whately, leader of the so-called Noetic School of inquiry at Oriel and later Archbishop of Dublin, Newman relinquished the office of vice-principal in 1836 to become tutor at Oriel. The school, a hotbed of liberal thinking, had been strongly influenced by John Stuart Mill and eighteenth-century rationalism, which stressed evidence, reasoning, and argumentation as the most appropriate paths to the embracement of Christianity. At the time of his fellowship at Oriel, Newman was still an avid Evangelical under the influence of Whately and the High Churchman Edward Hawkins, later provost of Oriel. However, Whately's insistence on logic and rhetoric, emphasizing the empirical evidences of Christianity over revelation, caused Newman to doubt evidentiary apologetics. Whately's interpretation of facts as an impartial judge went against his own notion of faith as a state of the heart. In 1827 his connection to Whately ended when Newman decided to oppose Sir Robert Peel's reelection to Parliament because of the politician's change of position regarding Catholic claims. Though appreciative of Whately's early guidance, their minds were "too different," and by 1829 "he [Whately] made himself dead to me."[12]

In 1829, Newman was appointed vicar of St. Mary's university church, where his "Parochial Sermons" drew praise for their thoroughness and scholarly temper. In their totality, they reflected his preference for "gentlemanly" education, a growing suspicion of the democratic man, and an increasing curiosity of church polity. During his tutorship at Oriel,

Edward Bouverie Pusey, who would later become Regis Professor of Hebrew and Canon at Christ Church, sent him a set of writings from the
Church Fathers to examine, the consequence of which drew him into a
lifelong study from which he concluded that the Anglican Church had ab-
dicated critical elements of established creed. In effect, the Reformation
had unwittingly abandoned much that remained true in Christianity.[13] In
the process of arriving at this conclusion, Newman relinquished much of
his Calvinism and, while nominally connected with the evangelical element in the Church, moved away from his Low Church connections, including membership in the Oxford Association and Bible Society.[14]

Newman's early years in residence at Oriel were lonely until he published several highly regarded articles that placed him in the company of
friends like Richard H. Froude, a fellow priest and tutor, whose mutual
interests centered on identifying a revised Protestant state of mind. With
the help of Froude, he "moved out of the shadow of liberalism" and grew
in his affection and criticism of the Anglican Church. As he explained, "I
felt dismay at her prospects, anger and sore at her do-nothing perplexity,"
and that if liberalism gained a foothold, he would need to find something
greater than the Reformation principles to save her.[15]

In the winter of 1832–1833, after resigning his posts at Oriel and St.
Mary's over religious differences with the provost, Newman embarked
on a Mediterranean voyage in the company of Froude and his father, the
archdeacon of Totnes. Their travels on the steamship *Hermes* brought
them to Gibraltar, Malta, the Ionian Islands, Sicily, Naples, and Rome.
At the time of his visit to Rome, Newman still considered the Catholic Church "polytheistic, degrading and idolatrous."[16] Nevertheless, he
learned much from Froude, who delighted in discussing the saints, the
Blessed Virgin, the Real Presence, and his scorn for "the Bible and the Bible only" religion of Protestantism. As a High Tory, Froude looked with
admiration on the Roman Church and challenged Newman's insistence
that it was anti-Christian and the papacy the Antichrist. During their voyage, they collaborated on a collection of religious poems published under
the title *Lyra Apostolica.*[17]

## OXFORD MOVEMENT

On his return to England, Newman along with several friends and associates joined in an effort to wean the Anglican Church from its Reformed heritage. When John Keble, a priest and professor of poetry at
Oxford, preached on "National Apostasy" at St. Mary's in 1833, it marked
the official beginning of the so-called Oxford Movement, with its aim of

finding a *via media*, or middle way, between Anglicanism and the Roman Church. The movement quickly became the focal point of an Anglo-Catholic revival seeking a type of Catholic reformation within the Church of England, involving greater theological consistency between Catholic and Protestant divines on a multitude of subjects, including the limits of reason. The effort pushed the Church of England in the direction of Catholicism without it becoming ensnared in popery and Romanism.

Ideologically, the Oxford Movement represented a conservative reaction to liberalism and the utilitarianism of Bentham. Protesting the reductionist naturalism and empiricism of post-Enlightenment England, it opposed the Catholic Church's metaphysical and supranaturalistic tendencies. Besides Keble, Froude, and Newman, the members of the group included William Palmer of Dublin and Worcester College; Arthur Philip Perceval, High Churchman and fellow of All Souls College; Charles Marriott, priest and fellow of Oriel College; Robert Wilberforce, fellow and tutor at Trinity College; and Isaac Williams, curate and Keble's successor as professor of poetry at Oxford. Others who joined included James Bowling Mozley, brother-in-law to Newman and editor of the *Christian Remembrancer*, who became Regis Professor of Divinity at Oxford; and Hugh James Rose, editor of the *British Magazine* and principal of King's College, who, because of his High Church position, eventually severed his relations with the movement.

Soon after Keble's sermon, Newman launched *Tracts for the Times* (1833–1841), a publication highlighting writings from a half-dozen contributing authors. Along with it, an Association of Friends of the Church organized, whose sympathies stood firm against any semblance of civil or state authority over the Church. The "tractarians," as they were called, defended the Church of England against utilitarian and nonconformist reformers and supported the revival of doctrines once held by the Anglican Church's great divines but now considered obsolete. Too frequently, explained the *Tract*'s editor, "in proportion as the maintenance of the [Anglican] Church has been secured by law, her ministers have been under the temptation of leaning on an arm of flesh instead of her own divinely-provided discipline, a temptation increased by political events and arrangements." The Church had purposely refrained from giving "the more gracious and consoling truths" to its members for the sake of sectarianism and at a cost of neglecting the very components of faith that the papacy had so successfully captured through its pastoral services.[18]

In the early years of the Oxford Movement, the *Tracts* were published as pamphlets; later they became book-length treatises. Published anonymously, they became a rallying point for those opposed to the Church's liberal tendencies. Newman authored twenty-four of the treatises and contributed to several others. Intending to uphold primitive Christianity and its earliest teachers, the tractarians hoped for a second Reformation—"a better Reformation, for it would be a return not to the sixteenth century, but to the seventeenth"—defending beliefs that rested not just on scripture, but on St. Ignatius's *Epistles* and on the Anglican *Prayer Book*.[19]

Altogether, the *Tracts* amounted to six volumes, the last being *Tract 90*. Some of the titles were:

> *The Catholic Church*
> *The Visible Church*
> *History of Popish Transubstantiation*
> *On Purgatory*
> *The Present Obligation of Primitive Practice*
> *Archbishop Ussher on Prayers for the Dead*
> *The Catholic Church a Witness against Real Illiberality*
> *The Necessity and Advantage of Frequent Communion*
> *The Athanasian Creed*
> *Faith and Obedience of Churchmen*
> *On Arguing concerning the Apostolical Succession*

Among the leaders of the movement was Edward Bouverie Pusey, who joined in 1835–1836 after sympathizing with its purposes. As a member of the High Church party within Anglicanism and more of an antiquarian than a theologian, he helped revive pre-Reformation ceremonial worship, including restoration of the penitential system, providing new meaning to the Eucharist, and revolutionizing various rituals of worship. His influence, felt almost instantaneously, gave gravity to the movement, making it a challenge to work "with precision the relation in which we stood to the Church of Rome." A scholar of the Church Fathers, Pusey's 1843 sermon "The Holy Eucharist, a Comfort to the Penitent" served as an influential source of conversion to Catholicism for a number of Anglicans, including Newman. So significant was this sermon that the term *Puseyism* often substituted as a form of identification for the movement. Still, Pusey refused to leave the Anglican Church.[20]

Newman claimed that his years as editor of the *Tracts* and the *British Critic* were the happiest in his life—a time when the Anglo-Catholic party became a force within the Church of England. It was then he felt "truly at home" in the Church.[21] Along with fellow tractarians, he lamented the schisms that had divided Christianity, causing different groups to emerge and show their sectarian hostility to one another. As ecclesiological conservatives, they held a Burkean reverence for the Anglican Church as an institution. The fact that it existed for so long suggested a level of validation that they willingly recognized, though it caused them considerable disappointment that so many legitimate dogmas had been left aside. Since real differences could not be concealed, they had no illusions that they might witness some great unity. Still, by focusing on the gospel, they hoped that at least several first steps might be taken to bring their Church closer to the Roman Church.[22]

Tracts 38 and 41, published in 1837 and 1838, the first being "Lectures on the Prophetical Office of the Church Viewed Relatively to Romanism and Popular Protestantism," and the latter, "Lectures on Justification," represented Newman's attempt to establish the Anglican Church as a *via media* between Romanism and continental Protestantism. The lectures consisted of a dialogue between Clericus (a cleric) presenting the tractarian point of view, and Laicus (a layman) seeking understanding. In dialogues reminiscent of Plato, Clericus accused continental Protestants of exercising a disproportionate influence over the Church of England, making it more Protestant than its founders had intended. As a consequence, he recommended a "second Reformation" in the belief that the Anglican Church had forgotten its founding principles. In particular, he identified practices that had erroneously been blamed on Catholic doctrine rather than on fanatics who had corrupted the Church's faith, worship, and discipline. As Clericus explained, the Anglican Church had been "faulty in faith and discipline."[23]

In the spring of 1839, Newman's standing within the Anglican Church was at its height. "I had supreme confidence in my controversial status, and I had a great and still growing success, in recommending it to others." This changed two years later when *Tract 90* (*Remarks on Certain Passages in the Thirty-Nine Articles*) suggested that Luther's criticisms of Catholic teachings had erroneously focused on popular exaggerations rather than on the teachings themselves. Since Protestantism and Roman Catholicism were real religions and the same in their fundamentals and agreed "in all but their later accidental errors," Newman saw no reason for the Anglican Church to forsake all that it held in common with the churches of Italy, France, and Spain. Those doctrines of the Roman Church that appeared wanting were, in fact, consistent with the *Articles*. Thus, it was important for the Anglican Church to cooperate with Rome "in all lawful things, if she would let us, and the rules of our own Church let us; and we thought there was no better way towards the restoration of doctrinal purity and unity."[24]

Newman interpreted the *Articles* as a protest against the worldliness of the Roman Church but regarded them as intellectually weak, since they were not actually in conflict with the authorized creed of the Roman Church. "While our *Prayer Book* is acknowledged on all hands to be of Catholic origin, our *Articles* also, the offspring of an uncatholic age, are, through God's good providence, to say the least, not uncatholic, and may be subscribed by those who aim at being catholic in heart and doctrine." This was reason enough to argue for the fundamental ecclesiastical identity of the Church of England as Anglo-Catholic rather than Protestant.[25]

*Tract 90* used the terms "Roman Church" and "Catholic Church" in a manner that left a high degree of ambiguity for its readers. There seemed to be no clarity in the proposed rapprochement as to whether the Anglican Church was to have separate but equal status with the Roman Church, meaning that the *Articles* were reconcilable with the Council of Trent, or whether the Anglican Church was expected to merge with the Roman Church as recognition of the latter's preeminence within the Catholic Church. Rather than demonstrate the compatibility of the *Articles* with the post-Tridentine theology of the Catholic Church, critics accused Newman of duplicity. He had become a spokesman for Romish doctrines (e.g., purgatory) at the expense of much honored sixteenth-century English Protestants who had sacrificed their lives for the cause. In effect, Newman threw his support to those Catholic doctrines and practices still evident in the Church of England and against the Erastian tendencies of the time.[26]

Reaction came swiftly as critics accused Newman of attempting to open the door for the teaching of Catholicism at Oxford. In their response, the heads of houses and proctors censured the *Tract*, and Bishop Richard Bagot directed an end to the discussion of the *Articles* as well as any further publications. Faced with criticism, Newman stood his ground and refused to withdraw *Tract 90* or to keep his silence. Writing to Bishop Bagot, he expressed the depth of his feelings on the matter: "I have nothing to be sorry for except having made your Lordship anxious, and others whom I am bound to revere. . . . I have never taken pleasure in seeming to be able to move a party, and whatever influence I have had, has been found, not sought after." He concluded from the experience that he had but two alternatives, the way to Rome, or the way to atheism, with Anglicanism the "half-way house on the one side, and Liberalism . . . on the other."[27]

## CONVERSION

After relinquishing his editorship of the *Tracts*, Newman returned to lay communion and, although claiming not to have contemplated leaving the Anglican Church, he certainly understood that his current position was outside the *Articles*. Nor was he aligned with Rome, due to its worship of the Virgin Mary and the saints, which he considered incompatible with the "One Infinite and Eternal." As a consequence, he resigned from the movement and retired to Littlemore, a village in the parish of St. Mary's, where Oriel College had built a chapel with financial support from his family. There he took up residence in the parsonage and lived a quasi-monastic life with several fellow tractarians who hoped for the day when they might again advance their ideas. The group included William Lockhart, John Dobree Dalgarins, Ambrose St. John, Frederick Oakeley, and Albany James Christie.[28]

By the end of 1841, Newman considered his membership in the Anglican Church on its "death-bed." He described it as "a tedious decline, with seasons of rallying and seasons of falling back." This remained his view of duty until his resignation from St. Mary's, when he concluded that he could no longer prove that the Anglican Communion was an integral part of the One Church. The nearest approach Newman could give to the reason for his resignation was the Church's repudiation of *Tract 90*. "If there ever was a case, in which an individual teacher has been put aside and virtually put away by a community, mine is one." With his own bishop against him, a factor he had not anticipated, he felt alienated from his former supporters and from the very principles he felt belonged with the Church.[29]

In 1843 Newman published "Oxford and Rome," in which he retracted many of his anti-Catholic statements. Concluding that the Church of Rome was the only true Church, the *via media* disappeared as a purposeful goal. A month later he delivered the last of his university sermons, "The Theory of Development in Religious Doctrine," using evolutionary theory to explain his evolving opinion of those Christian doctrines he had previously rejected. The sermon did little to endear him to his Protestant colleagues. Several months later came his sermon "The Parting of Friends," his last as an Anglican priest. Two years later, in 1845, the same year that French philosopher Joseph Ernest Renan (author of *The Life of Jesus*) broke from Catholicism, the Italian Passionist priest Dominic Barberi formally received Newman into communion, an act that caused his severance from family and friends, including many within the movement who accused him of "rearing at Littlemore a nest of Papists" who in due time transferred their allegiance to Rome.[30] In 1846 Newman traveled to Rome, where he was ordained by Cardinal Giacomo Filippo Fransoni and where Pius IX awarded him the degree of DD. On his return as an Oratorian, he moved to Edgbaston in the area of Birmingham where he established the Oratory of St. Philip Neri and carried out mission work. Except for a four-year assignment in Ireland, this remained his home for the next forty years.

With his conversion, Newman's genius "bloomed out with a force and freedom such as it never displayed in the Anglican Communion." Over the next several years, he wrote *Discourses to Mixed Congregations* (1849); *Certain Difficulties Felt by Anglicans in Catholic Teaching* (1850); and *The Present Position of Catholics in England* (1851), a set of lectures protesting the anti-Catholic claims of Dr. Achilli, an ex-Dominican friar, that precipitated a criminal proceeding against him for libel; and the novel *Loss and Gain* (1848), demonstrating there was no distinct line between his religious writings and his fictional works.[31]

Much of what is known of Newman's life up to his conversion was recounted in *Apologia pro Vita Sua* (1864), a confession of faith written in response to a long-winded exchange with Charles Kingsley, the Regis Chair of Modern History at Cambridge and private tutor to the Prince of Wales. A supporter of science and a fellow in both the Linnaean and Geological Societies, Kingsley precipitated a series of published letters and pamphlets between the two men. Newman used the exchange to explain his religious beliefs and ultimate conversion, which came with a certain amount of psychological theater no doubt fed by Kingsley's anti-Catholic sentiments.[32]

## IDEA OF A UNIVERSITY

In 1854 at the request of the Irish bishopric, Newman became rector of the Catholic University of Ireland, later known as University College, Dublin. During the four years of his administration, he prepared a volume of lectures that formed *The Idea of a University*. Written at two different times: the first series, prepared in 1852, comprised a set of lectures delivered prior to his appointment as rector; the second, written in 1859, was delivered during his rectorship. In them Newman explained his approach to Catholic education and the path he drew between freethinking and moral authority, the nature of the curriculum, the problem of specialization, the function of theology in the university, and the relation between theology and science. In many ways he tried to replicate the Oxford model; but his model also included structural elements of the Catholic University of Louvain (1834), whose governance lay in a central authority rather than in the hands of the individual colleges.[33] According to Newman, England's public-school system had been highly successful except for its exclusion of religion from the curriculum. Instruction most certainly improved the accuracy of mind, enabling gentlemen "to look out into the world right forward, steadily and truly, . . . to abstract, compare, analyze, divide, define, and reason, correctly." By engrafting Christianity, you added character.[34]

In Newman's day, education was valued much like a landed estate that remained in the family generation after generation, never to be sold without depleting the character and standing of its owner. A true education was one that prepared the individual to appreciate knowledge for its own sake, not for the sake of a discipline or specialized field of endeavor. Education was the cultivation of the intellect, which began with the seven liberal arts of the medieval university—the trivium consisting of grammar, rhetoric, and logic; and the quadrivium consisting of arithmetic, geometry, music, and astronomy. To this Newman added science and theology, albeit cautiously, aware that either one could threaten the integrity of liberal education with its "good sense, sobriety of thought, reasonableness, candour, self-command and steadiness of view." Thus, the cultivation of the intellect did not derive from the study of the seven liberal arts alone, but from training the mind how to think in other areas as well. The result, when exhibited, "is the clear, calm, accurate vision and comprehension of all things, as far as the finite mind can embrace them, each in its place, and with its own characteristics upon it." Implied in his description of the trained mind was the ability to meet complexity with imagination, clarity, wisdom, and the faculty of judgment.[35]

Newman remained a strong advocate of "liberal education," but the term requires clarification. What he called liberal education was "a comprehensive view of truth in all its branches, [and] . . . of their mutual bearings, and their respective values." This was knowledge that enlarged and illuminated the mind and grasped matters with a keen ability to reach into the heart. Acquiring a liberal education was the equivalent of having the capacity to think with reason irrespective of the temper of the moment, and with the ability to communicate with the power of speech and the pen. Newman's educated gentlemen treated knowledge in the context of religious duty. With knowledge its own reward, philosophy became its informing spirit, providing the essential bearings to effect moral progress. The terms "knowledge," "philosophy," "reason," and "philosophical morality" were set in the context of "Revelation," "Catholicism," and "the Church."[36]

Newman's Christian gentleman was someone who, divorced from the challenges of day-to-day living, had the luxury of quiet contemplation and, above all, loyalty to the past rather than to alterations introduced by public opinion. One has the impression he would have agreed with Bulwer Lytton's description of democracy as a "yawning grave" and that notions of loyalty, fealty, and authority had taken a ruinous fall with the excitement brought by its rise. While free discussion and judgment were tools for the Christian gentleman and held in check by tradition, authority, and loyalty, such checks were meaningless for the mass man, whose opinion was shaped by the press and its incessant alteration of long-held wisdom.[37] Newman's concept of the university represented a defense of the Oxonian theory of knowledge against Locke's utilitarianism, of medieval theocracy over the secular state, and the "ultramontanist" idea of papal supremacy over the democratic majority. Such ecclesiastical totalitarianism was his answer to apologetics—a moral posture that offered a social ethic more radical than the movement of Christian Socialism.[38]

Newman's academic curriculum included religion without the heavy hand of dogma. Man's pursuits required God-centeredness but not at the expense of other branches of knowledge. The university was dedicated to liberal education first and foremost, whose disciplines took no second seat to theology. This implied the freedom to indulge in research and publication without church interference, including censorship. Newman did not intend for the university to become the mouthpiece of Catholic theology. If it was religious training that a gentleman desired, there was always the seminary—an entirely separate entity. The university could not be a seat of learning if the intention was to have theology dominate. Unfettered research and the value of knowledge should not be hampered by theology or any other authority.

Catholic reaction to the book's publication left him confused and saddened. In his soaring eloquence for unhampered research, he had to be reminded of the safety net of Church authority that was needed at times to counter the capriciousness of private judgment. Considered much too liberal by the Irish bishopric, including Bishop Paul Cullen, who protested in a letter titled "Congregation for the Evangelization of Peoples," Newman was forced to resign his rectorship. In 1858 he attempted to establish a branch of the Oratory at Oxford, but this, too, was halted by the ultramontane Henry Edward Manning, the newly appointed archbishop of Westminster, who, like Newman, was a former tractarian and convert from the Anglican Church. According to Manning, sending sons to Oxford rather than to bona fide Catholic universities would subject them to unwanted dangers. Stymied in his efforts, Newman established the Birmingham Oratory, a school for gentlemen much like the English public school. Not until a hundred years later (1993) would the Oxford Oratory be established.[39]

To be sure, Newman was submissive to Rome, having accepted papal infallibility even before it became church doctrine. Privately, however, he feared that its official pronouncement would act as a deterrent to future conversions. On returning to England from Dublin, Newman became editor of the *Rambler*, a Catholic journal that questioned the reactionary tendencies of the Church, a topic most notably exemplified in his 1859 essay "On Consulting the Faithful in Matters of Doctrine." The publication caused considerable consternation for Pius IX and Cardinal Manning, who were suspicious of Newman's intentions. Elected as a liberal but subsequently frightened by the 1848 revolutions and the loss of the Papal States, Pius IX turned volte face, issuing the doctrine of the Immaculate Conception in 1854, his *Syllabus of Errors* in 1864 condemning the modernist tendencies of the age, and claiming papal infallibility in matters of faith and morals in 1869. Thus, when Newman wrote "Consulting the Faithful in Matters of Doctrine," he was reminded none too subtly that the bishops were responsible for testifying to the faith of the people, and therefore there was no reason to believe that their role did not or could not apply in the present as it had in the past.[40]

That many in the Oxford converts knew nothing of how the Roman Church operated remains an understatement. As a newly converted Catholic, Newman and those tractarians who joined him failed to grasp the mentality of their new religion. Though they connected with the Catholic ideal of the sacraments and apostolic succession, the papacy remained a black hole of incomprehension, a characteristic that eventually challenged them, and Newman in particular. Having accepted the Church, they were in no position to seek clarification, much less challenge, the apostolic chair on points of dogma.

## THE CONFLICT METAPHOR

By the time Darwin published his *Origin of Species* (1859), Newman had already established himself as a vocal champion of the compatibility between science and religion through two important addresses in 1855: "Christianity and Physical Science" and "Christianity and Scientific Investigation." Unlike what John William Draper would later argue in his *History of the Conflict between Religion and Science* (1874), and Andrew Dickson White in his *History of the Warfare of Science with Theology in Christendom* (1896), Newman saw no antagonism between the two. The perception of their incompatibility had come about due to a misunderstanding of their proper scope and relationship to each other. In his *The Idea of the University*, he divided knowledge into "natural" and "supernatural," the first being knowledge of nature or "that vast system of things, taken as a whole, of which we are cognizant by means of our natural powers," and the second, being that knowledge "of which the Creator Himself is the fulness, and which becomes known to us, not through our natural faculties, but by superadded and direct communication from Him." Both were genuine forms of knowledge; they represented "two great circles of knowledge" that rarely intersect and therefore "cannot on the whole contradict each other." This meant that the experts in each of these fields had no business judging the facts and truths in the other's field of knowledge, especially when they attempted to apply their disciplinary methods inappropriately beyond their proper sphere, that is, making theology inductive rather than deductive and the reverse for science. Knowledge of theological truths came from revelation, while the natural sciences appealed to Baconian and inductive methods. Rather than disparage one or the other, he insisted that each know its rightful place in the path to knowledge.[41]

As for evolutionary theory, Newman neither supported nor objected to Darwin's theory of natural selection, or any of the competing theories of transmutation. He was satisfied that if the biologists kept to their own discipline, there was no reason for him to object. He wrote in a letter to Pusey, "Mr. Darwin's theory need not be atheistical, be it true or not; it may simply be suggesting a larger idea of Divine Prescience and Skill."[42] In the final analysis, the theologian had nothing to fear from the scientist. Natural science offered no home for theology and was therefore unlikely to provide any basis for producing theology. Provided they respected each other's turf, neither Christian faith nor the scientist's line of investigation could produce contrary truths.

## GRAMMAR OF ASSENT

Newman's *Grammar of Assent* (1870) took twenty years to write. Given the stiltedness of its language, it might have been better had he spent a few additional years making it more readable. That said, Newman argued that the world of post-Enlightenment thought set the standard for evidence used for assent, but in real life the expectations of Whately and other positivists for such thoroughness in decision making were unrealistic. Most men did not decide day-to-day matters using formal reasoning. What proved to be logical was not always realizable. Instead, Newman proposed an approach to assent that applied to matters the common individual might not understand or be able to prove with the absolute certainty demanded by Locke and the British empiricists.

Considered the culmination of his preoccupation with the problem of faith, an issue he first addressed in the *Apologia pro Vita Sua*, Newman argued that faith could be considered certain based on evidence not demonstrated through propositions or rational evidence. Recognizing two forms of certainty—*objective* and *subjective*—he judged the latter as having the strength and assurance of the former even though it could not be demonstrated by evidence. It did not follow that the conclusions drawn from the latter were any less certain than the conclusions obtained by the former. Subjective certainty meant believing what the best reasoning failed to achieve. Here the concepts of *assent* and *inference* came into play. Assent was the acceptance of a proposition as true. Inference was a judgment made from a series of conditional beliefs or convictions that, by themselves, could neither claim nor demand belief. Both assent and inference were conditional, because the conclusions reached implied the assumption of premises. Of the two, Newman preferred judgments subjectively arrived at, since he doubted that absolute certitude could be reached strictly on grounds of reason. Inferences, on the other hand, could claim certitude even though they depended on lesser degrees of evidence.[43]

Newman also distinguished between *religious belief*, which resulted from human reason and will, and *divine faith*, a gift of grace. Divine faith, including the acceptance of Revelation involving God's communication to humankind, required the strongest degree of assent, excluding any doubt. It meant assenting to a doctrine as true "which we do not see, which we cannot prove, because God says it is true, who cannot lie."[44] What God revealed, He revealed with an absolute certainty equal to mathematic certainty. Divine faith not only accepted divinely revealed propositions but assented to those "messengers" (e.g., prophets, saints, popes) from God who stated propositions (e.g., infallibility, Trinity, incarnation, atonement, resurrection) to be certain and true. This was the outcome of an *informal* reasoning process that went on in everyday life and led to the acceptance of beliefs on equal status with those arrived through strictly experimental testing or formal logic. While there was no single piece of evidence that, by itself, made certain that the teachings of the Church were divinely revealed, each individual piece of accumulated evidence made more probable the certainty of the claim.[45] Given that most men were neither logical nor consistent in their thoughts and actions, mixing facts with prejudices and other impediments was destined to fail. Without the divine authority of revelation as taught through the Mother Church, there was only atheism. There was no other alternative.[46]

Even though the unlearned man could not understand the intricacies of dogma, he could believe it to be true because he believed in the Church. If man believed that the Lord was God, he believed all that was meant by its belief, even truths which had not come before him. He who believed in revelation believed in all its doctrines, even though he could not know them all. He embraced it all in his act of faith, including the Church as the infallible oracle of truth. Most good Catholics, perhaps even the majority, lived in a simple, firm belief in all that the Church taught for the very reason that it taught it. "There were whole nations in the Middle Ages thus steeped in the Catholic Faith, who never used its doctrines as matter for argument or research or changed the original belief of their childhood into the more scientific convictions of philosophy," Newman explained. "As there is a condition of mind which is characterized by invincible ignorance, so there is another which may be said to be possessed of invincible knowledge; and it would be paradoxical in me to deny to such a mental state the highest quality of religious faith,—I mean certitude."[47]

Newman also distinguished between *real* and *notional* assent. In real assent the individual *believed*, much like the martyrs or the uneducated woman who ruminated over her rosary beads. By contrast, in notional assent the philosopher explained himself through propositions and abstractions. Newman included in notional assent such things as rules of conduct, reflections on man and society, mathematical propositions, and legal judgments, as well as theological principles and doctrines.[48] Real assent, as distinct from notional assent, was an intellectual act in which the object was presented by way of the imagination. There was an imaging of the object by the individual, thus providing a direct apprehension or picture of Him whose presence was discerned. Newman's concept of real assent suggests that he was identifying belief with an inner sense whose feelings and emotions left the believer with an intimate experience of reverence. It was faith reduced to its essence—a sense felt by fingers moving slowly over the beads of the rosary that God was ever near, an aesthetic dimension that notional assent could never satisfy.[49]

Reminiscent of his long-standing feud with Whately, Newman argued that Christians need not affirm their faith on a rational basis of "I believe" but could more confidently state "I know." Stating "I know" for the ordinary believer was based more on a narrative that was lovingly held with little regard to what might be called a historical-critical account. Unlike Karl Barth, who saw the insecurity of man's existence and his ability to penetrate the unknown, Newman saw faith as an open textbook that, when properly used, ensured certainty.[50] "Can I attain to any more vivid assent to the Being of a God, than that which is given merely to notions of the intellect? Can I enter with a personal knowledge into the circle of truths which make up the great thought? Can I rise to what I have called an imaginative apprehension of it? Can I believe as if I saw?" Newman answered these questions by relying on phenomenology to explain how moral objects came through the senses where they were known by instinct. God might not be seen, but the evidence that lay in the phenomena and which impacted the senses provided the necessary certitude for belief.[51]

## Calculus of Probabilities

In *Essay on Ecclesiastical Miracles* (1843), followed by *Essay on the Development of Christian Doctrine* (1845), and *An Essay in Aid of a Grammar of Assent* (1870), publications that endeared him to Rome, Newman made the claim that miracles did not require proof, only "antecedent probability," meaning they were presumed to be true based on their biblical predecessors. Borrowing from the analogical and probabilistic reasoning of Bishop Joseph Butler, whose *Analogy of Religion* (1736) constructed the plausibility of a Christian God as the basis of belief, including miracles, Newman enraged critics and supporters alike, many of whom had concluded that so-called miracles were no longer essential to Christian belief. Anxious to reconcile science and religion, they viewed Newman's contribution to Christian faith not only as contempt for facts but as a form of dishonest antiscientific sophistry intended to sidestep rational investigation and the higher criticism. Newman's justification for miraculous apparitions represented monstrous deception of syllogistic nonsense that did little to square with the facts. Instead, it compelled conformity to the past and the mistaken belief that what was considered true once must be true for future generations as well, bestowing legendary credibility and certainty.

   Like Butler's, Newman's argument operated on the basis of probability, not facts. Butler considered it an imperfect form of information but essential for individuals of limited capacities. How was it possible, for example, for an uneducated or even moderately educated Catholic to *believe* in the Immaculate Conception, the Trinity, transubstantiation, or papal infallibility when the propositions that constituted these doctrines seemed oddly incomprehensible for intelligent acceptance? Was there an ideal of responsible believing? Must belief be based on evidence, however defined, or based on some "duty" or "responsibility"? What were the conditions under which a Christian forms and sustains his or her faith? How did one reach a conclusion that was reasonable to believe?[52]

Newman answered these questions by *inference* (formal, informal, and natural), which he drew from the convergence of "antecedent probabilities." In effect, he used calculus to arrive at what he identified as the *illative sense*, which represented the moment when the cumulative information gathered allowed for assent or belief. It was the convergence of probabilities from a wide variety of facts and observations that pointed to a conclusion. While this assent might not be the equivalent of logical or mathematical certainty, it was of equal or even higher value.[53] Faith was the reasoning of an enlightened mind, utilizing inferences grounded in premises held to be true; probability existed for those of weaker abilities and relied on presumptive inference. Without postulating a class-based rationale (although it is reasonable to make the connection), it seems clear that Newman made probability the equivalent of reason, an approach to belief that, while different from axioms and first principles, gave the common man access to a form of certitude, albeit different from the educated Christian gentleman's.[54]

Newman remained unapologetic with his central message: "That absolute certitude which we [are] able to possess, whether as to the truths of natural theology, or as to the facts of a revelation, [is] the result of an *assemblage* of concurring and converging possibilities . . . that probabilities which did not reach to logical certainty, might suffice for a mental certitude; that the certitude thus brought about might equal in measure and strength the certitude which was created by the strictest scientific demonstration."[55] He considered a proper assemblage of probabilities sufficient for mental certitude even if insufficient to justify logical certainty.[56]

As philosopher Frederick D. Aquino explained in his *Communities of Informed Judgment* (2004), Newman's illative sense functioned somewhere between sentiment and formal logic, rejecting Christianity as a religion either of sentiment or of evidence, with reason as the sole judge. The illative sense was a form of inner logic whose inferences were not constrained by formal rules. It resembled a communal wisdom that relied on impressions derived from sources deeper than consciousness and formal reasoning.[57] It was the product of intuition that included instinct, imagination, conscience, scripture, the church, antiquity, words of the wise, hereditary lessons, ethical truths, historical memories, legal and state maxims. When combined, they provided "the purgation of individual error"—the ultimate sanction of belief and action.[58] Newman sometimes described the illative sense as a form of genius obtained not from reasoning in the abstract but from a range of inferences and the converging of probabilities that determined what science could not determine. It was an exercise of the mind that proceeded to its conclusion by a method of reasoning analogous to mathematical calculus.[59]

Newman compared his convergence of probabilities with that of the polygon inscribed in a circle with its sides continually diminished to the point when it *nearly* becomes the circle, or the portrait artist filling in his sketch, which, over time, makes what was once only imaginative more concrete. Over time, the change became qualitatively clearer and real. In these examples there occurred a qualitative transition as probabilities converged. That which became "real" or "concluded" was predicated on accumulated evidence that nearly, but never, was absolute. Though incomplete by purely logical standards, it sufficed for drawing a conclusion. It was the imagination that ultimately "saw" a conclusion by bringing together the different threads, brushstrokes, or evidence to a critical threshold where the imaginative mind transformed it into a recognizable pattern or image.[60] As Newman explained it, the individual "passes on from point to point, gaining one by some indication; another on a probability; then availing itself of an association; then falling back on some received law; next seizing on testimony; then committing itself to some popular impression, or some inward instinct, or some obscure memory; and thus it makes progress not unlike a clamberer on a steep hill, who, by quick eye, prompt hand, and firm foot, ascends how he knows not himself, by personal endowments and by practice, rather than by rule, leaving no track behind him, and unable to teach another."[61]

In many ways, Newman's illative sense paralleled William James's search for unity of thought (he settled for the term *pluralism*) in an age where, in the battle between faith and reason, science had condemned faith as shameful.[62] As explained by D. H. Meyer's essay in the *American Quarterly*, "we have stopped proving things for which we cannot stop caring; are we, then, never justified in letting our cares carry us beyond our proofs? Have we no right to believe that which, as human beings with religious yearnings, we cannot help believing?"[63] Nor, presumably, was Newman's approach substantively different from the meta-analysis used in evidence-based medicine to arrive at a "best practice." By combining the results of individual clinical trials, some of which offered results too minor to draw any formal conclusion, it was possible to arrive at an operational level that gave certitude regarding a specific medication or procedure. It was the convergence of findings from numerous independent trials—large and small—that brought confidence to a treatment.[64]

Looking at Newman's or Butler's theology from the viewpoint of probability and mathematics, it appears evident that both men were more concerned with finding regularities in the face of imperfect knowledge than with identifying irregularities. By ignoring the irregularities in the data, they made belief the most predictable outcome. Even the presumed violation of natural laws seemed not intrinsically improbable to overcome. In this manner Newman's treatment of the convergence or accumulation of probabilities leading to unconditional assent turned into a statistical determinism reassuring the significance of God's ability to intervene in the world with miracles that violated the known physical laws.

Assent based on probability led Newman down more than one unanticipated rabbit hole. His claim, for example, that miracles did not require legal proof, due to the principle of "antecedent probability" (i.e., that miracles should be presumed true on the basis of their biblical precedents), precipitated considerable discussion on the use and misuse of probability.[65] Edwin Abbott, headmaster of the City of London School and a prolific writer on theology, rejected out of hand Newman's argument, stating that such claims were inappropriate for the worship of Christ. As a liberal Christian, miracles were interesting but did not (and should not) necessitate belief. If anything, they were an impediment. Accordingly, he described Newman's *Essay on Ecclesiastical Miracles* as an "abomination of intellectual desolation"—a mixture of sophistry and "that subtle and delicately-lubricated illative rhetoric" that unfortunately led from probability to "improbable belief." He accused Newman of using arguments and analogies that were "mere verbal pyramids balanced on their tops." Probabilistic thought had allowed Newman to make analogical leaps from positive probabilities to abetting unconditional assent to such troublesome and contentious claims as transubstantiation and papal infallibility.[66]

Despite criticism, *Grammar of Assent* remained Newman's weapon of choice in his fight against liberalism, including the higher critics whom he regarded as amateurs relying on historical evidence and the inductive sciences while wholly ignorant of the deductive nature of faith. His reading of the higher critics only confirmed this belief. Their adoption of scientific methods to study the Bible had done irreparable harm; their entry into the secular world of empiricism had devolved into a maze with no beginning or end. This included David Friedrich Strauss's *The Life of Christ Critically*

*Examined* (1836) and Ludwig Feurbach's *Essence of Christianity* (1841), which Newman accused of eroding the orthodox Christian message by forcing Christians to turn inward to search for a more individualized spirituality. "Tell men to gain notions of a Creator by His works," Newman insisted, "and if they were to set about it (which nobody does) they would be jaded and wearied by the labyrinth they were tracing. Their minds would be gorged and surfeited by the logical operation. . . . After all, man is not a reasoning animal; he is a seeing, feeling, contemplating, acting animal." In this sense theology that stood as a science was always notional, while religion, which was personal, imaginative and emotional, was real. This represented judgment based on the concreteness of the sense experience as distinct from the inference drawn from verbal argumentation. These views made Newman eagerly accepted by conservatives.[67]

## LATER YEARS

After taking the cardinal's hat, Newman's intellectual contributions contracted within the Catholic world. Though a Catholic through and through, he lacked the freedom of intellectual discussion, something he had valued in his *Idea of a University*. He longed for a greater license within the Church to discuss those theological matters that still needed examination. His letters and diary offer evidence of his private complaints against the Church's prerogative to end debate on questions that remained acute at the time. Papal infallibility blocked the very path of intellectual freedom that he had come to celebrate. It seems ironic that the person who pleaded for ecclesiastical authority over that of the state should have been treated so harshly by its ecclesiastical enforcers.[68]

From his cardinal's seat, Newman watched with dismay the energy created by liberalism, considering it the root cause of skepticism, the presumptuousness of private judgment, and the resulting impiety and human pride. He viewed the Enlightenment as an unchristian age where reason was given a standing that showed little or no recognition of people having been born with original sin. By giving in to the supremacy of reason and unlimited improvability, people had fatuously replaced God with human ego. Newman remained confident that the fruits of liberalism would prove ultimately destructive to humanity, leaving the individual with an inwardly hollow conscience attached to worldly desires, practical wisdom, and social virtues—all inattentive to God. Consequently, he viewed the world as turning to unbelief. Deceived by rationalistic faiths, those outside the Church faced an enormity of human catastrophes based on overestimation of rationality. Nor, for that matter, could the Bible provide authoritative prophecy. True authority came from the apostolic chair. This was the only authoritative instrument of Providence and the alternative to freedom of thought that had so undignified the race of man.[69]

As explained by political theorist and historian Russell Kirk, Newman was "devoted to the principle of aristocracy and the concept of loyalty to persons."[70] A sensitive and subtle person, he affirmed God's existence to be certain even though he could not find the logical grounds to explain it with satisfaction. In the tradition of Burke, he recognized the importance of faith, a conviction that he made clear in his writings. His spiritual and political conservatism served as a buffer between those like himself and the utilitarian ambitions to expand the power of education, which obviously reached across established class lines. In both religion and politics, he favored revealed religion rather than secular knowledge as the most direct access to moral improvement. Neither science nor the logic of words could bring certitude. Without a foundation in "first principles," science was nothing but an accumulation of unrelated facts—nothing with which to form lives.[71]

In 1890, after a long illness complicated by pneumonia, Newman died and was buried at the country house of the Oratory in Birmingham in the grave of his lifelong friend Ambrose St. John.

Most British and American Catholic intellectuals writing in the late nineteenth and early twentieth century were converts to Catholicism. These included Henry Manning, Orestes Brownson, Isaac Hecker, Evelyn Waugh, G. K. Chesterton, Martha Moore Avery, Augustus Welby Pugin, Katherine Burton, Christopher Dawson, Carlton Hays, Eric Gill, and Thomas Merton, among others. While the reasons for their conversions differed widely, it remains a curiosity why this occurred when, with the brief exception of the Roman Church's participation in the World's Parliament of Religions, the most evident characteristic of Catholicism at the time was its authoritarianism. As part of a romantic reaction to all forms of rationalism, Newman turned his back on the modern world. With Darwinism, eugenics, imperialism, and nationalism drawing allegiances from Anglo-American society, so too did papal infallibility, antimodernism, and acceptance of the Immaculate Conception. Not only did these converts attack Catholicism for its modernism, they invariably encountered distrust from the very community they had joined. This explains the excommunication of modernist theologian George Tyrrell and English biologist St. George Mivart for their views on evolution; Elizabeth Kite's support of eugenics; Dorothy Day's attention to nonviolence and social activism; and the criticism of the French philosopher Jacques Maritain for his refusal to support Franco in the Spanish Civil War. In explaining this phenomenon, Boston archbishop John Fitzpatrick observed that most converts failed to come into the fold through the "proper door," meaning they came by way of private judgment, which, for Catholicism, was too much of an antinomian endangerment.[72]

For all his pretense, Newman used the power of reason to denounce reason's ability to share the stage with Catholic dogma, which he accepted with a submissiveness that astounded critics and supporters alike. His readiness to make intellect a tool of belief, explained Gordon K. Lewis, was due to "a morbid self-distrust which led him to delight in the crucifixion of his own mind, to invite difficulties, to indulge in a self-abnegation that is reminiscent of the Augustinian Confessions." In sacrificing private judgment and reason for the authority of the Church and its traditions, he ignored the social and political history of Catholicism as if none of its historical roots had anything to do with the origination of its theological constructs—something that defied any substantive understanding of Judaism and Hellenism. Instead of showing an appreciation of the historical origins of Church doctrine, he chose to view the Reformation as the beginning of lawlessness, with liberalism and private judgment as its bastard offspring. "The tragedy of Newman," concluded Gordon K. Lewis, "was that his was a mind that was fascinated by the play of intellect yet ended in ruthlessly subordinating the claims of intellect to the demands of corporate tradition."[73]

When he made his bed in Catholicism, Newman found it difficult to reconcile himself to its dogmas not because he disbelieved them but because the arguments supporting them left him disappointed. While the Enlightenment's claims to rationality had been a source of Newman's criticism of liberalism, it was that same rationality that caused him to question the doctrines of eternal punishment, infallibility, and the Immaculate Conception. Having drunk the potion, he could not but affirm his faith in the authority of the apostolic chair. Many Anglicans viewed Newman's belated announcement of his acceptance of Rome as the culmination of a half dozen years as a disguised Catholic, someone who had foolishly traded his freedom of conscience for doctrinal certitude.

SELECTED WRITINGS

*The Arians of the Fourth Century* (1833)
*Tracts for the Times* (1833–1841)
*British Critic* (1836–1842)
*On the Prophetical Office of the Church* (1837)
*Lectures on Justification* (1838)
*Parochial and Plain Sermons* (1834–1843)
*Select Treatises of St. Athanasius* (1842, 1844)
*Lives of the English Saints* (1843–1844)
*Essays on Miracles* (1826, 1843)
*Oxford University Sermons* (1843)
*Sermons on Subjects of the Day* (1843)
*Historical Tracts of St. Athanasius* (1843)
*Essay on the Development of Christian Doctrine* (1845)
*Retraction of Anti-Catholic Statements* (1845)
*Loss and Gain* (1848)
*Faith and Prejudice and Other Unpublished Sermons* (1848–1873)
*Discourses to Mixed Congregations* (1849)
*Difficulties of Anglicans* (1850)
*The Present Position of Catholics in England* (1851)
*The Idea of a University* (1852, 1858)
*Cathedra Sempiterna* (1852)
*Callista* (1855)
*The Rambler* (ed., 1859–1860)
*Apologia pro Vita Sua* (1864)
*Letter to Dr. Pusey* (1865)
*The Dream of Gerontius* (1865)

# 3

## The Unknown
### Herbert Spencer

*In going down into the secrets of his own mind he has descended into the se-
crets of all minds. He learns that he who has mastered any law in his private
thoughts, is master to that extent of all men whose language he speaks, and of
all into whose language his own can be translated.*

—Ralph Waldo Emerson, "The American Scholar," 1849

THE ENGLISH PHILOSOPHER AND CLASSICAL liberal theorist Herbert
Spencer (1820–1903) grew up in a society dominated by the ideas
of Adam Smith in the sphere of economic policy and Jeremy Bentham
in politics and the positive law. An innovative and highly idiosyncratic
thinker with an encyclopedic love of data, he offered contributions to
the life of the mind that, as with Comte, were intended to incorporate all
knowledge. His adaptation of evolutionary thought to his so-called Synthetic philosophy broke down disciplinary walls and fenced-off realms of
inquiry, triggering an enormous impact on both Britain's liberal tradition
and the American business community, placing philosophy at the service of laissez-faire outcomes that forced labor and capital into seasons of
vengeful politics.[1] His free-market beliefs became the coin of American
oligarchs who justified the societal inequalities of modernity as the sine
qua non for humanity's progressive development. An almost forgotten
figure today, Spencer's reputation once rivaled Darwin's, who predicted
that Spencer "will be looked at as by far the greatest living philosopher in
England; perhaps equal to any that ever lived."[2]

Spencer formulated the elements of his philosophy in the early 1850s.
Published through subscription, they represented a prophetic effort to
construct a metaphysical system that synthesized all knowledge, including the future course of society, into a singular worldview. His synthetic
philosophy included *Principles of Psychology* (1855); *First Principles* (1860–
1862), which William James believed to be his greatest contribution; *The
Principles of Biology* (1864–1866); *The Principles of Psychology* (1872); *The
Principles of Ethics* (1879–1883); and *The Principles of Sociology* (1876–1896).
Together, they represented a universal system based on the principle of
competition ("survival of the fittest") while guaranteeing, under certain

conditions, that progress could be automatic, inevitable, and continuous.[3]

Spencer's writings caught the imagination of educated audiences everywhere. Backed with conjectures from astronomy, chemistry, physics, and the other sciences, he forced analogies between organisms and societies that gave credence to the interdependence of all structures and functions. His universal trending from the simple to the complex had its greatest impact in sociology and anthropology, where his ideas carried into the twentieth century. His organic analogies became corporate prescriptions for justifying, maintaining, and enforcing the status quo, that is, the adaptation of organisms to their environment as vindicated through individualism, laissez-faire policies, and the dismissal of governmental intervention. Considered one of the great Victorian thinkers and heir to the British school of empirical philosophy best reflected in the works of Bacon, Locke, Bentham, and Mill, Spencer defended humanity's self-serving acts not only because they produced the greatest happiness for the greatest number, but because they laid the groundwork for an ethical system that explained much of nineteenth-century British and American business and governmental beliefs and practices.[4]

## EARLY YOUTH

Born into a middle-class Derbyshire family whose ancestors included strains of French Huguenot and Bohemian Hussite Protestantism, Spencer was the first and only one of nine siblings to survive infancy. While his mother practiced a quiet and self-effacing Methodism, his father, a convert to Quakerism and an unconventional teacher, managed a private academy modeled on the theories of Swiss pedagogue Johann Heinrich Pestalozzi. Directing his lessons to the laws and properties of things, he typically began each class session with the question "Can you tell me the cause of this?"[5] From his lessons, Spencer learned that "every man who wished to know things really must rummage them out for himself in all sorts of ways, the odder, the more out of the way, the more difficult, all the better."[6]

Spencer's intellectual development owed much to the community of Derby, a textile and china manufacturing town in the English Midlands with a tradition of strong dissenting views. Similar to the provincial towns of Manchester, Leeds, and Birmingham, its scientific, philosophical, and literary societies were controlled by the clergy and gentry, who treated them as their personal fiefdom. The Derby Philosophical Society was a gentleman's organization formed in 1783 and boasted Erasmus Darwin as its first president. His theories, which were Lamarckian in context, carried far and wide across the English countryside. Other societies included the Derbyshire Agricultural Society, the Literary and Philosophical Society, the Mechanics' Institute, the County Museum and Natural History Society, the Young Men's Mutual Improvement Society, the Arboretum, Literary and Scientific Society. Each served as a portal of opportunity for the emerging middle class.[7]

Spencer subscribed as a youth to both the Philosophical Society's Library and the Methodist Library, giving him access to a wealth of scientific and philosophical periodicals, including the *Lancet, British and Foreign Medical Review, Medico-Chirurgical Review, Athenaeum, Mechanics' Magazine*, and *Chambers' Journal*. He also read history, personal narratives, and especially the details of battles and sieges. Because of his father's declining health, Spencer lived for a time with his uncle, the Reverend Thomas Spencer, at Hinton Charterhouse near Bath. An avowed free-trader and Chartist supporter, he served as editor of the *National Temperance Chronicle* and authored pamphlets on religion and politics. Spencer stayed with his uncle for three years, studying Euclid, Latin, Greek, grammar, algebra, chemistry, trigonometry, Arnott's *Physics*, Wood's *Mechanics*, and Martineau's *Tales of Political Economy*. He later admitted in his *Autobiography* that "none but the vaguest ideas of the contents of these books survive[d]." Where he did blossom beyond what boys commonly learned in school were concepts of physical principles, physics, chemistry, insect life, and medical, anatomical, and physiological information. Bright, self-confident, and at home with both a priori and a posteriori argumentation, he acquired a strong interest in science while ideas of the supernatural rapidly deflated.[8]

## BEGINNINGS OF A CAREER

After a false start trying his hand at teaching, Spencer was hired as a civil engineer with the London and Birmingham Railway. A year later he was promoted to the engineering staff of the Birmingham and Gloucester Railway, where, over a period of four years, he worked surveying, designing machinery, and providing other services. His tendency for "independent thinking," however, had a negative effect on his fellow workers, forcing managers to transfer him from one position to another. "Alien in culture, ideas, sentiments, and aims, from most of the young men with whom this new engagement brought me in contact, they regarded me as an oddity," he admitted in his *Autobiography*. "Constitutionally wanting in reticence, I never concealed my dissent from their opinions and feelings whenever I felt it."[9]

Spencer wrote his first article for the *Civil Engineer and Architect's Journal* in 1839. Others followed in quick succession, as he found the written word easier than conversation. After refusing a permanent post with the railroad, he returned to Derby, where he acquired an interest in plant specimens, making pencil sketches of fossils unearthed in railroad construction, and attending lectures on phrenology, which had become a popular topic within Derby's scientific community. From conversations with family members and his own study of individualism and freedom, he wrote a series of letters for the *Nonconformist* paper that addressed commercial restrictions, the Anglican Church, Poor Laws, colonization, national education, sanitary administration, and war, most of which he incorporated into his first book, *Social Statics*. Like his uncle, he also entered the political waters of Chartist agitation, advocating universal suffrage, triennial parliaments, vote by ballot, and other reforms.

After spending time at home in leisurely pursuits, Spencer resolved to try his luck as a professional writer. Moving to London, he wrote for the *Phrenological Journal* and the *Zoist* on mesmeric experiments, phrenomesmerism, and associated topics, eventually concluding that "the statements of phrenologists might contain adumbrations of truths [but] they did not express the truths themselves." Without a steady income and finding only the occasional odd job in engineering design work, he returned to Derby, where he planned a weekly paper, which failed for lack of financial backing.[10]

Following a brief time in Birmingham as an assistant editor of the *Pilot*, penning articles on the proper sphere of government, land nationalization, the place and role of women in society, and laissez-faire economics, Spencer returned once again to London, joining the staff of the *Economist*, a magazine originally established by the Anti-Corn Law League as a propaganda organ. He remained with the magazine from 1848 to 1853, drawing his ideas from the combined influences of evangelical Methodist and Quaker/Socinian rationalism and the laissez-faire beliefs of Thomas Hodgskin, the magazine's editor. As historian J. D. Y. Peel observed, Spencer's thinking was the projection of British history away from its authoritarian and aristocratic origins toward a national character that preferred capital accumulation, peace, and a more egalitarian society.[11]

## Social Statics

Those English thinkers preoccupied with the miseries and injustices stemming from the Industrial Revolution tended to reject the extreme formulas produced by the French Revolution. This explains the popularity of Jeremy Bentham's *Introduction to the Principles of Morals and Legislation* (1789) and John Stuart Mill's *Principles of Political Economy* (1848). It also explains why Spencer's *Social Statics*, an early example of science-based morality, was more favorably received than any of his later works. As a disciple of Lamarck, Spencer insisted that social evils resulted from the "non-adaptation of the constitution to conditions," namely, the placement of the individual in situations for which his powers did not fit. On the other hand, all changes toward "fitness" to the surrounding circumstances constituted progress, and "in virtue of this process, man will eventually become completely suited to his mode of life." To the extent that human faculties were molded into complete fitness for the social state, so surely did man have the potential to become perfect. "The modifications mankind have undergone, and are still undergoing," Spencer reasoned, "result from a law underlying the whole organic creation; and provided the human race continues, and the constitution of things remains the same, those modifications must end in completeness."[12]

Except for Comte's Religion of Humanity and his refusal to include psychology in his classification of the sciences, there was much that the two men held in common.[13] Nevertheless, Spencer remained forever touchy on the issue of intellectual borrowing and denied any indebtedness to Comte or his philosophy. "The disciples of M. Comte think that I am much indebted to him; and so I am, but in a way widely unlike that which they mean," he insisted. "Save in the adoption of his word 'altruism,' which I have defended, and in the adoption of his word 'sociology,' because there was no other available word (for both which adoptions I have been blamed), the only indebtedness I recognize is the indebtedness of antagonism."[14]

Having placed his confidence in the human ability to formulate individual and social characteristics from the effects of religion, custom, superstition, prejudice, mental tendencies, and the probabilities of future events, Spencer urged the identification of those moral forces upon which the social equilibrium and the continuance of the race depended. Against what he viewed were the failures of Lord Shaftesbury and Francis Hutchinson's *Moral Sense*, Thomas Read and James Beattie's *Common Sense*, Richard Price's *Understanding*, and Granville Sharpe's *Natural Equity*, he offered his own analysis of man's relationship to society. "Right principles of action become practicable, only as man becomes perfect," he opined, and "man becomes perfect, just in so far as he is able to obey them." Man can know only that the soul of the world is good and that "his part in it is to conform to the Law of the Whole." Even though progress was inevitable, it applied only to the outcome, not intermediary levels. For progress to succeed, there must be as few restrictions as possible.[15]

At the heart of *Social Statics* stood the "law of right social relationships,'" which stated that "every man has freedom to do all that he wills, provided he infringes not the equal freedom of any other man." In obeying the law, man demonstrated his justness. Important in ethics and an essential ingredient in politics and the law, it ensured society's greatness.

> In the social state the sphere of activity of each individual being limited by the spheres of activity of other individuals, it follows that the men who are to realize this greatest sum of happiness, must be men of whom each can obtain complete happiness within his own sphere of activity, without diminishing the spheres of activity required for the acquisition of happiness by others. For manifestly, if each or any of them cannot receive complete happiness without lessening the spheres of activity of one or more of the rest, he must either himself come short of complete happiness, or must make one or more do so; and hence under such circumstances, the sum total of happiness cannot be as great as is conceivable, or cannot be greatest happiness. Here then is the first of those fixed conditions to the obtainment of greatest happiness, necessitated by the social state.[16]

Operating on the assumption that the individual and the state had contrary interests, meaning that the role of the state too often undermined personal freedom, Spencer argued for the nonregulation of industry and opposition to the established church, colonization, and even public education. It was man's duty to forbid the state to administer religion or charity; it was equally important for the state to abstain from providing education, as it set the government on a course where children became wards of the state. The so-called right to education was not in the long-term interest of either the individual or the state. Education, he insisted, remained a parental responsibility.

The same restrictions applied to measures of public health. "Partly by weeding out those lowest in development and partly by subjecting those who remain to the never-ceasing discipline of experience," Spencer reasoned, "nature secures the growth of a race who shall both understand the conditions of existence and be able to act up to them."[17] Protecting individuals from their own ignorance meant nothing but disastrous consequences for the greater society. "Beings thus imperfect are nature's failures, and are recalled by her laws when found to be such. . . . If they are not sufficiently complete to live, they die, and it is best they should die." Suspending the law of equal freedom defeated the best of intentions, as sympathy for fellow persons came with unintended consequences. "Instead of diminishing suffering, it eventually increases it. It favours the multiplication of those worst fitted for existence and, by consequence, hinders the multiplication of those best fitted for existence." Government must limit its power to shielding its citizens from the aggressions of neighbors and from foreign governments. Anything beyond these two minimal responsibilities, and the state became an aggressor instead of a protector. Inserting itself in any action beyond these minimal responsibilities retarded adaption and delayed progress. The State must step aside and allow nature to take its course without interference. Then, and only then, could there be progress.[18]

Exemplary of society's ill-informed sympathy had been the passage of the so-called Poor Laws, whose "spurious philanthropy" had prevented "present misery" at the expense of "greater misery upon future generations." All that the Poor Laws had achieved was to delay the course of society from its ultimate destination. In their place, Spencer proposed "stern discipline," which, while admittedly cruel in the short term, promised to be kind overall—a purifying process for the well-being of humanity.[19]

The doctrine of laissez-faire held a central role in Spencer's thinking. Advocating on behalf of the self-reliant individual, he insisted that the state had no right to succor the poor, much less carry the mail or improve sanitation. Society advanced by means of "survival of the fittest," bringing early demise to the weak and intemperate but promising a cosmic redemption at the end of its benign purging. As explained by William James, Spencer's doctrine of laissez-faire was statistical in kind, constructed of collections of information where "the fate of the individual fact is swallowed up in that of the aggregate total." Despite Spencer's celebration of individualism, James believed that his philosophy minimized the role of the individual, whose survival depended on being dragged along in "fatal tow."[20]

## EVOLUTIONARY THOUGHT

In 1853 Spencer left the *Economist* and, supported by a small legacy from his uncle, embarked on a career as an independent writer. Although he could not recall the time or place when he first entertained any definite belief about the origin of the universe or of living things, he speculated that it had come from reading Lyell's *Principles of Geology* when he was twenty.[21] Another prelude came with his "Development Hypothesis," published in the *Leader* in 1852. By no means shy in self-esteem, he wrote his father, claiming that the article would "ultimately stand beside Newton's *Principia.*"[22] This was followed by "A Theory of Population Deduced from the General Law of Animal Fertility" published in the *Westminster Review,* which introduced the phrase "struggle for existence." Darwin would later adopt the phrase to explain his theory of natural selection. Finally, Spencer's theory of change from homogeneity to heterogeneity came a year afterward (1854) in "The Art of Education," which appeared in the *North British Review.*[23]

Spencer viewed matter as passing from homogeneity to heterogeneity, with dissolution occurring when resistance overcame equilibrium and lost its force. To be precise, "evolution is an integration of matter and concomitant dissipation of motion; during which the matter passes from an indefinite, incoherent homogeneity to a definite, coherent heterogeneity; and during which the retained motion undergoes a parallel transformation." Evolution did not extend forever, since the redistribution of matter and motion eventually and necessarily took place. Thus, evolution was but one aspect of a process that ultimately produced its opposite, dissolution. The state was an organism operating within the panorama of evolution and always seeking to adjust its diversity of functions to the environment with its goal of modifying egoistic impulses with altruistic interests. At any one time, some systems (e.g., societies) were in a state of integration, others in decay. As evolution moved inexorably toward greater complexity, those in a state of integration reached a state of adjustment or harmony between the inner condition of the organism and the external condition of its environment—a point of peaceful adjustment in accord with the use-inheritance contentions of Lamarck.[24]

In his superorganic view of the universe, Spencer theorized that the behavior of all life forms, including humans, was drawn into this scheme. The entire universe was enveloped in progressive development from homogeneity to heterogeneity. As explained by historian Goblet d'Alviella, "The fluctuations of the exchange are thus subject to the same law as the passage of a comet; while the victories of Alexander and the works of Shakespeare are reducible to the same factors as the Falls of Niagara and the spots on the sun."[25] Progress was no accident; it came through competition, struggle, and adaptation. The law of evolution penetrated every sphere of life, which American anthropologist Marvin Harris described as "the biologization of history without surrendering the Enlightenment's dream of universal progress."[26]

Spencer approached evolution in the context of eighteenth-century mechanics. A believer in Lamarckian use-inheritance, he adapted laissez-faire individualism to his evolutionary model, where good actions carried out by well-adjusted individuals promoted the greatest happiness. With his thought focused on the individual, and only secondarily on the species, he offered a nuanced understanding of established social and political theories. Nevertheless, his development hypothesis applied across the spectrum, from plants to politics, economics, and society, believing that all were affected by the idea of differentiation.

Spencer did little to adjust his ideas to Darwin's theory of nondirectional natural selection. Preferring a Lamarckian point of view, his law of evolution pictured an organism confronted by a different or challenging environment and reacting purposively to bring about a successful adaptation to the new set of circumstances. The life of any organism was one of continuous adjustment of its internal makeup to external conditions. The growing differentiation and the increasing heterogeneity from one generation to another resulted from the inheritance of acquired characteristics. This seemed to Spencer to be the natural inference from the facts he and his assistants collected. He could not imagine any other explanation; neither could his disciples, who regarded his philosophy with the surety of religion.[27]

With Darwin, evolution was a biological law; with Spencer it became a cosmic generalization that carried the day among social scientists, tracing the development of living organisms and societies from the homogeneous to the heterogeneous, from the simple to the complex, from the incoherent to the coherent, and from the indefinite to the definite. His conception of society as an organism was certainly not new. Since the time of Plato, it had served as a foundation for the advocacy of different forms of government. As a defender of liberalism, individualism, and laissez-faire, Spencer made frequent use of the biological analogy to explain how, as a social organism, society was subject to universal laws. As explained by sociologist and economist Werner Stark, Spencer viewed society in an organismic and quasi-biological manner, obeying "all the laws of structure, function and development which are characteristic, and which are constitutive, of organic life." Those functions that organs performed in the body were no different than units such as industry and labor that performed in the social organism—competing with one another, acting and reacting to the changing environment, and growing in proportion to their adjustment of functions. Stark compared Spencer to Goethe's Faust, "torn hither and thither by conflicting loyalties" as he conceived sociology first as organismic and then as cultural, the product of human, not natural forces, operating in a manner that cleared a path for some indeterminate cosmic goal.[28]

To be sure, Darwin and Spencer used similar language, including the phrase "survival of the fittest," an expression Spencer coined in 1852, but their approaches to evolution were decidedly different. For Spencer, evolution accounted for *all* change—from biology to psychology, sociology, and ethics. In his *First Principles*, published in 1862, three years after Darwin's *Origin*, Spencer gave only a brief notice to natural selection. The same applied to his *Principles of Biology* (1864–1867) as it, too, continued his conviction that organisms had the capacity for self-adjustment and consequent improvement.[29] Through adaptation, organisms established equilibrium with their changing environment. New conditions produced useful (direct) and random (indirect) variation in a species, but adaptive change was the primary cause of variation. Lamarckism as a theory offered the prospect of rapid progression if man was not indifferent to the consequences of his volitions should he interfere with the process.[30]

## The Knowable and the Unknown

With *First Principles* as his foundation, Spencer placed all knowledge on a deductive basis, declining to know or understand the true nature of things, only their appearance. One cannot know the nature of reality. "At the uttermost reach of discovery there arises, and must ever arise, the question—What lies beyond?" By continually seeking to know and being constantly reminded of the impossibility of knowing the ultimate nature of that which was manifested to humanity, Spencer arrived at the "Unknowable" (i.e., "the persistence of some Cause which transcends our knowledge or conception"), concluding that if science and religion were ever to be reconciled, the basis for that reconciliation would manifest itself to humankind as "utterly inscrutable."[31]

Spencer introduced the Unknowable seven years before Huxley coined the term *agnostic*. Neither the ultimate ideas of religion nor those of science could be fully comprehended; in their ultimate essence, neither could be completely known. "Ultimate religious ideas and ultimate scientific ideas, alike turn out to be merely symbols of the actual, not cognitions of it." The very nature of knowledge was relative. Still, there was a solution out of this difficulty.

> Common Sense asserts the existence of a reality; Objective Science proves that this reality cannot be what we think it; Subjective Science shows why we cannot think of it as it is, and yet are compelled to think of it as existing;

and in this assertion of a Reality utterly inscrutable in nature, Religion finds an assertion essentially coinciding with her own. We are obliged to regard every phenomenon as a manifestation of some Power by which we are acted upon; though Omnipresence is unthinkable, yet, as experience discloses no bounds to the diffusion of phenomena, we are unable to think of limits to the presence of this Power; while the criticisms of Science teach us that this Power is Incomprehensible. And this consciousness of an In-comprehensible Power, called Omnipresent from inability to assign its limits, is just that consciousness on which Religion dwells.[32]

Over the centuries, explained Spencer, both religion and science had undergone an "imperfect separation of their spheres and functions." In its purification religion continued to recognize a supreme verity. The same applied to science, which, after grouping the relations of phenom-ena into laws, progressed to causes that were abstract. In accomplishing this task, science was "slowly approaching . . . the inconceivable or un-thinkable." Each had relinquished ground that it falsely claimed while gaining from the other "that to which it had a right." Out of their compet-ing modes of consciousness emerged an Inscrutable Power whose nature transcended the limits of intelligence.[33] Having rejected the anthropo-morphic notion of God, Spencer substituted the Unknowable as recogni-tion of the absence of those conditions required for ultimate truth. Thus, while the Unknowable remained a vague and inscrutable something, it persisted in consciousness as a condition of experience—a positive but indefinite condition of knowledge.[34]

Spencer's Unknown comforted Victorians, in that it represented a line of demarcation between the unresolved nature of consciousness on the one hand and material existence on the other.[35] It celebrated the ultimate mysteriousness of the world, or what William James described as "the ex-istence of a Supreme Reality behind the veil." Once having recognized the mystery, however, Spencer dismissed it "with an affectionate good-bye" and proceeded to focus his attention on showing how society could move toward greater perfection. The infinite, absolute, impersonal, and inscrutable Unknowable represented Spencer's contribution to religion. Not a religious person, he settled on the ultimate mystery of existence, accepting that science could never displace religion but that evolution would eventually bring adjustment between the two.[36]

GATHERING STORM

Spencer convinced his generation that the entire fabric of the natural sciences, the social institutions, and even the mind and consciousness were subject to the law of evolution. This was the foundation on which the universe functioned and which he put into a coherent formula for his generation. His deductive hypothesis, which he corroborated rather than tested with facts, was opposite Darwin's inductive methodology. Though initially supportive, Darwin had difficulty understanding Spencer's reasoning and his deductive manner of treating every subject. As Spencer relied more and more on the immanent power of the Unknowable, Darwin became less and less supportive.[37] "If he had trained himself to observe more, even if at the expense, by the law of balancement, of some loss of thinking power, he would have been a wonderful man."[38] Notwithstanding Darwin's objections, Spencer transformed evolution into an all-embracing philosophy. With evidence generalized from Lamarck and borrowed from Comte's positivism, he brought the whole of knowledge into a singular worldview. Advanced as prophetic truth, the outcome of a multitude of superfluous facts, his synthetic philosophy proposed a complete system of knowledge. Working with only those facts that validated his formulae and a unilinear system constructed on the comparative method, the whole of the universe proceeded through an evolutionary process to arrive at predetermined conclusions.

That said, it seems remarkable that Spencer succeeded in convincing a generation of scholars of his unfailing assertions. This is explained in part by the mass of data arranged by assistants to buttress his points. "The material," explained Charles H. Cooley, "was collected under Spencer's direction by assistants, usually, I think, with a definite plan as to what he meant to get out of it."[39] Spencer relied on selective data to illustrate and corroborate his theory, not to test its accuracy. The very coherence of what became known as social Darwinism depended upon this continuity.[40]

As social Darwinism (i.e., Spencerianism) became part of a historical movement addressing the concept, theory, and philosophy of evolution, it entered the literature as a set of beliefs used to explain and defend the "natural order" of things. Some saw it guaranteeing progress and ensuring a constantly increasing perfection of man and/or the world; others saw it as God's method of creation, and still others as the application of a process that explained change in a universal manner. It was a power to which words such as "divine," "wise," "intelligent," "uniform," and "impersonal" were ascribed. From the Greeks onward, there had been notions of evolution and dissolution to explain the universe and its separate parts. Comte in France and Karl Marx in Germany stood as exponents of this new force, and each found in science a philosophy intended for the salvation of humankind. Like them, Spencer interpreted progress as no accident, only a necessity. "What we call evil and immorality must disappear. It is certain that man must become perfect."[41] He warned, however, that well-intentioned efforts to secure the safety of others' irresponsible acts only interfered with and delayed the process. Preserving the competitive process regardless of its seeming insensitivity ensured a highly integrated and progressively improved society.

Spencer's views were mimicked at home and abroad. His laissez-faire individualism fit admirably with American culture, making him the darling of the business community. The severity of his social philosophy, which was quite gloomy in its impact on the "unfit," offered both maximum freedom and happiness for those who survived. According to historian Vernon Louis Parrington, Spencer's disciples insisted that outside the complexities of evolution's competitive process, the theory "opened wide the doors of a vaster future," confirming what Americans had already identified as their common heritage.[42] As the laborer economist John R. Commons recalled, he was raised on "Hoosierism, Republicanism, Presbyterianism, and Spencerism."[43]

A generation or more of social scientists felt the full effects of their intoxication with Spencer's philosophy. Their science of society became a study of human customs, theology, and history fulfilling a preordained role. Dignified by evolution and the comparative method, their elaborate schemes of social development formulated the laws of growth for the Aryan races and relegated all non-Aryan peoples to either atavisms or outcasts from evolution's benign processes. Organic analogies and the comparative method produced fruitful explanations for the ways in which evolution institutionalized many distorted and falsified observations.[44]

Americans failed to distinguish between Darwin and Spencer. Without a blink of the eye, they confirmed that the evolutionary hypothesis worked on a grand scale. After reading both their works, Andrew Carnegie remarked: "Not only had I got rid of theology and the supernatural, but I had found the truth of evolution." Evolutionary progress in all forms became the byword of Carnegie's generation. In *The Gospel of Wealth*, he repeatedly referred to Spencer's "survival of the fittest," "the struggle for existence," and the "law of competition" as moral proof that the competitive struggle was good for the individual and the society.[45]

A. H. Lloyd of the University of Michigan called Spencer's philosophy one of "inbetween-ness" in that it fell between science and philosophy without satisfying either. Nevertheless, Spencer was a person whose

views could not be overlooked. His synthetic philosophy gathered followers in England, on the continent, and especially in America, where its advocates dominated the sciences and social sciences.[46]

Spencer's uncompromising individualism appealed to Americans.
Writers Hamlin Garland and Jack London were drawn to his ideas, hoping to free the genteel tradition from its theological inhibitions, while Columbia University economist/sociologist Frank H. Giddings regarded
Spencer as "the true founder of scientific sociology and as its greatest
constructive thinker."[47] Then again, sociologist Charles H. Cooley, eighth
president of the American Sociological Association, explained: "I imagine that nearly all of us who took up sociology between 1870, say, and
1890, did so at the instigation of Spencer." Though nearly all in the discipline "fell away from him sooner or later and more or less completely,"
his *Study of Sociology* (1896) did more to arouse interest in the discipline
that any publication before or since.[48]

Begun in 1862 and completed in 1896, Spencer's nine-volume *System
of Synthetic Philosophy* failed to bring the recognition he expected. A solitary figure whose ideas had long overstayed their welcome, he faced a
world immune to all but his belief in individualism. "I do not wonder
that, as he looked back over his magnificent life-work," wrote William
Henry Hudson in 1904, "his mind should have been darkened by the
doubt as to whether some of the truths to which he attached the greatest value might not, after all, have been set forth in vain."[49] One critic regarded the mass of information gathered on customs and manners as
little more than "a huge pile of cuttings . . . made to order" from various
travelers and extracted by the three assistants whom Mr. Spencer had employed.[50] Others were similarly harsh in their appraisal of his legacy. "It is
a pity that Mr. Spencer did not devote some years more of thought to his
work before publishing it," wrote one reviewer. "He might then have set
forth the truths it contains freed from the crude ideas with which they are
now mingled, and undisfigured by illegitimate corollaries."[51]

Long before Spencer completed his encyclopedic efforts, his synthetic
philosophy had all but perished as a newer generation of scientists and
social scientists took aim at his fragmentary proofs. A synthetic philosophy, however desirable, proved an impossible undertaking. "There are no
more Aristotles," wrote George Sarton, "and if one of these giants were to
come back, the immensity of accumulated knowledge would make him
feel like a pigmy."[52]

Just as scientists outgrew Spencer's science, finding it too philosophical and remote from the inductive method, so too did philosophers tire

of his evolutionary perfectionism. Writing in 1903, William James speculated that Spencer's ethical and political writings, especially the spirit of individualism in human life, were the most likely to endure, while his *Biology*, *Psychology*, and *Sociology* would probably become obsolete. Coarsely carried out, little remained of value. Despite the many imperfections in Spencer's philosophy, James admired "the bravery of his attempt [as] he sought to see truth as a whole. He brought us back to the old ideal philosophy, which since Locke's time had well-nigh taken flight; the ideal, namely, of a completely unified knowledge. . . . This was the original Greek ideal of philosophy, to which men surely must return."[53] British mathematician Thomas P. Kirkman, offered his own variation of Spencer's evolutionary formula: "Evolution is a change from a nohow-ish, untalkaboutable, all-alikeness, to a somehowish and in-general-talk-aboutable not-all-alikeness, by continuous something-elsifications and sticktogetherations."[54]

## LAST YEARS

A dyspeptic bachelor, Spencer lived out his final years in self-imposed isolation in Brighton. For those he continued to see, his conversations appeared as sound-bites from his books. Scrupulous in his details, his comments were usually measured to be the final word on any subject. As his doctrines faded, he grew sour, vain, and destitute of humor. Passionately devoted to his work, he divided his energies between finding facts to support his doctrines and mollifying his health with rest. Irritable and quick tempered, he showed little tolerance toward critics, refusing even to read authors with whom he disagreed. Such unflinching rigidness tended to be overly severe even to those who were sympathetic to his ideas.[55] His willingness to withdraw from conversation was never more evident than in the spring-operated, circular, fitted "ear stoppers" he sometimes wore. Once activated, they reduced the chatter of conversation around him to a mere hum. In this way he could detach himself from the conversation of friends and strangers in a matter of seconds. Content with the cessation of conversation, and not the least embarrassed by his unsociable disposition, he acted surprised that anyone would take umbrage with his action.[56]

Spencer died in 1903 at the age of eighty-four and, by any definition of the term, represented one of the most admired men of the Victorian Age, having spent much of his career in the earnest endeavor to classify men's minds. This attribution remains intact due largely to his terse phrase "survival of the fittest," which became a hallmark of the time and used randomly across disciplines. More than a million copies of his books sold, many translated into French, German, Spanish, Italian, and Russian.

Any effort to assess Spencer's importance is skewed by the fact that the very scholars who evaluated his life's work did so from the comfort of their narrow disciplines without appreciating the challenge of his integrated intellectual approach. In our present day, synthetic knowledge is little understood as scientists and social scientists gravitate toward ever-increasing specializations. So intense and authentic is this analytic research that general knowledge, however practical, is often relegated to the dustbin as faked or worthless.

The First World War represented a watershed in the acceptance of Spencer's philosophy that had expressed so clearly "the view of nature, life, and history which seemed to us once to be the pure reflection of an age of scientific discovery and industrial evolution."[57] Relegated to a rank of a second-rate philosopher who had overstayed his relevance, Spencer is seldom referenced except as some historical or transitional figure. Once considered masterpieces in the world of books, his writings "now line the back shelves of second-hand bookstores."[58] "Who now reads Spencer?" asked Talcott Parson in 1937. "It is difficult for us to realize how great a stir he made in the world. . . . We must agree with the verdict. Spencer is dead."[59]

## Selected Writings

"The Proper Sphere of Government" (1843)

*Social Statics; or, The Conditions Essential to Human Happiness Specified and the First of Them Developed* (1851)

"A Theory of Population" (1852)

*The Principles of Psychology* (1855)

*Education, Intellectual, Moral and Physical* (1861)

*First Principles* (1862)

*Principles of Biology* (1864, 1867)

*Principles of Psychology* (1870, 1880)

*The Study of Sociology* (1873)

*Descriptive Sociology* (1873–1881)

*Principles of Sociology* (1874–1896)

*The Data of Ethics* (1879)

*Essays, Scientific, Political and Speculative, first, second, and third series* (1858, 1863, 1891)

*Man versus the State* (1884)
*The Factors of Organic Evolution* (1893)
*Various Fragments* (1897)
*Facts and Comments* (1902)
*An Autobiography* (1904)

# 4

## Higher Intelligence
### Alfred Russel Wallace

*I am well aware that my scientific friends are somewhat puzzled to account for what they consider to be my delusion, and believe that it has injuriously af-fected whatever power I may have once possessed of dealing with the philoso-phy of Natural History.*
—Alfred Russel Wallace, *On Miracles and Modern Spiritualism*, 1875

AS A MEMBER OF THE scientific community, the British naturalist Al-fred Russel Wallace (1823–1913) was well attuned to the philosoph-ical and scientific issues of his day involving the nature and age of the earth, the centers of creation, the meaning of fossils, the geographical distribution and affinity of species, and the succession of types. Together with Charles Darwin, he stands as the recognized cofounder of the theory of natural selection. A spiritualized Owenite with interests in phrenology, life on Mars, ethnology, vaccination, women's rights, land reform, and so-cialism, he refused to forfeit his working-class values for acceptance into Britain's rigid class structure. Unfazed by their rejection, he affirmed his faith in Spiritualism, using it as a springboard for his progressive polit-ical beliefs and activities as well as his modified explanation of human evolution. A generous, deferential, and warm-hearted man, and author of twenty-two books and over five hundred articles, he won the admiration of nearly all who knew him.[1]

### EARLY YEARS

The seventh of nine children born into a lower-middle-class family in the Welsh village of Llanbadoc in Monmouthshire, Wallace grew up with few opportunities other than his own initiative. His father, Thomas Vere Wallace, an attorney for the Court of King's Bench, abandoned law for life as a "gentleman" until his marriage in 1807, when, to augment his income, he pooled his resources to publish a magazine devoted to art, antiquities, and general literature. After only a few issues, the publica-tion folded, saddling him with heavy debt. Without the means to make it right, he moved his growing family to Usk in southeast Wales, where the cost of living allowed them to live cheaply and in relative comfort. Even when supplemented by his wife's small dowry, occasional tutoring of pupils, and work in the town's library, he failed to resolve the family's financial status, which remained precarious at best. As a member of the Anglican Church, Thomas loved reading and occasionally wrote poetry but otherwise, according to his son, "possessed no special talent, either literary, artistic, or scientific." Quiet and even-tempered, he wore a beaver top hat about town and a much-weathered straw hat working in the family's vegetable garden.[2]

When Wallace was six, the family moved to Hertford in southern England, his memories of which included swimming in the river Lea, admiring the gear-works at the local grain mill, watching cricket matches, enjoying the rich meadows and parks, and spending time in the loft above the stable, where he and his playmates hid "forbidden treasures" of homemade popguns, spring-pistols, and cherrystone chains. As his parents were "old-fashioned" believers in the Church of England, he attended services twice on Sundays and listened to his father read from the Bible in the evenings. He also recalled attending the services of Dissenters, preferring their "vigorous and exciting style of preaching" to the "monotony" of his parents' religion. Though he spent his early childhood in a relatively orthodox religious environment, he admitted to having no awakened emotions or enduring impressions.[3]

Because of the family's impoverished situation, Wallace and his siblings were limited in their educational opportunities. His older brother William spent a year apprenticed to a firm of surveyors at Kingston in Herefordshire, and then with a London architect, where he learned the fundamentals of the building trade. His sister Fanny attended a French school at Lille before immigrating to the United States, where she taught French and English at Columbia College in Georgia; she returned to England in 1846. His brother John was apprenticed to a London builder, learning the trades of joiner, carpenter, and surveyor before immigrating to California, where he worked as a water engineer. His younger brother, Herbert, was placed with a trunk maker in Regent Street but, not liking the business world, joined Wallace in the Amazon. There he caught yellow fever and died at the age of twenty-two. Of the other children, one died when five months old, two others at ages six and eight.

At the Hertford Grammar School, which Wallace attended until age fourteen, Latin was the most wearisome of his studies, with history and geography not much better, as they were taught by rote, requiring little more than learning names and dates. "Whatever little knowledge of history I have ever acquired," he later admitted, "has been derived more from Shakespeare's plays and from good historical novels than from anything I learned at school." The constant stream of books circulating among family members due to his father's work as town librarian did more for his intellectual development than all his formal education.[4]

Because of the family's inability to pay for Wallace's continued education, the school remitted his fees on condition that he tutor the younger boys. His impoverishment led to painful remarks from fellow students, which he remembered as a "constant humiliation" in later years. Shamed by the ridicule of classmates, he left school angry at his treatment and the conditions that put him in that position. The experience left him mindful of the practice known as "saving face" common in Chinese and Japanese cultures, an expression that perhaps explained his work ethic and contempt of the British class system. Continued financial problems, including the eventual loss of the children's meager legacies, forced the family to move to an even smaller house on St. Andrew's Street in 1836, and then to Hoddesdon, where his father died in 1843.[5]

## FINDING A CAREER

Wallace entered the workforce in 1837 with only a modicum of formal education, assisting his brother John and later William. Surveying with John, whom he described as a man "of advanced liberal and philosophical opinions," brought Wallace face-to-face with the Midlands railway boom and the economic and social consequences of the General Enclosure Acts in England and Wales, which removed nearly seven million acres of commons land from collective use, turning them over to landowners who then charged rent.[6] The enclosure of the commons, to which the public theretofore had free passage and which the poor used as pasture for their domestic animals and fuel for their fires, resulted in agricultural depression, a dramatic increase in pauperism, and new rounds of landlord rents. Wallace viewed the legislation as "one of many acts of robbery" perpetuated by and on behalf of the landed gentry. As a result of this state-supported cruelty, farm families were reduced "from comfort to penury," forced to immigrate to towns and cities to find work or become "law-created paupers" driven to workhouses. This "all-embracing system of land-robbery" made an indelible impression on Wallace's life and his eventual preference for socialism. Later in life, encouraged by Henry George's *Progress and Poverty* (1879) and his single-tax theory, Wallace became president of the Land Nationalization Society and presented his own reform agenda in "Land Nationalization: Its Necessity and Its Aims" in 1882, and later in *Studies Scientific and Social*, published in 1900.[7]

Between jobs, Wallace spent his evenings at the Hall of Science off Tottenham Court Road in London, an Owenite institution for working-men, where he attended lectures, read papers, played dominoes, and drank coffee. As he recounted in his memoirs, the hall served as a mechanics institute "for advanced thinkers" among workmen and especially for followers of Welsh reformer Robert Owen, founder of the socialist movement in England. Owen's anti-Malthusian lectures, combined with his *New View of Society* (1813), became a heady influence on young Wallace, who adopted Owen's socialist doctrines. He also met Owen's eldest son, Robert Dale, who attacked the doctrine of eternal punishment taught by the Church of England and Dissenters. From his lectures on secularism, Wallace concluded "that the orthodox religion of the day was degrading and hideous, and that the only true and wholly beneficial religion was that which inculcated the service of humanity, and whose only dogma was the brotherhood of man." This attitude became the foundation for his religious skepticism and freethinking.[8] "Although I look upon Christianity as originating in an unusual spiritual influx," he admitted, "I am not disposed to consider [it] as essentially different from those which originated other great religious and philanthropic movements. It is probable that in your sense of the word I am not a Christian."[9] Wallace belonged to no organized church and was probably an agnostic before turning to Spiritualism as his religion of choice. His concept of "Inherent Power" eventually transitioned into an "Overruling Intelligence," both of which influenced his later views and modification of evolution.[10]

From his experiences at the Hall of Science, Wallace formulated his earliest political views, which, not surprisingly, were based on Owen's principle that "the character of every individual is formed for and not by himself, first by heredity, which gives him his natural disposition with all its powers and tendencies, its good and bad qualities; and, secondly, by environment, including education and surroundings from earliest infancy, which always modifies the original character for better or for worse." These two principles guided Wallace through life. "To urge that the will is, and remains through life, absolutely uninfluenced by character, environment, or education; or to claim, on the other hand, that it is wholly and absolutely determined by them—seem to me to be propositions which are alike essentially unthinkable and also entirely opposed to experience." Though he embraced the ideas of Herbert Spencer, whose *Social Statics* maintained that only by the process of adaptation was character produced, he found his later work virtually worthless. As he explained to Lester Ward, he thought Spencer's *Ethics of Social Life* (1891) was so "weak and illogical as to be absolutely childish."[11] Besides, Wallace could not forgive Spencer for his abandonment of land nationalization and misunderstanding of natural selection.[12] In the end, Wallace remained an admirer of Owen as his "first teacher in the philosophy of human nature and [his] first guide through the labyrinth of social science."[13]

During the seven years he worked with his brother John, Wallace became a close observer of the British class system, the reform ideas introduced in workingmen's clubs and mechanics institutes, and the deep ideological divisions that emerged among radicals, socialists, Malthusians, utopians, and other groups. An avid reader, he digested the works of William Paley's *Natural Theology*, John Frederic William Herschel's *A Preliminary Discourse on the Study of Natural Philosophy*, Robert Chambers's *Vestiges of the Natural History of Creation*, Thomas Paine's *Age of Reason*, and an assortment of pamphlets by socialists, vegetarians, secularists, utopians, and self-help advocates seeking to capture hearts and minds. He also spent his idle hours gaining insight into the trades, the ten-hour work system, the cost of living, and the strong morality that he so admired among the working classes. "I never once heard such foul language as was not uncommonly used among themselves by young men of a much higher class and much more education."[14]

Time and again in his autobiography, Wallace delighted in describing the geography of the land and the people he observed during his surveying work. He especially admired Lyell's *Principles of Geology*, which gave him a whole new perspective on the formations and strata that molded the land's surface. His rambles among the moors and mountains introduced him to the variety, beauty, and mysteries of nature, including the order (*scala naturae*) that naturalists believed underlay existence. He especially enjoyed gathering plant species, building a herbarium, and drying and organizing his collections. His interest in plants and catalogues fed his longing to visit the tropics, especially the equatorial forests of the Amazon.[15]

Coming of age in 1844, a year after his father's death, Wallace moved to London, where he wrote several short accounts of the manners and customs of the Welsh peasantry during his time in Brecknockshire and Glamorganshire. There, he obtained his first full-time employment as a master teacher at the Collegiate School at Leicester in the East Midlands, teaching reading, writing, arithmetic, surveying, drawing, and beginning

Latin. In his spare time, he made use of the library, where his choice of reading included William H. Prescott's *History of the Conquests of Mexico and Peru* and William Robertson's *History of America*. There, too, he attended several lecture-demonstrations on psychical research by Spencer Timothy Hall, a Nottinghamshire writer, lay homeopath, and mesmerist. Astonished by what he observed, he attempted to replicate the mesmeric trance on his younger students and succeeded with three of them. After reading *Constitution of Man* by Scottish phrenologist George Combe, the leading spokesman of the phrenological movement, he took an interest in phreno-mesmerism, which worked by touching the parts of the mesmerized patient's head that corresponded to the phrenological organs. Observing the subsequent changes in attitude and expression on patients' faces, he accepted phrenology as a true science and even had his own head professionally analyzed. Later, when journeying through South America, he would practice on the native peoples.[16]

While living in Leicester, Wallace met Henry Walter Bates, a hosiery manufacturer and amateur entomologist who became a major influence in his life, teaching him the fundamentals of natural history and encouraging the collection of plants and insects. Their friendship led to excursions through the region of Neath in Wales and speculating whether they could transform their hobby into a profession capable of supporting their needs. After deciding that collecting represented their true vocation, they planned a trip to the Amazon region of South America. What convinced them of this choice were the chronicles of earlier naturalists, including Darwin's *Voyage of the Beagle* (1839) and especially William H. Edwards's *A Voyage up the River Amazon* (1847), with its account of the people and vegetation. From the latter, they learned that the sale of rare and new species of insects, shells, birds, and mammals could pay for their expenses. With money advanced by Samuel Stevens of Bloomsbury, a natural history agent, and letters of support from various societies, they booked passage in the spring of 1848 for South America to collect zoological and biological specimens, confident that their collections would find a ready market among the myriad of societies in London and elsewhere.

Soon after their arrival in the port city of Balém do Pará, gateway to the Amazon, Wallace and Bates embarked on a study of the natural history of the river basin and its tributaries. As noted earlier, Wallace's younger brother, Herbert, came to assist in their explorations but died suddenly of fever. Despite this personal tragedy, Wallace accumulated a sizable collection of botanical and zoological specimens during his four years among the native tribes of Uaupès, exploring the remote regions of the Negro and Orinoco Rivers. In all, he and Bates traveled more than a thousand miles of river during their wanderings, and, while Bates remained six additional years exploring the region, Wallace boxed his collection and headed home. Two weeks into the voyage, the ship's cargo, including his entire collection of salable specimens, was engulfed in a mid-ocean fire, with all hands ordered into lifeboats. Before the day ended, the ship's masts had broken off and the decks burned away, leaving their small boats floating amid pieces of fiery wreckage. Ten days later they were picked up by a ship bound for London.[17]

Undeterred by the loss of his collections, Wallace became a frequent participant in discussions at the Zoological and Entomological Societies, and prepared *Travels on the Amazon and Rio Negro* (1853), published by the Royal Geographical Society. His publication, however, failed to garner him entrée into the elite scientific societies and clubs. Nor, for that matter, did he have the income to enjoy their membership had it been offered. Instead, having made connections with a few naturalists, including Darwin, he arranged travel to the Malay Archipelago (modern-day Indonesia), where he spent the next eight years collecting specimens and formulating a theory he later described as "the central and controlling incident of [his] life."[18]

## The Archipelago and Natural Selection

On his return to the tropics, Wallace picked up where he had left off in South America, hoping to discover a solution to the origin of species, a subject that had been on his mind for some time and enhanced by the variations he found among animals in different regions. Working out of Jesuit mission stations and private residences, he followed a set routine among the native peoples, some of whom, like the Dyaks, had practiced cannibalism.

Get up at half-past five, bath, and coffee. Sit down to arrange and put away my insects of the day before and set them in a safe place to dry. Charles mends our insect-nets, fills our pin-cushions, and gets ready for the day. Breakfast at eight; out to the jungle at nine. We have to walk about a quarter mile up a steep hill to reach it, and arrive dripping with perspiration. Then we wander about in the delightful shade along paths made by the Chinese wood-cutters till two or three in the afternoon, generally returning with fifty or sixty beetles, some very rare or beautiful, and perhaps a few butterflies. Change clothes and sit down to kill and pin insects, Charles doing the flies, wasps, and bugs; I do not trust him yet with beetles. Dinner at four, then at work again till six: coffee. Then read or talk, or if insects very numerous, work again till eight or nine. Then to bed.[19]

While working in Sarawak on the island of Borneo, Wallace's interest in variations among plants and animals in their geographical distribution led to his paper "On the Law That Has Regulated the Introduction of New Species" (later referred to as "The Sarawak Law Paper"), published in the *Annals and Magazine of Natural History* in 1855. Impressed with Chambers's *Vestiges*, and a convert to Lyell's uniformitarian geology, he explored the geographical distribution of species and their origin, taking note of the distribution of living and fossil species. He concluded, "Every species has come into existence coincident both in space and time with a pre-existing closely-allied species." He likewise observed that the *when* and *where* of species occurrence could only be through natural generation as suggested in Chambers's *Vestiges*. As for the *how*, that remained unresolved.[20]

Long before Darwin focused his attention on the natural history of man, Wallace had already collected information that would bear on arguments affecting the theories propounded by monogenists and polygenists respecting the origination of the human species. Despite warnings from the English zoologist Edward Blyth and geologist Charles Lyell that Wallace was encroaching in a highly sensitive area, Darwin chose to give it little account. In his correspondence with Wallace in 1857, he replied: "You ask whether I shall discuss Man: I think I shall avoid the whole subject, as so surrounded with prejudices, though I fully admit that it is the highest and most interesting problem for the naturalist."[21] Less troubled than his fellow Victorians, who he concluded were unnecessarily weighted down with theological predispositions and societal pressures, Wallace theorized that species were "mutable productions" and admitted that he "could not avoid the belief that man must come under the same law."[22] Today, scientists consider the Sarawak Law Paper one of the more significant milestones in the development of evolutionary theory. Ian McCalman referred to this publication as "the first ever British scientific paper to claim that animals had descended from a common ancestor and then produced closely similar variations which evolved into distinct species."[23]

In 1858, while recuperating from an attack of malarial fever in the Mollucas, Wallace remembered Malthus's *Essay on Population* and his observation that more life forms were produced than could possibly survive, a concept the author had applied to the human species where poverty and famine were natural outcomes of overpopulation. From both Malthus and Chambers's *Vestiges*, Wallace concluded that natural laws governed the universe and so defined the order of things that progression and continued divergence regulated the struggle for existence among life forms. Equally important, the violation of those laws could threaten individuals within the species.[24]

Much like Darwin, he experienced a flash of inspiration following his reading of Malthus, transforming the theory of population into a principle explaining how species evolved. Reasoning from economic theory to biology, he described how the book helped him formulate his theory.

> Vaguely thinking over the enormous and constant destruction [of animals] which this implied, it occurred to me to ask the question, why do some live and some die? And the answer was clearly, that on the whole the best fitted live. From the effects of disease the most healthy escaped; from enemies, the strongest, the swiftest, or the most cunning; from famine, the best hunters or those with the best digestion; and so on. Then it suddenly flashed upon me that this self-acting process would necessarily *improve the race*, because in every generation the inferior would inevitably be killed off and the superior remain—that is, *the fittest would survive*. Then at once I seemed to see the whole effect of this, that when changes of land and sea, or of climate, or of food supply, or of enemies occurred— and we know that such changes have always been taking place—and considering the amount of individual variation that my experience as a collector had shown me to exist, then it followed that all the changes necessary for the adaptation of the species to the changing conditions would be brought about; and as great changes in the environment are always slow, there would be ample time for the change to be effected by the survival of the best fitted in every generation.[25]

Surprised by what he learned, Wallace wrote Darwin, sharing with him an outline of his theory. Being away from his homeland for several years, he had no knowledge that Darwin had been developing his own theory of species variation. On receiving Wallace's packet from Ternate in the Dutch East Indies, Darwin immediately recognized that this distant naturalist had laid out virtually the same theory he had been struggling for years to explain. Here was a man isolated in a jungle environment who had come to the same conclusions on evolution by natural selection. To further complicate matters, not only did the essay explain it far better than he had in his own personal journal, but it included the contributions of Lyell and Malthus as well; even more surprising, he explained the process without the requirement of a Creator. Until receiving Wallace's materials, Darwin had no reason to either notice Wallace or be concerned with what he had been doing.

The impact of Wallace's letter can only be imagined. A relatively young and virtually unknown naturalist had arrived at a very similar conclusion, albeit even more provocative than Darwin had been writing in his own personal journals. And like Darwin, he discovered the evidence from plants and animals that lived on islands remote from the major continents. For both men, the explanation for differences within the panorama of living creatures did not require Lamarck's "volition" of the organism but simply the barriers of oceans, wind currents, and mountain ranges.[26] As varieties became separated over time, they constituted distinct breeding units. Writing to Lyell on the very day he received Wallace's manuscript, Darwin noted: "If Wallace had my manuscript sketch which was written out in 1842, he could not have made a better short abstract! Even his terms now stand as heads of my chapters."[27]

With the influence of Darwin's close friends, Joseph Dalton Hooker and Charles Lyell, both of Wallace's papers ("On the Law Which Has Regulated the Introduction of New Species" and "On the Tendency of Varieties to Depart Indefinitely from the Original Type") and Darwin's preliminary abstract were communicated to the Linnaean Society for presentation at its July 1, 1858, meeting, showing their co-discovery of the origin of species by natural selection. While both men had been unequivocal in explaining natural selection as the "force" responsible for speciation in all (excluding man) living organisms, it is noteworthy that Wallace deferred to Darwin, fourteen years his senior, and an educated gentleman of established reputation, as the prime discoverer and elaborator of the theory.[28] Recognizing that Darwin had worked on the theory for a good twenty years or more, he concluded that Darwin had a much greater grasp of the principle of divergence. "I could never have approached the completeness of his book, its vast accumulation of evidence, its overwhelming argument, and its admirable tone and spirit. I really feel thankful that it has not been left to me to give the theory to the world. Mr. Darwin has created a new science and a new philosophy; and I believe that never has such a complete illustration of a new branch of human knowledge been due to the labours and researches of a single man. Never have such vast masses of widely scattered and hitherto quite unconnected facts been combined into a system and brought to bear upon the establishment of such a grand and new and simple philosophy."[29]

Wallace did not return to England until 1862, bringing with him a collection of over 126,000 specimens, much of which added to the corpus
of Victorian anthropology. Once settled, he tried hard to find a place for
himself among the country's naturalists. Yet much had occurred during
his absence, and he returned at a time when Darwin and his coterie of
disciples were well in command of the theory. Signs of Darwin's preeminence were everywhere, and, even with co-ownership of natural selection, Wallace held none of the graces or benefits of Britain's class system,
a condition that remained a barrier to his acceptance into the scientific
community's inner circle. In fact, he found himself in the awkward position of being forced to live off lecturing, publishing, and editing man-
uscripts. Except to defend the theory of natural selection, he remained a
marginal figure among the gentlemen naturalists and their societies. Inattentive to and inexperienced with club politics, he navigated the peril-
ous waters of the scientific community as a practicing anthropologist, a
field collector of modest means, ready to discuss his observations in the
context of fact-based science. The absence of family wealth, education,
patrons, or the requisite breeding meant that his fellowship in the Royal
Society would not come until 1893.[30] Wallace was unprepared to make his
way in English society, and only through Darwin's patronage did he eventually receive a small government pension. Possessing little beyond his
skill as an empirical naturalist, he became a reluctant but grateful recipi-
ent of Darwin's favors.

## Divergence

Wallace contributed a long list of papers to the Zoological, Entomological, and Linnaean Societies of London, and while he continued to support
the theory of natural selection, he remained unsettled in thinking there
was no more to be learned or postulated. To be sure, evolution theory
was now secure, but he came to believe that natural selection represented
only one of several potential mechanisms of change. Darwin's choice
of the adjective "random" to describe variation was intended to mean
that variations did not occur because they were useful to the organism
in which they occurred. Chance alone was the source of creation—pure
blind indeterministic chance. This was his sole hypothesis—randomness
and no preordained design. Otherwise there would need to be some teleological explanation for the mutations and the random patterns that
arose. This point he explained in *The Variation of Animals and Plants under Domestication*: "Let an architect be compelled to build an edifice with

uncut stones, fallen from a precipice. The shape of each fragment may be called accidental; yet the shape of each has been determined by the force of gravity, the nature of the rock, and the slope of the precipice,—events and circumstances all of which depend on natural laws; but there is no relation between these laws and the purpose for which each fragment is used by the builder. In the same manner the variations of each creature are determined by fixed and immutable laws; but these bear no relation to the living structure which is slowly built up through the power of natural selection, whether this be natural or artificial selection."[31]

In their public statements and written words, Darwin and Wallace argued for natural selection as the only reasonable method of species descent and modification. However, all this changed in March 1864, when Wallace presented "The Origin of Human Races and the Antiquity of Man Deduced from the Theory of 'Natural Selection'" before the Anthropological Society of London. Referring to the ongoing feud between the monogenists and polygenists, he argued that there was indeed a single origin of the races of man with a divergence that occurred sometime prior to the development of man's mental and moral characteristics. Evolution had applied to the human species in two distinct phases: *First*, with man's physical form; and second, with the advent of mind when man no longer required further structural changes to the body. Among the higher specimens within the different races, changes to their intellect raised the level of the tribe from brute survival of the fittest to innovations in clothing, weapons, and tools, which, in turn, led to the extinction of those with lesser abilities. "Man has not only escaped natural selection himself, but he is actually able to take away some of that power from nature which before his appearance she universally exercised." In other words, a discontinuity occurred in the chance world of natural selection the moment the human species introduced mental characteristics into the evolutionary process.[32] Once this occurred, natural selection changed from a struggle for survival to cooperation, producing individuals who exhibited a higher moral sense.[33]

In his revision to natural selection, Wallace implied that the human species, alone among the multitude of species, underwent a modified process of evolution. In the childhood of the race, natural selection had operated on the body's physical appearance, but this ended after a time, leaving the physical characteristics more or less permanent while allowing subsequent changes to intelligence and moral development. In this manner, Wallace explained the development of the higher human faculties, which heretofore had eluded him. In one of his footnotes, Wallace recognized Spencer's *Social Statics* as having influenced his overall view. Thus, by distinguishing the human species from all other life forms and then incorporating Spencer's deductive principles, Wallace drew away from his original theory.

> While his external form will probably ever remained unchanged, except in the development of that perfect beauty which results from a healthy and well organized body . . . his mental constitution may continue to advance and improve till the world is again inhabited by a single homogeneous race, no individual of which will be inferior to the noblest specimens of existing humanity. Each one will then work out his own happiness in relation to that of his fellows; perfect freedom of action will be maintained, since the well balanced moral faculties will never permit any one to transgress on the equal freedom of others; restrictive laws will not be wanted, for each man will be guided by the best of laws; a thorough appreciation of the rights, and a perfect sympathy with the feelings, of all about him; compulsory-government will have died away as unnecessary . . . will be replaced by voluntary associations for all beneficial public purposes.[34]

Several years later, in his 1869 review of Lyell's revised editions of *Principles of Geology* and *Elements of Geology* in the *London Quarterly Review*, Wallace took a further step by introducing the idea of a "Higher Intelligence" to explain the development of the brain, hand, naked skin, and organs of speech. Not only did the savage have a brain with a capacity beyond his actual needs, but the same evidence of prepossession applied to the absence of hair from certain parts of the body, the specialization and perfection of the feet and hands, and the power, range and flexibility of the larynx, especially in the female. Arguing that natural selection failed to account for certain features in human development that extended beyond the purely physical changes (i.e., survival advantages) to the human body, he theorized that a spiritual explanation was required. His preference for the existence of a spiritual power represented a new and revolutionary addition to the minor correction to natural selection in his 1864 paper. "There yet seems to be evidence of a Power which has guided the action of those laws in definite directions and for special ends. . . . We must therefore admit the possibility, that in the development of the human race, a Higher Intelligence has guided the same laws for nobler ends."[35] In place of (or in addition to) Spencerian evolution, Wallace now included a spiritual world to explain the moral and intellectual development on the mind and society.[36] The evolution of the human mind represented the beginning stages of civilization, a point in time when the organic world came under the influence of teleological purposes. For Wallace, "a superior intelligence [had] guided the development of man in a definite direction, and for a special purpose."[37]

Most historians date the change in Wallace's beliefs to his 1864 paper before the Anthropological Society; others, however, have pointed out that the paper made no mention of any non-natural explanation for man's origin.[38] To be sure, having learned of Wallace's alleged volte-face, Darwin did not hold back from expressing disappointment in his friend's conclusions and reminded him that he was turning away from his own doctrine of natural selection. After being informed of Wallace's article planned for the *Quarterly Review,* Darwin wrote on March 27, 1869: "I hope you have not murdered too completely your own and my child."[39]

Wallace admitted this change in his thinking in a letter to Darwin in 1869: "My opinions on the subject have been modified solely by the consideration of a series of remarkable phenomena, physical and mental, which I have now had every opportunity of fully testing, and which demonstrate the existence of forces and influences not yet recognized by science." He went on to ask that Darwin suspend judgment until corroboration could be drawn from the evidence collected during séances.[40] "I have been writing a little on a *new branch* of Anthropology, and as I have taken your name in vain on the title-page I send you a copy. I fear you will be much shocked, but I can't help it; and before finally deciding that we are all mad I hope you will come and see some very curious phenomena which we can show you, among friends only. We meet every Friday evening, and hope you will come sometimes, as we wish for the fullest investigation, and shall be only too grateful to you or anyone else who will show us how and where we are deceived."[41] Disappointed in Wallace's interest in extrasensory experiences, Darwin responded: "As you expected, I differ grievously from you, and I am very sorry for it. I can see no necessity for calling in an additional and proximate cause in regard to man."[42]

In 1870 Wallace published *Contributions to the Theory of Natural Selection,* a collection of ten essays that examined more fully his revisions to the theory of natural selection. One of his essays involved a revision of his 1864 paper, to which he added a new conclusion suggesting that only a force independent of natural selection could explain the development of those qualities toward which the human species was tending. In the book's final essay, "The Limits of Natural Selection as Applied to Man," he made a further admission that his concept of theistic evolutionary theology would "probably excite some surprise among my readers to

find that I do not consider that all nature can be explained on the principles of which I am so ardent an advocate; and that I am now myself going to state objections, and to place limits, to the power of natural selection."[43] In essence, the origin of man's intellectual and moral nature could
not have derived from natural selection, since these attributes were not
required by the savage man to survive in his environment. "Natural selection could only have endowed savage man with a brain a few degrees
superior to that of an ape, whereas he actually possesses one very little
inferior to that of a philosopher." They were capabilities unnecessary for
the time being but implanted by "the controlling action" of a Higher Intelligence (i.e., Intelligent Design) in anticipation of man's future needs.[44]

Wallace denied any discontinuity between what he had earlier stated
regarding natural selection and his argument for a nonmaterial origin for
man's higher mental faculties. The latter simply amplified a teleological
or purposive connection behind man's creation. "I cannot admit that it
in any degree affects the truth or generality of Mr. Darwin's great discovery. It merely shows, that the laws of organic development have been occasionally used for a special end, just as man uses them for his special
ends; and, I do not see that the law of 'natural selection' can be said to
be disproved, if it can be shown that man does not owe his entire physical and mental development to its unaided action, any more than it is disproved by the existence of the poodle or the pouter pigeon, the production of which may have been equally beyond its undirected power."[45] In
seeking to state more clearly his position, Wallace remarked, "It therefore implies that the great laws which govern the material universe were
insufficient for this production, unless we consider (as we may fairly do)
that the controlling action of such higher intelligences is a necessary part
of those laws, just as the action of all surrounding organisms is one of
the agencies in organic development."[46] Despite denials, the publication
of *Contributions* marked Wallace's formal break from Darwin, thus drawing a line between natural selection and the teleological views that would
henceforth define change.[47]

Wallace was not alone in supplementing organic evolution with some
form of Intelligent Design. His defection troubled Darwin, but so did the
defection of his close friend and colleague Charles Lyell, whose support
of Wallace underscored the chasm that divided all of them when it came
to the admission of a Higher Intelligence. "I rather hail Wallace's sugges-
tion that there may be a Supreme Will and Power which may not abdicate
its functions of interference, but may guide the forces and laws of Nature," Lyell admitted to Darwin.[48]

Among American Protestants, theistic and telic change found a welcome place in their acceptance of evolutionary theory. Kindred in their effort to counteract the spread of a strictly materialistic interpretation of change, explanations ran the gamut from being overtly denominational in context, to expounding a theistic and purpose-driven process separate from organized religion. To borrow a concept from Ronald L. Numbers, evolutionary biology underwent a "privatization" that accommodated a host of bedfellows, each divining a view that interpreted the relationship between force and matter in highly idiosyncratic ways.[49]

In 1886 Wallace delivered a series of lectures sponsored by the Lowell Institute of Boston, which he later combined into *Darwinism*, published in 1889. The lectures, which explained and defended natural selection, also clarified his revised position. "None of my differences from Darwin imply any real divergence as to the overwhelming importance of the great principles of natural selection, while in several directions I believe that I have extended and strengthened it."[50] The Canadian-born physiologist George Romanes took issue with the claim, explaining that he had encountered several very distinct Wallaces: "The Wallace of Spiritualism and astrology, the Wallace of vaccination and the land-question, the Wallace of incapacity and absurdity."[51] Historian John R. Durant, on the other hand, argues that Wallace was consistent in his heterodoxy. An "outlier" throughout his life, he "had a knack of sitting on the wrong side of the scientific fence which would be infuriating if it were not always so transparently sincere."[52]

Historians Michael Flannery and Martin Fichman emphasize the intellectual unity of Wallace's scientific, spiritual, and political thinking, noting that Victorian society was filled with scientists/spiritualists like Robert Hare, William Crookes, William Fletcher Barrett, Cromwell F. Varley, and Oliver Lodge who managed to incorporate both components without contradiction. Wallace endeavored to demonstrate that in natural science, evolutionary philosophy, Spiritualism, and socialism were all part of an evolutionary teleology.[53]

## Spiritual Friends and Acquaintances

During his travels in the Amazon, Wallace remembered reading reports of strange happenings in the village of Hydesville in western New York, where "for the first time, intelligent communications" (i.e., rappings) took place between a nine-year-old girl, Kate Fox, and the spirit of a murdered man buried in the cellar of the house the family rented. Kate and her two sisters subsequently became highly sought mediums who claimed the ability to communicate with the spiritual world and, to prove their sincerity, submitted to numerous examinations intended to legitimize their claims. Within months, the phenomena had spread as the rappings were replicated in towns and cities across the United States. Before long, the Fox sisters and their imitators adopted Mesmer's novel *spirit-circle* (séance) as their laboratory to demonstrate and manifest messages from beyond the grave. The séance became the portal for all classes to communicate with family and friends on the Other Side. Within the darkened room of the spirit-circle formed individual and collective behaviors that were both highbrow and vulgar. In some circles, poems, essays, and commentaries were produced, allegedly written by dead poets, politicians, novelists, and divines affirming the continuance of their careers in the spirit-world. Corroboration by friends and relatives of their characteristic style lent identity and an imprimatur of authenticity. The séance and its accompanying materializations also entered households through religious literature, fiction, children's books, paintings, theater, musical performances, and church rituals. By describing these apparitions of the dead as "spirits," Spiritualism captured a more serious concept of the dead than the typical use of the term "ghost" and brought the world of spirits into everyday conversation.[54]

For the public, the reports seemed to confirm that science had at last unlocked the secrets of electricity and offered to the world a series of breakthrough techniques enabling communication over distances once thought impossible. The validations triggered an explosion of events that centered around the séance as the most appropriate method for connecting the natural and spiritual worlds. Before long, thousands of men and women were bringing solace to those grieving the loss of a child, sibling, parent, or partner.[55]

Not only were mediums capable of summoning the oracular thoughts of the world's notable leaders, but it was also possible to communicate in forms less dignified. Beginning with raps and knockings, the manifestations evolved into automatic writing, flying objects, levitated tables and chairs, ringing bells, veiled faces, articles removed from clothing, tickling, and touching. What started as a sober spiritual séance devolved into circuslike antics. These were not magisterial demonstrations of great minds imparting wisdom, but simple queries concerning personal family matters. What formerly had been in the hands of a few inspired revelators now became the property of all classes of willing participants—a democracy of hearts and minds. As Spiritualism expanded, the nature and sophistication of the experience became decidedly less spiritual and more like an open field of contact sports.

By 1870 twenty different spiritualist associations and 105 societies were operating in the United States, with several hundred mediums plying their newly discovered powers on the lecture circuit. Similar statistics confirmed Spiritualism's popularity in Great Britain and on the continent. Unlike spirit communications of former eras that were described as intuitive experiences of an individual or group, the spirit-world of the nineteenth century existed in the context of the new emerging sciences. Some like mesmerism stood their ground, having every expectation of reconciling their respective beliefs with empirical evidence. Others like phrenopathy, psychometry, and sarcognomy failed.[56]

The rappings marked a transition from understanding death as a predominantly religious phenomenon, not knowing with any assurance whether God had elected an individual for salvation, to a more secular view of death as part of a natural process independent of any religion-bound eschatology. Spiritualism provided an otherworldly existence free from the punitive God of the Judeo-Christian tradition. It satisfied the desire for immortality without the burden of eternal judgment. Communication by way of mediums provided a brief but much needed opportunity for the bereaved to learn that their loved one was well. Some even developed a pathological dependency on their mediums, insisting on a continuance of communication for years. Motives included feelings of guilt, attachment, and neglect. While skeptics and outright opponents cried "delusion," "insanity," "irreligion," "immorality," and "infidelity," supporters pushed forward what they believed to be a new science of the occult.

After returning home from the Archipelago, Wallace continued to read about these events, though he admitted being an "utter skeptic as to the existence of any preter-human or super-human intelligence."[57] From his knowledge of mesmerism, he knew there were mysteries connected with the human mind that modern science could not explain with satisfaction.[58] He remained a skeptic until the summer of 1865, when he attended a séance and witnessed "table turnings" and "distinct tappings."[59]

It was in the summer of 1865 that I first witnessed any of the phenomena of what is called Spiritualism, in the house of a friend,—a sceptic, a man of science, and a lawyer, with none but members of his own family present. Sitting at a good-sized round table, with our hands placed upon it, after a short time slight movements would commence—not often "turnings" or "tiltings," but a gentle intermittent movement, like steps, which after a time would bring the table quite across the room. Slight but distinct tapping sounds were also heard. The following notes

made at the time were intended to describe exactly what took place:—
"July 22nd, 1865.—Sat with my friend, his wife, and two daughters, at
a large loo table, by daylight. In about half an hour some faint motions
were perceived, and some faint taps heard. They gradually increased; the
taps became very distinct, and the table moved considerably, obliging us
all to shift our chairs. Then a curious vibratory motion of the table com-
menced, almost like the shivering of a living animal. I could feel it up
to my elbows. These phenomena were variously repeated for two hours.
On trying afterwards, we found the table could not be voluntarily moved
in the same manner without a great exertion of force, and we could discover no possible way of producing the taps while our hands were upon
the table."[60]

By 1866 Wallace was hosting weekly séances in his own home, con-
ducted by his sister Fanny Sims and mesmerist Miss Agnes Nichol. In
these and subsequent séances, he observed the drawing of ghost pictures,
levitation, musical sounds, table tilting, slate writing, rappings, and the
sudden appearance of flowers and fruit.[61] Satisfied with their authenticity, he became an outspoken advocate anxious to draw others into a world
where appearances did not necessarily align with the laws of the natural world, or at least those known at the time to be part of modern science. To the extent that light, heat, electricity, and magnetism were understood, and that an ether-type substance filled space, he felt there could
be any number of plausible reasons for linking the material and spiritual
worlds with some form of communication. Here was a puzzle that merited much more attention than traditional Christianity, whose ratiocina-
tions only added further disenchantment toward its dogma and creeds.

Wallace directed readers to the research of Baron Reichenbach on "Od-
Force," a reference to spiritual flames that allegedly surrounded living
bodies.[62] From there, he urged readers to look at Dr. William Gregory's
*Letters on Animal Magnetism*, Robert Dale Owen's *Footfalls on the Boundary of Another World*, Robert Hare's investigation of spirit manifestations,
and Daniel Dunglas Home's *Incidents of My Life*. For Wallace, Spiritualism furnished proof of the existence of ethereal beings and of their power
to act upon matter. More importantly, Spiritualism indicated that the "so-
called dead are still alive; that our friends are still with us, though unseen, and guide and strengthen us when, owing to absence of proper conditions, they cannot make their presence known."[63] From his numerous
observations and experiences, however, he concluded that man was a duality, consisting of both a physical body and an organized spiritual form

that evolved with the body; death was the separation of this duality without any change in the spirit, morally or intellectually; and progressive evolution was the destiny of each individual spirit.[64] "That after death man's spirit survives in an ethereal body, gifted with new powers, but mentally and morally the same individual as when clothed in flesh. That he commences from that moment a course of apparently endless progression, which is rapid, just in proportion as his mental and moral faculties have been exercised and cultivated while on earth. That his comparative happiness or misery will depend entirely on himself; just in proportion as his higher human faculties have taken part in all his pleasures here, will he find himself contented and happy in a state of existence in which they will have the fullest exercise."[65]

Wallace urged Spiritualism to be judged by the same standards used to judge any other hypothesis and thus took exception when his colleagues imposed conditions on what they would consider as proof. To this, Wallace responded, "Spiritualists are now profoundly indifferent to the opinion of men of science and would not go one step out of their way to convince them." He remained convinced that, given the variety of locations where Spiritualism had been observed—from private houses of eminent individuals, to open rooms in public buildings—the accounts were too overwhelming to dismiss them as the expression of fools or frauds. Not unlike John Henry Newman in his defense of miracles, Wallace believed that Spiritualism had been definitively demonstrated by the law of probabilities.[66]

Just as Wallace had once pushed phrenology unsuccessfully, he found Spiritualism anathema to the scientific community, if not more so because of the frauds uncovered among its most respected representatives, including admissions from the Fox sisters. Convinced nonetheless that the phenomena were real, and desirous of making it a new branch of anthropology, Wallace made repeated efforts to invite skeptics to examine the evidence. Thomas Huxley, William Carpenter, John Tyndall, and George Henry Lewes refused the challenge, although some would later agree to participate. These included Huxley, Darwin's cousin Francis Galton, George Darwin, John Tyndall, Hensleigh Wedgwood, Augustus de Morgan, and W. B. Carpenter. On January 16, 1874, even Darwin attended a séance at the home of his son Erasmus Alvey Darwin in London but left before it had concluded.[67]

It seems cruel that Wallace's many invitations to attend or to investigate séances were turned down. Whether in reaction to Wallace's strong identification with Spiritualism, his apparent willingness to break with

Darwin on the pivotal role of natural selection in the origin of man, his defense in court of several mediums exposed of fraud, differences of class, or some other reason, the rejections did little to soothe their perceived indignity. Lord Avebury remarked in a letter to Wallace, "As to Spiritualism, my difficulty is that nothing comes of it. What has been gained by your séances, compared to your studies?"[68] As for Huxley, his opinions seldom changed. As he explained to Wallace: "I am neither shocked nor disposed to issue a Commission of Lunacy against you. It may be all true, for anything I know to the contrary, but really I cannot get up any interest in the subject. I never cared for gossip in my life, and disembodied gossip, such as these worthy ghosts supply their friends with, is not more interesting to me than any other."[69] And, in a letter to the Committee of the Dialectical Society, Huxley minced few words: "But supposing the phenomena to be genuine—they do not interest me. If anybody would endow me with the faculty of listening to the chatter of old women and curates at the nearest cathedral town, I should decline the privilege, having better things to do. And if the folk in the spiritual world do not talk more wisely and sensibly than their friends report them to do, I put them in the same category."[70]

For those critics who pointed out the frivolous nature of the alleged communications, Wallace responded, arguing that "men are best educated by being left to suffer the natural consequences of their actions." In this manner he explained away the need for spirits to change the course of humanity by providing advice on future political directions, detecting crime, or naming in advance the winner of a derby. Quite simply, the commonplace communications received during séances came from spirits of "various grades and tastes" who were neither fools nor knaves but "continue[d] to talk after they [were] dead with just as little sense as when alive." Still, he did not regard Spiritualism as an idle curiosity. "It is a science of vast extent, having the widest, the most important, and the most practical issues, and as such should enlist the sympathies alike of moralists, philosophers, and politicians, and of all who have at heart the improvement of society and the permanent elevation of human nature." Thus, he remained curiously immune to critiques and to his own inconsistencies in the matter of Spiritualism's usefulness.[71]

When his efforts to make Spiritualism a "science" failed, Wallace settled on combining both evolution and Spiritualism into a religion. To be sure, he was not alone in mixing the two. According to Michael Flannery and Martin Fichman, Spiritualism complemented Wallace's larger teleological world that included intelligent evolution.[72] According to Fichman, "spiritualism and natural selection were never viewed by Wallace . . . as mutually exclusive . . . of a larger evolutionary teleology." Not holding with the afterlife described by Christianity, he viewed Spiritualism as offering the "only sure foundation for a true philosophy and a pure religion." It gave proof of a future state of existence minus divisive creeds, winged angels, golden harps, and orthodox Christianity's system of rewards and retributions.[73] Except for those few Victorians who held fast to the dysteleological implications of natural selection, it is arguable that the widespread acceptance of evolution could not have happened without acceptance of a Higher Intelligence that guided organic development to a special end or purpose.[74]

Given the overwhelming complexity and diversity Wallace found in the world, much of which science had brought to the notice of humanity, the *why* was left unanswered by both science and religion. "Science says: 'It is so. Ours not to reason why; but only to find out what is.' Religion says: 'God made it so'; and sometimes adds, 'it was God's will; it is impious to seek any other reason.'"[75] Wallace rejected both answers. In his *Man's Place in the Universe*, he postulated some "organizing spirits" or "ministering angels" whose "thought-transference" made it possible to influence the "cell-souls" to carry out their duties in accordance with some general design. "Some such conception as this—of delegated powers to beings of a very high, and to others of a very low grade of life and intellect—seems to me less grossly improbable than that an infinite Deity not only designed the whole of the cosmos, but that himself alone is the consciously acting power in every cell of every living thing that is or ever has been upon the earth."[76] This, he believed, represented the best teachings of modern Spiritualism and directed readers to three authors in particular: W. Stainton Moses (*Spirit Teachings*, 1898), V. C. Desertes (*Psychic Philosophy, as the Foundation of a Religion of Natural Law*, 1901), and the Swedenborgian mystic Thomas Lake Harris (*A Lyric of the Golden Age*, 1856).[77]

Having concluded that the universe was not a "chance product," Wallace accepted Spencer's explanation that some "universal immanent force" that was both infinite and eternal underlay both matter and spirit. But instead of a single infinite being, there were infinite grades of influence of higher beings upon lower. "Holding this opinion, I have suggested that this vast and wonderful universe, with its almost infinite variety of forms, motions, and reactions of part upon part, from suns and systems up to plant life, animal life, and the human living soul, has ever required and still requires the continuous coordinated agency of myriads of such intelligences."[78]

Though not reflective of his better works, his last three books, *The Wonderful Century* (1898), *Man's Place in the Universe* (1903), and *The*

*World of Life* (1911), summarized the last half-century of the scope and application of the theory of evolution; consolidated his persistent belief in Spiritualism; identified what had been accomplished and that which had been left undone, especially the shortsightedness of science in refusing to accept phrenology, mesmerism, and psychic phenomena; urged attention to the perennial problem of wealth and poverty; encouraged the study of man's spiritual life, and in particular, the potential for the role of mind in thought transference and in guiding evolution.

Spiritualism retained a special place in Wallace's revised interpretation of human evolution. Determined that natural selection could not explain the full depth of human evolution, he applied a teleological interpretation to *all* evolutionary processes.[79] With the publication of *The World of Life: A Manifestation of Creative Power, Directive Mind and Ultimate Purpose* (1910), he affirmed a spiritual causation for the *entire* substratum of evolution. In making this final transition, he endorsed a "vitalist" interpretation of life and a spiritual purpose that guided evolution. As Fichman explained, Wallace should be understood in the context of those Victorian thinkers who found both traditional Christianity and scientific naturalism "incapable of providing adequate guidelines for a holistic philosophy of man."[80] This disenchantment led him to pursue an alternate path that took him into a "World of Spirit," where man was destined to a "permanent progressive existence."[81]

SELECTED WRITINGS

"On the Law Which Has Regulated the Introduction of New Species" (1855)
"On the Tendency of Varieties to Depart Indefinitely from the Original Type"
    (1858)
"On the Zoological Geography of the Malay Archipelago" (1859)
"Remarks on the Rev. S. Haughton's Paper on the Bee's Cell, and on the Origin of
    Species" (1863)
"On the Physical Geography of the Malay Archipelago" (1863)
"On the Phenomena of Variation and Geographical Distribution as Illustrated by
    the Papilionidae of the Malayan Region" (1864)
*The Malay Archipelago* (1869)
*Contributions to the Theory of Natural Selection* (1870)
*The Geographical Distribution of Animals* (1876)
*Tropical Nature, and Other Essays* (1878)
*Island Life* (1881)

*Darwinism: An Exposition of the Theory of Natural Selection, with Some of Its Applications* (1889)

*Travels on the Amazon and Rio Negro* (1889)

*Man's Place in the Universe* (1904)

*My Life* (1905)

*The World of Life: A Manifestation of Creative Power, Directive Mind and Ultimate Purpose* (1910)

# 5

## Agnosticism
### Thomas Henry Huxley

*Extinguished theologians lie about the cradle of every science as the strangled*
*snakes beside that of Hercules; and history records that whenever science and*
*orthodoxy have been fairly opposed, the latter has been forced to retire from the*
*lists, bleeding and crushed if not annihilated; scotched, if not slain.*
    —Thomas H. Huxley, "The Origin of Species," 1860

THE ENGLISH ZOOLOGIST Thomas Henry Huxley (1825–1895), best
remembered as "Darwin's Bulldog," was part of a rising generation
of young and aspiring scientists who pinned their careers on the defense
of Darwin and his theory of natural selection as they sought membership
to the inner sanctums of the Linnaean Society, Royal Society, British Association for the Advancement of Science, and other "clubs" in the hands
of the nation's clerics and gentlemen naturalists. A brilliant thinker and
rhetorician, he belonged to an illustrious list of "Victorian sages" (e.g.,
Thomas Carlyle, Matthew Arnold, George Eliot, Jeremy Bentham, John
Stuart Mill, William Ewart Gladstone, Alfred Lord Tennyson, and Samuel
Taylor Coleridge) known for assembling a vision of the age and its culture.
Huxley's prose as well as his public demeanor conveyed the persona of
someone whose authority and reputation as a professional biologist gave
him license to a myriad of other disciplines. His *Evidence as to Man's Place
in Nature* (1863) and *Evolution and Ethics* (1893) were culturally defining
works of equal significance to Carlyle's *The French Revolution* (1837), Arnold's *Literature and Dogma* (1873), and Eliot's *Middlemarch* (1871).[1]

Huxley's advocacy on behalf of science and its reductionist methodology drew him into battles on behalf of evolution against orthodoxy, agnosticism against materialism, and the ascendancy of science curricula
in the universities. A trained scientist commanding the powers of per-
suasiveness and scholarly depth, he crusaded on behalf of education and
meritocracy to replace privilege and inheritance. Though he discovered
no new laws, he helped make the intellectual world safe for evolutionary
theory and, in the process, built an ethos of professionalism around science education and its disciplinary fields. A surgeon by profession, whose
investigations into natural history led to a stellar rise in the acceptance of

evolutionary theory, he adhered to only one kind of knowledge, namely, that found in the verifiable conclusions of the natural sciences. It was therefore wrong to claim certitude of a proposition unless one could produce evidence; it was equally wrong to demand belief when evidence was unavailable to substantiate it.

## EARLY LIFE

Born in the small country village of Ealing in Middlesex, the second-youngest of eight children, Huxley was compelled to leave school when he was ten, due to the family's financial difficulties. Undeterred, he educated himself in multiple disciplines; while inclined to mechanical engineering because of his drawing abilities, he was instead apprenticed to two of his brothers-in-law. The first, John Charles Cooke, was a practitioner and mesmerist in Coventry; the second, John Salt, was a North London practitioner who placed young Huxley in Sydenham College's anatomy school, where he observed his first postmortem examination at age thirteen. Demonstrating remarkable talent, Huxley was admitted on scholarship to Charing Cross Hospital Medical School, where he showed special interest in organic chemistry and physiology, which he described as "the mechanical engineering of living machines." He attributed much of his success at Charing to Thomas Wharton Jones, an ophthalmic surgeon and devoted student of anatomy and physiology, whose reputation had been sullied by his association with the infamous Burke and Hare body snatchers in Scotland. Under Jones's expert guidance, however, Huxley published his first paper in the *Medical Gazette* in 1845, explaining a hitherto unknown layer in the inner sheath of hair that became known since as "Huxley's layer."[2]

That same year, Huxley passed his first set of examinations, winning prizes for his achievements in anatomy and physiology. Being under twenty-one, too young for eligibility in the Royal College of Surgeons, he joined the Royal Navy's medical service, working at Haslar Hospital in Gosport treating invalided sailors. After qualifying as surgeon a year later, he was assigned by the navy to the position of assistant surgeon on the HMS *Rattlesnake*, a twenty-eight-gun ship whose complement of 180 officers and men served under the command of Captain Owen Stanley. In 1846 the ship's crew surveyed the inshore passage between Australia and the Great Barrier Reef, the Louisiade Archipelago, and the narrow Torres Straits separating New Guinea from Australia, a natural route for commerce between Australia and the Northern Hemisphere.[3]

Unlike Darwin, who, with his own valet, sailed as a gentleman companion to Captain Robert Fitzroy of the *Beagle*, Huxley traveled as a surgeon who, with time on his hands, joined in the work of John MacGillivray, the ship's naturalist, collecting marine specimens amid the antics of a hostile crew and a disdainful captain. Over the course of the ship's four-year voyage, he became a zealous advocate of zoological investigations and, when not dissecting marine animals brought up by tow-net, spent his time on shore perusing the libraries and museums of Sydney and communicating with the Linnaean and Royal societies. Not having the requisite social credentials, he found it necessary to send his first successful paper, "On the Anatomy and the Affinities of the Family of Medusae," to Captain Stanley's father, the bishop of Norwich, who communicated it to the Royal Society for publication in its *Philosophical Transactions*. It seems ironic that Huxley's initial success as a scientist required the support of a bishop, a factor that spoke to the patronage required for entrée into the nation's scientific community. For all intents and purposes, scientific research stood subordinate to both natural theology and the idealist metaphysics (e.g., Richard Owen) of parson-naturalists whose religious loyalties were usually incompatible with the independent pursuit of science.[4]

Following the ship's return, the admiralty assigned Huxley to the HMS *Fisgard*, a harbor flagship, which allowed him to continue with his research. Based on his paper on the Medusae and a succession of other highly prized publications, he was elected in 1851 (at age twenty-six) a Fellow of the Royal Society and received the society's prestigious Royal Medal the following year.

Huxley resigned his position in the navy in 1853 and set his sights on finding a position in Britain's rigid university system. But with no Oxbridge pedigree and only a few friends in high places (e.g., Joseph Dalton Hooker and John Tyndall), the task was far from easy. In the meantime, he made ends meet by teaching courses, writing articles, translating books, and seeking supplementary lectureships and honoraria while performing a dozen different nonremunerative but ingratiating activities that ultimately worked to his advantage. Between bouts of depression and anxiety, he became a successful public lecturer, fostered an exam-based approach for professional advancement, and authored articles that appeared regularly in the *Literary Gazette, Quarterly Journal of Microscopical Science, Proceedings of the Royal Institution,* and *Cyclopedia of Anatomy*. Recognized as a promising anatomist whose portfolio rivaled the work of Sir Richard Owen, he nonetheless struggled with unfulfilled aspirations.

Failing in his initial effort to obtain a professorship of natural history at the University of Toronto, Huxley wavered between eschewing British society altogether or scheming to be included. Driven by ambition and a voracious energy to succeed, he carried a love/hate attitude toward privileged authority. Above all else, he desired to place the appointment of university faculty in the hands of professionals who earned their credibility by democratically achieved merit.[5]

In 1854 Huxley's period of probation ended with his appointment as lecturer on natural history at the Royal School of Mines, where he remained for the next thirty-one years working on paleontology and projects to advance the professionalization of science. His workingmen's lectures began shortly afterward. A born teacher with superb rhetorical skills, he inspired as much as educated his audiences on the notion of evolution and its applications.[6] Two years later began his meteoric rise in reputation when he was appointed Fullerian Professor of Physiology at the Royal Institution (1863–1867) and Hunterian Professor (1863–1869) at the Royal College of Surgeons. In 1862 he was elected president of the Biological Section of the Royal Institution; in 1870, president of the British Association for the Advancement of Science; in 1869–1871, president of the Geological Society; in 1868–1871, the Ethnological Society; in 1883–1885, the Royal Society; and in 1884–1890, the Marine Biological Society. He also became honorary principal of the South London Working Men's College (1868–1880) and member of the first London School Board (1870–1872), where he demonstrated his commitment to education. Eminently successful at popularizing science, he did much to improve education in Great Britain and to defend Darwin's theory of natural selection from critics.

## The Making of an Acolyte

In lectures delivered at the Royal Institution in 1854 and 1855—"The Common Plan of Animal Forms" and "The Zoological Arguments Adduced in Favour of the Progressive Development of Animal Life in Time"—Huxley demonstrated a condition of mind regarding the progressive development of life that placed him in good stead with what Darwin suggested a few years later. Though he pieced together the fragments of animal and plant progression from simple to complex, he failed to discover an explanation for how it all worked. Darwin's *Origin* changed everything, expressing in a whole new manner what Buffon, Lamarck, Chambers, and Erasmus Darwin had earlier sought to establish, namely, an explanation for how species had descended from other species.

Assisted by the works of Malthus on population growth, Lyell's *Principles of Geology*, notions of progressive creation by Louis Agassiz, and the tantalizing arguments of Herbert Spencer, Darwin utilized the chance facts of variation, struggle for existence, and adaptation to bring new life to past theories of evolution.[7]

Reluctant to lead the fight to publicly communicate his nondirectional theory, Darwin looked to others to carry out the responsibility. Those who fit this challenge included biologists Huxley, George Romanes, and E. Ray Lankester; physicist John Tyndall; botanist Joseph Hooker; anthropologist John Lubbock; and mathematician William Kingdon Clifford. In the weeks before *Origin* was published, Darwin wrote to Wallace: "I think I told you before that Hooker is a complete convert. If I can convert Huxley, I shall be content."[8] As it turned out, Darwin had no reason to be concerned. Invited to write an anonymous review of *Origin* for the *Times*, Huxley jumped at the opportunity, followed by a second, much longer review in the *Westminster Review* in which he explained that natural selection was the only satisfactory explanation to date for the method of evolution.

> The "Origin" provided us with the working hypothesis we sought. Moreover, it did us the immense service of freeing us forever from the dilemma—refuse to accept the creation hypothesis, and what have you to propose that can be accepted by any cautious reasoner? In 1857 I had no answer ready, and I do not think that anyone else had. A year later, we reproached ourselves with dullness for being perplexed by such an enquiry. My reflection, when I first made myself master of the central idea of the "Origin" was, how exceedingly stupid not to have thought of that. I suppose that Columbus's companions said much the same when he made the egg to stand on end. The facts of variability, of the struggle for existence, of adaptation to conditions, were notorious enough; but none of us had suspected that the road to the heart of the species problem lay through them, until Darwin and Wallace dispelled the darkness, and the beacon-fire of the "Origin" guided the benighted.[9]

Huxley's endorsement came none too soon, as the *Edinburgh Review* and the *Quarterly Review* published reviews highly critical of the theory. The first, written anonymously by the biologist Sir Richard Owen, described the theory as wholly incompatible with religion and known scientific facts.[10] This was followed by Bishop Samuel Wilberforce of Oxford, a passionate debater who made no effort to conceal his distemper when it came to the theory. Huxley admired Owen's anatomical and paleontological contributions, but that same admiration did not extend to Wilberforce, whose clerical pretentiousness and ignorance of science had him spoiling for a fight. The moment came on June 30, 1860, at a meeting of the British Association for the Advancement of Science held at the Oxford University Museum when Wilberforce (coached by Owen) challenged Huxley to answer whether it was by his grandfather's or grandmother's side of the family that he was related to the ape. Huxley happily responded to the bishop's defense of creationism: "If there were an ancestor whom I should feel shame in recalling, it would be a man, a man of restless and versatile intellect who, not content with an equivocal success in his own sphere of activity, plunges into scientific questions with which he has no real acquaintance, only to obscure them by an aimless rhetoric and distract the attention of his hearers from the real point at issue by eloquent digressions and skilled appeals to religious prejudice."[11] Reportedly, ladies fainted and Captain Fitzroy of the *Beagle* held high a Bible to show his defiance of Huxley's behavior toward the bishop.[12] In a communication with Joseph Dalton Hooker following the debate, Huxley wrote: "I desire that the next generation may be less fettered by the gross and stupid superstitions of orthodoxy than mine has been. And I shall be well satisfied if I can succeed to however small an extent in bringing about this result."[13]

Both Wilberforce and Huxley were strong debaters and passionate in their beliefs. As legend and popular history portray, the triumphalist account of the Huxley/Wilberforce debate epitomized a conflict raging between the competing forces of scientific rationalism and religion, with Huxley depicted as "the archangel of truth" and Wilberforce as "the dark defender of the failing forces of authority, bigotry, and superstition."[14] Huxley's supporters embellished the event as a victory, while the friends of Wilberforce did the same, seeing the confrontation as a triumph of reason over rhetoric.[15] "In the minds of those of the audience best qualified to weigh biological arguments," wrote P. Chalmers Mitchell, "there was little doubt but that [Huxley] had refuted Owen, and simply dispelled the vaporous effusions of the Bishop."[16] Nevertheless, reports of the confrontation were purposively exaggerated, and, according to Peter Bowler, intended by the supporters of scientific rationalism "to bolster their own interpretation of the past in which science is ever triumphant in the 'war' against religion."[17]

What followed the Huxley/Wilberforce debate has often been depicted as a veritable armed camp pitting the warring parties of science and religion against each other, a view encouraged by John William Draper's *History of the Conflict between Religion and Science* and Andrew White's *History of the Warfare of Science with Theology in Christendom.*[18] The presumed standoff between these two camps, however, ignored the internecine issues within each, whose members were by no means of one mind regarding their respective principles. Within the scientific community, for example, there were positivists and unbelievers, the former, acolytes of Comte and Mill who hoped to backfill religion's retreat with an edifice built wholly by science and fulfilling the needs of mankind; the unbelievers were represented by Huxley and Spencer, who were skeptical of the ends and the means proposed by both sides. The positivists were conspicuous in their inability to formulate a consensus around their antimetaphysical approach to philosophy, its science of man, the classification of the sciences, and their evolutionary interpretation of history. What they professed publicly tended to collapse at the micro level, with no ground for a positivist synthesis. Agreed in principle on the supremacy of the inductive sciences and the motivating force of love toward fellow human beings, they forever chided one another with their impatience, their lack of self-assurance when it came to the source of moral virtues, their differences over whether man needed some form of religion to bind society together, and their determination to separate themselves from accusations of materialistic atheism.[19]

Among the British positivists, none was more controversial than Huxley, who fought all forms of clerical authority, judging it to have recklessly weakened the foundations of Christianity with its unwholesome pretentions. At the same time, he criticized the strict positivists for believing that science alone was enough to replace the virtues and morality typically associated with religion. For Huxley, positivism had overstated its case by equating itself with science. This mistaken claim caused him to describe Comte's positivism as "Catholicism *minus* Christianity."[20]

As revisionist historians have amply demonstrated, the confrontation between Huxley and Wilberforce was more vaudevillian in nature than a true depiction of relationship of science and religion at the time. In fact, many considered religious orthodoxy and science in "happy harmony," so much so that large numbers of gentleman naturalists were orthodox clergymen, such as botanist and geologist John Stevens Henslow, philosopher and theologian William Whewell (who coined the term "scientist" as a replacement for "natural philosopher"), geologist William Buckland, and paleontologist William Daniel Conybeare. Perhaps the combativeness of the age stemmed more from the effects of the higher criticism with its methodological revolt against Christian dogma, the migration of the Victorian working classes from mainstream churches, and the growing sectarianism within Christianity. Those differences that emerged between science and religion existed within a much broader social, philosophical, and political tug-of-war.[21] As a consequence, Victorian religion became more private than before—a taboo beyond the bounds of polite conversation. As Protestantism turned inward, it found solace not just in spirituality but, depending on class structure, in different forms of evangelicalism.[22]

Given the analysis of John Brooke and Geoffrey Cantor in their *Reconstructing Nature: The Engagement of Science and Religion* (1998), there is good reason to reject any canonical belief in the conflict thesis, suggesting instead a more nuanced picture of their relationship. The conflict was not just between scientists and religious believers but among those who disagreed within their respective groups regarding the cognitive content and intent of evolutionary theory. In fact, there was arguably less of a contest between science and religion than between the older and newer schools of biological philosophy, one based on the inductive sciences and the other on revealed religion. The stage that seemingly pitted Darwinian theory against religion was a generational feud between and among those who endorsed science as a branch of natural theology with its archetypes eternally present and forever fixed by Intelligent Design, and those younger intellectuals who, resenting the amateur credentials of science's theological spokesmen, intended for truths to be proved not by prophetic or intuitive insight but with evidence obtained by the inductive sciences. It set a university system whose sciences remained in the hands of clerics and gentlemen naturalists against those who sought entrée to university positions and insisted that respect as professionals in their fields was more important than class standing.[23]

## MAN'S PLACE IN NATURE

Long before the publication of *Origin*, naturalists had been hesitant to include the human species as a part of the zoological classification system. Even the broadest minds feared saying or writing anything that might question the religious barrier separating man from the lower creatures. Such had been the unhappy experience of Sir William Lawrence's book *Lectures on Physiology, Zoology, and the Natural History of Man* (1822). Even someone as revered as Owen avoided anatomical comparisons for or against the descent of man. By contrast, Huxley reveled in the opportunity to compare and confront the scriptural account of creation with that of evolution. While many members of the clergy hoped to reconcile scripture and evolution, he would have none of it. Instead, he opted to channel his advocacy for human evolution by studying the anatomy of the brain and toe of apes, which he explained in "The Relation of Man to the Rest of the Animal Kingdom" (1861), published in the *Natural History Review*. A crowd-pleaser, the article became a determined response to the war of words that had transpired between himself and Wilberforce. Starting with a series of lectures to workingmen and members of the Philosophical Institution of Edinburgh on "The Relation of Man to the Lower Animals," and later expanded into a volume called *Man's Place in Nature* (1863), Huxley stated the obvious.

> It will be admitted that some knowledge of man's position in the animate world is an indispensable preliminary to the proper understanding of his relations to the universe; and this again resolves itself in the long run into an enquiry into the nature and the closeness of the ties which connect him with those singular creatures whose history has been sketched in the preceding pages. The importance of such an enquiry is, indeed, intuitively manifest. Brought face to face with these blurred copies of himself, the least thoughtful of men is conscious of a certain shock; due perhaps not so much to disgust at the aspect of what looks like an insulting caricature, as to the awakening of a sudden and profound mistrust of time-honoured theories and strongly rooted prejudices regarding his own position in nature, and his relations to the underworld of life; while that which remains a dim suspicion for the unthinking, becomes a vast argument, fraught with the deepest consequences, for all who are acquainted with the recent progress of the anatomical and physiological sciences.[24]

After surveying the literature describing the gibbons and orangutans in Eastern Asia, along with chimpanzees and gorillas in Western Africa, Huxley proceeded to compare their anatomy to that of humans and turned to the question that occupied many minds, namely, the place which both occupied in nature. "Whence our race has come; what are the limits of our power over nature, and of nature's power over us; to what goal we are tending; are the problems which present themselves anew and with undiminished interest to every man born into the world?" In answering these riddles, Huxley claimed a structural unity of man with the rest of the animal world, particularly with the primates. With their close physical resemblance made clearer every day through the fossil record, Huxley placed man in the same order of animals as primates, hoping over time to discover their "missing links," namely, those common ancestors of man and the primate. Until such evidence was found, he and others turned their attention to the mental powers of man and the higher animals, cultural artifacts, the presumed mental capacities of the races based on facial angle, brain size, disease characteristics, and other comparisons. In this regard, he supported natural selection as being as "near an approximation to the truth as . . . the Copernican hypothesis was to the true theory of the planetary motions." Unconcerned that Darwin had not yet applied his theory to ethnological questions, Huxley, along with Wallace and French naturalist Félix-Archimède Pouchet, supported the common descent of man from preexisting species.[25]

Apart from those who stood firmly with Christian orthodoxy, Huxley's position was generally adopted, as subsequent studies supported his argument for the closeness of man's structural affinity. The mode of origin as well as man's early stages of development were considered identical with those immediately below him in the scale. As he explained, humans were "far nearer the apes than the apes are to the dog." Like many of his contemporaries, however, Huxley was careful to stress the important differences not just in the structure of human and primate brains but in their respective sizes and weights—differences that were also used to separate the lowest and highest humans.[26]

## DARWINISM

Biographer Janet Browne identified Charles Lyell, Joseph Hooker, Asa Gray, and Huxley as Darwin's "Four Musketeers." Together they proceeded to advocate a mutual goal of advancing evolution while masking their own differences.[27] Huxley's guardianship of Darwin's intellectual property, for which he introduced the term "Darwinism" in the April 1860 issue of the *Westminster Review*, was evidenced time and again in statements to the press, in public lectures, and in his writings. Surprisingly, however, Huxley avoided using the term himself, because of its association with matters that neither he nor Darwin supported.[28] The term "Darwinism"—social, biological, and philosophical—contained loaded concepts whose hermeneutic options seemed limitless, capturing in its worldview elements of Spiritualism, naturalism, materialism, and positivism. The connection between Darwinism and sociopolitical evolution was not something to which Darwin gave his consent; nevertheless, in the hands of others, including many of his strongest supporters, it became a topic with immediate and long-range implications, including imperialism, racism, and sexism.[29]

The fact that Robert Chambers's *Vestiges of the Natural History of Creation* continued to sell after *Origin* appeared is evidence that the scientific credibility of natural selection competed with other options that appealed just as powerfully to the imagination of the reading public. So utterly convoluted was this situation that David L. Hull remarked: "A scientist can be a Darwinian without accepting all or even a large proportion of the elements of Darwinism. Conversely, a scientist can by and large accept the tenets of Darwinism without being a Darwinian."[30] Darwinism proved rich in analogies and images, leaving virtual vacuums for those speculative in their thinking to fill with their particular vision. From the Darwinism of Wallace and Gray to its different meanings when used by Huxley, Romanes, and Hodge, the word acquired a messiness that perplexed the most petulant scholars. Loaded with meaning, the term became both a noun and an adjective—a banner attached to numerous "isms" including "Spencerism," "Haeckelism," "Weismannism," "Neo-Lamarckism," and "Neo-Darwinism."

Evolutionists called themselves "Darwinists" or "Darwinians" to acknowledge their deference to Darwin, using his popularity to wrest control of the scientific community from clerics and amateur naturalists. Despite their personal objections to natural selection as the precise mechanism for evolution, they repressed any open criticism, for fear that it would diminish their efforts to use evolutionism as the catalyst for reform of the scientific community. "In the end the success of Darwinism rested not on a general acceptance of the selection theory," explains historian Peter J. Bowler, "but on the exploitation of evolutionism by those who were determined to establish science as a new source of authority in Western civilization."[31] As explained by English historian Leslie Stephen, "Darwinism . . . acted like a leaven affecting the whole development of modern thought. . . . We classify the ablest thinkers by the relation which their opinions bear to it, and, whatever its ultimate fate, no one can doubt that it will be the most conspicuous factor in the history of modern speculation."[32]

As noted earlier, Huxley embraced natural selection as the most reasonable explanation for the changes known to have taken place in species. Nevertheless, he distinguished between evolution and Darwin's explanation as to how it had come about, never claiming that the hypothesis was correct.

There is no fault to be found with Mr. Darwin's method, then; but it is another question whether he has fulfilled all the conditions imposed by that method. Is it satisfactorily proved, in fact, that species may be originated by selection? that there is such a thing as natural selection? that none of the phenomena exhibited by species are inconsistent with the origin of species in this way? If these questions can be answered in the affirmative, Mr. Darwin's view steps out of the ranks of hypotheses into those of proved theories; but so long as the evidence at present adduced falls short of enforcing that affirmation, so long, to our minds, must the new doctrine be content to remain among the former—an extremely valuable, and in the highest degree probable, doctrine, indeed the only extant hypothesis which is worth anything in a scientific point of view; but still a hypothesis, and not yet the theory of species.

After much consideration, and with assuredly no bias against Mr. Darwin's views, it is our clear conviction that, as the evidence stands, it is not absolutely proven that a group of animals, having all the characters exhibited by species in nature, has ever been originated by selection, whether artificial or natural.[33]

Later, when awarded the Darwin Medal by the Royal Society, in 1894, Huxley offered a much similar statement. "I am sincerely of the opinion that the views which were propounded by Mr. Darwin thirty-four years ago may be understood hereafter as constituting an epoch in the intellectual history of the human race. They will modify the whole system of our thought and opinion, our most intimate convictions. But I do not know, I do not think anybody knows, whether the particular views he held will be hereafter fortified by the experience of the ages which come after us. . . . Whether the particular form in which he has put before us the Darwinian doctrines may be such as to be destined to survive or not, is more, I venture to think, than anybody is capable at this present moment of saying."[34]

By 1865 the term "Darwinism" had become problematic; by 1869 its socio-cognitive value had been repackaged to include a range of meanings beyond anything that Darwin or Huxley ever imagined. The Huxley who in April 1860 in the *Westminster Review* used the term to express his approval of the *Origin* and commend descent by natural means was *not* the Huxley who, in 1871, placed "Darwinism" in quotation marks as a way of dissociating himself from its meaning.[35] Huxley's response to Darwin's chance universe was to point out that "chance variations" resulted from the operation of definite but undefined laws that in no way eliminated the element of teleology. With these words, the term "chance variations" morphed into what John C. Greene identified as a "hidden system of laws, elements, and forces which had produced them." It was that revised definition that drew pragmatists Charles Peirce and William James to examine more closely Darwin's theory.[36]

Huxley remained a stalwart defender of the general principle of evolution, which he willingly identified with Darwinism. As he remarked in a course of lectures in 1906. "I really believe that the alternative is either Darwinism or nothing, for I do not know of any rational conception or theory of the organic universe which has any scientific position at all beside Mr. Darwin's." Nevertheless, he admitted to accepting the theory "provisionally, in exactly the same way as I accept any other hypothesis."[37] Huxley did not waver from defending Darwin's theory before the public but filtered it through a series of casuistic explanations that resulted in an outcome significantly different from what Darwin himself had put forward. What passed for Darwinism turned out to be a combination of concepts, most of which offered a purposive and even inevitable progressive process.

## X-CLUB

There was a personal dimension in the struggle to support evolution that involved a tightly knit group of professionals held together by personal loyalties and dedicated to seeking professional identity for themselves. This explains why, when a group of convivial friends from the Ethnological Society of London met for dinner at St. George's Hotel in 1864 to discuss the political and theological divisiveness of the times, they formed a dining club, better known as the "X Club," dedicated to defending evolutionary theory, advocate a naturalistic explanation for the world, and advance the professionalization of science. Most of the club's initial members (Huxley, Tyndall, Hooker, Lubbock, Spencer, William Spottiswoode, Thomas Hirst, Edward Frankland, and George Busk) shared the experience of being outside the privileged world of clerics and gentlemen naturalists. Huxley christened the group the Blastodermic Club, hoping that it would eventually become an acknowledged source of authority within scientific circles. Committed to the pursuit of knowledge through a combination of work and a sense of duty, its members sought jobs in engineering, teaching, surveying, medicine, and similar trades, often delaying marriage for the sake of their careers. Living with untamed ambition at the edges of Britain's class system, they sought nominations and patronage positions, assisted each other as willing allies when the opportunity permitted, shared their defeats, and celebrated their successes. This included seeking election to coveted positions, reviewing each other's work, providing endorsements, and winning awards.[38]

The X Club, consisting of an informal but well-connected circle of young scientists eager on building a mystique surrounding Darwin and his theory, became a "Trojan horse" in the inner sanctum of Britain's class-structured scientific circles. Meeting monthly from October to June for twenty years, it served as a staging ground for the advancement of professional science at the expense of the Anglican establishment. Over time, it succeeded in filling chairs and administrative positions thereby advancing the professionalization of science. As a symbol of its success, three members (Huxley, Hooker, and Spottiswoode) were elected presidents of the Royal Society. The club also exercised its power to force awarding the prestigious Copley Medal to Darwin when the society's membership thought it ought to have been awarded first to Adam Sedgwick.[39] Huxley's leadership in the X Club on the one hand and his association with Norman Lockyer and the journal *Nature* on the other made him one of the more formidable scientific power brokers of his generation.

## AGNOSTICISM

In his *Origins of Agnosticism*, historian Bernard Lightman identified three phases to the word *agnosticism*. The first, from 1869 to 1877, involved little application outside discussion among members of the Metaphysical Club (1869–1880) to which Huxley belonged; the *second*, from 1878 to 1883, when the term entered the lexicon in articles appearing in the press; and the *third*, beginning in 1889, when Huxley sought unsuccessfully to control its meaning.[40]

R. H. Hutton, editor of the *Spectator*, reported that Huxley first coined the term *agnosticism* at a meeting in the home of James Knowles on Chapham Common in 1869, borrowing it from St. Paul's reference to the altar "of the unknown God." Huxley, on the other hand, remembered differently, recalling that he first used the term as antithetic to *gnostic*, meaning those "who profess to know so much about the very things of which I was ignorant."[41] With it, he intended to distance himself from unbelievers like Hume, Locke, and Kant, who were associated with stark materialism, as well as from Spencer's Unknowable. In fact, Huxley thought little of Spencer's term, commenting, "There are many topics about which I know nothing; and which, so far as I can see, are out of reach of my faculties. But whether these things are knowable by anyone else is exactly one of these matters which is beyond my knowledge, though I may have a tolerably strong opinion as to the probabilities of the case."[42]

In their discussions regarding certitude, the Metaphysical Club's members initially employed words such as "unknown," "skepticism," and "doubt" to express their frustration with Christian dogma and the ecclesiastical authority employed to justify it. The age-old certainties concerning man and the universe no longer held the same currency as before. Since the Enlightenment, the *philosophes* had viewed God as unnecessary to account for the natural order, and, while there was nothing especially new in this attitude, the nature of unbelief reached new intensity by the second half of the nineteenth century. Science and evolutionary theory now dominated the Western mind, but with no single model on which to hang its hat, there being no consensus to the question "Why?" As Darwin himself observed, with natural selection there was no more evidence of design "than in the course which the wind blows."[43] As a consequence, club members adopted Huxley's invented term, using it as a rhetorical weapon in their struggle with religious orthodoxy. Standing apart from atheism's outright denial of God's existence, the term represented a "safe zone" between accusations coming from the scientific materialist and the Christian believer—a neutral position free from a debate that seemed to be going nowhere.

During the second period when agnosticism became popular currency, the word took on meanings that were seldom consistent in purpose or intent. These included those simply indifferent to religion and uncaring as to the issue of God's existence; those who believed it impossible for anyone to know whether God existed; those who had no belief in God but did not feel they could disprove his existence; and those who perhaps had a religious attitude but no assurance that God existed. Some critics even condemned it as materialistic philosophy and a form of infidelity hostile to religion and ethics; others were just as convinced it represented an acceptable position to hold, even for church communicants.[44]

Bernard Lightman took issue with the long-held assumption that the epistemological positions of agnosticism and skepticism were the logical outcomes of materialistic science and biblical criticism. Focusing on the leaders of the agnostic movement, which included Spencer, Huxley, Tyndall, Henry Mansel, and William Clifford, he provided textual evidence of their hostile but not irreligious skepticism toward Christian orthodoxy. Overall, many agnostics genuinely hoped to preserve those aspects of religion that could be affirmed intellectually. Their arguments were not against religion per se, or justifying science at the expense of religion, but with attacking ecclesiasticism, which had played a role far beyond its pretended hegemony.[45]

Agnostics were preoccupied with the limits of knowledge, some siding more with science; others with religion. They pictured a thin veil lying between man and his ability to answer with conviction the *why* of creation along with the criterion for progress, direction, and limitations.[46] For Spencer, Huxley, Tyndall, Mansel, and Samuel Laing, the epistemological basis for their respective agnosticisms differed, but they all showed a willingness to build a coherent set of beliefs that were both scientifically responsible and spiritually satisfying. As representative of the milder school of agnosticism, Spencer had used his choice term *Unknowable* with the reverence of religion, recognizing the ultimate mysteriousness of the universe.[47] For those for whom science weighed more heavily, their unwillingness to accept revelation or a priori knowledge left them with an equal sense of the world's impenetrable mystery. Lightman argued that, in either case, and despite inconsistencies, agnosticism represented an "apologetic tool" used by the rising middle class "to wrest cultural and social prestige from the clergy."[48]

Throughout this period, Huxley held his silence while a high-profile war of words ensued between Spencer and British jurist Frederic Harrison, a fellow member of the Metaphysical Society, both of whom were unbelievers, followed by a Catholic response from John Henry Newman suggesting his *Grammar of Assent* "as the antidote to poisonous agnostic ideas."[49] The Spencerian agnostics, namely, those whose agnosticism inclined toward theism, carried the day. Their Unknown was a spiritually tainted agnosticism that seemed more appealing for the time.[50]

Huxley did not claim ownership of the term until twenty years after its first appearance, when he attempted to set the record straight by using it in philosophical and argumentative discourse when evidence proved insufficient for certitude. With it, he encouraged a habit of mind rather than a formalized belief. It served as a weapon for the intellect to consider before choosing to affirm or deny. It also represented an attack on those who were comfortable with leaving superstition and hazy metaphysical dogmas in control of the facts.

Agnosticism, in fact, is not a creed but a method, the essence of which lies in a rigorous application of a single principle. That principle is of great antiquity; it is as old as Socrates; as old as the writer who said, "Try all things, hold fast by that which is good"; it is the foundation of the

Reformation, which simply illustrated the axiom that every man should be able to give reason for the faith that is in him; it is the great principle of Descartes; it is the fundamental axiom of modern science. Positively the principle may be expressed: In matters of the intellect, follow your reason as far as it will take you, without regard to any other consideration. And negatively: In matters of the intellect, do not pretend that conclusions are certain which are not demonstrated or demonstrable. That I take to be the agnostic faith, which, if a man keep whole and undented, he shall not be ashamed to look the universe in the face, whatever the future may have in store for him.[51]

Huxley's agnosticism amounted to this: "That it is wrong for a man to say that he is certain of the objective truth of any proposition unless he can produce evidence which logically justifies that certainty." Though he doubted the certainty that theologians of his time professed, he did not deny the possibility that a theological proposition might or could be true.[52]

Every variety of philosophical and theological opinion was represented there, and expressed itself with entire openness; most of my colleagues were -ists of one sort or another; and, however kind and friendly they might be, I, the man without a rag of a label to cover himself with, could not fail to have some sort of the uneasy feelings which must have beset the historical fox when, after leaving the trap in which his tail remained, he presented himself to his normally elongated companions. So I took thought and invented what I conceived to be the appropriate title of "agnostic." It came into my head as suggestively antithetic to the "gnostic" of Church history, who professed to know so much about the very things of which I was ignorant; and I took the earliest opportunity of parading it at our Society, to show that I, too, had a tail, like the other foxes. To my great satisfaction, the term took; and when the *Spectator* had stood godfather to it, any suspicion in the minds of respectable people, that knowledge of its parentage might have awakened, was, of course, completely lulled.[53]

As an agnostic, Huxley stood apart from the purveyors of religious orthodoxy. Newman's assertion that faith could not rest on reason astounded him. He was equally surprised to learn of Newman's endorsement of miracles based on the law of probabilities.[54] Huxley's principal feud, however, was with the Comtean positivists, whom he accused of replacing religious orthodoxy with a Religion of Humanity that he found just as repulsive as the papal chair in Catholic orthodoxy.[55]

Huxley valued the methodological superiority of science over the biblical explanation of life and applied evolutionary theory to explain distinct stages in the historical development of its texts. But rather than suggest that the Bible was either obsolete or insignificant, he chose to view it in much the same way geologists treated fossils to explain changes in the natural world.[56] "The present antagonism between theology and science does not arise from any assumption by the men of science that all theology must necessarily be excluded from science," he admitted, "but simply because they are unable to allow that reason and morality have two weights and two measures; and that the belief in a proposition, because authority tells you it is true, or because you wish to believe it, which is a high crime and misdemeanor when the subject matter of reasoning is of one kind, becomes under the *alias* of 'faith' the greatest of all virtues when the subject matter of reasoning is of another kind." As for serving God or science, Huxley responded: "Let him not imagine he is, or can be, both a true son of the Church and a loyal soldier of science."[57]

Huxley's harshest critics categorized him as an outspoken materialist.[58] Yet, if obliged to choose between the extremes of materialism and idealism, he gladly accepted the latter as the preferred choice for the scientific man. The brain may be the machinery by which the material universe becomes conscious of itself, but even if this conception of the universe was true, "we should . . . still [be] bound by the limits of thought, still unable to refute the arguments of pure idealism. The more completely the materialistic position is admitted, the easier it is to show that the idealistic position is unassailable, if the idealist confines himself within the limits of positive knowledge."[59]

Huxley did not affirm teleology outright or the argument from design but felt that the theory of evolution had progressed beyond crude mechanics with the element of "chance" only in form or appearance. Ultimately, there was no incongruity between evolution and the expectations of teleology. Still, he insisted that the God question could not be settled with the scientific method. In effect, science was out of its depth in addressing realms of ultimate meaning or value. "There is a wider teleology," he maintained, "which is not touched by the doctrine of evolution but is actually based on the fundamental proposition of evolution. This proposition is that the whole world, living and not living, is the result of mutual interaction, according to definite laws, of the forces possessed by the molecules of which the primitive nebulosity of the universe was composed [and whose] mechanical dispositions [were] fixed beforehand by intelligent appointment and kept in action by a power at the center."[60]

To the extent that unbelievers found themselves in a quarrelsome discussion with believers, they just as often found their fellow unbelievers even more challenging. What makes Huxley's position so profoundly different from his colleagues' is the fact that his agnosticism was anchored in genuine doubt rather than in faith in some formulation of God or matter. It appealed to those who, out of honesty and humility, found themselves unable to accept any of the existing creeds. It represented with almost existential acuity the inability to know the ultimate order or purpose of the world. As an agnostic, Huxley insisted that the God question could not be settled by scientific methods, and thus, he chose not to divide the world into the realm of phenomena, which was the basis of science, and a metaphysical realm belonging wholly to religion and philosophy. Instead, explains Christopher Clausen, Huxley divided the world "into those things about which we have knowledge and those things about which we do not, and probably cannot, know anything at all." This explains why critics found it difficult to locate a point of weakness in his position. For the proponents of religious orthodoxy, his agnosticism appeared to be a carefully concealed variation of atheism.[61]

American and British positivists applied the words *agnosticism* and *Unknowable* with a degree of soft-spoken reverence, but the terms remained too abstract to constitute a collective sigh of relief from the population at large. Given the presumption in the words that many things were simply beyond proof and arguably beyond caring, their usage prompted an existential foreboding that the future might be something other than that foretold by science's evolutionary theory. The quest for certainty stalled not by proclamations of outright infidelity by a few atheists, but by a persistent mood of uncertainty that ate away at any hopeful signs of any empirically founded assurances attributed to science's presumed familiarity with the cosmos.

Hoping to rein in its true purpose and meaning, Huxley discovered too late that the word had taken on a life of its own. Thus, while agnosticism became part of conventional wisdom in the closing decades of the nineteenth century, Huxley failed to give it a definitive meaning or definition. In fact, it entered the public domain with a branding that was attributed more to Spencer than to Huxley.[62]

## Ethics of the Cosmos

The late Victorians remained divided on the "chicken or egg" relationship between faith and morals. Were God and religion essential to the development of moral laws? Did they create the impulse for man's conscience and pursuit of righteousness, or could moral laws derive from man's inner nature? And if the stakes were not high enough, was a depersonalized cosmic theism (e.g., Spencer's Unknowable) the equivalent of the spiritually comforting anthropomorphic God of Christianity? The quarrel among the positivists included indiscriminate labeling and name-calling, best represented by Huxley's refusal to countenance broad pronouncements on cosmic questions and his epitomizing Comte's Religion of Humanity as "Catholicism *minus* Christianity."[63]

Though he denied there was sufficient evidence for claiming the existence of the soul and an afterlife, Huxley avoided being pegged a materialist for fear of harming the dignity and responsibility of the individual. Morality was something that depended not on physiology but on an instinct that service to mankind (i.e., altruism) was the only meaningful purpose of life. "I repudiate, as philosophical error, the doctrine of Materialism as I understand it, just as I repudiate the doctrine of Spiritualism . . . and my reason for thus doing is, in both cases, the same; namely, that whatever their differences, Materialists and Spiritualists agree in making very positive assertions about matters of which I am certain I know nothing, and about which I believe they are, in truth, just as ignorant."[64]

Huxley found morality so entangled with religion and politics that it required the "dexterity of an egg-dancer" to make sense of the current state of things.[65] Looking at the forces of evil, sorrow, and suffering in the world, he concluded that modern humanity was simply retreading the worn paths of prior civilizations. Religion was no source of moral authority; instead, morality was the outcome of one's culture. The cosmic process was non-moral, meaning that as civilization advanced, the ethical person was challenged to counter the negative and sinister forces at work in the struggle for existence. To demonstrate this point, his Romanes Lecture in 1893, titled "Evolution and Ethics," began with the premise that the forces of the cosmos were no grounds for virtue. If the cosmos were to stand in judgment before the tribunal of ethicists, it would "stand condemned," suggesting the denial of any ethical element in the order of nature. "The science of ethics professes to furnish us with a reasoned rule of life; to tell us what is right action and why it is so. Whatever difference of opinion may exist among experts, there is a consensus that the ape and tiger methods of the struggle of existence are not reconcilable with sound ethical principles." Though this view of life seemed to leave man utterly despondent, Huxley insisted that humanity's role was to fight the cosmos rather than imitate it. One could expect no help or sympathy from the cosmos. In becoming civilized, man ventured on an undertaking for which he alone was the responsible party. Civilization thus became man's effort to escape the world of survival of the fittest. By exercising self-restraint and cooperation, he could rise above the strict biological needs of the species by using his energy and intelligence to modify the conditions of existence. Ultimately, cosmic evolution would be counterbalanced by dissolution, and to this end, he showed stoicism.[66]

Huxley regretted using the phrase "survival of the fittest," as it connoted that "fittest" was also "best," implying perfection by means of a struggle for existence by the strongest and most assertive over the weaker. True social progress, he concluded, meant checking the cosmic process and "the substitution for it of another, which may be called the ethical process," the end of which was the survival not of those who might happen to be the fittest but "of those who are ethically the best." "In place of ruthless self-assertion it demands self-restraint; in place of thrusting aside, or treading down, all competitors, it requires that the individual shall not merely respect, but shall help his fellows; its influence is directed, not so much to the survival of the fittest, as to the fitting of as many as possible to survive. It repudiates the gladiatorial theory of existence. . . . Laws and moral precepts are directed to the end of curbing the cosmic process and reminding the individual of his duty to the community, to the protection and influence of which he owes, if not existence itself, at least the life of something better than a brutal savage."[67]

No believer in a static or cyclical view of the universe, Huxley held that at every moment the cosmos was in a state of "transitory adjustment" or "impermanence." Man had evolved over the centuries from savage to a "member of an organized polity." But nature was amoral, which meant that if man was to make progress, he would need to depend on his own energies and intelligence to make it happen. Having worked to the "headship of the sentient world" by succeeding in the struggle for existence using "axe and rope," man passed from the anarchy of struggle to a more "reasoned rule of life." Over time, the conscience of man "revolted against the moral indifference of nature." In this manner, the ethical progress of man and of society formed when man succeeded in creating an "artificial world within the cosmos"—when intelligence was used to modify the "instincts of savagery in civilized men."[68] Although he refused to accept the Bible as authentic revelation, he supported its being read and studied in the schools.[69]

Huxley's Romanes Lecture came at a time when many had begun to view Buddhism as the most admirable of the non-Christian religions, winning adherents across the East/West divide. With terms and concepts introduced into general use in moral, philosophical, and religious discussion due largely to the contributions of British Eastern scholar Rhys Davids, Huxley introduced an analytical and comparative connection between the distinctive philosophical ideas present in this two-thousand-year-old religion and Western metaphysics. Attributing to Buddhism a deeper understanding of life's imponderables than that espoused by Western philosophers, he endorsed many of Buddhism's humanistic values, especially those founded in empirical thought.[70]

Huxley viewed the consummation of evolution as reached not in man himself but in man as a member of an organized polity, a view that placed him uncomfortably close to Wallace's revision to natural selection. It suggested the application of intelligence and will guided by "sound principles of investigation and organized in common effort" that curbed the savage instincts in man.[71] Through much of humankind's early evolution, its success had been largely indebted to those qualities people shared with the rest of the animal kingdom. But to the degree that humans passed from struggle for existence and survival of the fittest, which was not reconcilable with ethical principles, to social organization, marked the beginning of a purely intellectual process that was in harmony with the moral sense—the ethical ideal of the just and the good. Evident in the book of Job, the Buddhist sutras, and the poets of Greece, the endless cycles of events metamorphosed into a world soul striving to improve amid the reality of evil and the grim realities of practical life.

But what is the part played by evolution in ethics? For Huxley, Greek and Indian thought set out from common ground, developed under very different physical conditions, and eventually converged to the same end. The new hero is not the soldier but the monk. Where the "best" and the "fittest" once held the connotation of the world of "root, hog, or die," social or ethical progress meant checking the cosmic process, which meant the survival not of those who happened to be the fittest but of those who were ethically the best. In place of ruthless competition, there was the creation of laws and moral precepts intended to curb the cosmic process. "The history of civilization," explained Huxley, "details the steps by which men have succeeded in building up an artificial world within the cosmos."[72] Essentially, Huxley's honesty forced him to be suspicious of evolutionary ethics. A true ethic, one that reflected the hopes and purposes of civilization, demanded the rejection of natural selection's "red in tooth and claw" as the rule of human behavior.

SCIENCE AS EDUCATION

During the time of Huxley's self-education, science was not taught as a formal subject in the public schools, and educators made little provision for it in the universities, except for medical students, who received a modicum of instruction in botany, chemistry, and physiology. In all of Europe, there were less than a dozen professorships in science. Even in 1854, when he was appointed to the chair of natural history in the Royal School of Mines, no laboratory existed to accompany instruction. Lectures alone sufficed, and any physical or practical acquaintance students had with the subject matter was done apart from class. "I am set there to teach natural history without a biological laboratory and without the means of shewing a single dissection," he complained. Not until 1872 did he develop a laboratory course, which became the model of courses given subsequently. In addressing an audience in St. Martin's Hall in London, he remarked that with the exception of those few who had received a medical education, "there is not one who could tell men what is the meaning and use of an act . . . of breathing—or who could state in precise terms why it is that a confined atmosphere is injurious to health."[73]

All this changed with Huxley's compelling arguments. In lectures in Liverpool, University College in London, the University of Aberdeen, and Johns Hopkins University, and before the International Medical Congress, he spoke eloquently on the necessity of science being a part of a liberal education. In 1880 he, chemist Henry Enfield Roscoe, and physicist Balfour Stewart served as general editors for a series of "science primers" written for the public and published by Macmillan. All three men insisted that chemistry, physics, botany, and zoology should be part of a student's general education, and not simply the purview of a professional medical education. In addition, Huxley, Tyndall, and Spencer formed an advisory committee for books chosen for inclusion in the International Scientific Series (published by D. Appleton and Company of New York between 1872 and 1909), which became the professional scientists' principal outlet for the dissemination of science to the general population. The series included the writings of Darwin, Bagehot, Buckle, Helmholtz, Huxley, Lecky, and Tyndall. As part of the series, Huxley's *Manual of the Anatomy of Vertebrated Animals* (1871), *Manual of the Anatomy of Invertebrated Animals* (1877), and *The Crayfish: An Introduction to the Study of Biology* (1880) for decades were used as introductions to the study of zoology. Over time Huxley became "a one-man industry with his days filled with scientific research and teaching, and the rest of his hours devoted to lectures, meetings, and writing to advance the interests of professional scientists and earn extra income to support his family."[74] In none of his many contributions did he ever once discuss the role of natural selection. Instead, his purpose was to infuse the principle of naturalism into science.[75]

Peter Bowler has argued that while Huxley emerged as a principal catalyst for evolution's popular acceptance, he was a "non-Darwinian," on the grounds that he rejected both gradualism and the theory of natural selection. In fact, in his efforts to find a place for science in British education, natural selection made no appearance in any of his textbooks.[76] Even as Darwin's self-appointed "Bulldog," the question remains how much Huxley held to the theory. Jacques Barzun called Huxley imbued "with an evangelical passion to overstate his conclusions, but . . . neither stupid nor dishonest. He had the highest kind of courage, and a Calvinistic desire to be chosen for the right reason, which for him was the possession of truth."[77] While true to his empiricist epistemology and his skepticism of metaphysics and any argument from Design or special creation, his coining of the term *agnosticism* carried over into Darwin's natural selection and the nature of evolutionary change. Though the public voice and defender of the reclusive Darwin, he chose to dwell on the idea of evolution generally rather than on the chance-driven mechanism of natural selection. He remained, explains Bowler, "a classic example of a pseudo-Darwinian." For all his bombast, that which stimulated him into action seemed more directly connected to evolutionism as a concept, not to the selection theory.[78]

## SELECTED WRITINGS

*The Scientific Memoirs of Thomas Henry Huxley* (1898)
*Collected Essays by T. H. Huxley* (1893–1895)
*The Oceanic Hydrozoa* (1859)
*Evidence as to Man's Place in Nature* (1863)
*On Our Knowledge of the Causes of Organic Phenomena; Being Six Lectures to Working Men* (1863)
*Lectures on the Elements of Comparative Anatomy: On the Classification of Animals and the Vertebrate Skull* (1864)
*An Elementary Atlas of Comparative Osteology* (1864)
*Lessons in Elementary Physiology* (1866)
*An Introduction to the Classification of Animals* (1869)

*A Manual of the Anatomy of Vertebrated Animals* (1871)
*A Course of Practical Instruction in Elementary Biology* (1875)
*A Manual of the Anatomy of Invertebrated Animals* (1877)
*Lay Sermons, Essays, and Reviews* (1877)
*American Addresses, with a Lecture on the Study of Biology* (1877)
*Physiography, an Introduction to the Study of Zoology* (1880)
*Introductory Primer* (1880)

# 6

## Cosmic Theism
### John Fiske

*For my own part . . . I believe in the immortality of the soul, not in the sense
in which I accept the demonstrable truths of science, but as a supreme act of
faith in the reasonableness of God's work. Such a belief, relating to regions
quite inaccessible to experience, cannot of course be clothed in terms of definite
and tangible meaning. . . . But on such grounds, if on no other, the faith in
immortality is likely to be shared by all who look upon the genesis of the highest
spiritual qualities in man as the goal of Nature's creative work.*

    —John Fiske, *Cosmic Philosophy*, 1874

CONFRONTED BY THE THEORY OF evolution and the harsh findings
of the higher criticism, Christian orthodoxy had its sturdy confidence seriously eroded and its certitude perceptibly diminished. Darwin's
nondirectional universe came as a heavy blow to conventional thinking,
which included the concept of Design. Orthodoxy had faced earlier challenges from the eighteenth-century *philosophes* regarding miracles and
the Trinity, but the challenges to the late Victorians proved far more serious, throwing doubt not just on Christianity's anthropomorphic God but
on the unity and purposefulness of history, man's moral sense, reward
for virtue, sanctity of life, and immortality—beliefs that had stood their
ground for centuries. Now the choice was between belief and disbelief, a
crisis deemed more ominous than ever before. The term *agnostic* coined
by Huxley in 1869 became one more symbol of society's distrust in Christianity's rhetoricians. But Huxley's agnosticism paled before Robert G.
Ingersoll's humanistic rationalism, which carried the implications even
further when he proclaimed: "The agnostic does not simply say, 'I do not
know.' He goes another step, and says, with great emphasis, that *you* do
not know." The agnostic not only accepted personal responsibility for not
knowing but concluded that the world of the believer was, in fact, a world
of shadows.[1] Historian D. H. Meyer said it best when he observed that
"doubt was no longer a matter of personal bafflement but a badge of intellectual honesty."[2]

The American philosopher and historian John Fiske (1842–1901) spoke for those Victorians who longed for spiritual unity and purpose in the universe without the artifices of organized religion. Too much a Christian to acquiesce to Darwin's nondirectional implications, he allayed the fears of his countrymen by interpreting evolution as a positive force in the modern world, bringing comfort and reassurance that the universe, however lonely it appeared, remained in the hands of a well-meaning Deity. A brilliant popularizer and an authoritative spokesman for the synthetic philosophy of Spencer, he introduced a form of scientific theism that claimed a single, cosmic vision. In doing so he united the facts of science with an intelligent but depersonalized God who harmonized man's moral efforts with the seemingly benign nature of evolution. An ardent champion of Spencer, he sought to reconcile evolution with centuries of passionately held and intuitively derived truths. Above all else, he advanced the liberal tradition in American Christianity using the methods of science to demonstrate the validity of notions concerning God, man, and history. He spoke to a generation of Americans anxious to square evolution with the foundations of Christianity and the nation's destiny.

## Formative Years

Born in Hartford, Connecticut, John Fiske was baptized Edmund Fisk Green. His family came from freethinking Quakers who eventually joined the Congregational Church, a reflection of the fluid nature of class and religion in American Protestantism. Hartford offered Edmund a larger-than-life view of a community that was middle-class and prosperous, where poverty was rare, and society not yet stratified. The town's religious life centered around six churches: two Congregational, one Episcopal, one Baptist, and two Methodist. In all six, preaching followed the "strictest evangelical character," breathing the grim theology of Calvin and Edwards at the expense of the more humanizing aspects of Unitarianism.[3]

His father, Edmund Brewster Green, a graduate of Wesleyan University, had been a successful lawyer and judge of the Superior Court of Middlesex County. A restless man who envied the fortunes of those around him, he left the bar to become editor and proprietor of the *New England Review*, a weekly Whig journal. Later he worked as private secretary to Henry Clay, before joining in the frenzy of the gold rush. On his way to San Francisco to claim his share of fortune, he had a change of heart and settled in Panama to publish the semiweekly *Panama Herald*, where he died shortly afterward of cholera. Coping with her husband's frequent absences, Edmund's mother had started a successful career teaching in private schools for young ladies in Hartford and New York City.

Given his parents' lifestyle, which seemed always in transition, Edmund spent most of his youth at the home of his maternal grandparents in Middletown, seventeen miles south of Hartford, which, like New Haven, Providence, and Boston, reflected the region's strong Puritan roots. Edmund's grandfather John Fisk worked as the town clerk and treasurer, clerk of the superior court, county treasurer, and clerk of probate—all simultaneously. Known affectionately as the town's "walking encyclopedia," he served as an ideal role model to his grandson, nurturing his inquiring mind with Charles Rollin's *Ancient History*, Oliver Goldsmith's *History of Greece*, Edward Gibbon's *Decline and Fall of the Roman Empire*, and William Robertson's *History of the Reign of the Emperor Charles V*. From this auspicious beginning, the boy turned to *Plutarch's Lives* and Jared Sparks's *Life of Washington*, followed by the works of Calvin, Edwards, Shakespeare, Milton, Pope, and Walter Scott. In this enriched and nurturing environment, the young prodigy with red hair and freckles blossomed, and by age seven had read nearly two hundred volumes on subjects ranging from natural history and philosophy to chemistry, astronomy, grammar, and mathematics. By nine he was enrolled in a private preparatory school for boys, after which he studied without a tutor, teaching himself French, Italian, Portuguese, and German, before learning Hebrew and Sanskrit. He also became proficient on the piano, with his favorite musical choices rich in the Christian tradition.[4]

When Edmund was twelve, his mother remarried. Unwilling to move to New York City, he chose to remain with his grandparents, who had provided the only real home he had ever known. After making this decision, he changed his name to "John Fisk" in honor of his grandfather and the Fisk family. The addition of the letter "e" to his surname did not occur until college, when school officials inadvertently added the letter in his official transcript. Because the Fisk family history included ancestors with that spelling, he formalized the additional change.

Shortly after his mother's marriage, the family decided to send Fiske to Betts Academy in Stamford, whose daily regimen, modeled after Britain's public schools, was highly structured and disciplined. "I get up at 5½ o'clock every morning, am dressed and ready for prayers in 15 minutes. At 6 o'clock we have breakfast. From 8 till 10, I study Greek. Then there is half an hour recess. From 10½ till 12, I study mathematics. From 2 till 4 Latin. At 6 o'clock we have supper. From 7½ to 8¼, I study Latin Prose. From 8½ to 9, I read. The play hours are from 7 to 8 A.M., from 1 to 2 and from 4 to 6 P.M. Every Wednesday morning we draw. Every Saturday morning we speak or write compositions. Wednesday and Saturday afternoons we go on an excursion."[5]

During his time at the academy, a strict evangelical school requiring attendance at church and daily prayers, Fiske informed his family of the seriousness of his religious feelings and formally joined the North Congregational Church. Besides singing in the choir, he taught Sunday school and participated in Bible class and revival meetings. Much to his grandparents' amusement, he sometimes impersonated the minister, a preacher of strict orthodoxy, acting out his sermons.[6]

By age fifteen, after completing his studies at Betts, where he earned the school's highest honors, Fiske set his sights on Yale and acquired a private tutor, Rev. Henry M. Colton, to prepare him for the examination. Colton convinced him to postpone college for two years, suggesting that he was too young to benefit from the experience. In the summer of 1859, Fiske took the examination and passed "very credibly," missing only one question. Awarded a certificate of admission, he again decided to postpone college, this time choosing Harvard, where he intended to seek admission at the sophomore or even junior level.[7]

Along with his studies, which included reading some of Britain's positivist thinkers, Fiske began questioning the sincerity of his Calvinistic faith—a matter coincident with the rise of evolutionary philosophy and the troubling issues emerging from the higher criticism—which included challenges to the inspiration of the Bible and the binding force of church dogma. Often during these times of doubt, he turned to John Langdon Dudley, pastor of the South Congregational Church in Middletown, for a sympathetic ear. He also sought help from Joseph Whitcomb Ellis, a liberal-minded Swedenborgian who offered the use of his library. According to biographer John Spencer Clark, "[Fiske's] whole religious nature was deeply stirred by the manifest incongruities between Revelation as asserted by dogma and the verifiable revelations unearthed by science and history."[8] Writing to his mother, he explained his dilemma of trying to align belief in the Trinity with Mosaic cosmogony, noting that "if the system is true, orthodoxy, Unitarianism, and Swedenborgianism are alike false."[9] As he explained, "With more mature thought, I came to see the great spiritual truth enshrouded in these dogmas; and a wider acquaintance with the philosophy of history, led me to see that the dogmatic coverings of this great truth had been of immense service in its protection and its development while knowledge was slowly being organized through science, for its verification in human experience. And now the

Christian world is beginning to see that religious and social progress consists mainly in the freeing of this great spiritual truth from the dogmatic wrappings it has outgrown."[10]

Fiske endeavored to retain his religion by reading Hugh Miller's *Testimony of the Rocks*, James Barr Walker's *Philosophy of the Plan of Salvation* (1845), Francis Wayland's *The Elements of Intellectual Philosophy* (1854), Isaac Taylor's *The World of Mind* (1858), and even Horace Bushnell's *Nature and the Supernatural* (1858). To balance out these authors, he chose Henry T. Buckle's *History of Civilization in England* (1871) with its emphasis on science over metaphysics, the superiority of natural forces over intuitive forces, and the questioning of accepted philosophic conclusions and religious beliefs. Buckle proved to be a greater stimulant, causing him to favor the role of nature on civilized man and the discoveries of science. His joy in reading Humboldt's *Cosmos* (1852), Herschel's *Outlines of Astronomy* (1849), and Asa Gray's *Structural and Systematic Botany* (1857) were preludes to his discovery of Darwin's *Origin of Species* (1859). In later correspondence with Darwin, he recounted reading the *Origin* when he was seventeen, having just previously read Agassiz's *Essay on Classification* "with deep dissatisfaction at its pseudo-Platonic attempt to make metaphysical abstractions do the work of physical forces." By contrast, he was exulted with the *Origin*, "reading and re-reading it till I almost knew it by heart."[11]

Given the harshness he witnessed in the pastoral sermons of his minister at the North Church who condemned the sciences along with the findings of the higher criticism as harbingers of infidelity, Fiske absented himself from the communion service and eventually withdrew from church attendance altogether. His decision carried consequences in the conservative community where charity extended to the "moral delinquent" but not to the "infidel." Treating Fiske's action as the latter, the Rev. Jeremiah Taylor publicly called him out for being an atheist and used for evidence his library of books that included the works of the positivists. Socially ostracized by the same congregation that had earlier welcomed his presence, he left Middletown to prepare for life at Cambridge.[12]

## COMTE'S LITTLE ACRE

Wise beyond his years, Fiske entered Harvard in 1860 as a sophomore and with a desire to study comparative philology along with ancient and modern history, literature, and philosophy. Though his teachers were astonished at the breadth of his knowledge, some feared his influence on fellow students, given the suspicion that he had imbibed too heavily in positivist thinking. And indeed, he had. Having discovered an announcement at the Old Corner Bookstore in Boston of Spencer's proposed synthetic philosophy, he subscribed to the series.[13] The English philosopher and sociologist became one of Fiske's favorite authors; Spencer's philosophy furnished him with the materials to explain, interpret, rationalize, and advocate on behalf of evolution's implications in social, religious, and economic spheres. Fiske's admiration was effusive: "Herbert Spencer has been surpassed by no thinker that ever lived, and has been rivaled only by Aristotle, Berkeley, and Kant." Recognizing that the Englishman's ideas had much to offer, Fiske chose to become his apostle and interpreter to American audiences.[14]

By junior year Fiske was known among his classmates for a personal library that included Auguste Comte, John Stuart Mill, George Henry Lewes, George Grote, Henry Thomas Buckle, John Frederick Herschel, Herbert Spencer, Alexander Bain, Robert W. Mackay, Charles Darwin, and Charles Lyell—authors whose views had become increasingly popular among students but open to suspicion from President Cornelius C. Felton, the school's Eliot Professor of Greek literature, who had no qualms expressing his preference for classical instruction. What provisions existed for scientific instruction were meager at best, a fact made evident by the absence of any questions on science in his entrance examination.

Notwithstanding his scholarship and much-admired library, Fiske was closely watched for potential disciplinary issues, the most serious of which occurred when he was discovered reading Comte during church services. Identified by tutors as a dangerous influence ("the young atheist of Cambridge"), he was accused of undermining the faith of his fellow students. Even though Harvard was considered the most liberal college in New England, its *Orders and Regulations* required compulsory attendance at religious services for all students, and while eighteen absences from lectures could result in censure, the absence from three church services was punishable with dismissal.[15]

Brought before the college on charges of disseminating infidelity and disrespecting the Christian faith, Fiske made no excuse for his action. However, when Felton indicated his intention to suspend him for a year, faculty opposition prevented the action, especially following Fiske's public apology. Felton reversed his decision but minced few words in his letter to Fiske's family: "Your son's good character in general, and his faithful attention to his studies, induced the faculty to limit the censure to a Public Admonition. I have only to add, that while we claim no right to interfere with the private opinion of any student, we should feel it our duty to request the removal of any one who should undertake to undermine the faith of his associates. I hope you will caution your son upon this point; for any attempt to spread the mischievous opinions which he fancies he has established in his own mind, would lead to an instant communication to his guardian to take him away."[16]

At a time when Henry Adams, another of Harvard's graduates, was serving as secretary to his father, the US ambassador in London during the Civil War, the precocious Fiske followed the debates surrounding the theory of evolution in England and the United States. Anxious to understand the influence of Comtean positivism, he prepared a critical review of Buckle's *History of Civilization* for the *National Quarterly Review* in 1861 and two years later penned "The Evolution of Language" for the *North American Review*. The American writer and publisher Edward L. Youmans, an ardent proselytizer for evolution, encouraged Fiske to send the Buckle article to Spencer. Taking his advice, Fiske wrote to Spencer (their correspondence lasted decades) revealing his decision to leave Christianity. "I was brought up in the most repulsive form of Calvinism in which I remained until I was sixteen years of age. My skepticism, excited in 1858 by geological speculations, was confirmed in the following year by the work of Mr. Buckle."[17] Similarly, he revealed the reasoning that had eventually led him to Spencer's theory of evolution.

> Having successively adopted and rejected the system of almost every philosopher from Descartes to Professor Ferrier, I began the year 1860 with Comte, Mill, and Lewes. I then favored the scheme of acquiring a general knowledge of all the sciences in their hierarchical order as laid down by Comte, which scheme was eventually carried out. I first noticed your name in Mr. Lewes's little exposition of Comte early in 1860, and the extract from "Social Statics" there given led me to put down my name for "First Principles," before there could have been as yet more than a dozen subscribers. It is unnecessary to enter into further details. The influence of your writings is apparent alike in every line of my writings and every sentence of my conversation: so inextricably have they become intertwined with my own thinking, that frequently on making a new generalization, I scarcely know whether to credit myself with it or not.[18]

Fiske graduated from Harvard on July 15, 1863. Had he not received deductions for his class absences, he would have stood first in his class; instead, he ranked forty-seventh out of 112.[19]

FINDING A CAREER

Newly married and in search of a career, Fiske returned to Harvard for his LLB in 1865, whereupon he joined the Suffolk bar and opened an office in Boston. To his disappointment, he found law much less entertaining than Huxley's *Man's Place in Nature*, Stuart Mill's *Principles of Political Economy*, Youmans's *Chemistry*, and Draper's *Intellectual Development of Europe*. Here were individuals who recounted the structures of ancient and modern society, penetrated the beliefs of different societies, traced the origin of laws, and explained how thought developed over time. What could one not like?

With few clients forthcoming, Fiske gave himself to reading fiction interspersed with his usual fare of philology, history, science, and philosophy. He also continued reading the positivists and delighted in the literary styles of historians William H. Prescott, John Lothrop Motley, and Francis Parkman, as they applied evolutionary theory to the historical process. Counseled by Spencer's statement regarding "the continuous adjustment of internal relations to external relations," he abandoned law altogether and moved his family into his grandparents' home in Middleton, where he cobbled together a career reviewing books and explaining how the doctrine of evolution had become the "master key to all social phenomena." The fact that he had begun to correspond with many of the great minds of the Western world became an overriding factor in his decision to pursue a career in scientific and philosophic studies. "When I [heard] the stuff that people talk when they have nothing in them to let out you can't imagine how dreadfully low and worthless their pursuits and ideas seemed to me. O, my dear! There is nothing in this world like SCIENCE; nothing so divine as the life of a scholar!" Before long, he built a successful and highly remunerative career lecturing and writing for the *North American Review, Atlantic Monthly, Christian Examiner, Nation, New York World*, and *Boston Advertiser*.[20]

In 1866 Harvard's alumni established a Board of Overseers, vesting it with oversight of the university. Perceiving it as the beginning of a major effort to reform the university, Fiske moved his family to Cambridge to be part of the movement. Coincidental with his move was his publication "University Reform" in the *Atlantic Monthly* (April 1867), followed by "Liberal Education" in the *North American Review* (July 1868), both welcomed by the Harvard community.

The year 1869 was memorable for Fiske, as it signaled the beginning of Charles William Eliot's presidency (1869–1909) and his own appointment as lecturer of positive philosophy (1869–1871) and instructor in history (1870), teaching the very philosophy he had been forbidden to study as a student. Along with Fiske, Eliot appointed Ralph Waldo Emerson and James Elliot Cabot as University lecturers of philosophy for the academic year 1869–1870. The lectures, delivered in Holden Chapel, were part of Eliot's plan to transition Harvard's instruction to another level.

With the notable exception of those who vigorously opposed his appointment, Fiske's lectures were highly regarded by students and faculty alike. Eliot remained unperturbed by the criticism, believing Fiske had removed the negative aspects of Comte's philosophy by making it more in harmony with the works of Spencer, Huxley, Lyell, Mill, and Bain. In his second year, wide discussion again followed his lectures as Fiske traced the law of evolution and combated the idea that British positivism was synonymous with the philosophy of Comte. The Board of Overseers, which at the time considered Darwinism, positivism, and Comtism a toxic combination that insulted divinely revealed religion, accused him of being an atheist and a materialist. Essentially, Fiske became a scapegoat for the board's suspicion that Eliot's reform policies had gone too far. According to Fiske's biographer, however, there was nothing in Fiske's lectures to suggest a denial of God's existence. "What he denies is the power of the finite mind to conceive God. What he affirms is the existence of a Divine Being transcending the power of the human mind in any way to measure or to limit."[21] The other plausible reason for the board's hostility stemmed from its admiration of Louis Agassiz, whose anti-evolutionary bias weighed heavily in matters concerning the sinecure of a professorship.[22]

Fiske's appointment as an instructor in American history came at a time when Eliot had begun advocating for a less proscribed curriculum, a cause that would later result in his much-debated elective system. But what might have developed into a regular appointment failed to materialize. Nowhere except at the University of Michigan did students receive instruction in American history in a form other than a rote textbook approach. As explained by historian Albert Hart, "the world was not yet ready for Fiske in 1868," evidenced by the fact that none of his four successors at Harvard persisted in teaching American history as a specialty. This, Hart explained, was due to the fact that "the dignity of their national history was not yet manifest."[23]

The Board's continued negativity toward Fiske ended any possibility of a permanent position. Knowing that the lectureship could not continue, Eliot offered Fiske the position of assistant librarian, where, from 1872 to 1879, he devoted himself to writing a history of the American people in the context of evolutionary theory.[24] As Vernon Parrington explained, "he called himself a philosopher, but he meant by the term not a metaphysician, but a cosmic historian whose business was to interpret the universe in the light of the great laws that science was revealing."[25] Combining the law of gravitation with the law of biological variation, survival of the fittest, and the conservation of energy, he proceeded to explain Spencer's unitary cosmos, devoting his life "to their illustration in the origins and foundation of our national commonwealth."[26] As he reflected, "From the sentimental aspect it is worthy of notice, that only eight years ago I was threatened with dismissal from college if caught talking Comtism to anyone."[27]

## COSMIC PHILOSOPHY

In 1874, at the age of thirty-two, Fiske published his four-volume *Outlines of Cosmic Philosophy, Based on the Doctrine of Evolution, with Criticisms of the Positive Philosophy* revealing how the law of evolution encompassed the full range of matter. The book's chapters consisted of expanded versions of thirty-five lectures delivered at Harvard between 1869 and 1871 and later repeated before appreciative audiences in Boston, New York, Milwaukee, and London. As Fiske explained to his listening and reading audiences, until the middle of the eighteenth century, the different dissenting creeds within Christianity had formulated the intellectual framework for the Western world. This framework included a Divine Creator, the origin of man, and his endowment with rational consciousness, followed by his fall and redemption. All were explained using a combination of incredible stories, dogmatic affirmations, and the personal superintendence and goodwill of a distinctly anthropomorphic Creator and Sustainer. This changed with Newton's law of gravitation, Lavoisier's discovery of the indestructibility of matter, the conservation of energy demonstrated by German and English physicists, the findings of the higher criticism, and eventually by Darwin's theory of evolution by natural selection.

Spencer's synthetic philosophy demonstrated that patterns existed in the universe that man, with knowledge obtained from the sciences, now had the ability to decipher. This philosophy was not the product of romantic naturalism with its eternal and static orders, but the affirmation of a set of laws that accounted for the origin, structure, and evolution of the universe. It fell to Spencer to extend evolution's application to the entire universe and, behind it, to an infinite Unknowable power as its source and sustainer. Having propounded the concept of universal cosmic evolution, Spencer formulated a dynamic law of the continuous redistribution and integration of matter and motion, which brought all phenomena within a framework of scientific laws.[28]

With this as his prolegomena, Fiske viewed evolution as an all-embracing law offering an optimistic future based on the concept of an immanent (not absentee) God, albeit with distinctly nonanthropomorphic attributes. A philosophic work written in consideration of the country's economic advances, *Outlines* addresses three fundamental issues: the cosmic universe, including its origin and meaning; man's physical, moral, and intellectual development and destiny; and the omnipresent, omnipotent, and transcending power that lay behind the cosmos as its ultimate cause.

Fiske made no claim to having created a new system of philosophy; rather, he considered his cosmic system an interpretation of the works of Spencer to which he added several contributions—all intended to repudiate any atheistic-materialistic suppositions of Comte and affirm instead the presence of an infinite power transcending all. Fiske viewed his *Outlines* as proof of Spencer's independence from Comte's materialistic ideas by separating out Spencer's teleological Unknown from Comte's Religion of Humanity. More importantly, his *Outlines* presented his own interpretation of the nature of the Ultimate Cause ("Cosmic Theism"), the gulf between mind and matter, and the "higher realms of human thinking," which he attributed to the part played by infancy in the development from brute to man. His theistic approach to matter and spirit called attention to the significance of prolonged infancy in the species' evolution from brute to civilized man.[29]

Fiske portrayed the genesis of man in three phases: Darwin's natural selection, which produced the physical man; Wallace's explanation for the evolution of intelligence; and his own contribution about prolonged infancy. The struggle for existence, having succeeded in bringing forth the human species, "has done its work and will presently cease," notwithstanding notable "inferiorities" that produced "a wide interval between the highest and lowest degrees of completeness" among the races. Still, the human species seemed destined for even higher levels of spiritual perfection.[30] As a consummate synthesizer of contemporary beliefs, Fiske drew on the British positivists to explain how progressiveness in human nature had stopped short among half the peoples of the world, including Africans, Polynesians, Native Americans, Chinese, and peoples of the East generally. "It is only in the Aryan and some of the Semitic races, together with the Hungarians and other Finnic tribes subjected to Aryan

influences, that we can find evidences of a persistent tendency to progress." Success had not been inherent in the race but due to favorable circumstances that occurred with the integration of matter and the concomitant dissipation of motion. Some species thrived in the struggle for life
and acquired new capacities, while others were less fortunate.[31]

Those differences that existed between higher and lower races resembled similar differences between humans and the chimpanzees and gibbons, namely, the anatomical size and composition of the brain. Borrowing from Wallace's revision to the theory of natural selection, Fiske
recounted how, after a period of time, the physical changes to man resulting from the struggle for existence were replaced by psychical evolution determined by the heterogeneity of the social environment. As the
brain reached a certain cubic capacity, "a kind of Rubicon" was crossed,
at which point a new chapter in man's psychical evolution began. "Increase in social complexity renders possible . . . fresh associations of ideas
in greater and greater variety and abundance, so that the decomposition
and recombination of thoughts involved in abstraction and generalization
is facilitated; and along with this, the definiteness and the plasticity of
thought is increased, and the contents of the mind become representative in higher and higher degrees." Those attributes that natural selection
preserved included what Wallace identified as the capacity for cooperation, self-restraint, sympathy for others, a sense of right, and intelligent
foresight.[32]

Fiske added to Wallace's explanation with the observation that humans
were born into the world more helpless than any other creatures, allowing for the development of nerve connections essential for more complex
intelligence. Prolonged infancy "tended gradually to strengthen the relationship of the children to the mother, and eventually to parents, and
thus give rise to the permanent organization of the family."[33] This additional contribution to human evolution helped to justify the "goodness"
behind the evolutionary process.

> It has been shown that the genesis of Man was due to a change in the di-
> rection of the working of natural selection, whereby psychical variations
> were selected to the neglect of physical variations. It has been shown that
> one chief result of this change was the lengthening of infancy, whereby
> Man appeared on the scene as a plastic creature capable of unlimited psy-
> chical progress. It has been shown that one chief result of the lengthen-
> ing of infancy was the origination of the family and of human society en-
> dowed with rudimentary moral ideas and moral sentiments. It has been

shown that through these cooperating processes the difference between Man and all lower creatures has come to be a difference in kind transcending all other differences; and his appearance upon the earth marked the beginning of the final stage in the process of development, the last act in the great drama of creation; and that all the remaining work of evolution must consist in the perfecting of the creature thus marvelously produced. . . . Man is coming to an end, and his future development will be accomplished through the direct adaptation of his wonderfully plastic intelligence to the circumstances in which it is placed. Hence it has appeared that war and all forms of strife, having ceased to discharge their normal function, and having thus become unnecessary, will slowly die out; that the feelings and habits adapted to ages of strife will ultimately perish from disuse; and that a stage of civilization will be reached in which human sympathy shall be all in all, and the spirit of Christ shall reign supreme throughout the length and breadth of the earth.[34]

Building on Spencer's explanation of ever-greater complexity, Fiske further explained the significance of prolonged infancy in humans in his essay "The Meaning of Infancy" (1883). "As mental life became more complex and various, as the things to be learned kept ever multiplying, less and less could be done before birth, more and more must be left to be done in the earlier years of life. So instead of being born with a few simple capacities thoroughly organized, man came at last to be born with the germs of many complex capacities which were reserved to be unfolded and enhanced or checked and stifled by the incidents of personal experience in each individual. In this simple yet wonderful way, there has been provided for man a long period during which his mind is plastic and malleable, and the length of this period has increased with civilization until it now covers nearly one third of our lives."[35]

Not surprisingly, scientists and social scientists viewed race differences as an inevitable consequence of evolutionary change. Looking at the three principal human stocks—Caucasian, Negroid, and Mongolian—and their subdivisions, the races and ethnicities became the subject of numerous environmental and hereditarian discussions. Given the uneasiness of post-Reconstruction politics, the continuing Indian wars, and the increased numbers of immigrants arriving daily from non-Anglo-Saxon nations, scientists and social scientists found it easy to focus on race and racial characteristics. With sizable numbers of the southerners seeking to overturn Reconstruction policies and worries among northerners that lax immigration laws had opened the nation's gates to inferior races, both sections of the country looked for solutions that would justify legislation minimizing each other's concerns.

Fiske's career in public lecturing reinforced the Aryan and Teutonic sources of American institutions and the enduring image of the Anglo-Saxon imprint on history, religion, science, language, and philosophy. Like Spencer, he charted racial differences by observing the mass and structural complexity of the brain, noting that the difference in the volume or cubic capacity of brain between the highest and lowest man was "at least six times as great as the difference between the lowest man and the highest ape."[36] In his study of brain capacity, he was fond of quoting Galton's *Tropical South Africa* (1851), and the comparison he made of the primitive Damara seeking a solution to a simple mathematical problem and the dilemma of Galton's dog Dinah. "Once while I was watching a Damara floundering hopelessly in a calculation on one side of me, I observed Dinah, my spaniel, equally embarrassed on the other. She was overlooking half a dozen of her new-born puppies, which had been removed two or three times from her, and her anxiety was excessive, as she tried to find out if they were all present, or if any were still missing. She kept puzzling and running her eyes over them, backwards and forwards, but could not satisfy herself. She evidently had a vague notion of brain. Taking the two as they stood, dog and Damara, the comparison reflected no great honour on the man."[37]

As president of the Immigration Restriction League in the 1890s, Fiske gave his blessings to the importance of Anglo-Saxon birthright in America. He also gave his blessing to the change taking place in the New England conscience regarding the Negro's place in nature. With both New England and the South feeling the effects of their respective race issues—one affecting racial lines in the South due to the Fourteenth and Fifteenth Amendments, and the other desiring to stop the flow of immigration—they found common cause. The solution they agreed upon was for the South to disfranchise the African American and allow the North to impose restrictions on the masses of illiterate immigrants flowing into its eastern ports.[38]

For all his connections with Wallace in terms of the latter's revised ideas on natural selection as it applied to the human species, it's hard to imagine that Wallace would have had any sympathy for the jingoistic nativism that Fiske advocated in his role as president of the Immigration Restriction League. Here, the socialism of Wallace and the Teutonic folkmote (people's assembly) of Fiske took divergent routes, with the latter viewing the drama of American civilization becoming the crowning feature of evolution. "As a purveyor of Victorian science to the American people, he did a useful and important work," concluded historian Vernon Parrington, but his attempt to reinterpret the nation's past proved less fruitful due in large measure to his handicap of "inadequate knowledge and an inadequate philosophy."[39]

## COSMIC RELIGION

As noted above, Fiske considered his *Outlines* as furthering the work of Darwin and Spencer. To the extent that Darwin had furnished proof of evolution in the organic world and Spencer had expanded evolution to the inorganic world as well, and to an Unknown underlying power, Fiske saw even more. A true reading of Darwin's theory, he suggested, demonstrated "the slow and subtle process of evolution as the way in which God makes things come to pass." Out of the struggle for existence, which continued unabated for countless centuries, "the whole creation has been groaning and travailing together in order to bring forth that last consummate specimen of God's handiwork, the Human Soul." Asked whether man should be regarded "as in any higher sense the object of Divine care than a pig," Fiske responded that the Darwinian theory "shows us distinctly for the first time how the creation and the perfecting of Man is the goal toward which Nature's work has all the while been tending." Evolution did not cancel man's faith; instead, it gave added support. It illuminated the process not by eliminating God but by enhancing his glory and reconciling evolution with immortality.[40]

As Fiske's writings affirm, evolution was rarely popularized in the manner that reflected Darwin's theory of natural selection, with its nondirectional and nonprogressive prospective. Instead, evolution became a contrivance subject to the direct action of a caring God. Even those with close personal ties to Darwin chose to give lip service to his nondirectional theory while supporting the progressive nature of evolution at both the micro and macro levels. Many adopted elements of Lamarckism, associating evolution with goal-directed, purposive objectives. Their explanations typically preserved free will and individual responsibility while, at the same time, associating evolution with progressive change. Popularizers like Grant Allen, Samuel Butler, Edward Clodd, Richard Procter, Edward L. Youmans, and Benjamin Kidd embraced theistic and teleological approaches not just for the natural world but for the entire physical universe. As James Moore argued in *Post-Darwinian Controversies*, those nineteenth-century orthodox Christians who accepted Darwin's theory did so because they considered it modestly compatible with the concept of divine immanence or with a broader teleology that included a belief that God acted uniformly throughout nature.[41]

None felt bad about their choice, since Darwin's several editions of *Origin* carried multiple associations that, for some, suggested a transcendent Designer and an ultimately purposive structure to nature.[42] Each edition of the *Origin* contained alterations, the most important being Darwin's conceding alternative mechanisms, including small elements of Neo-Lamarckism, a subject that kept the scientific community in continuous debate over the arguments for and against selection. Congregationalists like Henry Ward Beecher and Lyman Abbott embraced Darwin's theory, arguing that it reinforced the inevitability of progress and the march toward perfection that was part of God's plan.[43] As Henry Ward Beecher explained in his *Evolution and Religion*, "I regard evolution as being the discovery of the Divine method of creation" and "far from being in antagonism with true religion, will develop it with more power than any other presentation of science that ever has occurred in this world."[44] A pronounced evolutionist, Abbott claimed that Jesus represented what humanity was becoming.[45] Even John Henry Newman weighed in on the matter, writing to a friend: "I see nothing in the theory of evolution inconsistent with an Almighty God and Protector."[46]

Just as deism had become the rightful heir to revealed religion during the Enlightenment, evolution provided the nineteenth century with a lawbound substitute for Christianity's view of human nature. Evolutionary theory, along with the higher criticism, provided formidable evidence that Christianity represented a manifestly false history of the world, of miracles, and of man's early history. In a series of lectures delivered at the Concord Summer School of Philosophy and subsequently published as *The Destiny of Man* (1884) and *The Idea of God* (1885), Fiske replaced the anthropomorphic deity of his Calvinist past with something more knowable than Spencer's Unknowable. He identified a more conciliatory cosmology that he called *Cosmic Theism*, with its divinely destined law of progress minus theology.

Fiske regarded three possible ways to contemplate the universe. *First* was viewing the world as having no orderly progression, no ultimate law, and no reasonableness except what humans made of it. This constituted what the philosopher and mathematician Chauncey Wright described as "cosmical weather"—a world utterly blind and irrational. *Second* were those who held to an underlying unity and the manifestation of an Omnipresent Energy that was neither personal nor anthropomorphic and whose events exhibited an "orderly progression, but not toward any goal recognizable by us"—a worldview identified as pantheistic. *Third* were those who, while accepting that the manifestation of an Omnipresent Energy was above man's comprehension, believed in the reasonableness of the universe and an orderly progression toward a goal recognizable by human intelligence, though barely. It was this latter option that Fiske proposed in *Outlines*, arguing that the presence of God was "an all-pervading fact of life." Ultimately, he concluded that the process of evolution represented "the working out of a mighty teleology of which our finite understandings can fathom but the scantiest rudiments." Change came by force of a law built on the labors of man's intellect working in concert with an undefined but intelligent telic force.[47]

Fiske differed from Spencer in believing that Christianity was by no means unimportant to a proper understanding of evolution. The Christian conception of God simply required a transition from its outdated anthropomorphism to a concept that transcended finite experience. Evolution had a noble role for religion. More so than other philosophies, it represented the soft hand of a divinely ordained, predetermined, and inevitable force working within the context of knowable laws and increasing differentiation and complexity. "We see Man still the crown and glory of the universe and the chief object of divine care," Fiske assured readers. "We see the chief agency which produced him—natural selection which always works through strife—ceasing to operate upon him."[48] Here was faith in God, in progress, and in the moral law. As historian David W. Marcell explained, Fiske molded his scientific inquiry to fit a predetermined, essentially theological conclusion.[49]

Fiske claimed there was little in the way of trustworthy evidence that separated the historical Jesus from the Christ of Christian dogma with its doctrines on resurrection, ascension, apocalypse, miracles, and the Pauline theory of a future life. In effect, Christianity had become an "historical monstrosity" filled with polemical and unblushing heresies whose preposterous explanations violated the very basis of sober scientific thinking. Lacking authenticity, the Christian world had been forced to rely on the untrustworthy gossip of chroniclers years after the actual occurrence of the events they professed to record. The early gospels threw light on Christian opinion but offered only vague and uncritical information on Jesus himself. Thus, the historical Jesus remained hidden from view. In effect, dogmatic purpose had obscured Christianity's historical meaning. Insisting on a more factual and naturalistic history than that seen through the lens of biblically based Protestantism, Fiske challenged readers to find harmony (i.e., synthesis) in science and religion. He urged consideration of a *doxological science*, meaning a science that reinforced the wisdom and power of a modified and accommodating Christian form of Darwinism.[50]

Approaching religion from the perspective of a philosopher with the heart of a poet, Fiske regarded Christianity as the highest expression yet attained in the spiritual development of mankind, steadily undergoing purification through scientific criticism. Ultimately, he predicted Christianity would leave its anthropomorphic clothes and ecclesiastical accretions behind and transition into a more rational faith, replacing the spread of atheism and materialism.[51] Regarding the human being "as the consummate fruition of creative energy, and the chief object of Divine care," he discounted the materialistic assumption that the life of the soul ended with the life of the body. He doubted, however, that humans would succeed in making the soul's immortality a matter of scientific fact. The soul would remain in the purview of religion and not science.[52] "Though science must destroy mythology, it can never destroy religion."[53]

Anthropomorphic religion rested upon unsupported theories of causation, a mistaken conception of law, and was incompatible with science. "Instead of enlightening, it only mystifies us; and, so far from consoling, it tends to drive us to cynical despair." Cosmic Theism was neither atheism nor positivism, but a form of theism that was higher and purer than the anthropomorphism defended by theologians. It represented a power "to which no limit in time or space is conceivable, of which all phenomena, as presented in consciousness, are manifestations, but which we can know only through these manifestations."[54] Unlike Comte, who had assigned Humanity as the object of religious contemplation and worship, Fiske posited the God of Christianity freed from the "illegitimate formulas" that had rendered it comprehensible.[55] Fiske was America's great synthesizer, explaining the world in a manner that soothed the Victorian's crisis of faith. His Cosmic Theism stood as guardian, consoling all who would listen that evolution was a slow process requiring a combination of patience and a willingness not to interfere with the natural processes.[56]

On December 19, 1900, Fiske delivered the Ingersoll Lecture "Life Everlasting" in Sanders Theatre, Cambridge. Intended as the completion of his philosophic studies issued under the titles "The Destiny of Man Viewed in Light of His Origin," "The Idea of God as Affected by Modern Knowledge," and "Through Nature to God," he recounted how the Christian doctrine had fused the moral significance of Jewish thought with Hellenic mysticism. The belief that the human soul survived the death of the body had been challenged by the Enlightenment, followed by Comte's positive philosophy, Darwin's dysteleology, the agnosticism of Huxley, and the Unknown of Spencer. "The position that science irrevocably condemns such a belief seems at first sight a very strong one and has unquestionably had a good deal of weight with many minds of the present generation," he admitted. Given that human powers of framing conceptions were limited by experience, the condition of a future life seemed impossible, except for those mediums who claimed evidence of the presence of disembodied spirits with which they held communication. Such claims, Fiske felt, hardly merited notice in philosophic discussion.[57]

So, one question remained: Was such a belief untenable, if not absurd? Fiske answered no, since the study of light and other radiant forces had furnished information that "the luminiferous ether" could be a world crowded with disembodied souls or consciousness that survived the death of the material body. Open to the proposition that consciousness was a product of molecular motion outside the nervous system and therefore could claim a special kind of existence, it remained within the realm of probability that consciousness could exist without the body. "The considerations adduced . . . must convince us that we are at perfect liberty to treat the question of man's immortality in the disinterested spirit of the naturalist." For himself, he believed in a Divine Purpose that aimed at the "perfection of the higher spiritual attributes of humanity." In time, he hoped that the study of evolution would eventually supply the basis for a more comprehensive and satisfying Natural Theology.[58]

## Historical Publications

Aided by his librarian position, Fiske uncovered what he considered to be one of the great epochs in history, namely, the transplanting to the New World of the Old World's social and political institutions—the "legitimate evolutionary outcome from what he had affirmed was the greatest event in human history since the birth of Christ: the voyage of Columbus into the Sea of Darkness in 1492."[59] Publications came in rapid spurts, and, except for George Bancroft, he probably penned more than any other American historian.[60]

Fiske's success as a historian came not just as a writer but as a lecturer, a talent eminently demonstrated in a series of lectures on American history given at the Old South Church. "His engaging voice, his fullness, his cogency, his humor, his beautiful language, his power of statement," remarked historian Albert Hart, "made him one of the most popular

speakers of his time" and provided a handsome livelihood that continued throughout his career.[61] Between 1888 and 1893, he delivered over
five hundred lectures on various philosophical and historical subjects.
Making upwards of $10,000 annually from his lectures, "he was a verita-
ble Chautauqua, a peripatetic chair of history and philosophy [who] cheer-
fully accommodated his menu to the taste of his audiences." Voluminous
as they may have been, his lectures were hastily formulated and often
lacked accuracy. Inspiring thousands with his handiwork, he left much to
be desired in the soundness of his ideas.[62] An amateur par excellence, his
popularization of history and philosophy soothed the worries of the aver-
age man but did nothing for his reputation as a historian.[63]

Fiske's historical approach became not just a record of the interplay of
forces objectified in a preordained plan, but a paean to the genius of the
Anglo-Saxon people. No other race had proven so successful in balancing
the concepts of liberty and union. For that reason alone, it was essential
for those non-English elements who immigrated to America to be culturally (if not biologically) assimilated to the Anglo-American norm. To this
end, his election as president of the Immigration Restriction League in
1894 gave visible evidence of the efforts to transform scientific theory into
legislative policy.

Like Spencer, who "found" data to support his scheme of evolution,
Fiske often insisted on unproven or implied analogies when there were
none in evidence. "Fiske was brave enough in the announcement of his
formula," observed historian Henry Steele Commager, "but timid in its
application. . . . His philosophy of history, in short, was promising, but
the promise was never fulfilled."[64] Still, he had a talent for finding common ground on his panoramic journey through American history. And
while he did not always retain his purported evolutionary theme, everywhere in his writings were lessons to be learned, character identified,
suppositions made, and predictions offered in a manner that was matter-
of-fact and humorous, if not always faithful to the evidence. Fiske's failure
to make use of original sources, observed J. B. Sanders, kept him from
ranking among America's great historians.[65] Professor Hart put it more
harshly. "[Fiske] is so swift and so sure of his own judgment that one is
tempted to forget how many are the unhewn forests of tangled questions
in which nobody has arrived at certainly. . . . Who knows? Certainly not
Mr. Fiske."[66]

Nevertheless, it was Fiske, the popularizer of the nation's historical
foundations, who conveyed to the country's schoolchildren and to eager
listeners the glad tidings of evolutionary philosophy. No longer did the

future rest on man's limited reasoning or intuition but on scientific discovery, the universal application of evolution, and the oversight of an unknown but beneficent Creator. "The Enlightenment had built a Heavenly City, and Transcendentalism a Utopia," explains Commager; Fiske's evolution "held out to man the dazzling prospect of a future more glorious than anything which either had imagined, and its promise carried conviction."[67]

The life and times of Fiske intersected with much of the turmoil in late nineteenth-century philosophic, scientific, and religious thinking as Americans struggled make the connection between the human and the rest of the natural world. A popularizer of evolution, Fiske viewed it as a creative process that would ultimately define the human's place in the universe. The universe might remain incomprehensible, but it was nonetheless good, and Fiske saw his purpose in explaining that fact. What he identified as cosmic law was none other than the impact of social evolution on human society, revealing the progression of the human species from savagery to civilization in an inevitable upward assent. Behind the day-to-day unfolding of seemingly impersonal and amoral forces stood a beneficent, reasonable, and omniscient Creator. While Henry and Brooks Adams were revealing in their writings a universe marked by disorder, randomness, and entropy (second law of thermodynamics), Fiske's "gospel of good cheer" consoled his audiences with all the confidence of a loving father and assurance that there was nothing to fear of the future, because evolution, for all its seeming chaos, promised a telic outcome.[68]

Fiske's interests ranged far and wide in pursuit of understanding, and while his youth was spent absorbing the wisdom of Emerson and other New England thinkers, his adulthood was spent following the diverse tributaries created by the sciences in their shaping of the modern mind. Too much a New Englander to deny his spiritual obligations, he nonetheless ignored the revealed word of the Bible, as well as the bleakness of a mechanistic universe, for a genial God in evolution's shaping of humanity. A popularizer of science and history to the English-speaking world, he made Darwin's *Origin* and Spencer's *Synthetic Philosophy* respectable to all classes. Far from eliminating God, he illuminated the manifestations of a Divine Power and recast the evolved man with the dignity of a spiritually advanced object of perfectibility.

## Selected Writings

*The Progress from Brute to Man* (1871)

*Myths and Myth Makers* (1872)

*Outlines of Cosmic Philosophy* (1874)

*The Unseen World* (1876)

*Darwinism and Other Essays* (1879)

*Excursions of an Evolutionist* (1883)

*The Destiny of Man Viewed in the Light of His Origin* (1884)

*American Political Ideas Viewed from the Standpoint of Universal History* (1885)

*The Idea of God as Affected by Modern Knowledge* (1885)

*The Critical Period of American History, 1783–89* (1888)

*The Beginnings of New England* (1889)

*The War of Independence* (1889)

*Civil Government in the United States* (1890)

*The American Revolution* (1891)

*The Discovery of America* (1892)

*The United States History for Schools* (1895)

*Old Virginia and Her Neighbors* (1897)

*Dutch and Quaker Colonies in America* (1899)

*Origin of Evil* (1899)

*A Century of Science and Other Essays* (1899)

*Through Nature to God* (1899)

*The Mississippi Valley in the Civil War* (1900)

*Life Everlasting* (1901)

*Essays, Literary and Historical* (1902)

*New France and New England* (1902)

# 7

# Will to Believe
## William James

*We of the nineteenth century, with our evolutionary theories and our mechanical philosophies, already know nature too impartially and too well to worship unreservedly any God of whose character she can be an adequate expression. . . . Visible nature is all plasticity and indifference,—a moral multiverse, as one might call it, and not a moral universe. To such a harlot we owe no allegiance.*

—William James, "Is Life Worth Living?" 1895

I T IS THE FORTUNE OF a few gifted individuals that their words change the world intellectually, artistically, and sometimes even materially. Ralph Waldo Emerson was such a figure; so, too, was the philosopher and psychologist William James (1842–1910) whose contributions bridged the nineteenth and twentieth centuries. Arthur O. Lovejoy compared James to Emerson, believing they were the most influential of America's philosophers and the only two with wide international standing, leaving as their legacy generations of disciples anxious to carry forward their ideas.[1] Emerson was much beloved by Henry James Sr. and his family when William was only twelve. His complete writings were among William's most treasured possessions, and the stepping-off point for his own belief system. As Frederic I. Carpenter explains, he marked and annotated Emerson's books, placing them into three categories: those that revealed unique contributions; those he considered counter to his own philosophy; and those that supported his action-oriented pragmatism. He read Emerson not just out of general interest, being that he was the nation's intellectual godfather, but because his ideas on individuality and freedom remained such vital issues for his own generation. "Throughout his life," explains Carpenter, "James praised the pragmatic Emerson, but disapproved the transcendentalist."[2]

James's admiration of Emerson remained strong provided he endorsed the interaction of thought and experience, and so long as his divination of experience pointed to the future. Emerson's *Representative Men* (1850), a paean to Emanuel Swedenborg's "doctrine of uses," stood for the ascendant role of ideas transformed into purposive action. When, however, his words were lost in billowy clouds of transcendental fluff, James lost interest. It was not that he disapproved Emerson's ideals or ends, but that their abstractness was often misplaced. Emerson declared truth to be ideal and undefinable; James insisted it was specific, definable, and embodied in its use. Neither had a systematic quality, suggesting the unfinished nature of the universe. Neither was anxious to make commitments for future generations, binding them to a particular belief or rule of conduct.[3]

James's spiritual insight bore a relationship not only to Emerson and to his father's Swedenborgian mysticism, but to a highly personal desire to find adequate grounding for moral values and endeavors outside the philosophic and religious systems current in his day, especially those that implied an inevitable trending toward some fixed goal. In doing this, he developed a biological and empirical naturalism sufficiently comprehensive to accommodate free will and the fulfillment of its desires. As a champion of individualism and the instrumental application of thought to human knowledge, he stoked a level of nonconformity that offered fresh alternatives to the dogmatic philosophizing of his day, including a distrust of final truth, an emphasis upon the novelties of nature, and the adoption of mind as an active instrument in the body's interaction with the environment. An imaginative and open-minded thinker gifted with the discerning eye of an artist, the curiosity and skepticism of a scientist, and the heart of a humanist, James celebrated the practical benefits of belief, the determining factor of experience in the conduct of life, and each person's ability to affect the future in a meaningful way. Provisional in his views, he advocated a form of pluralism that functioned as a solvent to life's competing propositions, claiming a middle course between empiricism and rationalism.

To understand James requires a discussion of freedom, self, mysticism, ethics, and the nature of belief. Richard M. Gale captures this in what he called a tension between James's "Promethean pragmatism" and his "anti-Promethean mysticism" which exposed two different sides of his personality. On one side, he exuded an expansive, abstract and technical self; on the other, a highly intuitive, experiential, and spiritual self. As the nation's representative philosopher, he charmed critics and acolytes alike with his command of information, his ability to reduce issues to concrete terms, his avoidance of verbal conflict, and support of ideas that were always meaningful in their consequences.[4]

## The Making of a Mind

William James, the Scots-Irishman and patriarch of the James family, immigrated to Albany, New York, in 1789, where he made a fortune investing in business and real estate, including the Erie Canal, leaving to his heirs a trust fund estimated at three million dollars. Henry James Sr., one of William's twelve children and a person of independent mind, refused to accept what his father intended for him as a vocation. Disinherited, he had to fight in the courts for more than a decade before receiving his portion of the estate, which enabled him to live a life unconditioned by the expediency of making a living. In place of having to choose a career to provide for his family, he became a theologian, lecturer, and writer, assembling a very idiosyncratic set of theological and social assets reflective of the spirituality of Swedenborg and the socialism of Charles Fourier, best represented in his *Substance and Shadow* (1863) and *Society the Redeemed Form of Man* (1879). His children included William (b. 1842); Henry (b. 1843), the novelist and man of letters; Garth Wilkinson (b. 1845) named for his father's Swedenborgian colleague in England; Robertson (b. 1846), a chronic alcoholic and museum curator; and Alice (b. 1848), who suffered from lifelong invalidism but whose literary gifts brought her closest to her two older brothers.

As "the unquiet son of an unquiet father," William grew up in a bustling household filled with the untamed competitiveness of three male siblings, and where family meals were animated by youthful horseplay interspersed with adult discussions on morals, literature, and the arts. His education benefited from his father's wide-ranging philosophical and theological interests, which included books on multiple subjects and visits to the household by Emerson, Henry David Thoreau, J. J. G. Wilkerson, Bronson Alcott, and others of his father's generation. Freed from the standard fare of local schoolmasters, his education followed the trail of the family's sojourns, where he and his siblings were deposited with a succession of private tutors in New York, London, Switzerland, and Paris.[5]

Despite his father's disapproval, William initially intended a life of painting and studied for a time with William Morris Hunt and his pupil, John La Farge, in Newport. After a year he abandoned the effort and, at the age of nineteen, enrolled in the Lawrence Scientific School at Harvard, where he studied anatomy under Jeffries Wyman and Louis Agassiz, followed by Harvard Medical School in 1864, where he took courses from Charles Eliot in chemistry and physiology from Edouard Brown-Séquard and Oliver Wendell Holmes, before breaking from his studies to join an expedition to Brazil with Agassiz. On his return, and between bouts of depression, eye troubles, and digestive disorders, he resumed his medical studies, which included an internship at the Massachusetts General Hospital. His principal diversion was his association with a group of young intellectuals (Oliver Wendell Holmes Jr., John Dewey, Chauncey Wright, Nicholas St. John Green, and Charles Sanders Peirce) who met regularly for conversation in what they called the Metaphysical Club. Not unlike his father's Saturday Club (which included Emerson, Nathaniel Hawthorne, Henry Wadsworth Longfellow, Richard Henry Dana Jr., James Russell Lowell, and Charles Eliot Norton), the Metaphysical Club became a breeding ground for discourse that eventually drew him into philosophy and psychology. In 1867 he chose yet another moratorium from his medical studies to read philosophy and attend university lectures in Germany. Not until 1869 did he complete his medical degree, an anomaly of sorts, since he never practiced medicine. No doubt the weight of being the oldest son complicated his search for identity and autonomy of person.[6]

Soon after receiving his degree, William experienced a highly personal and existential crisis that threw his life into inner turmoil. Like his father, who had faced a similar sickness of the soul (what Swedenborg called "vastation") when the family was living in England in 1844, William underwent his own sickness, which began around 1869. Troubled by the specter of scientific determinism and his own struggle to underscore the meaning of free will, of voluntary choices, and a refusal to accept resignation or fate, he found comfort in French philosopher Charles Renouvier's Neo-Kantian essay on human freedom and his own Armenian bias for free will. It was Renouvier's philosophy that unburdened James from the dilemma of determinism by calling for the reenergizing of one's personal powers.[7]

James began his career in 1872, choosing not to practice medicine but instead to become an instructor of physiology at his alma mater, where he devoted himself to the study of the human mind, much of it during the heyday of Charles Eliot's presidency. As a physiologist, he came early to distrust the positivist philosophies of his day, drawn instead to the nature of experience as perceived from within, and approaching his subject "with that freshness and lucidity of vision which comes alone to the man who is permitted to follow his soul's affinities whithersoever they lead him."[8] Physiology led him to the emerging science of psychology, which, three years into his appointment, he began teaching. By 1878 he had contracted with Henry Holt publishers to write *Principles of Psychology*, which took twelve years to complete. Though unable to follow his father's spiritual journey into Swedenborgianism, his science became increasingly subjected to spiritual filters that eventually led to his disavowal of reductionist science in favor of a philosophy rooted between idealism and empiricism.

## Pragmatic Theory

James was a radical empiricist to the core, relying on experience as the best and most appropriate pathway to truth. In his radical empiricism, he abandoned the duality of knower and known to better understand what organisms do in contact with objects, that is, making consciousness the moment of experience with the physical world. To use James's own words, "the body is the storm centre, the origin of coordinates, the constant place of stress in all that experience-train."[9] Man was an organism that could be understood only within the natural environment. Unlike Locke, for whom the mind was a tabula rasa, soaking up sensations before connecting them to perceptions and choices, James viewed the mind as an active (i.e., creative) component in the meaning of experience. He came to the issue naturally due to his enrollment in the Lawrence Scientific School, where Asa Gray and Louis Agassiz differed over Darwin's *Origin of Species* and his first two publications, which critiqued Huxley's radical materialism.[10]

Several years later in "Remarks on Spencer's Definition of Mind as Correspondence" (1878), James made a similar argument against the Neo-Lamarckism of Herbert Spencer when he called for a coercive "adjustment of inner to outer relations," a picture drawn so vast and simple that it proved "noxious" as a fail-safe formula.[11] Instead, James presented an alternative in the form of Darwin's independent forces being responsible for generating and selecting variations distinct from those environmental pressures that maintained or reinforced variations. Matthew Crippen described it in this fashion: "James does on the epistemological level what Darwin does on the phylogenetic one. He allows for a separation between that which generates new content and that which causes it to inhere."[12] Ralph Barton Perry described James's view of the mind somewhat differently, explaining that it "gropes about, advances and recoils, making many random efforts and many failures."[13]

James's articulation of pragmatic theory began with his 1898 address at Berkeley titled "Philosophical Conceptions and Practical Results," later expanded and published as *Pragmatism, A New Name for Some Old Ways of Thinking* (1907). With this and other publications, pragmatic philosophy earned a place in American philosophy, although the length and depth of that influence remains to this day a heavily contested topic, not the least of which concerns Charles Peirce's differences that led to his adoption of the term "pragmaticism" in 1904 as a means of distinguishing his own brand of thinking.[14] Unlike James, who interpreted pragmatism broadly as an overall theory of truth and a psychology of the conscious self, Peirce insisted on limiting pragmatism to a philosophical method of clarifying ideas by considering what effects they might have of a practical nature. Still, there was much on which they agreed, including their understanding that "God" was a hypothesis that reasoning could never assure certainty.[15]

Pragmatism represented a philosophical movement whose theory of knowledge was based on the practical, voluntary, workable, and useful consequences of one's choices. Neither religious nor antireligious in its intentionality, it nonetheless favored religion, if only for its affirmative rather than skeptical or agnostic outlook on life. Nevertheless, ultimate reality lay in the immediate experience, which James described this way: "My philosophy is what I call a radical empiricism . . . which represents order as being gradually won and always in the making. . . . It rejects all doctrines of the Absolute."[16]

Pragmatism humanized truth by leaving the term "unfinished" in much the same condition as Helen Evers's *The House the Pecks Built*. Truth remained an approximation sufficient in its probability to be counted as agreeing to certain ways of working for the fulfillment of human purposes. Truth is what could happen to an idea as the result of an individual's actions and social practices. "If there is to be truth . . . both realities and beliefs about them must conspire to make it."[17] Pragmatic truth carried practical verification in its uses, becoming "truth's cash-value in experiential terms." There was no single, comprehensive definition of truth; nor could there be. Rather than transcending experience, truth was mutable to situations. "The practical value of true ideas is thus primarily derived from the practical importance of their objects to us. Their objects are, indeed, not important at all times."[18] Pragmatic truths were time-dependent, admitted to degrees of probability, and "worked" if they led to beneficial consequences in experience.[19]

*WILL TO BELIEVE*

James's *Will to Believe*, an address to the Philosophical Clubs of Yale and Brown Universities published in 1896, represented a defense of faith (not necessarily religious faith) in which the individual made a voluntarily adopted statement true or possible in the absence of certitude. It represented an act of consent, trusting to believe what appeared as a real possibility. There was a transference made by the individual in what "ought" to what "is." By acting "as if" something was true, even with limited evidence, the individual could make truth happen. This was "the slope of good will on which the larger questions of life men habitually live."[20] As

James explained, it was "the readiness to act in a cause the prosperous issue of which is not certified to us in advance." In a world of indetermin-
ism, there was room for possibility and even probability. Even without
guarantees, goals were possible.[21]

Written in response to Huxley and William K. Clifford, who questioned any commitment to belief without sufficient evidence (judging
such assent as self-deception if not intellectual dishonesty), James argued that in choices of great personal significance, it was far better to rely
on intuition than to suspend judgment. The consequences of avoiding
moral choice could have much more severe outcomes. Choosing a specific course of action with insufficient evidence did not constitute self-
deception or conceal the truth of the situation. Besides, it could eventually lead to belief, a condition not optional for those who suspended
judgment based on unprovable evidence.[22] Even though one cannot always prove with reason and therefore cannot know with complete confidence that something is true, a seeker of truth can still believe, making
judgment a method and a justification for action. Belief was not fiction
but operated within a combination of inferences, experiences, and intuition. "Faith means belief in something concerning which doubt is still
theoretically possible; and as the test of belief is willingness to act, one
may say that faith is the readiness to act in a cause the prosperous issue
of which is not certified to us in advance."[23] Though he did not discuss
the existence of God or advocate belief in religion, his secular advocacy
of belief offered affirmation of its importance as a broad and unparochial
act of intention. This was in no way a defense of irrationality or wishful
thinking, but the willingness to act on options which the intellect was unable by itself to resolve.[24]

In its functioning, faith played an important part of reality. "Moral
questions immediately present themselves as questions whose solutions
cannot wait for a sensible proof," he wrote. "A moral question is a question not of what sensibly exists, but of what is good, or would be good
if it did exist."[25] In acting on belief, or willing to believe, one creates the
reality.

A conception of the world arises in you somehow, no matter how. Is it
true or not? you ask.
It might be true somewhere, you say, for it is not self-contradictory.
It may be true, you continue, even here and now.
It is *fit* to be true, it would be *well if it were true*, it *ought* to be true, you
presently feel.

It *must* be true, something persuasive in you whispers next; and then as
a final result—

It shall be *held for true*, you decide; it *shall* be as if true, for you.

And your acting thus may in certain special cases be a means of making
it securely true in the end.[26]

Faith was an instrument, a form of commitment for which one typically preferred to have as much knowledge as possible, but which seldom
offered an ideal set of circumstances before a decision was necessary. As
James in quoting Kierkegaard stated, "we live forwards . . . but we understand backwards."[27] It was not James's intention to replace religious
faith; rather to unveil the sources of its power, its connectedness with the
world, and to avoid the loneliness of the soul in its existential contact with
the indeterminate vastness of the universe. Different in terms of its wish-
fulness, James's *Will to Believe* stood within the philosophical tradition of
Pascal's desperate wagering for the existence of God. Neither, however,
served to illuminate the other. The former looked to the ethical, cultural,
and aesthetic values brought into existence by a system of belief, while
the latter represented simply a risk/benefit calculation devoid of any "passional" and intrinsic meaning for belief.[28]

As John Hick explained in his *Philosophy of Religion* (1990), James argued "that the existence or nonexistence of God, of which there can be
no conclusive evidence either way, was a matter of such momentous importance that anyone who so desired had the right to stake one's life upon
the God hypothesis." For Hick, who categorized James's position as a
form of traditional theism, this amounted to "an unrestricted license for
wishful thinking."[29] Actually, James had a much broader view of belief
that was suggestive and fluid. His was an "open universe" where choices
made a difference, ideals were realizable, and humans were encouraged
to engage the world in a participative and liberating manner. As James explained in his lecture "Pragmatism and Religion," man must be willing
"to live on a scheme of uncertified possibilities which he trusts [and] willing to pay with his own person, if need be, for the realization of the ideals which he frames."[30] He invited readers to embrace life, allowing their
hopes to outlive their fears. "Be not afraid of life," he told the Harvard
Young Men's Christian Association in 1895, "Believe that life *is* worth living, and your belief will help create the fact."[31]

Despite criticism from Bertrand Russell for lacking the technical rigor
of a true philosophy, James's *Will to Believe* or what he sometimes called
the "*right* to believe," did not include beliefs that either contradicted

known facts or violated logic. Instead it acted as a form of therapy designed to release constructive action on the part of the doer. It represented a judgment about the truth-value in belief, the worth of life, and an emotive statement on the implied goodness of the world.[32] Belief was an experience to be lived rather than an affirmation of any defined doctrine. As for the historical definition and attributes of God, these had no basis other than a mechanically deduced vision erected as "aftereffects, secondary accretions upon those phenomena of vital conversation with the unseen divine . . . [that occur] in the lives of humble private men."[33]

Recognizing that most data used to prove a scientific truth were gained in the laboratory *after* the truth itself was conjectured, he applied the same to faith, arguing that it is possible to will oneself into a belief by not only acting as if it were real but by generating data to support it. "Suppose I am climbing in the Alps, and . . . work myself into a position from which the only escape is by a terrible leap. Being without similar experience, I have no evidence of my ability to perform it successfully; but hope and confidence in myself make me sure I shall not miss my aim. . . . But suppose that, on the contrary, the emotions of fear and mistrust preponderate . . . why, then I shall hesitate so long that at last, exhausted and trembling, and launching myself in a moment of despair, I miss my foothold and roll into the abyss. In this case . . . the part of wisdom clearly is to believe what one desires; for the belief is one of the indispensable preliminary conditions of the realization of its object."[34]

Regardless of the perspective one might have conceiving the universe, it was important for the individual to act "as if he were individually helping to create the actuality of the truth whose metaphysical reality he is willing to assume." Anything less than "passional assent" was shameful. If every good man decided to wait for certitude, stagnation would ensue. The willingness to believe more than to disbelieve was the only practical approach between beliefs and action. Either gain from belief or lose what possibilities it might convey from its benefits. This was the logic of action, the choice to dare, to risk the chance of failure, or to do nothing and allow opportunity to slip by.[35]

Throughout his life, James remained a radical empiricist, upholding his belief in experience as the most reliable guide to truth. Truth for James, especially if it agreed with reality, was better to believe than not. It became a guide to conduct, a justification that life was worth living, and a realization that truth may change or, at the very least, newer theories may develop that challenge existing guides to conduct. There was a certain catholicity in his temperament and a healthy-mindedness in his ideas. Indeed, his seriousness as a philosopher and his readiness to argue his position radiate from his persona. As Arthur O. Lovejoy observed, James "found a place in which a man is imperatively called upon to take sides." Thus, while modestly calling pragmatism "a new name for some old ways of thinking," he was continually surprised by the bewilderment it caused in some men's minds.[36]

## *VARIETIES OF RELIGIOUS EXPERIENCE*

*The Will to Believe* and *The Varieties of Religious Experience* (1902) contain James's most important thoughts on religion. In the former, as noted above, he suggested that when given a choice between two hypotheses, neither of which offered sufficient evidence or assurance, it was important not to suspend judgment but to choose that which most satisfied the individual's emotional and practical needs. In *Varieties*, James focused on the psychology or mental phenomena that accompanied the experience of religious belief. Though most religious thinkers purported to believe in a part of selfhood that was permanent, immaterial, indestructible, and dwelling freely with the physical body, giving it a certain value or purpose beyond death, James made no such claim. Instead, the self was a fact of experience whose essential reality was in the consciousness of the moment.

James's *Varieties*, which he delivered at Edinburgh in 1899–1901 as part of the Gifford Lectures on Natural Religion, was a virtual tour de force, representing a synthesis of mind, faith, and belief. In it, James responded to three related questions: What does religion do? Whence did it come? And was it important that its claims be literally and objectively true? As a physiologist, psychologist, and philosopher, whose distinctive roles had not yet been defined by professionals, he chose to glide from one discipline to the other without setting off alarms from those interested in establishing distinct disciplinary boundaries and constraints. He emphasized the "experience" an individual went through in response to a life crisis and the transition from the "sick soul" to a state of "healthy mindedness," either through a "once born" or "twice born" process of restoration.[37]

James regarded the statements of theologians and philosophers regarding religion as ambiguous at best. Unless one could understand religion from the perspective of the subject, an experience of feeling rather than thought, of action rather than contemplation, it carried little meaning. Similarly, he rejected the theological argument of God as Absolute. All that was required to meet the practical needs of belief was that God be "both other and larger than our conscious selves. . . . It need not be infinite, it need not be solitary."[38] Above all else, this "otherness" needed to act catalytically to make individuals choose principled action that brought meaning to their existence. Whatever or however defined, God needed to be reasonable and useful. Without God, explained Gary Alexander, "James thinks that we will not be as moral as we possibly can be."[39]

James used the term "God" reluctantly, preferring a broader perspective that replaced religion's mythical dogmas and absolutes with *humanism*, a term looking to human experience for moral guidance, love, justice, peace, and social responsibility. In this sense, God should be understood as a reference for humanity and its ideals. God became a symbol of commitment to human ideals rather than belief in a supernatural entity. Quoting A. Eustace Haydon, who, along with John Dewey, was one of the signers of *The Humanist Manifesto I*, "More needful than faith in God is faith that man can give love, justice, peace, and all his beloved moral values embodiment in human relations. Denial of this faith is the only real atheism. Without it, belief in all the galaxies of gods is mere futility. With it, and the practice that flows from it, man need not mourn the passing of the gods."[40]

Given that the existence of God could not be demonstrated or disproven by traditional means, James nevertheless insisted that the quality of life caused by belief carried significant meaning to its consequences. James accepted the term *God* provided it implied something *more* in the relation between the individual and the universe and resulted as well in a morally transformative experience. It did not, however, demand the preoccupation demonstrated by organized religion, including God's anthropomorphism, interventionism, and redemptive attributes. A difference existed between the God of *revealed* religion, whose attributes were caught up in theological dogmatics, and the God of *natural* religion, whose belief involved a connectedness to the panorama of life and in the aggregate of human experience. In other words, God was a concept broader than the religions that claimed ownership. James's picture of the universe was always in an unfinished state, forever coming to terms with its different elements, wrestling with moral will and the ongoing experiences of struggle, faith, and salvation. "Because God is not the absolute, but is himself a part when the system is conceived pluralistically," he wrote "his functions can be taken as not wholly dissimilar to those of the smaller parts,—as similar to our functions consequently."[41]

James took exception to Huxley's notion of agnosticism. In "The Sentiment of Rationality," an address delivered before the Harvard Philosophical Club in 1880 and published in the *Princeton Review* in 1882, he insisted that man must "take nothing as an equivalent for life but the fullness of living itself." When he chooses to be only a visitor and not a dweller, "he will never carry the philosophic yoke upon his shoulders." The choice of suspending judgment or belief was not an option. The same applied to Spencer's Unknown. "There can be no greater incongruity than for a disciple of Spencer to proclaim with one breath that the substance of things is unknowable, and with the next that the thought of it should inspire us with awe, reverence, and a willingness to add our co-operative push in the direction toward which its manifestations seem to be drifting. The unknowable may be unfathomed, but if it makes such distinct demands upon our activity, we surely are not ignorant of its essential quality."[42] As for atheists who considered God a discredited myth that no longer deserved meaningful discussion, James offered a more nuanced approach. Pragmatism's melioristic approach looked not at religion's pernicious role in the history of human relations or its blindness to modern science, but in the richness of its diversity, its contributions to art and philosophy, and particularly its usefulness in serving human needs. God may be a delusion, but if belief benefited the individual and society, the metaphysical issues as to whether God exists or not should take a back seat, since this was an unanswerable question. The trouble with claiming ownership of Truth with a capital "T" was its distraction from people working for the common good. "The real power of the pragmatic approach," wrote Andrew Fiala, "is that it reminds us that human life occurs within the shared practices and norms of a community." It celebrates the shared values and communal practices that result from those who practice religion's rituals and beliefs.[43] Though some forms of religiosity were clearly harmful, necessitating some level of control, such misdeeds did not justify intolerance to the whole of religion's diversity.

James made sympathetic references to Jesus but did not identify with the term "Christian." Having rejected abstract notions of an Absolute for a finite God who worked in partnership with humanity, James left no room for notions of Christ and divine revelation. Instead, he constructed a framework in which belief was not a matter of contemplation but of action and where the individual stood as a participant in the world and not simply as a spectator. Standing inside and not outside the decision-making process, humans made choices that became acts of faith, hoping that the future would confirm what they had the courage to risk.

## PLURALISM

James rejected the God of orthodoxy because he found Him devoid of any practical purpose or meaning. Mere existence commanded no reverence. Instead, God needed to be a co-laborer with people in building a moral universe. Such a finite God, explained philosopher David Paulsen, was "pragmatically richer than belief in an absolutely unlimited God in that it provides greater virility and impetus to our moral endeavors."[44] James admitted to having "no living sense of commerce with a God. I envy those who have for I know the addition of such a sense would help me immensely."[45] Busying himself instead with the prospect of improving the human condition individually and communally, he chose pluralism to either a death-of-God approach or placing in God too much control. The relevance of the traditional all-knowing and all-powerful God was irrelevant to human existence, but belief in God resulted in a moral and ethically more meaningful existence. If God was the missing factor in bringing unification to human ideals and choices, then he urged humans to use it.[46]

Except for Nietzsche, few philosophers aside from James chose polytheism as a serious alternative to the monotheistic tradition in Western philosophy. He first made mention of this option in *Varieties* when expressing his compatibility with a pluralistic universe. "Theism, whenever it has erected itself into a systematic philosophy of the universe, has shown a reluctance to let God be anything less than All-in-All. In other words, philosophic theism has always shown a tendency to become pantheistic and monistic, and to consider the world as one unit of absolute fact; and this has been at variance with popular or practical theism, which latter has ever been more or less frankly pluralistic, not to say polytheistic, and shown itself perfectly well satisfied with a universe composed of many original principles, provided we be only allowed to believe that the divine principle remains supreme, and that the others are subordinate."[47]

James's endorsement of both pluralism and polytheism was a response to the monistic worldview that seemed to turn life into a Greek tragedy with little room for free will. The only alternative, he explained, was "to cut loose from the monistic assumption altogether and to allow the world to have existed from its origin in pluralistic form, as an aggregate or collection of higher and lower things and principles, rather than an absolute unitary fact."[48] This became his solution to the moral problem of evil and God its ultimate source. "Given the enormity of human . . . suffering," explained Richard A. S. Hall, "James believes that God's goodness can be salvaged only if he is conceived of as limited in his natural powers."[49] Polytheism destroyed the divine hegemony of an all-powerful God by opening the possibility to a more mystical and democratic theism, a degree of tolerance to other systems, and opposition to a more sovereign and monistic state of religious experience.

James was a religious pluralist who valued those religions that connected belief with ethics or moral values. It was not the existence or non-
existence of God or an eternal moral law that counted, but the empathy
humans expressed toward each other and the moral obligation of making things better.[50] In his use of the term "plural universe," James implied a universe composed of many minds as distinct from one absolute
mind. James's pluralism was a matter of no small importance, as he applied the term in complex and varying ways to his epistemology, ethics,
and views on religion.[51] Pluralism was something to be celebrated rather
than regretted. He encouraged individuals to venture into religious pluralism (doxastic religious pluralism) provided that the resulting fermenta-
tion supported the ideals of tolerance and healthy competition.[52]

James's pluralism contrasted sharply with the monism of Paul Carus,
the stoicism of Buddhism, the dualism of Christian scholasticism, the
absolutism of Josiah Royce, and the determinism of Calvinism. Desiring that pragmatism steer a middle course between the competing systems, he salvaged what terms he could from the religious point of view,
albeit expunged of their negative attributes. Still, at the end of the day, he
seemed to vacillate between human sufficiency and reliance on "otherness" that transcended personal experience.

IMMORTALITY

James's interest in immortality was, by his own admission, "a secondary
point," though he sympathized with those who found it an urgent impulse. The only thing he could attest with any intellectual clearness was
that "we can experience union with something larger than ourselves and
in that union find our greater peace."[53] He accepted immortality within
the framework of the pragmatist's will to believe but was not personally
troubled by it or his own mortality. "God is the producer of immortality; and whoever has doubts of immortality is written down as an atheist
without farther trial. I have said nothing in my [Ingersoll] lectures about
immortality or the belief therein, for to me it seems a secondary point.
If our ideals are only cared for in 'eternity,' I do not see why we might
not be willing to resign their care to other hands than ours. Yet I sym-
pathize with the urgent impulse to be present ourselves, and in the conflict of impulses, both of them so vague yet both of them noble, I know
not how to decide. It seems to me that it is eminently a case for facts to
testify. Facts, I think, are yet lacking to prove 'spirit-return.' . . . I consequently leave the matter open, with this brief word to save the reader

from a possible perplexity as to why immortality got no mention in the body of this book."[54]

Philosopher Ralph Barton Perry suggested that James tended toward belief in immortality in his later years, experiencing a "growing faith in its reality."[55] One is reminded, however, of the French novelist Roger Martin du Gard's *Jean Barois*, whose titular protagonist, when faced with the immediacy of death in a sudden and unexpected traffic accident along the Boulevard Saint-Germain, burst out with the words "Hail, Mary, full of grace . . ." Alarmed by what he interpreted as a momentary but alarming weakness, Barois prepared a testament of his beliefs in the event that another such event might cause him to revert in a weakened state to his former faith.[56] James admitted to the possibility of immortality, though certainly not in a manner compatible with Western religious tradition. Recognizing that belief in immortality represented one of the "great spiritual needs of man," he found it disconcerting that mainline religions had constituted themselves its "official guardians" that included the pretended power of withholding it from those who did not accept their teachings.[57]

James recognized that immortality constituted "a pungent craving" and offered two points he suspected might "rob the notion of much of its old power to draw belief." While most physiologists agreed that thought was a function of the brain, meaning that mental phenomena did not exist as independent variables in the world, James considered it possible that the life of the mind might continue when the brain itself was dead. The flaw in strict scientific reasoning was to state that thought was a function of the brain. "When we think of the law that thought is a function of the brain, we are not required to think of productive function only; *we are entitled also to consider permissive or transmissive function*." Thus, consciousness could, in ways now unknown, continue intact and compatible "with the supernatural life behind the veil hereafter." "Just how the process of transmission may be carried on, is indeed unimaginable; but the outer relations, so to speak, of the process, encourage our belief. Consciousness in this process does not have to be generated *de novo* in a vast number of places. It exists already, behind the scenes, coeval with the world. The transmission-theory not only avoids in this way multiplying miracles, but it puts itself in touch with general idealistic philosophy better than the production-theory does. It should always be reckoned a good thing when science and philosophy thus meet."[58]

In his explanation of the transmission-theory, James referenced mediums who allegedly could identify an individual's private thoughts or an apparition of something happening hundreds of miles away. He likewise referred to the "influx" referenced by Swedenborgians to describe special insight, and Kant, whom he quoted: "The death of the body may indeed be the end of the sensational use of our mind, but only the beginning of the intellectual use. . . . The body would thus be not the cause of our thinking, but merely a condition restrictive thereof, and, although essential to our sensuous and animal consciousness, it may be regarded as an impeder of our pure spiritual life."[59]

On the other hand, James playfully questioned how such an "intolerable number" of spiritual beings could exist if immortality were indeed true. The world would include "inconceivable billions of fellow-strivers," including "hosts of Hottentots" and others among the animal kingdom, all of whom would make for an "inconveniently crowded stage." "Life is a good thing on a reasonably copious scale; but the very heavens themselves, and the cosmic times and spaces, would stand aghast, we think, at the notion of preserving eternally such an ever-swelling plethora and glut of it." While Christians might not have use for the heathen and the "swarms of alien kinsmen," he questioned whether this reasoning applied to God. If humans wished to claim immortality, they should at least be tolerant (i.e., democratic) to the claims of immortality made by *all* its members—past, present, and future. Not doing so would "be letting blindness lay down the law of sight."[60]

Given James's affirmation of the will to believe, individuals were justified in adopting immortality even with the lack of sufficient evidence other than a personal "leap" to belief. If believing in immortality helped in coping with life and making the world a morally better place, then it was a ready-made solution. The metaphysical need to believe in immortality, explains Sami Pihlström at the University of Helsinki, "flow[s] from our mortality and the sorrow, distress, fear, horror, anxiety, or angst caused by it."[61] It would be difficult to state whether James's search for immortality was a success or failure. Certainly, the idea of transhuman consciousness remained an ever-present hope. His was not the absolute mind of Carus's monism but plural seas of consciousness (a cosmic consciousness "like islands in the sea") that he set forth in his Ingersoll Lecture "Human Immortality."[62]

Overall, critics accused James of being too credulous, of accepting or at least admitting to the possibility of some form of paranormal communication (i.e., telepathy, clairvoyance, or premonition). James's friend Richard Hodgson likened the quality of the evidence to two distant persons who had only dead-drunk servants to act as their messengers.[63] To be sure, James did not commit himself to Spiritualism to the degree that

Wallace had. At the same time that he expressed his astonishment with what he had seen from the medium Leonora Piper, he was equally strong in his condemnation of Blavatsky when she was called out by Richard Hodgson for deceit. As he remarked in his presidential address to the Society of Psychical Research in 1896: "A universal proposition can be made untrue by a particular instance. If you wish to upset the law that all crows are black, you mustn't seek to show that no crows are; it is enough if you prove one single crow to be white. My own white crow is Mrs. Piper." This is to say that despite his adherence to the general concept of empiricism, he never saw it necessary to denounce his metaphysical pluralism.[64]

## MELIORISM

Over the years, James became increasingly anti-institutional and anarchistic in his thinking, alarmed by the number of people who had accepted a deterministic world where the individual became the mere plaything of external forces. Championing personal freedom and active participation in the pursuit of democratic ideals, he spoke out publicly of his opposition to the events of the 1890s, especially the Spanish-American War, the invasion of the Philippines, the Dreyfus affair in France, attempts to annex Hawaii, and US meddling in Venezuelan affairs. Increasingly, he saw anonymous forces—government, military, corporations—assuming control over individual lives.[65] Already identified with psychical research, opposition to medical licensure laws, and support of mind-cure medicine, he came to politics naturally through his father's Christian socialism, Fourierism, and Swedenborgianism. Like his father, he advocated a passional vision that was deeply anti-institutional and exemplified by his participation in the Anti-Imperialistic League, his numerous letters to editors on social and political issues, and his public statements before the Massachusetts Legislature against medical licensing. So strong was his reaction that he confided to William Dean Howells in 1900, "I am becoming more and more an individualist and anarchist and believer in small systems of things exclusively."[66]

Meliorism became James's personal choice to combat the extremes of optimism and pessimism. In a pluralistic universe where God was finite and contingent within a given environment, God and humanity labored together to realize change. Seen as subordinating the "true" for the "good" in his escape from abstractions, he emphasized the power of the ideal in making individual actions morally worthwhile and infusing what Scott R. Stroud of the University of Texas at Austin identifies as an "experiential integrity" between the individual and his work activity.[67] On the whole, explains religious scholar Wayne Proudfoot, "pragmatism inclines to meliorism, which stands between optimism and pessimism, where salvation is not assured."[68]

In addressing the question of how individuals were able to draw upon their own personal forces to overcome crises of will that kept them from acting out their hopes and goals, James's comments were reminiscent of Theodore Roosevelt's "Strenuous Life" speech before the Hamilton Club of Chicago in 1899. "Let us therefore boldly face the life of strife," Roosevelt urged, "resolute to do our duty well and manfully; resolute to uphold righteousness by deed and by word; resolute to be both honest and brave, to serve high ideals, yet to use practical methods."[69] In other words, James's will to believe lent itself to invigorating those intent on transforming their inner ideals. It began with doubt, moved to action, and ended with belief. By convincing themselves that belief in action could make a positive difference, they changed their lives and those of others. Belief produced a transformative effect on the individual and on society. Being a meliorist meant placing possibility at the heart of meaning and what purposeful and sometimes even strenuous activities might produce. As Perry explained, "James attached intrinsic value to heroic action, and praised the life of conflict and struggle for the personal qualities it engendered."[70] James applauded the "strenuous life," but without the aggressiveness and martial virtues of empire-building. His activism came without the bellicose policies and injustices that accompanied the nation's raw use of power.[71]

Much like his father, James insisted on a path to personal freedom separate from formal institutions and corporate entities that compartmentalized and controlled how persons thought and acted. While his father drew his main ideas from Swedenborg, James drew upon pragmatic philosophy as his method of choice for weighing truths and values. Philosophy was no longer an exercise of academics but a method of meliorist change that made room for hope and the possibility of a better world. His was a call to arms against institutions and theories that encouraged passiveness, acquiescence, and neglect of social evils. Instead of a single network or institutional philosophy, he offered a philosophy that gave everyone the self-determined opportunity to contribute to the realization of American ideals. Through individual and small group action distinct from the state or church, everyone could become a force in the affairs of man and society.[72]

A forceful player in the biological and medical sciences, psychology, philosophy, and religion, James was gifted with the ability to bring wholly different and illuminating perspectives into each of the disciplines. Rich in the diversity of his experiences and knowledge, he gave to the study of man a distinctive worldview. Although Van Wyck Brooks accused him of "destroying ethical morality and leaving the American mind to its own devices which, compared to the European . . . were hopelessly low-class," Whitehead considered James one of the world's four greatest philosophers (along with Plato, Aristotle, and Leibniz) and his philosophy of pragmatism an equal to Francis Bacon's experimentalism in human thinking.[73] As these two extremes suggest, James impelled readers in different directions and sometimes for opposite reasons. For some, his philosophy represented the application of Darwin's evolutionary theory to the definition of truth; for others, it provided a foundation for scientific positivism; and still others viewed it as a license to believe and make judgments without depending on abstract reasoning or on facts.

James was no system maker dealing with broad generalizations; instead, he gloried in the things that could not be analyzed or systematized, preferring the novelty and multiplicity of life and the richness of data that defied easy scheme making. His radical empiricism was itself an attack on the monistic philosophizing of his generation. Unlike Spencer, who in his senior years found his once highly touted synthetic philosophy crumbling before a generation of philosophers and social scientists, James found his ideas continuing to gain supporters even when he moved into metaphysical areas not typically recognized among devotees of science. His intense devotion to the search for truth and his treatment of all data found to be significant made him one of the most influential psychologists in his day and, as Dewey foretold, one of the greatest psychologists of all time.[74]

A virtual artist of the mind, this teacher of physiology and son of a Swedenborgian theologian felt impelled to treat the functioning brain and nervous system as an integrated organ of sensations and an instrument of action. In doing so, he brought the natural sciences within the portals of psychology and philosophy. Like an impressionistic painter, those distinctions he made between the material and the metaphysical, the objective and subjective, faded in the glare of light, suggesting forms hardly recognizable close up but exposing meaning and significance when viewed with the proper perspective. As a physiologist and philosopher, he expanded the boundaries of the mind by driving home the point that life was decided moment to moment and not as the dull mechanical outcome of a determinant chain of events. "In no revival of a past experience," he wrote, "are all the items of our thought equally operative in determining what the next thought shall be."[75] One understood life not by reducing it to intellectual categories or mechanical principles but by grasping intuitively the connection between the individual as knower and the individual as doer. It meant rejecting an absolute distinction between subject and object by recognizing the right to believe and running the risk of error, that is, the courage to risk success and failure in the experience of testing or experimentation. James never claimed to be an ethical teacher, but he conveyed a moral atmosphere in his works that showed fully the character of the man.

## Selected Writings

*The Principles of Psychology* (1890)
*Psychology, Briefer Course* (1892)
*The Will to Believe, and Other Essays in Popular Philosophy* (1897)
*Human Immortality: Two Supposed Objections to the Doctrine* (1897)
*Talks to Teachers on Psychology and to Students on Some of Life's Ideals* (1899)
*Varieties of Religious Experience: A Study in Human Nature* (1902)
*Pragmatism: A New Name for Some Old Ways of Thinking* (1907)
*A Pluralistic Universe* (1909)
*The Meaning of Truth: A Sequel to "Pragmatism"* (1909)
*Some Problems of Philosophy: A Beginning of an Introduction to Philosophy* (1911)
*Memories and Studies* (1911)
*Essays in Radical Empiricism* (1912)
*Letters of William James* (1920)
*Collected Essays and Reviews* (1920)
*The Correspondence of William James* (1992–2004)

# 8

## Telesis
### Lester Frank Ward

*Had religion been true to its nature and function, as wide as morality and hu-*
*manity, it should have been the bond of unity to hold mankind together in one*
*brotherhood, linking them in good feeling, good will, and good work toward*
*one another; but it has in reality been that which has most divided men, and*
*the cause of more hatreds, more disorders, more persecutions, more bloodshed,*
*more cruelties, than most other causes put together.*

—Henry Maudsley, "Materialism and Its Lessons," 1879

WHAT COMTE WAS TO FRANCE, and Spencer to England, Lester Frank Ward (1841–1913) was to the positivist tradition, which
he carried into the vanguard of American sociology in ways that Comte
and Spencer would have hesitated to follow, if not vociferously declined.
Known as both the "Aristotle" and "Nestor" of American sociologists, he
lived two lives, one as a paleobotanist and the other as a social philosopher. The former was his vocation, the latter his avocation, for which he
became better known. Cut from the same cloth as Comte, Spencer, and
Huxley, his *Dynamic Sociology* (1883), *The Psychic Factors of Civilization*
(1893), *Outlines of Sociology* (1898), *Pure Sociology* (1903), and *Applied Sociology* (1906) set forth a system of philosophy that was cosmic in nature,
viewing creation as having no beginning or end, and forever undergoing change. Rather than be drawn into special studies, he dwelt on social
forces that influenced the whole of society in its scope of purpose. Clearly,
it was this synthetic aspect of knowledge more than specialized studies
that appealed to him. Integration was much more important than differentiation. Coming to sociology at a point in time when Spencer was at the
height of his influence, he challenged the Englishman's laissez-faire approach to human problems as unscientific and morally reprehensible, insisting that organized society had the means not only to identify the key
forces in society but to manipulate them to accelerate human progress.
Though fond of identifying society as still in the "stone age of politics," he
visualized the state as a potential catalyst for positive social change.[1]

Historians identify three periods of theorization in Ward's intellectual
worldview. The first, indicated by his *Dynamic Sociology* (1883), focused

on Spencer's impact on evolutionary thinking. Often viewed as the best of his many works, it was written while Spencer was still working on his *Principles of Sociology*. Until then, few had approached the subject with such extensive understanding. The book transformed positivism into a form of invention rather than an indifferent and mechanical form of human progress. He identified his theory of social forces and the differences between feeling and function and contrasted these with the guiding influence of the intellect, including the superiority of artificial or teleological processes over natural or genetic processes. He did so by correlating psychic factors to social questions and the degree to which governments could take information and use it for addressing problems.

The second, represented by his *Psychic Factors of Civilization* (1893), took the ideas earlier hinted at in his *Dynamic Sociology* (1883) to a new level of explanation. Considered a contribution to both psychology and sociology, *Psychic Factors* represents Ward's effort to place a psychological overlay to the purely physiological view of the world. The mind had both a subjective and an objective side, resulting in a social synthesis. The forces of society were truly psychic and under the control of a directive agent.

The third, *Pure Sociology* (1903), demonstrated how society could modify itself for the betterment of mankind. The book explains Ward's concept of synergy and creative synthesis. With these and other books and articles on human society and the mind of man, he artfully crafted an explanation of social scientists carrying out their role observing, theorizing, forecasting, and shaping the impact of constructive intelligence. In doing so, he introduced the terms "telesis," "sociocracy," "synergy," "meliorism," and "teleology," giving them special significance and demonstrating his claim that sociology was not just a science but the mechanism for human progress. Purposeful in his role for sociology, he made it the accelerant for social change.[2]

## YOUTHFUL YEARS

Born in 1841, the year William Henry Harrison became the ninth president of the United States, Lester Frank Ward was the youngest of Justice and Silence Ward's ten children. His paternal parentage was of an old New England descent; some of his ancestors had held public office. His mother, the daughter of a clergyman, claimed an equally respectful lineage, including the president of Lewisburg College in Pennsylvania. Lester's father worked as a mechanic and millwright, moving his family as jobs materialized. The year Ward was born, the family lived in Joliet, Illinois, a canal town some forty miles south of Chicago, where his father built several locks on the Illinois and Michigan Canal. A year later, they located in Cass, Illinois (Downers Grove), where Justice contracted to build a ten-mile towpath along the Des Plaines River. It was in Cass that Lester's education began, with reading at an early age from *Olney's Geography* and *McGuffey's Readers*. When Lester was nine, the family moved once again, this time to Norton's Mill near St. Charles in Missouri, and from there to Iowa. Following Justice's death in 1857, the family returned to St. Charles, where Lester and his brother Erastus kept a "bachelors' hall" and supported themselves by farming in the summer to pay for schooling in the winter. In 1860 Lester taught in a country school, saving enough to enroll at Susquehanna Collegiate Institute in Bradford County, Pennsylvania, where, because of his self-education, he advanced quickly through his studies.[3]

In 1861 Lester and Erastus moved to Myersburg, Pennsylvania, where they worked briefly in a wagon hub factory owned by their older brother Cyrenus. When the business failed, their attention turned to the War of Rebellion and their enlistment in the Army of the Potomac, where Lester wrote of his war experiences. In letters to the *Bradford Argus* in 1862–1863, he recounted his involvement at the Battle of Chancellorsville. The letters tell the story of being wounded in the right knee while other "friendly peacemakers" passed through both thighs. After lying unattended and exposed for three hours to "howling missiles of death," he spent his convalescence in the hospital of the Third Corps near Potomac Creek in the District of Columbia before being discharged in 1864 with a physical disability.[4] In a letter dated April 10, 1865, to the *Daily National Republican*, he took exception to Grant's offer of pardon to the "crime-stained" Confederate leadership. Identifying himself as "One Who has Bled to Punish Traitors," he urged the nation's leadership to "deal out condign punishment to the guilty leaders, not in wrath nor in vengeance, but in justice, in honor, in wisdom, pardoning only the deluded victims of ignorance and slavery."[5]

After the war, Ward obtained a government position as a clerk in the Treasury Department and later became chief of the Division of Navigation and Immigration, followed by the position of librarian for the United States Bureau of Statistics. In 1881 the soldier, geologist, and longtime friend Major John Wesley Powell offered Ward the choice of working for the Bureau of American Ethnology as a linguist or for the United States Geological Survey as a geologist. With credentials that prepared him for both, he chose the Geological Survey, and his subsequent publications about North American geology grew at a fast pace, including contributions to *The Century Dictionary* and *Webster's International Dictionary*. In 1892 he became the Survey's chief paleontologist.[6]

Possessed of a thorough grounding in botany and geology at the time he started his duties with the Survey, Ward authored a *Guide to the Flora of Washington and Vicinity*, followed by articles in the *American Naturalist* and other magazines, before drifting into paleobotany. He produced a series of papers, including "Evolution in the Vegetable Kingdom," "Historical View of the Fossil Flora of the Globe," "Botanical View of the Fossil Flora of the Globe," "Geographical Distribution of Fossil Plants," and numerous others. Combined, they demonstrated his newfound influence in the field of paleobotanical literature.

Living in Washington provided Ward the opportunity to expand his education with formal study at Columbian (George Washington) University, which he attended in the evenings, receiving his AB (1869), LLB (1871), AM (1872), and honorary LLD (1897). A strong believer in the importance of education, he planned and executed a systematic reading of the great masters in philosophy, religion, and the sciences. Those whom he especially admired included Bacon, Kant, Draper, Agassiz, Lyell, Haeckel, Comte, and Spencer. He counted both Spencer and Haeckel among his friends. "Mr. Herbert Spencer has received, and probably deserves, the title of England's greatest philosopher," Ward once wrote, "and when we reach England's greatest in any achievement of mind, we have usually also reached the world's greatest."[7]

## RELIGIOUS BELIEFS

In 1870 Ward and his wife, Lizzie, helped launch the *Iconoclast*, a four-page monthly paper founded by the short-lived political society in Washington called the National Liberal Reform League, which, according to historian Steven L. Piott, was dedicated to "the establishment of the principles of mental, moral, and religious liberty as embodied in the Declaration of Independence."[8] Ward edited the paper and wrote much of its content, noting the errors of theological dogmatism and searching for a religion free from superstition. Using the paper as his pulpit, he assailed organized religion for its doctrinal errors and opposition to the teaching of science in the schools and universities.[9] Nor did he trust religion to write its own history, since it had crafted too many half-truths calculated to benefit its view of the world. "Our aim," he explained, "shall be to secure the largest possible mental liberty for all and to oppose only those who are the opponents of liberty."[10]

Ward was especially critical of revealed religion, which he viewed as directly opposed to human progress. Religion was not supernatural, but the product of natural selection. The belief in spiritual beings had originated out of fear that the individual and race sensed danger from "unknown and uncontrollable agencies."[11] Though he respected the spiritual values of religion, he deplored the way it had replaced truth with error. "Pretended revelation" had proven prejudicial to the social improvement of humankind, with its support of divine right, witchcraft, capital punishment, polygamy, war, and the institution of slavery, which both the Old and the New Testaments supported.[12] Agreeing with John William Draper, Andrew Dickinson White, and William Lecky, he insisted that if organized religion held its grip on society, civilization would decline proportionally. "Rome, once the proud center of a resplendent civilization, now abjectly crouches at the feet of a Christian pontiff, while the genius of empire and civilization, ever accompanying mental liberty, is enshrined in more infidel France, Germany, England, and America."[13] "A religion that holds forth a bundle of dogmas, and requires an implicit subscription to them on pain of future damnation; that marks out the limit of human thought, and declares 'thus far shalt thou go and no farther'; that sets up, as an infallible standard and guide to action, the writings of men who lived centuries ago; that devotes its attention not to the encouragement of temporal employments, but to the contemplation of a future life, is one of the greatest enemies of human progress, and it should be the effort of every good man feeling the force of this fact to labor for the restriction of its deadly influence."[14]

Ward seldom used the term *God*. As with Laplace, he considered the God hypothesis unnecessary. One of the few instances he did use the term was in *Pure Sociology* where God was likened to a monistic atom of unquantifiable energy.

Nature is not only a becoming, it is a striving. The universal energy never ceases to act and its ceaseless activity constantly creates. The quantity of matter, mass, and motion in the universe is unchangeable, everything else changes—position, direction, velocity, path, combination, form. To say with Schopenhauer that matter is causality involves an ellipsis. It is not matter, but collision that constitutes the only cause. This eternal pelting of atoms, this driving of the elements, this pressure at every point, this struggle of all created things, this universal nisus of nature pushing

into existence all material forms and storing itself up in them as properties, as life, as feeling, as thought, this is the hylozoism of the philosophers, the self-activity of Hegel, the will of Schopenhauer, the atom soul
of Haeckel; it is the soul of the universe, the spirit of Nature, the "First
Cause" of both religion and science—it is God.[15]

As a philosopher, Ward did not believe in personal immortality except
for the immortality of deeds "The real immortality," he was fond of re-
peating, "is the immortality of achievement."[16] In this regard, Ward spoke
out against the popular belief that religion was proxy for morality. "Away
with this bug-bear," he responded emphatically. "If a man is moral and
upright, he is so whether within or without the church. If he is mean
and unprincipled, it is the same. . . . History proves this. A thousand
daily events demonstrate it."[17] The cosmos manifested itself in a myriad
of structures functioning according to their own nature but in harmony
with one another and expressive of a common, monistic, spiritual, and
creative energy. It was this kinship in the cosmos—a microcosm within
the macrocosm—that produced man's ethics. "The true crown of a system of scientific philosophy is not an Ethics which seeks to restrain and
circumscribe activity, but a Sociology which aims at the liberation of action through the directive agency of intelligence."[18]

Ward's religiosity did not adhere to existing theological or ecclesiastical structures. Yet, it would be wrong to describe him as irreligious, for
he admired the beauty and unity that religion inspired. Moreover, he recognized the need for religion, and like Paul Carus of Open Court Publishing Company, hoped that a scientifically based religion might suffice.
Science was the great Iconoclast. Initiated by men like Galileo and Newton, and continued by Cuvier, Humboldt, Agassiz, and Huxley, it toppled
"the old systems, both of government and of religion, and threaten[ed] to
rebuild the entire frame-work of society itself."[19] Much like Haeckel and
Carus, Ward was a monist who believed in the absolute continuity of nature whose law was evolution. "All the phenomena of all the sciences conform to one law—Evolution—are the result of one process—Organization." Ward's concept of the cosmos was one that was forever evolving,
forever changing, without beginning or end—the conscious striving of
the individual and race to ever higher goals.[20]

When the nation's favorite preacher, Henry Ward Beecher, remarked
that if religion was a fiction with no existence beyond the grave, he would
seal his mouth rather than disclose the information, Ward remonstrated
with equal vigor. "This may do very well for clergymen, but for our part

we would be very glad to know the truth, whatever it be. We believe in the superiority of truth over error . . . and if we knew the truth respecting this matter, we would hasten to proclaim it to the world, even if it should dash all men's cherished hopes of future bliss to the earth. The difference between us and Mr. Beecher, is this: that though neither knows anything at all about it, he goes about preaching immortality while we say nothing, but humbly acknowledge our ignorance."[21]

## COMTE AND SPENCER

Ward accepted Comte's classification of the sciences from mathematics to astronomy, physics, chemistry, biology, and sociology. He also credited him with introducing and justifying sociology's role in the hierarchy—its capacity to classify data, demonstrate the uniformity of social phenomena, and then apply the collected data to the betterment of society. Sociology implied a relation of parts in which all aspects of the material universe were connected. As man had no knowledge of anything but phenomena, he knew neither the essence nor the real mode of production of any fact but only its relation to other facts. Such relations were constant, meaning that they were always the same in the same circumstances. That which linked phenomena together, uniting them as antecedent and consequent, were *laws*. They were all that man knew respecting phenomena, since their essential nature and their ultimate causation remained unknown and inscrutable. Matter was a "thing in itself" whose "ultimate nature is not known."[22]

Ward described Comte's classification of the sciences as "the most sublime, interesting, and important idea of the nineteenth century."[23] His achievement brought a world of independent facts into a set form or order that better explained the universe. Formulated around the law of gravitation, the nebular hypothesis, and the development theory, the sciences approached nearer to unification than ever before. Nevertheless, Ward took exception to Comte's disparagement of the role of the hypothesis, insisting that the search for efficient (not final) causes and explanations was perfectly within the realm of human responsibility. Science gave man the ability to foresee the future, and he fulfilled that responsibility for the sake of the whole of humanity. Choosing not to do this struck "a fatal blow at all true progress in human knowledge."[24]

Just as Ward had criticized Comte for his disparagement of the importance of the hypothesis, he criticized Spencer for giving so little importance to the value of invention. "This is the faculty that has the chief value in sociology," he insisted. "It is the one that has produced nearly all the effects that distinguish man from an animal." Invention, or what Ward preferred to call *social art*, drove people to do things in the interest of both the individual and the greater society. Ward also criticized Spencer for his failure to appreciate social integration. The latter's extreme individualism had prevented him from seeing the benefits of collective action. "[Spencer] did not perceive that the fundamental distinction which he so clearly pointed out between the animal and the social organism necessarily reverses the direction of social evolution and causes it to work for the good of the individual."[25] While praising *Principles of Biology* as the "gem" of Spencer's synthetic philosophy, ranking it as a masterpiece, he judged its author "a very poor observer," as he had seemingly "subordinated and practically sacrificed his perceptive to his reflective capacities."[26]

In looking back over the history of humankind, Ward observed that the "highest wisdom" had been "to learn and then to follow the ways of nature" and rebuke as "meddlers" those who would set out in a different direction. Consequently, any efforts to use government to intervene in what were thought to be the "immutable laws of nature" were deemed illogical, if not harmful. Government was made to "let society alone, and thus allow the laws of nature to work out their beneficent results." In this scheme of things, laissez-faire became the watchword imposed on any ameliorative effort thought to be injurious. The laws of nature "must be left wholly untouched," so its advocates insisted, believing that survival of the fittest would ultimately correct abuses, sharpen wits, and develop the brain, leaving the unfit to drop out of the competition. Explicit in this scheme of Spencer and his disciples was the belief that social reform was "unscientific" and that public charities had perpetuated in their kindness the least-worthy elements in society. Competition being the law of nature, all progress resulted from allowing it to function without interference. Thus, as sociology developed as a discipline, it became a forceful teacher insisting that society must be based on the biological law of competition.[27]

## MIND

Calling out laissez-faire as "a gospel of inaction," Ward set himself the task of formulating a more progressive approach. After conceding to the truthfulness of the doctrines of the survival of the fittest and natural selection in explaining the organic world, he insisted that they failed to account for the mind, which introduced a "new power" into the cosmos. Here was a faculty that allowed human intelligence to transform the human habitat. No other animal possessed a comparable ability. "If we inquire more closely into the mode by which the intellect operates," he explained, "we shall find that it serves as a guiding power to those natural forces with which it is acquainted (and no others), directing them into channels of human advantage." What was called civilization was an "inventive process" requiring artificial intervention of mind into the processes of nature. "If nature's process is rightly named *natural* selection, man's process is *artificial* selection." The same instrumentality of the mind that allowed humans to defend themselves from their enemies also allowed those same powers to protect the weak against adverse forces. Unlike the rest of the animal kingdom, people had developed the sentiments of equity, beneficence, and benevolence. These were strictly human traits, and although many evolutionists and sociologists refused to recognize them, they clearly demonstrated the human's uniqueness among the species. The mind, fortified with knowledge, was the single reliable mechanism for directive improvement. Acquiring information and understanding the forces of nature enabled one to secure the end sought. It was information embraced in the word "science" and diffused through education that proved to be truly progressive.[28]

Aided by the principle of evolution, Ward took the information obtained from each of the sciences and brought them together in a homogeneous system of knowledge.[29] "My thesis," he wrote, "is that the subject-matter of sociology is human *achievement*. It is not what men are but what they do. It is not the structure but the function." This approach, unique among his contemporaries, concerned the practical aspects of sociology, meaning its application and the artificial means of accelerating the process to some specific end. With the use of "creative synthesis," a term Ward borrowed from German philosopher Wilhelm Maximilian Wundt, he set the mind to work against the forces of nature with daring and confidence that the outcome would more than compensate for the effort. The mind was a creative force capable of detecting and differentiating stimuli from the environment and directing them toward a higher end. Synergy, a creative force resulting from the collaboration, competition, and interaction of the forces of nature, resulted in a social dynamic that took place at the crossroads of this fusion and forged a modification to the environment that was preservative, reproductive, and spiritual.[30]

Ward questioned how naturalistic philosophers could have shut their eyes to the role of intelligence. "Nothing is easier than to show that the unrestricted competition of nature does not secure the survival of the fittest but only of the actually fittest, and in every attempt, man makes to obtain something fitter than this actual fittest he succeeds, as witness improved breeds of animals and grafts of fruits." Using this line of reasoning, he advocated government's right to "meddle" with the laws of trade, business, and the natural laws if only to understand them more thoroughly and endeavor to control their outcomes. Government must be allowed the right to protect its citizens, enforce codes of morals, improve the healing art, and devise improvements to man's earthly condition. Truth came not just from the rational study of nature but by creatively controlling those forces that involved the senseless destruction of the weak. "When nature comes to be regarded as passive and man as active, instead of the reverse as now, when human action is recognized as the most important of all forms of action, and when the power of the human intellect over vital, psychic and social phenomena is practically conceded, then, and then only, can man justly claim to have risen out of the animal and fully to have entered the human stage of development."[31]

Given Ward's strong opinion on the role of hypothesis and inventiveness, he had little difficulty attributing the biological origin and development of the mind to the action of natural selection and therefore not of God or some intelligent force. Having determined that the mind was a function of the body and a natural product of evolution, he regarded it like any other organic objects that had developed "in the midst of an infinite series of antecedents and consequences." No less than plants, it was a part of nature and modified by the continuum of forces operating in it. "Nature has made great progress in developing organized beings and is assumed to be still working in this direction."[32]

*Dynamic sociology*, a term that Ward preferred to *positivism*, depicted human progress as something wholly different from natural selection. Here is where art surpassed nature by moving away from it. Rather than imitate nature, dynamic sociology bent nature to man's purposes. Progress derived from two sources: uncontrolled and unknown laws and what he called the *progress of art*, meaning the result of "foresight and intelligent direction." This latter force required zealous husbanding "by the deliberative foresight of enlightened intellect." Unless this was done, the individual and society would drift under purely natural influences. "The era of teleological or artificial progress has not yet begun," Ward noted. In fact, it might never begin. "But, until it does so," he warned, "society is as liable to succumb to an adverse wave of reaction, and suffer extinction, as is any race or species of animals or plants; and we know that this is constantly occurring."[33] "In short, man has not yet ceased to be an animal, and is still under the control of external nature and not under the control of his own mind. It is natural selection that has created intellect; it is natural selection that has developed it to its present condition, and it is intellect as a product of natural selection that has guided man up to his present position. The principle of artificial selection which he has been taught by nature, and has applied to other creatures, more as an art than as a science, to his immense advantage, he has not yet thought of applying to himself. Not until he does this can he claim any real distinction from the other animals."[34]

The principle of *telesis* formed a fundamental component of Ward's thinking about the mind, since it hypothesized that for evolution to succeed, its energy must be redirected. "Telic" meant progress that came not from unorganized forces but from those artificial efforts to secure a greater good for man. This implied conscious control by the mind that was far superior to unconscious control by nature, since nature was wasteful and moved slowly. Mind, a "dynamic agent" informed by experience, personal feelings, desires, and aspirations, became a guide or "directive agent." Aware of ends and means, it had the wisdom (or unwisdom) to prosecute its intentions. When artfully employed, the mind shaped the world by controlling human progress artificially. Education, namely the study of science, was the instrument of social progress.[35]

Left on its own, nature remained undirected and wasteful; when directed by an informed mind, nature's wastefulness turned constructive. It became telic in the sense that the forces of nature were put to work for ethical, aesthetic, and intellectual ends. Of even greater importance than individual telesis was collective or social telesis, where ends were attained through the economy of many minds comprehending the environment and concentrating the best science to the attainment of improvements meant to affect the larger community. A telic society, operating for the general welfare and not just for specific individuals or groups, formed combinations of thought that added to morals, religion, codes of conduct, and culture. Granted that some of the best achievements were the work of a few original minds, true genius came through social changes that accelerated civilization's advancement.

Ward distinguished between *theo-teleology* and *anthropo-teleology*—the former suggested that human progress stemmed from divine arrangement, much like what Wallace identified as an explanation for man's special evolution. Ward, on the other hand, chose the latter, insisting that progress could be explained mechanically through the application of human intelligence rather than any Higher Intelligence. Still, there was much in Ward's concept of the uniqueness and power of the human mind that resonated with Wallace. With the development of the mind, humanity had the capacity to impose itself as a natural force on society. There was as much propriety in the use of the word "anthropo-teleology" as those who supposed the purposes of a deity. Humans were a product of nature whose acts emanated from motives that lay within each individual and were performed "in obedience to plans, designs, and purposes, which exist in the minds of individuals."[36]

During Wallace's American tour, he developed a close friendship with Ward, who at the time was serving as government paleobotanist in Washington. Despite Wallace's persistent defense of Spiritualism and Ward's outspoken agnosticism, they both came together on their criticism of capitalism and the advocacy of equality of opportunity for the masses.[37]

## Neo-Lamarckism

Arguably the most prominent of the classical liberals, Spencer minimized the role of the state to the extent that William Dunning in his *A History of Political Theories from Rousseau to Spencer* (1920) referred to his political theory as anarchistic. So extreme were his restraints that he not only opposed all forms of social and industrial regulation but even objected to public support of education. Only when the individual could pursue his own self-interest was the greatest progress possible. Spencer and his disciples insisted that government would always remain an inferior entity, preying upon society's weaker elements. This explains why Spencer advocated for a laissez-faire environment to remove the corrupt and selfish interests of authority. According to Ward, however, those who appealed for governmental inactivity often did so to further exploit society's less fortunate members. Here was the dividing line between Spencer and Ward.[38]

As contrasting ideologies competed for recognition, American social scientists sought common ground with their British counterparts. On one side, conservatives like William G. Sumner, John Fiske, Edward L. Youmans, Edwin L. Godkin, and Andrew Carnegie set out to rationalize the nation's social inequalities using the Manchester school of economic thought; on the other, reformers like Ward, Henry George, Henry Demarest Lloyd, Thorstein Veblen, Washington Gladden, and Richard T. Ely chose to explain the limitations of that school of thought on wages, profits, and rent. In their standoff of opposing principles were the advocates of economic individualism with its limited role for the state, and those for whom cooperation and a centralized state constituted the road to societal improvement. For the latter, the state acted as representative of the organic whole, devoted to the common good and general welfare. As Joseph L. Blau explained, there were "social" Darwinists like William Graham Sumner and "unsocial" Darwinists like Lester Ward.[39]

Both Comte and Spencer were avowed believers in the inheritance of acquired characteristics. Lamarck's explanation for the process of physical evolution fit nicely into the social science perspective in that it allowed a role for human behavior and its interaction with the environment to explain the mechanism of change. His argument that the needs of an organism brought about "an inclination towards the actions appropriate to their satisfaction" and subsequent modifications that passed on through heredity gave rise to a science of human behavior that gave humans a central role in their development. Almost immediately, modified forms of Neo-Lamarckism sprang up within and outside the scientific communities where their advocates, especially in the United States, sought a more deliberative role for humans in the evolutionary process.[40]

Representative of America's Neo-Lamarckians, Ward emphasized the role of cooperative activity as a sign not just of social progress but of the inability of natural selection to extend evolutionary development beyond the lower animals. Natural selection explained the life and death of species below humans and perhaps even the cunning of the human species, but it could not explain those artifacts that had rendered the human being unfit in the struggle for existence.[41] Aligned with him were W. J. McGee, first president of the American Anthropological Association, John Wesley Powell, director of the US Geological Survey and Bureau of Ethnology, and Granville Stanley Hall, president of Clark University. The inheritance of acquired characteristics fit nicely with American social theorists in much the same way that Spencer's individualism played into the hands of Manchesterian economic theory. Far more than with Darwin, for whom there was admiration but no widespread acceptance of his theory of natural selection, American social scientists, particularly those who were reform-minded, felt comfortable with a modified Lamarckian doctrine to explain the inheritance of acquired traits.[42]

Ward refused to accept a "chance" universe, believing it bred stagnation and stifled progress, yielding only contentment (or pessimism) and inaction. Nature was neither friendly nor hostile to humanity, neither favoring nor discriminating. While man could not increase or diminish the powers inherent in nature, he did have the ability to direct them by increasing or diminishing their impact. "He can focalize the rays of the sun; he can divert the courses of the rivers; he can direct the currents of the air; he can vary temperatures; he can change water to steam and set the steam to work in propelling machinery or ships or railroad trains; he can utilize electricity. His power over nature is unlimited. He can make it his servant and appropriate to his own use all the mighty forces of the universe."[43]

With advanced civilization came the adoption of the spirit of *meliorism* and, with it, the liberty of opinion and the freedom to investigate, possess, and subjugate the powers of nature to one's personal or collective use. "It is only because all nature is a domain of rigid law, of absolute impartiality, and devoid of all moral quality and all intelligence, that man can hope to carve out of it his fortune or shape his destiny." There is no fixed way of doing things. The outcome depends entirely upon the initiative of whoever first launched it. There was no telling what humans could discover, much less do. The human was the only social being known to be endowed with life, feeling, and thought.[44] Thus, for Ward, natural selection explained humans' early development, but Lamarckism explained how evolution progressed following the development of the higher faculties.[45]

American society seemed predisposed to accept Neo-Lamarckism for the very reason that it seemed more compatible with its general scheme of the world. The inheritance of acquired characteristics explained how societies grew and how the mental faculties, particularly those of the Anglo-Saxon race, developed capacities far in advance of the rest of humankind. Truly, the idea of the inheritance of acquired characteristics explained the full measure of the mental faculties, racial differences, and of the social behavior of persons. Whether identified as Neo-Lamarckian or as Social Darwinism, the response of the organism to its environment proved to be the telling mechanism whereby habits became instincts ("race instincts" and "race habits") causing social development to take a specific direction.

Ward accepted the fact that many would remain skeptical if not outright distrustful of government, but there was no reason to exclude the possibility that government could be made useful, protective, and interventionist on behalf of humanity.[46] Admitting to government's corrosive history and that some governments continued to use their powers to injure their citizens, he nonetheless insisted that government had the capacity to grow in general intelligence and enlightenment, acquiring scientifically based functions that acted for the benefit of society. True, many legislators had proven to be "mere bunglers," knowing little of the laws of society. Until now, society and its legislators had lived in "the 'stone age' of the art of government." But to the degree that social art could be directed by science, progressive legislation had the potential to bring millions of individuals together in common cause.[47]

Ward viewed society as a "compound organism" whose actions exhibited the combined individual forces of its members. The challenge was whether man could control those social forces to his advantage. Could he, using telic foresight, succeed in harmonizing the myriad of individual forces to bring the greatest advantage to the whole? Having attacked the defenders of laissez-faire with their let-alone policies creating positive harm to the body politic, he looked to scientifically based legislation that would redirect the forces of the state to secure the greatest benefits to its people.[48]

## SOCIOCRACY

When Alfred Wallace read Ward's *Psychic Factors of Civilization*, he was particularly taken with the author's opposition to Spencer's individualism, a position that closely aligned with his own beliefs. "How dreadfully Herbert Spencer has fallen off in his *Justice*," Wallace wrote to his friend. He noted that much of Ward's book formed "an excellent work on the Scientific Basis of Socialism which would have great value as a weapon against the individualist school, and would enlighten many who are now blinded by the prestige of Spencer and the Political Economists." As noted in an earlier chapter, Wallace expressed his interest in land nationalization and, after reading Henry George's *Progress and Poverty* and Edward Bellamy's *Looking Backward* and *Equality*, declared himself a socialist.[49] Ward, who preferred not to call himself a socialist, suggested in its stead the term *sociocracy*, by which he meant a society devoid of inequalities, and benefits distributed according to merit.[50] Unlike Marx, Ward had no interest in class struggle; nor was he interested in expropriating the instruments of production. His approach remained progressively hopeful that a socialized society would be realized incrementally from the steady determination of human perseverance.[51] Sociocracy was not to be confounded with socialism or with competitive individualism. In his *Outlines of Sociology*, he made clear the distinctions:

1. Individualism has created artificial inequalities.
2. Socialism seeks to create artificial equalities.
3. Sociocracy recognizes natural inequalities and aims to abolish artificial inequalities.
4. Individualism confers benefits on those only who have the ability to obtain them, by superior power, cunning, intelligence, or the accident of position.

5. Socialism would confer the same benefits on all alike and aims to secure equality of fruition.

6. Sociocracy would confer benefits in strict proportion to merit but insists upon equality of opportunity as the only means of determining the degree of merit.[52]

Ward forecasted that all governments (e.g., autocracy, monarchy, aristocracy, plutocracy) would eventually transition through democracy on their way to sociocracy, which he defined as a government that operated purely on behalf of society's interests. In contrast to those democratic governments that were largely party-run governments, sociocracy focused entirely on the needs of the people. Resting on the science of sociology to investigate the facts, it prevented any special group from benefiting over another. Instead, it operated "for the best interests of society at large."[53] Provided this took place, Ward predicted that the bulk of government activity would devolve into a form of investigation into the nature of humankind. Much like an academy of science, or a statistical bureau, scientific experts would constitute the future workforce of government. Hence the term *social physics*, by which Ward meant that future laws would result from recommendations carefully worked out in a clinical setting. Sociology became the means for adjusting the institutional framework of society to the inherent social forces residing in man. In a sociocratic society, citizens were expected to act on the findings of experts.[54]

Sociocracy, the final step in political evolution, made government the ideal agency to remove partisanship and hypocrisy from governing. Under it, Ward envisioned an enlightened government that guarded and furthered individual and collective interests.[55] In this ideal world, legislators worked with sociologists to fuse scientific lawmaking. Reflective of Comte's Religion of Humanity, the sociologist applied scientific evidence to control and redirect the unruly aspects of social forces to more positive ends. Here, education carried out by the state ensured that useful information would extend to all classes. Rather than leave the social system to the wiles of nature, uninspired and drifting by chance, sociology became man's artificial intrusion into the natural process, promoting a telic approach to legislation. Believing that progress would be obtained "in proportion to the degree and universality of intelligence," he insisted that "no effort or expense would be spared to impart to every citizen an equal and adequate amount of useful knowledge."[56]

Ward threw himself into the relationship of the individual to society with all the energy he could muster. Though he did not, like Marx, erect a detailed structure of his ideal government, he identified those positive elements that ought to exist in his *Applied Sociology*, which he intended as the "crown" of his system. Between those who accepted evolution as God's means of progression and those who emphasized man's blundering in helplessness except to mimic nature's benign neglect, Ward offered *meliorism*, which injected purposive intelligence into the functions of the state. The purpose of sociology and its place at the summit of the sciences required that it deal "in a thoroughly scientific way with all the facts and phenomena of society."[57]

## ACADEMIC SOCIOLOGY

When Ward announced his intent to resign from government service in 1906, William Herbert Perry Faunce, president of Brown University, offered him a position on the faculty. For the next seven years, Ward taught three elective classes for upperclassmen and graduate students. "Of all the men who flourished in America during the period centering around the year 1900, whom will the after world wish to know intimately more than Dr. Ward?" This remark by Harry L. Koopman, university librarian at Brown, speaks to Ward's reputation as a teacher and scholar during the years he was on the faculty.[58] According to one of his students, "every lecture was a recapitulation of evolution; not that tremendous striving of nature, with its waste and failures, its trials and errors, its barbarous natural selection; but the superior artificial selection which charms the reasoning mind of man."[59] "I had read everything that Spencer had published," remarked Albion W. Small at the University of Chicago, "but the elements of his method that afterward seemed to me most useful failed to find me at first." After reading *Dynamic Sociology*, however, Small found it acted as a reagent to ideas long stirring in his mind. "The moment I began to turn the leaves of the book, I was aware of feelings as the alchemists might have felt two or three centuries earlier if they had stumbled upon the 'philosophers' stone.'"[60] It caused Small to think of physical and psychical phenomena as equally real and as equally instrumental as causation within human beings.

The Department of Social Sciences at Brown University became deeply invested in Ward's approach and used his *Pure Sociology* as a textbook for its undergraduate class. A more simplified edition of it came out in 1905 as *The Text Book of Sociology*. Ward dominated the field of sociology in its early years. During his lifetime his books were translated into German, French, Spanish, Italian, Russian, Polish, and Japanese.[61]

His ideas spread through university faculty in the Midwest and East, lasting into the 1930s, where he was rediscovered by New Deal liberals who projected his sociocracy into FDR's programs. Of the top five sociology departments in the United States—Chicago, Columbia, Wisconsin, Minnesota, and Michigan—four of the five were in the Midwest, the stronghold of populism and progressivism, with Chicago supplying more than half the presidents of the American Sociological Society. By contrast to the social Darwinist conservatism of East Coast schools, the Midwest looked to sociology as a science of social reconstruction. Only five sociologists contributed more than a single textbook to American sociology by 1908: Spencer, Ward, Albion W. Small, Franklin H. Giddings, and John Bascom.[62]

Unlike European sociology, which advanced the collective concept of society as a "super individual organism" obeying either the Comtean laws of progress or Spencerian laws of evolution, American sociology tended to favor a form of unreflective individualism that addressed the changing environment in the form of pragmatism, economic determinism, legal realism, and other forms of liberal-conservative movements.[63] Sociology became a representation of middle-class aspirations in the United States, which, not having to contend with an established aristocracy or state church, divided between pro-business Hamiltonians who supported eastern businessmen, industrialists, and financiers, and Jeffersonians who represented small-town businessmen and farmers.

One of the true sociological giants of the nineteenth century, Ward offset the reigning mechanistic theories of evolution by adding a "psychic factor" to human development. Accepting Spencer's cosmology and biology, he nonetheless chose to reject altogether his sociology, believing that human progress could and should be artificially controlled. As a founder of modern psychological sociology, he introduced the power of life's subjective elements and their contribution to the betterment of society.[64] Sociology was not just the sum of generalizations derived from the natural sciences, but a creative new science that, embracing all truth, assisted the state in securing the welfare of man.[65] He saw the future as one founded on an intelligent use of government, whose political synergy brought cooperation between opposing groups. Society could be brought under a consciously planned form of control that was telic, guided by an informed social science and sustained through education.[66]

"Throughout Ward's work ran one dominating and organizing thought," explained Franklin Giddings: "Human society, as we who live now know it, is not the passive product of unconscious forces. It lies within the domain of cosmic law, but so does the mind of man: and this mind has knowingly, artfully, adapted and readapted its environment, and with reflective intelligence has begun to shape it into an instrument wherewith to fulfill man's will."[67] A pragmatist when it came to society, Ward constantly sought freedom from doubt along with the consequences of meaning and truth by turning the practical improvements of society toward higher moral purposes. The moral imperative was in making knowledge work for social betterment, a factor that aligned with the views of Charles Sanders Peirce and William James.[68]

## SELECTED WRITINGS

*Dynamic Sociology* (1883)
*Neo-Darwinism and Neo-Lamarckism* (1891)
*The Psychic Factors of Civilization* (1893)
*Contributions to Social Philosophy* (1895–1897)
*Outlines of Sociology* (1898)
*Pure Sociology* (1903)
*Applied Sociology* (1906)
*Social Classes in the Light of Modern Sociological Theory* (1908)
*Glimpses of the Cosmos* (1913–1918)

# 9

## Entheism
## Paul Carus

*Science is divine; science is a revelation of God. Through science God commu-*
*nicates with us. In science he speaks to us. Science gives us information con-*
*cerning the truth; and the truth reveals his will.*

> —Paul Carus, "Science a Religious Revelation," 1893

INDEBTED TO THE WORKS OF Auguste Comte, Henri de Saint-Simon, and Pierre-Simon Laplace, positivists in post–Civil War America stressed the importance of theory and observation in arriving at authentic verifiable knowledge. All knowledge, whether scientific, philosophical, or religious, was discernible in a concise and exhaustive manner through natural laws, rather than from unquantifiable a priori or intuitive thought. One particularly outspoken advocate of this positivist tradition was the Illinois publisher and editor Paul Carus (1852–1919), who, in answer to the charge that religion and science were incompatible, constructed a religion of science replete with cosmological assurances intended to offset skepticism, materialism, and the dysteleological implications of natural selection. Carus insisted on a form of idealistic monism, suggesting that religion and science *must* be compatible or the domains of both would shatter. A radical in substance but a conservative in style, he followed the path of Comte in rejecting orthodoxy's dogmas but retaining its traditional terminology and even its rituals.[1] The medium for Carus's lifelong discussion of religion and science was the Open Court Publishing Company of Chicago, whose magazines the *Open Court* (1887–1936) and the *Monist* (1890–1936) provided the means for lively communication between and among a world-class group of American, European, and Asian scholars—some established, others on the rise.

### EARLY YEARS

The son of a Lutheran pastor who rose through the ranks of the Reformed Church to become the first superintendent general of the church in Prussia, Paul Carus grew up in Ilsenburg am Harz, where he attended the gymnasia at Posen and Stettin, studying under the direction of the scholar Hermann Günther Grassmann, whose encyclopedic curiosity and proficiency in mathematics introduced Carus to the philosophy of form, linguistics, and the study of Sanskrit.

From the gymnasia, Carus pursued his studies at the universities of Greifswald, Strassburg, and Tübingen, which at the time were expanding their transmission of knowledge by including the sciences (*Wissenschaft*) in their curricula. This, plus newer studies and interpretations of the Bible and the publication of Darwin's *Origin of Species*, resulted in a whole new set of standards for acquiring certitude. Initially intent on entering the ministry, Carus experienced a crisis of faith and, unable to subscribe to his father's orthodoxy, turned to the study of philosophy, philology, and the natural sciences. Aspiring to become a teacher, he set his mind on constructing a worldview compatible with what he discovered in the sciences.

After earning his doctor of philosophy in classical philology in 1876, Carus served briefly in the Twelfth Saxon Artillery Regiment in Mertz, before accepting an appointment to the military academy of the Royal Corps of Cadets in Dresden, where he held the position of Oberlehrer, or senior teacher of Latin, German, and history. Anxious to express his support of biblical research, he wrote a pamphlet in 1880 praising the literary beauty of scripture in a manner reflective of the higher critics and cautioning that it not be read in any strict literal sense. Faced with backlash from his peers, he chose to resign his position rather than retract his beliefs.[2]

After leaving the academy, Carus traveled the continent before residing briefly in England, where he learned the basics of the English language prior to immigrating to the United States in 1885. Like many young adults in his day, he intended to test his abilities and aspirations in America, believing it offered the opportune place and time to make his mark in the world. Soon after his arrival, he found initial employment teaching German in the Boston schools. A short time later, he moved to New York, where he was employed as coeditor for publisher Verlag von S. Zickel's *Novellen-schatz und Familien-blätter*. On occasion, Carus also contributed poetry to the *Index*, a leftwing Unitarian magazine published by the Free Religious Association and supported by the philosopher and economist Henry George, author of *Progress and Poverty* (1879).[3]

*MONISM AND MELIORISM*

Carus's next effort to express his philosophy, specifically the matter of causality and ethics, came with his first monograph, a fifty-five-page booklet titled *Monism and Meliorism* (1885), published by F. W. Christern, a German bookseller in New York City. In it Carus explained monism (sometimes called "New Positivism," "Philosophy of Science," and "New Realism") as standing for a conception of the world that traced everything, including the soul of man, to a single source or principle. Monism conceived of the world as "one inseparable and indivisible entirety" continually corroborated by the progress of science. Meliorism, on the other hand, stood for a view of life that, rejecting both optimism and pessimism, found purpose in man's "aspiration . . . to some higher state of existence." The world was neither completely good nor evil, but subject to improvement following the path of biological and social evolution.[4]

Appreciative of the groundbreaking work of Comte's progressive school of positivism, Carus nonetheless accused Comte and his disciples of being agnostic to the core, even to the point of failing to identify a "touchstone" by which to distinguish whether matter was a positive fact or an illusion. Instead of addressing this basic problem in philosophy, Comte declared it "unsolvable." In similar fashion Herbert Spencer had collected and systematized data on the material world, but his efforts had ended in the *Unknown*. "We have high respect for Mr. Spencer as a man and a thinker," wrote Carus, "but it is a great pity that with all his brilliant talents . . . he is a dilettante. . . . Mr. Spencer, as a thinker, follows the principle of Hedonism; he shirks the toil of research and engages in such subjects only as can easily be woven into feuilletonistic essays."[5] Kant, on the other hand, did not shirk from the challenge of identifying whether matter was a positive fact or an illusion, constructing a philosophy that stood its ground against the Spiritualism of George Berkeley and the crass materialism of Étienne Bonnot de Condillac, Baron d'Holbach, and the French encyclopedists. "What Luther did for religion, and Copernicus for science, Kant has done for philosophic thought," explained Carus. He inaugurated a new philosophic spirit and a set of new humanitarian ideals based on individual freedom and human rights.[6]

Notwithstanding his admiration for Kant, Carus concluded that he, too, had failed to solve the problem satisfactorily, having lost himself in "the intricate paths and windings of his strange idealism." In his *Critique of Pure Reason* (1781), Kant showed that time and space were not realities but mere *phenomena*, and that beliefs about the soul, world, and God that had stood for more than a thousand years were *noumena*, that is, concepts.[7] Kant offered both an atheistic and a theistic approach, likening God to the sea in its vastness and grandeur. "The diver strikes down into its depth and the sailor swims on the surface," explained Carus. "The one finds precious pearls and corals in its abysses; the other encompasses a cognizance of its extension but declares it to be a stormy and sterile water-desert, wherein no precious things are to be found." The sailor in this analogy represented pure reason, while the diver spoke on behalf of human emotions. But this, according to Carus, was not sufficient. "If the philosopher is not able to combine both, he will be either a shallow rationalist, keeping constantly on the surface, thus gathering his cognition superficially, or a thoughtless zealot, a prejudiced and one-sided bigot." With Kant's failure to find the higher unity he had been searching, "the universality of the law [was] lost, and all the affairs of the world, instead of being one uninterrupted chain of causes and effects [were] dissolved into unaccountable and innumerable particularities."[8]

Carus's choice method for binding the loose ends left by prior philosophers was to add monism to the philosophy of positivism. "True positivism is monistic," he insisted, and "true monism is positive." As a monist, Carus rejected the terms "first" and "final" causes, insisting they were complicit with outdated theology. The idea of a first cause in the sense of a Creator was a contradiction. Similarly, the term "final cause" was invented on the supposition that a first cause assumed some transcendent power had arranged the world to accomplish some specific end or purpose. Instead, he substituted the term *finis*, an idea that affirmed a purpose or an ideal toward which the cosmos was moving.[9] "Only by knowing the *finis*, the *whither* of the development of the world, can we find out the nature and *character* of the final principle of the cosmos, which represents the *whence* of all movement in the universe, the ultimate ground and source from which all activity starts. Now, if the tendency of amelioration prevails everywhere, we should apply this law to the final principle, which pervades the macrocosm. So the aspiration towards ever higher aims on the high road of infinitude and eternity seems to be the inmost, the sublimest and grandest characteristic of this final interior of nature, the groundwork of the world."[10]

Monism implied a unity or principle that permeated the cosmos, inclusive of all things spiritual and material toward which evolution tended. "Things are not single existences, but form one entire whole," and all tendencies, while seemingly different, aspired toward the same *finis*. In the world of monism, spirit and matter were mere abstractions—the oneness of existence with no differences of kind, no Creator or created, no supernatural or natural. Carus's initial idea of monism reflected the positions taken by Ernst Mach and Ernst Haeckel in that he rejected dualism as unscientific, proclaiming instead a oneness of truth and the unity of the universe. Monism denied any split between the subjective and objective—the enigma that had proved satisfying yet so incomprehensible. On the other hand, he rejected both materialism and agnosticism, appealing instead to the philosophy of *forms* introduced by his mentor Grassmann, who maintained that the noumena and phenomena were one.[11] God, the human spirit, and the universe were one, replacing the egocentric consciousness of the human being with the consciousness of the All-One. Reality was indivisible even between the organic and inorganic.[12]

In its most basic identity, monism represents a belief that mind and matter are simply different aspects of a single substance, though it is not always clear whether the attributes of that substance are more similar to the attributes of mind or to matter. Holding that religion (when approached scientifically) and science were two sides of the same coin, Carus argued that a proper study of both resulted in "one law only in the world which in its purely formal relations is the condition of all uniformities in the world."[13] For lack of better word, the eternal laws of *form* stood for Carus's God, whom he defined as the *principle* of form. God was the sum of the omnipresent laws or forms, which he explained in his motto on the title page of his *Fundamental Problems* (1891):

Not agnosticism but positive Science
Not mysticism but clear thought,
Neither supernaturalism nor materialism
But a unitary conception of the world
Not dogma but Religion, Not creed but faith.[14]

God was not a "person," only an expression of pious sentiment interwoven with numerous errors. If the word *God* was to remain in the lexicon, it was human duty "to eliminate the false notions and to point out the truth which it contains." In his *Idea of God* (1888), he created a new word for God, which he labeled *entheism*, denoting a monistic God that was immanent but not transcendent, different from and superior to nature, yet pervading all nature.[15] Entheism stood for the indestructible something in everything that exists. It constituted the direction of evolution and the growth of life, the actuality that could not be lost in any changes that took place in the universe. "It is eternal, and it is in him we live and move and have our being."[16]

While Christian theologians based the ethics of their religion on the Ten Commandments (i.e., the authority of an anthropomorphic God), the Spencerians on the subjective principle of happiness or hedonism, and still others on utilitarianism and asceticism, Carus insisted that a life worth living was one "full of active aspiration for something higher and better," which he called *meliorism*.[17] Meliorism was not a regulative law but a natural law representing the very core and inmost quality of the world. The purpose of an organism's existence was always something higher than itself—a characteristic that pervaded all organic nature. Organisms could not exist but under the principle of meliorism. Though the world was full of evil and misery, over time all being would become good and perfect as evolution tended toward a constant amelioration that, in turn, led to "the interminable, infinite path of progress, not as Darwin says, merely ruled by the famous law of the struggle for life, but enhanced by the *strife for the ideal*."[18]

## Edward G. Hegeler

Carus's monograph came to the attention of Edward G. Hegeler (1835–1910), who, along with his schoolmate and business partner Frederick William Matthiessen (1835–1918), emigrated to the United States in 1857, where they started a highly successful zinc smelter and manufacturing operation near LaSalle, Illinois, utilizing the zinc deposits at Mineral Point, Wisconsin, to supply their needs. Hegeler was also an amateur philosopher, whose generosity helped support the New York Society for Ethical Culture (1876) and the Free Religious Association of Boston (1869), which were devoted to finding truth in some yet-to-be-determined middle ground between scientific rationalism and religious faith. An inquiring thinker, Hegeler devoted a considerable portion of his wealth to advocate for his own idiosyncratic belief in monism by founding the Open Court Publishing Company, which he dedicated to placing religion and ethics on a scientific basis. His choice of editor was Benjamin Franklin Underwood (1839–1914), an outspoken materialist and agnostic who had been editor of the *Index*, a magazine published by the Free Religious Association. Underwood authored numerous pamphlets, including *Darwinism: What It Is and the Proofs in Favor of It* (1875), *The Crimes and Cruelties of Christianity* (1877), *Woman: Her Past and Present, Her Rights and Wrongs* (1877); *The Influence of Christianity on Civilization* (1889); and *Herbert Spencer's Synthetic Philosophy* (1891).[19]

When Underwood reached out to Hegeler for support of the financially troubled *Index*, he received instead an offer to start a new magazine that would replace the eclectic nature of the *Index* with a more purposeful philosophy that harmonized with what they both believed was a shared vision of monism. A freethinker and champion of materialistic philosophy, Underwood seemed a likely match for Hegeler's intentions, but differences arose almost immediately, due largely to Underwood's extreme form of materialism and his insistence on maintaining full control over the magazine's editorial and managerial responsibilities. Hegeler, however, insisted on being more than just the publisher, and as their respective interpretation of monism became more visibly divergent, and because both men were strong-willed, it was only a matter of time before their differences became less and less tolerable.[20]

Much to his regret, Underwood had introduced Hegeler to Paul Carus, speaking highly of his monograph and gifting the publisher with a short book of poems written by the young man. Hegeler not only appreciated the gift but, finding himself in agreement with most of what Carus had written, offered him employment as a tutor for his children and the position of coeditor of the *Open Court*. The latter appointment, made without consulting Underwood, precipitated a deep distrust in their relationship and an even greater resentment toward Carus, whom Underwood considered an unprincipled conniver. While the Underwoods (Benjamin and his wife, Sara) worked out of the offices of the Open Court Company in Chicago, several hours by train from the Hegeler family home in LaSalle, Carus lived with the Hegelers, benefited from daily conversations with the publisher, and began courting the family's eldest daughter, Mary. To further complicate matters, Carus wrote a series of articles on religion and science, which Hegeler personally edited and directed Underwood to publish, insisting they were important contributions. Seen from Underwood's point of view, the articles "were an irritation and an embarrassment."[21] As Underwood would later explain, he viewed Carus's efforts to resuscitate the role of religion, and especially Christianity, in the modern world wholly at odds with the magazine's original purpose. Viewing Christianity as "one of the great evils" of the world, he saw no reason why it might change for the better because of science. Christianity was no better informed than pagan superstition and therefore destined to become obsolete and forgotten.[22]

Feeling disadvantaged by his lack of direct communication with Hegeler and by what he perceived as the publisher's undisguised admiration for Carus, Underwood accused Hegeler of using the journal to advance the work of one author, a preference that violated the very definition of the word "open" in the magazine's name. Underwood's insistence on preserving the philosophical neutrality of the journal became a point of contention that ran counter to Hegeler's missionary bias toward monism and quickly became a pretext as well for his personal animosity toward Carus. Feeling he had reached an impasse for which there was no real solution, Underwood resigned, whereupon Hegeler appointed Carus as editor. Soon afterward, Carus and Mary Hegeler married, and for the next thirty-two years, Carus served as editor of the *Open Court* and its sister journal, the *Monist*, which he started in 1890.[23]

## The Open Court

In his first issue as editor of the *Open Court*, Carus announced his (and Hegeler's) intention of using the journal to advance the philosophy of monism by replacing the superstitions and falsehoods of religious ortho-doxy with a more spiritualized and scientifically verifiable faith—a posi-tion substantively different from that which Underwood thought Hegeler had originally agreed upon. As Carus explained, the *Open Court* "dis-cusses the philosophical problems of God and soul, of life and death, and life after death, the problems of the origin of man and the significance of religion, and the nature of morality, occasionally including political and social life without, however, entering into party questions."[24] Clearly, Hegeler had found someone whose philosophy was more in harmony with his own and who, without disagreement, would devote the magazine to the work of reconciling religion with science, rather than treating them as perennial enemies. A thinker in his own right, Hegeler authored nu-merous articles in the *Open Court*, including "The Basis of Ethics," "Hap-piness and Ethics," "The Kernel of Religion," "The Soul," and "What the Monistic Religion Is to Me."

Despite Carus's strong personal advocacy of monistic philosophy, he transformed the *Open Court* and the *Monist* into lively centers of debate around issues of the day. His cadre of scholars included evolutionary bi-ologist George John Romanes; geologist and explorer John Wesley Pow-ell; geologist Joseph LeConte; philosopher and theologian Francis Elling-wood Abbot; French psychologist Alfred Binet; botanist, paleontologist, and sociologist Lester Frank Ward; German biologist and philosopher Ernst Haeckel; Dutch botanist and geneticist Hugo de Vries; philosopher and psychologist John Dewey; philosopher and intellectual historian Ar-thur O. Lovejoy; essayist and playwright T. S. Eliot; Japanese Zen Bud-dhist D. T. Suzuki; and British philosopher and logician Bertrand Russell. Among his favorites were the Sanskrit scholar and philologist Friedrich Max Müller; the Austrian physicist and philosopher Ernst Mach; and the truculent philosopher, logician, and mathematician Charles Saunders

Peirce. Gracious and courteous to all, including William James, whose pragmatic philosophy he vigorously opposed, he transformed the journals into forums of open discussion on some of philosophy's most contentious subjects.[25]

By 1903, the *Open Court* had a circulation of 3,000, and the *Monist* a circulation of 750. Their combined circulation never exceeded 5,600.[26]

## RELIGION AND SCIENCE

In 1893 Carus published his *Religion of Science* with the intention of preserving all that proved good and true in religion while discarding its irrational elements and errors. From *Monism and Meliorism*, which he had written eight years earlier, to *The Religion of Science*, Carus had traveled a considerable distance from his earlier agnosticism to an almost missionary passion for reconciling the purposes of science and religion. Admitting that America's churches were not as conservative as their dogmas pretended to be, he set out to retain their warmth and enthusiasm while using the higher criticism to remove their "sectarian narrowness and dogmatic crudities." In essence, *The Religion of Science* represented a protest against the "pagan spirit" within church orthodoxy that had brought it in conflict with science. But rather than encourage a new sect, he urged the establishment of an "invisible church" whose members acknowledged "that truth has not been revealed once and once only, but that we are constantly facing the revelation of truth, and that the scientific method of searching for truth is the same in religious matters as in other fields." He cared not that those who acknowledged this invisible church called themselves Christians, Jews, Buddhists, Moslems, or simply freethinkers.[27]

This volte-face in thinking represented a significant change from Carus's earlier beliefs. Now, the Open Court Publishing Company served as the operational center for the reformation of religion under the influence of science and the law of evolution. Science was slowly transforming all aspects of life with truths verified by rational proof, experience, and experiment. While doing away with ignorance and bigotry, science was not, as some critics claimed, ushering in an age of irreligion. Instead, it was proving the human origin of the Bible, the outdated anthropomorphism of the old God-conception, and discrediting the traditional theory of a soul-entity. The age was one of transition—the disintegration of dogma and the reconstruction of faith on the foundation of science. The truth of evolution as a general principle of all life meant not the destruction of the old but the building of a higher and truer religion. "We are too much convinced of the truth of evolution as a general principle of all life, not to apply it also to the spiritual domains of civilization, morality and religion." The path to truth naturally passed through periods of myth, allegory, parables, and mysticism before transitioning to a scientific understanding. This was the law of evolution.[28]

Traditional religions were the "harbingers" preparing the way through parable, mythology, and allegory for their eventual fulfillment in science. Founded prior to the scientific methods of inquiry, they had relied on prophets for explanations and guidance. Even in their imperfect form, they provided solace to mankind. Indifferent to the historical Jesus, which he considered sufficiently addressed by the reverent but scientific and critical research of Heinrich Julius Holtzmann, a professor of theology at the University of Strasburg, Carus admired the Christ-ideal with its legends and poetical visions representing mankind's aspiration toward perfection. There was a distinction between the Christ-ideal and the Christian worship of Christ, which he equated to paganism. Unfortunately, most Christians had chosen the latter, making their religion a "fetish worship" significantly different from the actual injunctions of Christ.[29]

Besides the distinction between the historical Jesus and the Christ-ideal, Carus noted a difference between "Christian prayer," which he described as a superstitious trust in miracles, and "Christ's prayer," which he defined as an effort to change the individual's will, not God's will. Unlike the techniques of self-help and auto-suggestion recommended by the advocates of New Thought, prayer had to be lived, not simply spoken. It was not an incantation but an act of self-discipline that attuned the will of a person to the will of God. True Christianity was not just a moral factor in the world, but *the* moral factor in the evolution of mankind." To their discredit, however, most Christians preferred blind belief over investigation. Their distrust of the inductive sciences ("sense-information") made their acceptance of God's revelation one-sided, trusting the wisdom of Isaiah at the expense of Darwin.[30]

The often-made claim that the God of the old religion was dead, and that the leaves of its dogmatic opinions were falling to the ground, was not a dreary depiction of a future empty of purpose, but a sign that a new religion was stirring, whose branches would soon grow in the hearts of mankind. The new religion would be an ethical one—realistic for its love of truth and its ennoblement of human life. Similarly, the new ethics was not founded on the authority of a power foreign to humanity but "upon a more correct understanding of man and man's natural tendency to progress and raise himself to a higher plane of work, and to a nobler activity."

The hoped-for triumph of a better future did not mean revolution or dis-respect for the old but an evolution with "due reverence for the merits of the past."[31]

Carus accused most of those who called themselves Christians of liv-ing outside the Christianity of Christ and the religion of science. Prefer-ring to believe in their mythology, they carried on their lives ignorant of religion's esoteric spirit and the individual's personal relation to the "All-being" that quieted the troubles and anxieties of life. "We live to perform work. We have a mission. There are duties imposed upon us," Carus in-sisted. There could be no genuine happiness other than "the rapture of the God moving in us." The abyss that separated the religion of science from the orthodox religions of the world remained broad and deep, but concealed behind its many artifices, Christianity was a "cosmic religion . . . founded in the constitution of the universe."[32]

The dogmatic and miraculous faiths of the past were gone. Rent by the effects of the higher criticism and challenged by the implications of the theory of natural selection, church doctrines appeared as so many an-cient artifacts dragged along in the baggage as humanity marched into the future. "Why can it not be acknowledged that tenets which our fathers considered as truths of divine revelation, were after all their personal and private opinions only?" Carus asked. Science had caused church dogma to drift into a sea of opinion, speculation, and doubt, as if there never had been a fixed and orthodox faith in the world. While in previous times ministers preached to audiences who believed the Bible to be a divine book, many now had ceased to accept it. Such freedom in thinking about spiritual things challenged the functions and mission of the Christian churches. As the moral instructor of mankind, the church "should not be dragged along behind the triumphant march of humanity but should deploy in front with the vanguard of science!"[33] Carus considered him-self a preacher who belonged to no church and pledged to no dogma or creed; instead, he taught the religion of humanity, which pledged to be faithful to facts verified by experiment. "If Christianity means the dogma-tism of the Church, it is an historical religion which will disappear in the course of time; if it means the doctrine of Christ, the fulfillment of the law through love, it will be the religion of mankind."[34]

With religion defined as "a conviction that regulates man's conduct, af-fords comfort in affliction, and consecrates all the purposes of life," and science as "the methodical search for truth," Carus aspired to find truth using the most reliable scientific methods. Rejecting all manner of past revelations, dogmas, creeds, and rituals, there remained only those truths discoverable by the application of the scientific method. Much like Comte's "Religion of Humanity," Carus did not object to the continued use of sacraments, ceremonies, and rituals so long as they represented the outward form of a spiritual relationship between man and God. If used, they could not imply any intrinsic or mystical power; nor were they indispensable to belief.[35] Again, like Comte, Carus treated scientists as society's newest prophets, who alone had the authority to validate truths. As prophets, they spoke not of God, or of religion, but only the results of their investigations. They had the responsibility to discover the moral law of nature and its corollaries, all of which formed the harmonious system of regularity.[36]

Carus's radical convictions were governed by a conservative instinct to reinterpret traditional dogmas scientifically, including the retention of the terms *God* and *immortality*. He considered *God* to be one of the most interesting expressions in the human language. Whether a truth or a hallucination of the mind, the term benefited from a unique history whose origins lay shrouded in obscurity. Nevertheless, it carried enormous influence in Platonic, Aristotelian, and Neo-Platonic philosophies that considered God the creator of the world and master of man's fate. So varied was the idea of God, explained Carus, that "we make bold to say that every single individual has a conception of his own." In viewing its various meanings through history, he chose theism as the more reasonable view in that God had been cleansed of its cruder anthropomorphic attributes.[37]

Having lost the supernatural religion of his youth and finding little satisfaction in skepticism and atheism, Carus retraced his steps to the inspiring and spiritual significance of God minus any anthropomorphic sense of fatherly love or the dispenser of destinies. God was the eternal norm of truth and righteousness, a superpersonal "All" found not in theology but in a philosophical concept he termed *theonomy*.[38] Carus likened God to that law, form, or principle that stood for the natural law. God was the outcome of the philosophy of forms—the authority or law of the cosmos, the "author of the moral ought." God was the eternal law in the world that made harmony, evolution, aspiration, and morality possible. To conceive God as a person was the equivalent of poetry, not science.[39]

As for "immortality," Carus insisted that the souls of the dead continued to communicate with the living, but only in their minds. No thought was gone forever but remained a reality in the soul-life of humanity, which consisted of "the immortalized precipitate of the sentiments, ideas, and acts done in past years, dating back to the beginning of soul-life upon earth." Every thought remained part of the whole. Past and present lived together in the soul-life, which was real. "It is the kingdom of God of which Jesus said that it is within us" and not the "ghost-immortality" of the Christian doctrine of resurrection, which Carus dismissed as a crude allegorical expression.[40]

"All our ancestors live in us," Carus explained, "their souls are with us and will remain with us even unto the end of the world. And so, we shall live even though the body dies." The soul neither began with birth nor ended with death; it existed wherever ideas were thought "and shall exist wherever they are thought again; for not only our body is our self, but mainly our ideas. Our true self was spiritual in nature." Seen in this light, each individual soul-life was part of a greater whole, which, in the scheme of evolution, evolved to ever higher planes of spiritual existence. The soul's immortality was a scientific truth whose continuance lay not in the Christian scheme of the body's resurrection but in the incarnation of God in "the soul of our soul." Eternal and ever evolving, the "soul of our soul" was "not our individual self, but God in us."[41]

Carus faced tough criticism for his *Religion of Science*, accused of offering a "conglomeration of self-contradictory ideas."[42] Undeterred, he insisted there was a power in the world that man was obliged to recognize as the "norm of truth and the standard of right conduct." Claiming that his life's work was to uphold the "cosmic order" or "universal Logos" as an eternal abiding reality of the moral law, he declared God a "superindividual reality" scientifically provable by evidence. Without such a God, "science would be mere verbiage, religion meaningless, and ethics an impossibility." God was "the measure of goodness and the moral law of life"—the unity of the universe and the harmony in its order. The God of the religion of science was not a new God but the old God of the Jews and the God of every prophet, only purified.[43]

Not surprisingly, many of the very people who supported Carus's religion of science rejected his use of the terms *God* and *immortality* as inconsistent with the facts of science. Unperturbed by the criticism, Carus insisted that the terms contained altogether different meanings from those used by the historical religions. Free of all supernaturalism and anthropomorphism, God stood for the ultimate authority by which man regulated his conduct. Carus used the term *entheism*, which defined God not as an object of worship but as the law of Nature. Alternative terms were "Morality," "the Good," "the Ethical law," or "the Natural Aspiration for the Ideal."[44]

Though he affirmed the ethics of Christ, it was clear that Carus was not Christian in any traditional sense of the term. Christ and Christianity represented opposite systems of belief. There are two kinds of Christianity: the one was spiritual in nature, teaching the life and death of Christ; the other was organizational and claimed the acceptance of certain dogmas as indispensable conditions for salvation. The former represented the soul of civilization, while the latter proved to be "an embarrassing dead weight on the feet of mankind, obstructing all progress and higher development."[45] Ultimately, Carus despaired of Christianity ever fulfilling its cosmic purpose as the religion of universal truth, since it continued to cling to its mythology and failed to see any meaning deeper than its fictions. Christianity had not sufficiently matured to receive and accept the truth.[46]

## World's Parliament of Religions

The World's Parliament of Religions, which opened in September 1893 during the Columbian Exposition in Chicago, made a lasting impression on Carus. The first global gathering of its kind in the modern world, it left a legacy in both the West and the East by shifting the marginally understood history and culture of Asia into the maelstrom of global thinking on missionary work, westernization, science, evolution, industrialization, colonialism, imperialism, comparative religions, and racism.

Carus presented three papers during the course of the exposition: "The Philosophy of the Tool," "Our Need of Philosophy," and "Science a Religious Revelation." In the latter paper, he predicted that although science would someday prove that God was not a person, it could not deny the existence of a power that enforced conduct. In a word, God was the "authority of conduct."[47] In former times, religion had found truths by insight, inspiration, or intuition, a method common among the prophets and sages of the great religions, like Zarathustra, Confucius, Buddha, Socrates, and Moses. Nevertheless, it was important for humankind to appreciate the grandeur of evolution; the more one studied it, the more one found that science preserved the spirit of religion and enhanced its truths.[48]

Over the course of the parliament's schedule of events, which he helped plan, Carus made numerous personal and professional connections. These included Shaku Soyen, the lord abbot of a Japanese Zen monastery; Protap Chunder Mozoomdar, leader of the Hindu reform movement and author of *The Oriental Christ* (1869); Virchand Gandhi, a popular lecturer of the Jain faith; Anagarika Dharmapala, a Sri Lankan Buddhist, reformer, and co-creator of the Theosophical Society; and Indian Hindu monk Swami Vivekananda, a nationalist credited with raising Hinduism to a major world status in India. When the parliament ended, many of these delegates accepted Carus's invitation to visit his home in LaSalle.

As noted earlier, until the meeting of the parliament, the principal work of the Open Court Publishing Company had been to find a middle ground in the ongoing feud between religion and science. Following his encounter with Eastern religions at the exposition, Carus became the nation's self-appointed ambassador to facilitate a renaissance using his role as publisher and editor. Indicative of the parliament's influence on his thinking, Carus revised the masthead of the *Open Court* from "A Weekly Journal Devoted to the Religion of Science" to "A Monthly Magazine Devoted to the Science of Religion, the Religion of Science, and the extension of the Religious Parliament Idea."[49]

Following the close of the seventeen-day event, the parliament formed the Committee of the World's Religious Parliament Extension to promote its cause. As the extension's secretary, Carus pursued the noble principle of mutual tolerance set forth by the parliament, ensuring that its goal would endure for generations to come. Already, he observed, the old names of Catholic, Protestant, Anglican, Dissenter, Baptist, Methodist, Independent, Calvinist, and Armenian had lost their spell. "How sane and healthy all this is," Carus observed. "We are now in sight of the goal, for we see that whatever becomes of the names, union will come by conserving and promoting all that is true and good in each. . . . Our present aim must be to get mutual tolerance which subsists already between the sections of Christendom." He saw no reason why mutual tolerance could not extend among all religious groups. While rituals and symbols varied according to taste, "the essence of religion can only be one and must remain one and the same among all nations, in all climes, and under all conditions."[50]

Two years after the Chicago event, the Pan-American Congress of Religion and Education met at the Horticultural Gardens Pavilion in Toronto, Canada. Through the generosity of Mrs. Caroline E. Haskell, an endowment was established at the University of Chicago to create a Lectureship on Comparative Religions, with lectures delivered in India and Chicago. Finally, plans were put in place for a Religious Parliament to be held in Paris in 1900, to which all religions would be invited.[51]

*THE GOSPEL OF BUDDHA*

Following the parliament, the number of articles published on the subject of Eastern religion and philosophy in the *Open Court* and the *Monist* multiplied several fold before leveling off in 1906. Carus's pre-1893 references to Buddhism treated it as an equal with Christianity, though still superstitious and focused on resignation (i.e., Nirvana). After the World's Fair, he became an active enthusiast of non-Christian religions, and while he never repudiated Christianity altogether, he most certainly criticized its intolerant behavior toward Eastern religions and philosophies. Carus's interaction with Eastern philosophy, especially Buddhism, was facilitated by the addition of Shaku Soyen's translator Daisetz Teitaro Suzuki to his editorial staff. From 1897 to 1908, Suzuki lived with the Carus family, where he performed editorial duties and translated numerous works of Eastern philosophies and religions and would become an internationally recognized Zen scholar. In all, the Open Court Company published thirty-eight books on Buddhism, including the widely popular *The Gospel of Buddha* (1894), a compilation of tracts favored by reform-minded Buddhists. According to historian Harold Henderson, the *Open Court* and the *Monist* magazines gave Eastern religions more extensive and sympathetic coverage than any other publication in the United States.[52]

Being neither a Buddhist nor a scholar of comparative religions, Carus relied on translations for his understanding of the Buddhist texts used in his *Gospel*. "Suffice it to say," observes Martin J. Verhoeven, "Carus chose his European sources wisely."[53] This included works from Max Müller's fifty-one volumes of *Sacred Books of the East* (1879–1910); Samuel Beal's *Travels of Fah-hian ad Sung-Yun* (1869), *A Catena of Buddhist Scriptures from the Chinese* (1871), *The Romantic Legend of Sakya Buddha* (1875), *Buddhist Canon* (1878); *A Life of Buddha by Asvaghosha Bodhisattva* (1879), and *An Abstract of Four Lectures on Buddhist Literature in China* (1882); and Thomas William Rhys Davids's *Buddhism* (1877), *Buddhist Suttas from the Pali* (1881), and *Vinaya Texts* (1881–1885); and *Questions of King Milinda* (1890–1894), which Rhys Davids translated in collaboration with Herman Oldenberg. To be sure, most of these early translators were missionaries and unapologetic in their belief in Christianity's destined place above the world's heathen religions. Although indebted to these scholars for their translations, Carus did not share their views that the Eastern religions were agnostic, pantheistic, or even atheistic. On the contrary, all religions required a stripping away of their myths, dogmas, and rituals.

Of all the translations, Müller's works were the most frequently cited in the *Gospel*. A graduate of Leipzig University in 1843 in the field of Sanskrit, and one of the founders of comparative religions, Müller spent his entire professional life at Oxford. Like Carus, he strongly believed in religion grounded in science and looked to removing layers of dogmatic accretion that over time had corrupted Christianity's original purity. Consequently, both Carus and Müller exhibited a greater appreciation of Buddhism than their contemporaries. To the extent the West's missionaries dismissed Buddhism as unqualified to even be identified as a religion, Carus and Müller insisted on Buddhism's positive spirit. How could one condemn a religion that critics claimed had no God but whose way to Nirvana consisted of "right faith (orthodoxy), right judgment (logic), right language (veracity), right purpose (honesty), right practice (religious life), right obedience (lawful life), right memory, and right meditation"?[54]

Carus presented to the West a worldview not of historical Buddhism, but of an advanced form of scientific Buddhism intended to strengthen its compatibility with post-Enlightenment science, including the implications of evolutionary theory. According to Thomas A. Tweed, Carus was probably "more influential in stimulating and sustaining American interest in Buddhism than any other person living in the United States."[55] The fact that his choice of material fit comfortably with countries like Japan that were undergoing modernization gave the book added gravitas. Stripped of miracle stories, superstitions, revelations, and supernatural cosmologies, the *Gospel of Buddha* received a warm reception in the East and, like Henry Steel Olcott's *Catechism*, was adopted as the official text in Buddhist schools in Japan and Ceylon.[56]

According to Martin J. Verhoeven, Carus's encounter with Buddhists at the World's Parliament in Chicago "gave birth to a modern Buddhism in the United States . . . that would leave its imprint on the religious landscape of America well into the next century." The success of his *Gospel* also played a role in the "second flowering" of Buddhism in the 1960s through the work of Suzuki at Columbia University and the beat generation's embrace of Eastern philosophy, especially Zen. Today, over a hundred years later and into the fifth generation of the Carus/Hegeler family enterprise, Buddhism remains a centerpiece of the Open Court's publishing interests with the 2004 edition of *The Gospel of Buddha*.[57]

## Christianity and Buddhism

Carus focused much of his early attention on the possible Buddhist origin of Christianity, noting that many of those most competent to speak on the subject were reticent to even countenance the idea. To be sure, clear differences existed in their belief systems, but Carus found it remarkable that scholars supposed no historical connection. Countering this argument was the fact that Buddha lived in the fifth century before

Christ and that the Buddhist canon had been settled by 250 BC. While it remained possible that in the later phases of Buddhism's development, some Christian ideas and modes of worship might have been imported into Northern India and influenced Buddhism (e.g., the legend of St. Thomas's visit to India), it was just as likely that the story of St. Thomas was a Christianized Buddhist legend due to the latter's commercial relations and exchange of thought between India and Judea before the appearance of Christ. During Ashoka's time, official legations had been dispatched from India to neighboring countries and to Western Asia for spreading Buddha's teachings. "There cannot be the slightest doubt," Carus argued, "that Buddhist missionaries were sent to Western Asia in the third century before the Christian era and must have made attempts to preach Buddhism. . . . It would be strange if Buddhist missionaries had gone to all neighboring countries except to Palestine, and that all kinds of Buddhist stories and wise saws were translated into other tongues, but not the essential doctrines of their sacred literature."[58]

Carus discovered two fundamental truths in Buddhism and Christianity, namely, that life existed in the renunciation of one's personality ("He that loseth his life shall find it" Matt. 10:39) and that the good of man is only in his union with God and through God to each other ("As thou art in me and I in thee, that they also may be one in us"; John 17:21).[59] Other similarities existed as well.

Both experienced similar sects and heresies;
both were religions and not philosophies;
both contained exaggerated and legendary tales;
both used religious symbols and art productions;
both abandoned a pessimistic outlook on life; and
both sent out missionaries into all quarters of the world.

Both Jesus and Buddha were of royal, not priestly lineage whose childhood was jeopardized;
both led a life of poverty and wandered without a home, family or property;
both were viewed as saviors of the world;
both were teachers;
both were tempted by the "evil one";
both confessed a mission and preached a gospel;
both refused to countenance superstitions;
both were attributed with miracles;
both allegedly walked on water;

both were tied to asceticism;
both were fond of parables and aphorisms;
both had sayings that showed strong similarities; and
both shared the idea of a world-savior.[60]

Carus felt confident that Buddhism stood for positivism, having built its religious goals on a scientific methodology.[61] "It demands no belief in the impossible; it dispenses with miracles, [and] it assumes no authority except the illumination of a right comprehension of the facts of existence."[62] Buddhism was a "religion of enlightenment" whose Buddha Gautama was "the first positivist, the first humanitarian, the first radical freethinker, the first iconoclast, and the first prophet of the Religion of Science."[63]

Time and again, Carus wavered between the two religions, praising one, then the other, criticizing one, then the other. "Whatever may be said in favor of Buddhism, its profundity, its cosmic universality, and the loftiness of its morality," he observed, "the great strength of Christianity lies in the lesson of Golgotha, which means, salvation lies not alone in the attainment of the truth, but in struggling for it, in living for it, in suffering for it, and in dying for it."[64] Over time, Carus grew increasingly attentive to Buddhism's rejection of ego-driven desires in its search for God in humankind. Still, there is no indication that he embraced it as his faith. Having abandoned the orthodoxy of his father, he chose not to treat religion as a personal belief system, but rather as an object of scientific investigation, with himself as its official investigator. If pushed, however, the evidence suggested that Buddhism stood at the top of his preferred list of belief systems.

Carus held a position that was simultaneously Kantian, Christian, and Buddhist, cherry-picking those elements of each that served his needs. "In a certain sense I am a Buddhist," he explained, "for I adopt the main doctrines of Buddha as to the non-existence of the atman or ego-soul, and the irrationality of the belief in a creation of the world by a big ego-deity out of nothing." However, "should . . . the question arise whether I belong to one of the Buddhist sects, I would have to answer, 'No, I am not a Buddhist.'"[65]

Ultimately, Carus chose not to press the idea that Christianity was influenced by Buddhism, regarding it as only a hypothesis. The elements of Christianity were certainly not new and could have been scrounged from multiple sources, including the idea of the Logos from Neo-Platonism, the God-idea from Jewish tradition, baptism from an Essenian rite, communion from a Dionysian cult, and the world-savior from Buddhism. One could reasonably argue that "the evolution of both religions may have taken place independently, according to a natural law."[66]

As a monist and a Darwinist, Carus insisted that rivalry among the world's religions would eventually result in a clarification of their respective belief systems.

> Mankind is destined to have one religion, as it will have one moral ideal and one universal language, and the decision as to which religion will at last be universally accepted, cannot come about by accident. Science will spread, maybe, slowly but unfailingly, and the universal acceptance of a scientific world conception bodes the dawn of the Religion of Truth,—a religion based upon plain statements of fact unalloyed with myth or allegory. In the eventual conditions of religious life, there may be a difference of rituals and symbols, nay, even of names, according to taste, historical tradition, and individual preference, but in all essentials there will be one religion only, for there is only one truth, which remains one and the same among all nations, in all climes, and under all conditions. The law of the survival of the fittest holds good also in the domain of spiritual institutions. And let us remember that the greatest power lies not in numbers, not in wealth, not in political influence, but in truth. Whatever may be the fate of the various faiths of the world, we may be sure that the truth will prevail in the end.[67]

It was no use defending old orthodoxy or agnosticism; only that orthodoxy which reconciled with science had any future. "We must broaden both our science and our religion until our religion becomes scientific, and our science religious," Carus insisted. True science could not be antireligious, and true religion could not be antiscientific. "If you want a Religion that is truly catholic, let it be in accord with Science." In their respective roles, science searched for Truth and formulated the facts of experience into natural laws, while religion sought to apply Truth to life. Without science, religion was mere superstition. Science was the equivalent of Jacob's ladder, which "at its bottom touches the world of sense, while its top reaches into the heaven of spirit."[68]

## Pragmatism

For reality to be meaningful, Carus insisted on using nonempirical categories that he referred to as "forms," which stood for "supreme reality."

They were the uniformities or laws that shaped the world.[69] Without objective criteria there could be no path to objective or scientific truth. Thus, when the American philosopher and psychologist William James remarked that "truth happens to an idea," referring to an attribute that might or might not occur, Carus took issue, condemning it as a crass and unenlightened form of subjective empiricism. Instead he equated truth with forms that were universal, preexistent, absolute, immutable, and of intrinsic value regardless of the situation. If, as James explained, truth was "whatever proves itself to be good in the way of belief, and good, too, for definite, assignable reasons," then what is it that makes a useful lie true?[70] Similarly, if "truth *happens* to an idea," how is it that an idea could be both true and untrue?[71]

Carus insisted that truth was not an artifice made by humans, but discoverable. It was rigid, not plastic, and "independent of our likes and dislikes." The truth of yesterday must be the truth of tomorrow. Ptolemaic astronomy was never true and would never be true even though it satisfied scientific inquiry at the time. If James was correct, the followers of Ptolemy need not have troubled themselves with the inconsistencies they found.[72] Carus rejected James's utilitarian approach to truth because it made something universal and objective into a relative and highly subjective "personal equation." Science stood or fell with the objectivity of truth, insisted Carus. "If truth were mere opinion, if my truth might be different from your truth, even though all errors due to a difference of terminology were excluded, if both our truths in spite of being contradictory might be truths, truth would be subjective. It would appear different in different minds, and even in the same mind truth would be subject to change. Objective truth would be impossible." This Carus could not accept.[73]

Carus's opposition to James was never more intense than in the area of ethics, where he criticized pragmatic philosophy for becoming "the fashionable free thought of the day . . . closely connected with negativism and hedonism."[74] He condemned it as an expediency grounded in a temporary pleasure or happiness, neither of which was "sufficient to make a complete and worthy human life."[75] While materialism led to hedonism, and Spiritualism led to asceticism, neither answered the search for truth.

First, to inquire after truth.
Second, to accept the truth.
Third, to reject what is untrue.
Fourth, to trust in truth.
And fifth, to live the truth.[76]

The two factors necessary for establishing a scientific truth included sense experience and a method or means of handling the material identified by sense activity. This meant classifying, measuring, tracing cause and effect, and arranging the outcome into an understandable and harmonious system. Arriving at a scientific truth required distinguishing between form and substance, between the formal sciences (e.g., arithmetic, geometry, pure mechanics, logic) and the sciences that investigate concrete things (e.g., chemistry, physiology). The formal sciences became the organ of thought that supplied the sciences with concrete phenomena used to arrive at a conviction. Once experience verified the results of the sciences, one could be assured there could be no conflict, for the world was a unitary system, not one of chaos. Once a truth was proven to be true, it remained true forever. The consistency of the world was universal and eternal. "What is true here is true everywhere, and what is true now is true forever."[77]

The philosophy of the future, he insisted, should focus on the importance of memory as the soul builder, science as the search instrument for objective truth, the unitary world-conception he called monism, and God as a "super-personality." Opposed to agnosticism, which he called *ne-science*, and pragmatism, which had lost itself in pluralism and subjectivism, he celebrated the work of Schiller and Goethe, whom he identified along with Plato as the "prophets of the philosophy of form."[78]

Although admitting that religion had suffered from the accumulated baggage of superstitions, dogmas and rituals acquired over time and sapping its purpose, he refused nonetheless to discount it altogether, particularly given the unity and harmony it brought to mankind. He intended to use scientific enquiry to save religion from itself. "Armed with his philosophy of forms," explained historian Donald Harvey Meyer, "Carus moved bravely into the field of religion. He believed that truth was one, that science was the search for truth, and therefore that religion must be based on science." Science became the source of new revelation, replacing older revelations with undisputable conclusions grounded in factual data.[79] The universe constituted a unitary whole while man, whose personality or self-embraced body (living matter), soul (the psychic qualities of the organism), mind (intelligent portion of feelings), and spirit (combining feelings and intellectual functions), found harmony with the whole.[80] Man was not the sum total of matter but rather of form which consisted of those thought structures that embodied his aspirations, purposes, and will. "Man's life is like a tapestry adorned with divers patterns. The warp is the reality of actual facts while the woof is supplied by our spiritual comprehension, our thoughts and aspirations."[81]

Carus's prior emphasis on forms became increasingly important in later years while his aspirations for the advent of monistic philosophy ever more distant. As Harold Henderson explained, a new generation of thinkers first questioned and then rejected "Carus's formal certainties in philosophy, physics, and even mathematics."[82] From the pragmatists who he considered anti-intellectual and from the relativity physicists who criticized objectivity and scientific truth, he faced challenges that began cordially and professionally but ended in a corrosive indifference, as if Carus's issues were no longer relevant.

Carus's status as a philosopher diminished as philosophy became a recognized discipline with its own coterie of professionals. Taken for granted as a wannabe scholar, Carus faced increasing criticism from the very scholars he had nurtured in his magazines. His enduring significance, concluded Martin Verhoeven, was "in introducing and interpreting others' thoughts, particularly the religious thought of Asia, to an American audience."[83] The more philosophy became a specialized field of study, the more they viewed him as an outsider. "The public to which he spoke," noted Donald Harvey Meyer, "was deaf to his voice" while the intellectuals he had long supported found him "too simple." Eventually his ideas regarding the unity of truth, cause and effect, and the preservation of matter and energy, were viewed as contradictory and crudely formulated.[84] While grateful for their access to his journals, Carus's stable of authors eventually turned on him. "It is the constant indoor life, the lack of acquaintance with the real needs of practical life, and the close confinement to a special mode of work," Carus observed, "that tends to make scholars one-sided, and if professional pride and personal vanity are added, a peculiar disease originates, which, in one word, we call *scholaromania*."[85]

Carus's trove of seventy-five books and over fifteen hundred articles ranged in subject matter from mathematics and biblical criticism to poetry, translations of Eastern writings, Zoroastrian lore, and psychology. Unfortunately, recognition of his scholarship came in fits and spurts, sometimes enthusiastically but often grudgingly, condescendingly, and with qualifications. At best, he was given faint praise as a "gifted amateur" in a world of budding scholars. Despite his prodigious output, he remained relatively obscure in philosophical circles, viewed condescendingly as an amateur philosopher, a dilettante who offered a confused and not particularly helpful contribution to and analysis of the science, philosophy, and religion of his day.[86]

## SELECTED WRITINGS

*Monism and Meliorism, a Philosophical Essay on Causality and Ethics* (1885)

*Fundamental Problems* (1889)

*The Soul of Man: An Investigation of the Facts of Physiological and Experimental Psychology* (1891)

*Monism: Its Scope and Import* (1891)

*The Religion of Science* (1893)

*The Gospel of Buddha* (1894)

*Buddhism and Its Christian Critics* (1894)

*The Dawn of a New Era and Other Essays* (1899)

*The Surd of Metaphysics* (1903)

*Kant and Spencer: A Study of the Fallacies of Agnosticism* (1904)

*The Bride of Christ: A Study in Christian Legend Lore* (1908)

*The Foundations of Mathematics* (1908)

*God; An Enquiry into the Nature of Man's Highest Ideal and a Solution of the Problem from the Standpoint of Science* (1908)

*Philosophy as a Science: A Synopsis of the Writings of Paul Carus* (1909)

*The Philosophy of Form* (1911)

# 10

## Roads Not Taken

*The West is preparing to add its fables to those of the East. The valleys of the Ganges, the Nile, and the Rhine having yielded their crop, it remains to be seen what the valleys of the Amazon, the Platte, the Orinoco, the St. Lawrence, and the Mississippi will produce. Perchance, when, in the course of ages, American liberty has become a fiction of the past—as it is to some extent a fiction of the present—the poets of the world will be inspired by American mythology.*

—Henry David Thoreau, "Walking," 1851

EACH OF THE "GRAND NARRATIVES" chosen for this study sought to reset the terms and conditions of Western civilization's role in the advance of history. Accompanying them was an optimism that made a caricature of the proposition advanced by Andrew White and John Draper that science and religion were at war. Indeed, the options proposed by the intellectuals in this book reveal how the relationship between these two citadels of learning was much more nuanced. The cosmos now appeared as an organism—not the deist's static universe—that was infinite, transcendent, and progressive. How else to explain Paul Carus's divinity of science or William James's will to believe? It's no surprise, however, that many important narratives have been left out of this study—some deliberately, others by circumstance, or sheer oversight. They include the hedonistic calculus of Jeremy Bentham, the creative evolution of Henri Bergson, the absolutism of Josiah Royce, the Scottish School of common sense of James McCosh, and the St. Louis Hegelians of William T. Harris, to mention a few. Also, excluded from the mix was the spiritual cosmology inspired by the scientist and mystic Emanuel Swedenborg, whose influence in the first half of the nineteenth century had caused Emerson's generation to identify the period as "The Age of Swedenborg."[1]

Of those not chosen, a good number had been allied with idealism. This philosophy had once defined American philosophy but lost its long ascendency in the second half of the nineteenth century. That it had flourished among New England's elite was easily understood. That it had advocates in the Midwest contemporaneous with Billy the Kid and Jesse James seems counterintuitive. Yet Henry David Thoreau's essay

"Walking," which grew out of different entries in his journal, treated the West as symbolic of an ideal world, a concept reinforced by Bronson Alcott's belief that the philosophical fountainhead of America's future lay in the Mississippi Valley. This was the same valley where the Plato Club, the American Akadêmê, William T. Harris's St. Louis Hegelians, and Paul Carus's Open Court Publishing Company stood as sentinels against the crass materialism of the age.[2]

Midwest Platonism was never more popular than at the Plato Club in Jacksonville, Illinois (known as the "Athens of the West"), which claimed nearly four hundred members. Formed in 1866, it flourished for more than thirty years, attracting teachers and hosting a broad array of lecturers, like Ralph Waldo Emerson, Bronson Alcott, William T. Harris, Denton J. Snider, Horace H. Morgan, and Thomas Davidson. The town's attraction to Plato was due mainly to the presence of Dr. Hiram K. Jones (1818–1903), a physician who lectured on philosophy at Illinois College, the town's private liberal arts school, where Jones shared his passion for metaphysics with all who would listen.[3]

Another latter-day Platonist was General Ethan Allen Hitchcock (1798–1870), a West Point graduate and career officer in the United States Army who had served as staff officer to Lincoln and Secretary of War Stanton. Known to his friends as the "Hermetic Initiate," Hitchcock was a dedicated researcher whose alchemic collection of science, philosophy and mystical books has been preserved by the St. Louis Mercantile Library at the University of Missouri-St. Louis. The author of *Remarks on Alchemy and the Alchemists, Indicating a Method of Discovering the True Nature of Hermetic Philosophy* (1857) and *Swedenborg, a Hermetic Philosopher* (1858), he suggested that alchemy belonged to the legitimate field of allegory, setting forth the transformation of the human soul.[4] As Hitchcock explained, the Alchemists had pursued wisdom, not rare metals—a thesis looking at broader issues of intent. Having read numerous works on alchemy, he concluded that they were a product of symbolic writing, much like *Gulliver's Travels*, the adventures of *Robinson Crusoe*, or the Joel Chandler Harris's *Tales of Uncle Remus and Brer Rabbit*. Teaching by means of similitude, parable, fable, allegory, and symbolism, Hitchcock brought innovative ideas and opinions before the public using guarded language to avoid the consequences of potential civil or religious retribution. Thus, books dealing with the "elixir of life" and the "philosopher's stone" were religious in nature and written to avoid discovery. The Alchemists were Protestants at a time when their beliefs could not be practiced openly. Neither pretenders nor imposters, they were searchers after truth,

believing that true knowledge of the One could not be openly taught. Instead, they resorted to numbers, figures, and allegories.[5]

Another prominent idealist was the attorney Thomas Moore Johnson
(1851–1919) of Osceola, Missouri, president of the Council of the Hermetic Brotherhood of Luxor and editor of the *Platonist* (1884–1888). Published monthly, the magazine stood at the forefront of a national revival
in Platonic thinking, elucidating the practical application of Platonic ethics. The journal included articles on theosophical philosophy, philologi-
cal investigations, translations, interpretations, and utterances of gifted
individuals—all intended to teach harmony between pure Christianity
and the esoteric doctrines of ancient faiths.[6] According to Johnson, one of
the earliest members of the Theosophical Society (1875), Platonism was
a method or discipline more than a system. "It embraced the higher nature of man by unfolding the mysteries of the interior being." Though not
esteemed among those who favored scientific knowledge, its proponents
believed that to the extent Platonists gathered wisdom from the ancient
schools and combined it with modern thinking, it could extract what was
precious from each. "The philosophic discipline," Johnson wrote, "un-
folds the interior nature of the soul, arouses the dormant truth there in-
humed, brings into activity the spiritual faculty, and enables us to peruse
the arcane of the higher life."[7]

The journal struggled to survive by extending its reading audience to
those interested in the occult and Eastern mysteries by including reviews
of George Wyld's *Theosophy and the Higher Life* (1880) and articles from
the *Theosophist* published in India by Helena Blavatsky and Henry Steel
Olcott.[8] Other articles symptomatic of this broadening trend included reviews of Giles B. Stebbins's *After Dogmatic Theology, What? Materialism,
or a Spiritual Philosophy and Natural Religion* (1880); William Oxley, *The
Philosophy of Spirit* (1881), which sought to combine the Vaishnavas of
the Bhagavad Gita with the adepts of Tibet; and Alfred Percy Sinnett, *The
Occult World* (1881), which explained the Hindu adepts who wielded the
scepter of occultism in India.[9]

## CONCORD SCHOOL OF PHILOSOPHY

Another legacy from the first half of the nineteenth century was the Concord School of Philosophy, which dated from 1842, when Bronson Alcott met with fellow philosophers to discuss opening a summer program at his Orchard House organized around Platonic Idealism. Not
until 1878, however, following a conversation with Dr. Hiram K. Jones of

Jacksonville, did the enterprise became a reality. Incentivized by memories of the Transcendentalists, the school opened in 1879 with financial support from W. T. Harris and Louisa May Alcott. Based on the idea of Plato's Academy, it offered lectures and readings on the Transcendentalists, the Neo-Platonists, and Hegelians. Decidedly more highbrow than the Chautauqua Institution founded in 1874 by Lewis Miller and John Heyl Vincent, the School represented a marriage between New England Transcendentalists and the circle of Midwest Platonists under the leadership of Harris.[10]

With advice and help from Emerson, Harvard mathematician Benjamin Peirce (a close friend of Carus), reformer and philanthropist Ednah D. Cheney, and educator and philosopher Harris, the school offered a term of five weeks with "professors" Alcott, Harris, Jones, David A. Wasson, and Cheney lecturing from Monday through Friday on Christian Theism, speculative philosophy, Platonic philosophy, political philosophy, and the history and morals of art.[11] Saturdays were given over to guest lecturers Franklin B. Sanborn (*Philanthropy and Social Science*), Thomas W. Higginson (*Modern Literature*), Thomas Davidson (*Greek Life and Literature*), and George H. Howison (*Philosophy from Leibnitz to Hegel*), who spoke on their favorite topics. During the years that followed, lecturers included Protap Chunder Mozoomdar on the *Upanishads*, John Fiske on immortality, Dr. J. S. Kedney on the higher criticism, Mrs. Cheney on Nirvana, Dr. Frederic H. Hedge on ghosts, and Harris on skepticism and agnosticism.

The school had no examinations and no limitation of age, sex, or residence for those who subscribed. The cost was $15 for the entire program, with board obtained in the village from $6 to $12 a week.[12] Though some feared the school's radical heritage might bleed into its lectures, the actual outcome was far more sublime, dignified, and conservative. Nearly four-fifths of the attendees were women from the conservative Midwest; some were teachers; others were wives of professional men. According to Louisa Alcott, they "roost on our steps like hens waiting for corn."[13]

## American Akadêmê

When the Concord School refused to relocate its summer program farther west to better accommodate its midwestern participants, Dr. Hiram K. Jones organized the American Akadêmê in Jacksonville in 1883. Intended as a winter program distinct from the Concord's summer program, it convened the third Tuesday of each month from September through June at the residence of Dr. Jones.[14] Within a year it claimed 180 members, and by 1892 there were 422 associates from across the continent, including visitors from France and Australia.[15]

The Akadêmê's purpose was "to promote the knowledge of Philosophic Truth, and to cooperate with the dissemination of such knowledge, with a view to the elevation of the mind from the sphere of the sensuous life into that of virtue and justice, and into communion with the diviner ideas and natures."[16] At a meeting of Akadêmê members on May 20, 1884, the members hotly debated the theory of evolution's usefulness in explaining the origination of life, the universe, and whether every particle of matter was under its power. Not only were members sharply divided on acceptance of Darwin's theory, but the majority declared that the doctrine could in no way be accepted until certain gaps that were "still yawning widely" were successfully bridged. By contrast, Mrs. Lizzie Jones's lecture on Prof. Henry Drummond's *Natural Law in the Spiritual World* uniformly condemned the rising influence of materialism and skepticism concerning anything supernatural.[17]

## THEOSOPHY

The religious scholar Stephen Prothero has suggested that the early years of Theosophy (or, as some called it, "Theosophical Idealism") represented an attempt to "gentrify" the spiritualist tradition in America. Until then, the central ritual of American Spiritualism had been the séance, with all its unruliness and bad behavior. His thesis bears consideration given how quickly the so-called Hydesville and Rochester rappings of the Fox sisters in 1848 set a bar so low for believability that medium communication with spirits seldom rose above the conjuror's touch. Theosophy postulated a more advanced form of Spiritualism that appealed to the nation's cosmopolitan elites looking to replace the séance's untethered and raucous manifestations. As Prothero explained, Theosophy was not as much devoted to promoting Asian religious traditions as it was an attempt to lift Spiritualism from its more vulgar aspects.[18]

Best known as cofounder and first president of the Theosophical Society (1875),[19] and credited with the Buddhist revival in South Asia, Henry Steel Olcott was born in Orange, New Jersey, of Presbyterian parents. He came of age at a time when the "burned-over district" in western New York was making its imprint on American society by way of Mormonism, Stirpiculture, Millerism, perfectionism, and the rappings of the Fox sisters. A dropout from the College of the City of New York, Olcott gravitated to the cause of Spiritualism in 1852, authoring articles in the *Spiritual Telegraph* before becoming a correspondent for Greeley's *Tribune* and the *Mark Lane Express*, where he mixed his spiritualist beliefs with anti-slavery and other reform issues.

Not a man to be taken lightly, Olcott enlisted in the Union army, where he was assigned to examine corruption in military arsenals and shipyards before being appointed by the War Department to an investigative commission to examine the assassination of President Lincoln. After the war he practiced law and advocated for civil service reform. Like others of his generation, he looked upon spirit communication as a popular form of healing the intellectual sores stemming from the war's high mortality. Having no satisfactory reason to deny the phenomenon, he remained a spiritualist for decades, albeit one who had grown tired of its vulgar and fraudulent practices.[20]

Olcott's fascination with spiritualistic phenomena included the investigations of the scientist Robert Hare (1781–1858), who initially undertook to expose Spiritualism but concluded that the manifestations were real; and the work of William Crookes (1832–1919), the discoverer of Roentgen rays, who announced his acceptance of spirit manifestations. In 1874, as a reporter for the *New York Daily Graphic*, Olcott and newspaper artist Alfred Kappes visited the farmstead of William, Horatio, and Mary Eddy in Chittenden, Vermont, to investigate the family's alleged manifestations. According to Olcott, several generations of the Eddy family had experienced spirit materializations in one form or another. Supposedly, they lived three distinct lives: one external in a manner common to all; a second, where they saw spiritual things while in a normal condition; and a third, where they experienced "events" in the state of deep trance.[21]

Olcott met Helena Petrovna Blavatsky at the Eddy family farm in Chittenden. Born in the Ukraine, she had married young and, after deserting her husband in 1848, traveled through much of Europe, the Middle East, and West Asia. With the assistance of the Scottish medium Daniel D. Home she converted to Spiritualism in the 1850s. In 1873, at the age of forty-two, and no longer receiving support from her family, she moved to New York, where she supported herself writing advertising literature.[22] A chain-smoking Bohemian, she traveled to Vermont to defend the authenticity of the Eddy brothers' manifestations against the claims of New York physician George Miller Beard, who had called them frauds. When Olcott met Blavatsky, they discovered a shared interest in Spiritualism, and cooperated on a series of articles in the *Spiritual Scientist* that cemented their relationship and marked their separation from the

Spiritualist movement, which remained fixated on rappings, levitating tables, voices, and spirit-pictures. The combination of Blavatsky's charisma
and Olcott's careful planning gave them an ideal platform from which to
launch Theosophy, a form of Neo-Spiritualism that drew its wisdom from
divine knowledge transferred directly to Blavatsky from a secret brotherhood of monks living in the Tibetan highlands.[23]

Drawing on the work of Rhys Davids and Max Müller, who had transformed their Eastern interests into academic fields of study, Olcott and
Blavatsky proceeded to replace the séance with a modern manifestation
of Brahmanism and Buddhism that brought together many of the nation's esoteric traditions, including Gnosticism, the Mystery Schools of
the Classical World, the Concord School of Philosophy, and the Platonist
and Neo-Platonist societies of the Midwest.[24]

## Isis Unveiled

Blavatsky's *Isis Unveiled: A Master-Key to the Mysteries of Ancient and Modern Science and Theology* (1877), followed by *The Secret Doctrine* (1888), presented the belief system of Theosophy revealed to her by Tibetan monks.
Alexander Wilder, who edited *Isis Unveiled* for the publisher and provided
a thirty-six-page introduction, took issue with contemporary claims that
Christianity represented the "bright lamp of modern science." The struggle between science and theology had shown both to have feet of clay.[25]
Theosophy included a healthy mix of karma and reincarnation; telepathic
communication; Darwinian-style evolutionary theories; and romantic images generated by Rhys Davids's translations of Pali texts.[26] Influenced by
the Neo-Platonists, Blavatsky and Olcott stressed the importance of hermetic philosophy as the key to understanding the connection between
science and theology. In the case of evolution, science had provided evidence of its truth, and so did the ancient myths. Like many of the Neo-
Platonists of the time, Blavatsky believed the secrets of the universe could
be discovered in Pythagorean numerals and ancient symbols. While evolutionary theory explained how life changed, it did not necessitate a materialist point of view, since nature consisted of matter, spirit, and soul.[27]

In their writings Olcott and Blavatsky offered the mysticism of the East
as the answer to the West's crisis in faith. The practical and evolutionary
cosmology in Eastern religions rested on the proposition of ascent for every living organism, thus providing a comforting response to Darwin's
theory of natural selection. The use of science, pseudoscience, and particularly the rhetoric of evolution allowed Theosophy to claim legitimacy as

a part of normative science, thus bringing together religion, science, and rationality as proof of Theosophy's relevance. By giving Spiritualism a scientific basis, Olcott and Blavatsky effectively replaced the séance and its magicians/mediums with a much-needed respectability demanded by the educated elite.[28]

Theosophy operated at the intersection of science, occult research, and the law of progressive evolution, offering one more option for humankind to participate in modernity. It contextualized esotericism within the framework of enlightenment science, romanticism, philosophy, and theology. Purported to be the esoteric wisdom of the world's most revered religious prophets (Moses, Krishna, Lao-tzu, Confucius, Buddha, and Christ) handed down through an ancient brotherhood of gifted adepts, mahatmas, or masters, Theosophy became a worldwide movement that had drawn into its fold such luminaries as George Bernard Shaw, Lyman Frank Baum, James Henry Cousins, William Butler Yeats, Lewis Carroll, Sir Arthur Conan Doyle, Jack London, James Joyce, D. H. Lawrence, T. S. Eliot, Thornton Wilder, Kurt Vonnegut, Lewis Carroll, Susan B. Anthony, and Thomas Edison. Interestingly, Alfred Russel Wallace would have none of it. Writing to his longtime friend Mrs. Fisher (Arabella Buckley) in 1897, he noted: "I have tried several Reincarnation and Theosophy books, but *cannot* read them or take any interest in them. They are so purely imaginative, and do not seem to me rational."[29]

## THE BUDDHIST CATECHISM

In 1880 Olcott traveled to Ceylon, where he publicly announced his conversion to Buddhism. Revered as the "White Buddhist," he brokered a religious tradition that was Buddhist in name but included "the religious beliefs and behaviors of American Protestant modernists, the cultural assumptions of European academic Orientalists, and the social class preoccupations of New York City's metropolitan gentry."[30]

In 1881 Olcott wrote the *Buddhist Catechism*, a westernized version of Buddhist thought that Olcott introduced into Ceylon's educational system and later into Burma, India, and Japan. Much like the catechisms common in both Catholic and Protestant denominations, it used a question-and-answer approach to explain Buddhist beliefs. The *Catechism* went through multiple revisions before becoming the accepted authority in Ceylon, and subsequently translated into French (1883), English (1885), and German (1886). As explained by Prothero, Olcott joined with other Eastern reformers in defining religion in ethical and moral terms, rather than in ritualistic creeds. Olcott projected a reform type of Buddhism that featured the wisdom of its ancient texts and their grounding in reason, common sense, and the discovery of modern science, including the law of evolution.[31]

In the book's thirty-fourth edition, published in 1904, Olcott expanded his list of questions and answers, grouping them into five separate categories, one of which included the reconciliation of Buddhism with science.

194. Q. *Are there any dogmas in Buddhism which we are required to accept on faith?*

A. No: we are earnestly enjoined to accept nothing whatever on faith; whether it be written in books, handed down from our ancestors, or taught by the sages.

325. Q. *Has Buddhism any right to be considered a scientific religion, or may it be classified as a "revealed" one?*

A. Most emphatically it is not a revealed religion. The Buddha did not so preach, nor is he so understood. On the contrary, he gave it out as the statement of eternal truths, which his predecessors had taught like himself.

331. Q. *Is Buddhism opposed to education, and to the study of science?*

A. Quite the contrary: in the Siga'lowa'da Sutta, by a discourse preached by the Buddha he specified as one of the duties of a teacher that he should give his pupils "instruction in science and lore." The Buddha's higher teachings are for the enlightened and wise, and the thoughtful.[32]

The 1904 edition also included references to evolution, identifying it among the Four Noble Truths, which included "the miseries of evolutionary existence resulting in births and deaths, life after life." (#121); escaping bad Karma and moving toward higher evolution as a result of deeds of merit (#139); demonstrating that Buddhism accorded with the theory of gradual evolution of the perfected man (#233); and that "the principle of evolution, guided by Karma, individual and collective, will evolve another universe with its contents, as our universe was evolved out of the Akasha"

(#367). Olcott's evolution correlated to aspects of positivism but not with the Darwinian universe that was without design, progress, or destiny. Like most scientists, liberal clergy, and college-educated Protestants, Olcott adopted a concept of evolution that replaced revealed religion with an optimistic worldview.[33]

Contemporaneous with the popularity of Theosophy and a westernized version of Buddhism came the founding of Mary Baker Eddy's Church of Christ, Scientist (CCS) and New Thought, whose early spokespersons (e.g., Horatio Dresser, Henry Wood, William Walker Atkinson, and Ralph Waldo Trine) infused large amounts of Buddhist thinking into their writings. While Christianity continued to struggle with the existential challenges stemming from the higher criticism and the consequences of natural selection, these examples of late nineteenth-century idealism encountered the world with a sophisticated set of beliefs intent on minimizing the tensions arising from the creeping effects of Western science and technology. As noted by David L. McMahan, "perhaps no major tradition has attempted to adopt scientific discourse more vigorously than Buddhism."[34]

It took two world wars for these grand narratives to lose their relevancy—not that the matters they addressed could have been solved to anyone's satisfaction, but that postmodern society stopped probing them with any expectation of discovering some final explanation. Unlike their predecessors, the postmodernists learned to live with ambiguity and make decisions based on a wide range of disassembled information. They realized that many of life's questions had no answers, and unlike in previous eras, they seemed no longer troubled by the new reality.

Even with large portions of the West's population literate, elites continue to play a significant role in driving its core values. John Brockman suggested in *The Third Culture* (1995) that a new generation of scientific intellectuals distinct from the traditional stable of creative minds now communicates with the literate public on matters bordering the frontiers of knowledge, including the origins of life, mind, and the universe. If true, and it seems to be, intellectuals from physics, evolutionary biology, philosophy, AI, computer science, and psychology have entered the conversation, altering how we look at ourselves and the universe. Accompanying these new perspectives has been the realization that the world no longer fits the neat categories our brains created to understand it. Leaving

aside Henry Adams's amusement that the "grand narratives" were mis-
takenly likened to fixed stars capable of explaining the past and predicting
the future, one is reminded of the observation made by historian John
Lukacs that the authority given to science was inflated to the degree that
it disconnected the objectivity of the researcher from any fallibility as a
human being. Lukacs wisely noted our limitations by calling subjectivity
and objectivity "two sides of the same debased coin."[35]

Although educated and affluent elites continue into the present day
utilizing their assets to influence public opinion, others have garnered attention by impugning rather than supporting the democratic traditions
of civility, free press, regulated capitalism, voter rights, and the concreteness of our sense perceptions. These discredited but otherwise influential individuals have seen their ideas metastasized into social media, ca-
ble, and talk radio to the point of polarizing every issue and making a
mockery of a common identity or consensual set of core values. Their unruly and undemocratic behavior, augmented by growing inequality and
economic insecurity, have conditioned millions to accept over-drawn par-
tisan perceptions, resentments, and deepening fears of one another. The
etiquette that once managed discourse has been discarded as caricatures
of contending opinions gnaw at the very roots of what is left of the West's
weakened institutions. Thus, guarantees of a stable future are much less
probable today than ever before. The late nineteenth- and early twentieth-
century quest for certitude, however flawed it may have been, proved
much more genuine by comparison to the tribalism, fragmentation, and
loss of vision that mark our current condition.[36]

# Notes

## Introduction

1. Henry Adams, *The Education of Henry Adams: An Autobiography* (Boston: Houghton Mifflin, 1918), 231–32.

2. Read Mark Noll, *America's God: From Jonathan Edwards to Abraham Lincoln* (New York: Oxford University Press, 2002).

3. Van A. Harvey, "Is There an Ethics of Belief?" *Journal of Religion* 49 (1969), 41.

4. Read Van A. Harvey, *The Historian and the Believer* (New York: Macmillan, 1965); Stephen Maitzen, "Two Views of Religious Certitude," *Religious Studies* 28 (1992), 65–74.

5. W. K. Clifford, "The Ethics of Belief," in Walter Kaufman (ed.), *Religion from Tolstoy to Camus* (New York: Harper and Row, 1961), 204–6; Sherrie Lyons, *Species, Serpents, Spirits, and Skulls: Science at the Margins in the Victorian Age* (New York: SUNY Press, 2009), 1–16, 171–202.

6. Read Richard J. Helmstadter and Bernard Lightman, *Victorian Faith in Crisis: Essays on Continuity and Change in Nineteenth-Century Religious Belief* (Stanford: Stanford University Press, 1990).

7. Henry S. Nash, "Religion, Revelation and Moral Certitude," *Biblical World* 31 (1908), 369.

8. Read Randall Collins, *Conflict Sociology* (New York: Academic Press, 1975); James Davison Hunter, *Culture Wars* (New York: Basic Books, 1991); G. Therborn, *The Ideology of Power and the Power of Ideology* (London: Verso, 1980).

9. Lance St. John Butler, *Victorian Doubt: Literary and Cultural Discourses* (New York: Harvester Wheatsheaf, 1990), 1.

10. Susan Budd, *Varieties of Unbelief: Atheists and Agnostics in English Society* (London: Heinemann Educational Books, 1977); A. N. Wilson, *God's Funeral* (London: John Murray, 1999).

11. Timothy Larsen, *Crisis of Doubt: Honest Faith in Nineteenth-Century England* (Oxford: Oxford University Press, 2006).

12. John Henry Newman, *Apologia pro Vita Sua* (London: Longman, Green, Longman, Roberts and Green, 1864), 374.

13. Fraser Watts, "Are Science and Religion in Conflict?" *Zygon* 32 (1997), 125–39.

14. Andrew Cunningham, "Getting the Game Right: Some Plain Words on the Identity and Invention of Science," *Studies in the History and Philosophy of Science* 19 (1988), 384. See also Peter Harrison, *The Bible, Protestantism, and the Rise of Natural Science* (Cambridge: Cambridge University Press, 1988); John Brooke, *Science and Religion: Some Historical Perspectives* (Cambridge: Cambridge University Press, 1991).

15. Sydney Ross, "'Scientist': The Story of a Word," *Annals of Science*, 18 (1962), 65–88; Frank M. Turner, "The Victorian Conflict Between Science and Religion: A Professional Dimension," *Isis*, 69 (1978), 360.

16. Peter Harrison, "Science and Religion: Constructing the Boundaries," *Journal of Religion*, 86 (2006), 85; Frank M. Turner, "The Victorian Conflict between Science and Religion: A Professional Dimension," *Isis*, 69 (1978), 356–76.

17. The anonymously published *Vestiges of the Natural History of Creation* had been written by Robert Chambers, an Edinburgh writer and publisher of *Chambers' Edinburgh Journal*. In it he proposed a vast sequence of developmental change in the universe, with the eventual appearance of man through progressive change from primates. Read William Paley, *Natural Theology; or, Evidence of the Existence and Attributes of the Deity* (London: C. Knight, 1836); Aileen Fyfe, "The Reception of William Paley's Natural Theology in the University of Cambridge," *British Journal for the History of Science*, 30 (1997), 321–35; J. Topham, "Science and Popular Education in the 1830s: The Role of the Bridgewater Treatises," *British Journal for the History of Science*, 25 (1992), 397–430; John Robson, "The Fiat and Finger of God: The Bridgewater Treatises," in Bernard Lightman and Frank Turner (eds.), *Victorian Faith in Crisis: Essays on Continuity and Change in Nineteenth-Century Belief* (Stanford: Stanford University Press, 1990), 71–125.

18. See John Dewey, *The Quest for Certainty* (New York: Putnam's, 1960), 1–73; John Dewey, *The Influence of Darwin on Philosophy* (Bloomington: Indiana University Press, 1910), 1–19.

19. James Moore, "Deconstructing Darwinism: The Politics of Evolution in the 1860s," *Journal of the History of Biology*, 24 (1991), 353–408.

20. John Passmore, "Darwin's Impact on British Metaphysics," *Victorian Studies*, 3 (1959), 51.

21. E. Manier, *The Young Darwin and His Cultural Circle* (Dordrecht, Holland: D. Reidel Pub. Co., 1978); S. Silvan Schweber, "The Young Darwin," *Journal of the History of Biology*, 12 (1979), 175–92; Keith Thomson, *The Young Charles Darwin* (New Haven: Yale University Press, 2009).

22. Neal C. Gillespie, *Charles Darwin and the Problem of Creation* (Chicago: University of Chicago Press, 1979).

23. James R. Moore, *The Post-Darwinian Controversies: A Study of the Protestant Struggle to Come to Terms with Darwin in Great Britain and America, 1870–1900* (Cambridge: Cambridge University Press, 1979).

24. Daniel C. Dennett, *Darwin's Dangerous Idea: Evolution and the Meanings of Life* (London: Allen Lane, 1995), 21–22.

25. Darwin admitted at the time of his recommendation to the post on the *Beagle*, he had not "the least doubt the strict and literal truth of every word in the Bible." Quoted in Nora Barlow (ed.), *The Autobiography of Charles Darwin, 1809–1882* (New York: Harcourt, Brace, 1958), 57.

26. Francis Darwin (ed.), *The Life and Letters of Charles Darwin*, 2 vols. (New York: D. Appleton, 1896), 1:147.

27. For examples, see James C. Livingston, "Darwin, Darwinism, and Theology: Recent Studies," *Religious Studies Review*, 8 (1982), 105–16; Maurice Mandelbaum, "Darwin's Religious Views," *Journal of the History of Ideas*, 19 (1958), 363–78; Dov Ospovat, "God and Natural Selection: The Darwinian Idea of Design," *Journal of the History of Biology*, 15 (1980), 169–95; Frank Burch Brown, "The Evolution of Darwin's Theism," *Journal of the History of Biology*, 19 (1986), 1–45.

28. Francis Darwin (ed.), *The Life and Letters of Charles Darwin Including an Autobiographical Chapter*, 2 vols. (New York: Appleton, 1898), 2:105.

29. Darwin to Gray, November 26, 1860, "Darwin Correspondence Project," https://www.darwinproject.ac.uk/letter/entry-2998, accessed January 24, 2016.

30. Quoted in Nora Barlow (ed.), *Autobiography of Charles Darwin*, 94.

31. Van A. Harvey, "The Ethics of Belief Reconsidered," *Journal of Religion*, 59 (1979), 408.

32. John C. Greene, "Darwin and Religion," *Proceedings of the American Philosophical Society*, 103 (1959), 721.

33. Asa Gray, *Natural Science and Religion: Two Lectures* (New York: Scribner's, 1880). See also Vernon L. Kellogg, *Darwinism To-Day: A Discussion of Present-Day Scientific Criticism of the Darwinian Selection Theories, Together with a Brief Account of the Principal Other Auxiliary and Alternative Theories of Species-Forming* (London: Bell, 1907).

34. Alfred Russel Wallace, *Darwinism: An Exposition of the Theory of Natural Selection, with Some of Its Applications* (London: Macmillan, 1889), viii.

35. The religious aspects of the Darwinian controversy are also examined in Bert James Lowenberg's "The Reaction of American Scientists to Darwinism," *American Historical Review*, 38 (1933), 687–701; "The Controversy over Evolution in New England, 1859–1873," *New England Quarterly*, 8 (1935), 232–57; "Darwinism Comes to America, 1859–1900," *Mississippi Valley Historical Review*, 28 (1941), 339–68.

36. Bernard Lightman, "Darwin and the Popularization of Evolution," *Notes and Records of the Royal Society of London*, 64 (2010), 11–16.

37. St. George Jackson Mivart quoted in Thomas H. Huxley, "Mr. Darwin's Critics," in *Darwiniana: Essays* (New York: D. Appleton and Co., 1893), 122–23.

38. The term "dysteleology" was invented by Haeckel to explain the purposelessness in natural selection. Read Edward Aveling, *The Creed of an Atheist* (London: Free Thought, 1881), *The Student's Darwin* (London: Free Thought, 1881); *Works of Robert G. Ingersoll*, 13 vols. (New York: Dresden, 1909–15), 4:463–64; Ernst Haeckel, *Riddle of the Universe at the Close of the Nineteenth Century* (New York: Harper and Brothers, 1900).

39. Donald Harvey Meyer, "American Intellectuals and the Victorian Crisis of Faith," *American Quarterly*, 27 (1975), 591.

40. Stow Persons, *Free Religion: An American Faith* (Boston: Beacon, 1963 [1947]), 57.

41. Quoted in Charles A. Madison, "Henry George, Prophet of Human Rights," *South Atlantic Quarterly*, 43 (1944), 360.

42. Henry Adams, *The Education of Henry Adams* (New York: Modern Library, 1918), 237.

43. Quoted in Paul Carus, *The Dawn of a New Religious Era, and Other Essays* (Chicago: Open Court, 1899), 7.

44. Quoted in Paul Carus, "The Dawn of a New Religious Era," *Monist*, 4 (1894), 8.

45. Richard Hughes Seager, "Pluralism and the American Mainstream: The View from the World's Parliament of Religions," *Harvard Theological Review*, 82 (1989), 301–24.

46. Carus, *Dawn of a New Religious Era, and Other Essays*, 6.

47. David L. McMahan, "Modernity and the Early Discourse of Scientific Buddhism," *Journal of the American Academy of Religion*, 72 (2004), 898.

48. Carus, "Dawn of a New Religious Era," 1, 16–17.

49. Amy Kittelstrom, "The International Social Turn: Unity and Brotherhood at the World's Parliament of Religions, Chicago, 1893," *Religion and American Culture; A Journal of Interpretation*, 19 (2009), 244.

50. W. M. Simon, "Auguste Comte's English Disciples," *Victorian Studies*, 8 (1964), 162.

51. Auguste Comte, *The Positive Philosophy of Auguste Comte*, trans. Harriet Martineau (New York: AMS Press, 1974 [1855]), 1:27.

52. Read Gillis J. Harp, *Positivist Republic: Auguste Comte and the Reconstruction of American Liberalism, 1865–1920* (University Park: Pennsylvania State University Press, 1995).

53. John Henry Newman, *An Essay in Aid of a Grammar of Assent* (New York: Catholic Publication Society, 1870), 100–101, 210.

54. Charles H. Cooley, "Reflections upon the Sociology of Herbert Spencer," *American Journal of Sociology*, 26 (1920), 135.

55. Comte, *Cours de philosophie positive* (Paris: Bachelier, 1841), 3:296; Herbert Spencer, *Principles of Psychology*, 2nd ed. (London, 1870), 1:422.

56. Wallace, *Darwinism: An Exposition of the Theory of Natural Selection with Some of Its Applications* (London, 1889), 477–78.

57. Alfred Russel Wallace, "A Defense of Modern Spiritualism," *Fortnightly Review*, 15 (1874), 785–808. Read also Malcolm J. Kotter, "Alfred Russel Wallace, the Origins of Man, and Spiritualism," *Isis* 65 (1974), 145–92; Roger Smith, "Alfred Russel Wallace: Philosophy of Nature and Man," *British Journal of the History of Science*, 6 (1972), 177–99; Wilma George, *Biologist Philosopher: A Study of the Life and Writings of Alfred Russel Wallace* (London: Abelard-Schuman, 1964); Janet Oppenheim, *The Other World: Spiritualism and Psychical Research in England, 1850–1914* (Cambridge: Cambridge University Press, 1985).

58. Thomas H. Huxley, *Collected Essays*, 9 vols. (New York: Greenwood, 1968 [1898]), 4:47, 9:56.

59. John Spencer Clark, *The Life and Letters of John Fiske*, 2 vols. (Boston: Houghton Mifflin, 1917), 1:372.

60. Richard M. Gale, *The Divided Self of William James* (Cambridge: Cambridge University Press, 1999).

61. James O. Pawelski, "William James and the Journey toward Unification," *Transactions of the Charles S. Peirce Society*, 40 (2004), 795.

62. Lester F. Ward, *Dynamic Sociology, or Applied Social Science, as Based upon Statical Sociology and the Less Complex Sciences* (New York: D. Appleton, 1883), 35, 36.

63. Ward, *Dynamic Sociology*, 28.

64. Bernhard J. Stern, "The Liberal Views of Lester F. Ward," *Scientific Monthly*, 71 (1950), 102.

65. Lester Frank Ward, *Applied Sociology: A Treatise on the Conscious Improvement of Society by Society* (Boston: Ginn, 1906), 7.

66. Paul Carus, *The Religion of Science*, 2nd ed. (Chicago: Open Court, 1896), 72–73.

## Chapter 1

1. *Discours sur l'esprit positif* (Paris: V. Dalmont, 1844), translated as *A Discourse on the Positive Spirit* (London: Reeves, 1903); *Discours sur l'ensemble du positivism* (Paris: Mathias, 1848), translated as *General View of Positivism* (London: Trübner, 1865); *Système de politique positive, ou Traité de sociologie instituant la religion de l'Humanité*, 4 vols. (Paris: Carilian-Goeury, 1851–1854), translated as *System of Positive Polity* (London: Longmans, Green, 1875–1877); *Catéchisme positiviste* (Paris: self-published, 1852), translated as *The Catechism of Positive Religion* (London: Trübner, 1891); *Appel aux conservateurs* (Paris: self-published, 1855), translated as *Appeal to Conservatives* (London: Trübner, 1889); and *Synthèse subjective* (Paris: self-published, 1856), translated as *Subjective Synthesis* (London: Kegan Paul, 1891).

2. Read Mary Pickering, *Auguste Comte: An Intellectual Biography*, 3 vols. (Cambridge: Cambridge University Press, 2005, 2009); Gillis J. Harp, *Positivist Republic: Auguste Comte and the Reconstruction of American Liberalism, 1865–1920* (University Park: Pennsylvania State University Press, 1995).

3. H. B. Acton, "Comte's Positivism and the Science of Society," *Philosophy*, 26 (1951), 295.

4. Read Frank Edward Manuel, *The New World of Henri Saint-Simon* (Cambridge: Harvard University Press, 1956); Arthur John Booth, *Saint-Simon and Saint-Simonism: A Chapter in the History of Socialism in France* (London: Longmans, Green, Reader and Dyer, 1871); Mathurin Marius Dondo, *The French Faust: Henri de Saint-Simon* (New York: Philosophical Library, 1935).

5. Gillian Lindt Gollin, "Theories of the Good Society: Four Views on Religion and Social Change," *Journal for the Scientific Study of Religion*, 9 (1970), 1–4.

6. Read Henri de Saint-Simon, *The New Christianity* (London: B. D. Cousins and P. Wilson, 1834).

7. Eric W. Smithner, "Descartes and Auguste Comte," *French Review*, 41 (1968), 632–33; W. M. Simon, *European Positivism in the Nineteenth Century* (Ithaca: Cornell University Press, 1963), 28, 122.

8. The creator of the science of sociology, Comte coined the term in the forty-seventh lesson of his *Course in Positive Philosophy*.

9. Auguste Comte, *A General View of Positivism; or, Summary Exposition of the System of Thought and Life, Adapted to the Great Western Republic, formed of the Five Advanced Nations, the French, Italian, Spanish, British, and German, Which since the time of Charlemagne, have always constituted a Political Whole* (London: George Routledge, 1910 [1848]), 28, 32–34, 56–57.

10. Auguste Comte, *The Positive Philosophy*, translated and condensed by Harriet Martineau (New York: Calvin Blanchard, 1858), 436.

11. In many ways, Comte's life, and particularly his frustration in being recognized by contemporaries, mirrored the life and times of Charles Fourier, who battled similar feelings of abandonment.

12. Richard Vernon, "Auguste Comte and 'Development': A Note," *History and Theory*, 17 (1978), 323–26; Auguste Comte, *Cours de philosophie positive*, 2 vols. (Paris: J. B. Baillière et fils, 1875), 2:124.

13. Auguste Comte, *Social Physics: From the Positive Philosophy* (New York: Calvin Blanchard, 1856), 406.

14. Comte, *Positive Philosophy*, 440.

15. Charles D. Cashdollar, "Auguste Comte and the American Reformed Theologians," *Journal of the History of Ideas*, 39 (1978), 73–74.

16. Comte, *Positive Philosophy*, 25–26.

17. Comte, *Catechism of Positive Religion*, 169.

18. Comte inveighed against the opinion that psychology should be included among the sciences, arguing that introspection lacked legitimacy as a scientific method for understanding nature's laws. It offered no basis for philosophy; nor could it stand as a discipline. In its place, Comte substituted the cerebral functions set forth by Broussais and the phrenology of Franz Gall. This explains his reductionist endorsement of phrenology's division of the brain into the regions of propensities, sentiments, and intellect. The brain, "an apparatus of organs" grew more complex with the affective and intellectual functions. "A full contemplation of Gall's doctrine," he wrote, "convinces us of its faithful representation of the intellectual and moral nature of Man and animals." From his perspective, Gall's cerebral theory destroyed the metaphysical "fancies" of previous centuries concerning the origin of mankind's social tendencies. Read W. M. Simon, "The 'Two Cultures' in Nineteenth-Century France: Victor Cousin and Auguste Comte," *Journal of the History of Ideas*, 26 (1965), 46; See Comte, *The Positive Philosophy*, 2:136; Simon, *European Positivism in the Nineteenth Century*, 122–23; John Stuart Mill, *Auguste Comte and Positivism* (London: N. Trübner and Co., 1866), 65.

19. Comte, *Positive Philosophy*, 49, 54.

20. Read Arthur Lovejoy, *The Great Chain of Being; A Study of the History of an Idea* (New York: Harper and Row, 1965).

21. Comte, *Positive Philosophy*, 484.

22. Auguste Comte, *A General View of Positivism* (London: Reeves and Turner, 1880), 41, 44–47.

23. Comte, *Positive Philosophy*, 473–74.

24. Quoted in Mary Pickering, *Auguste Comte*, vol. 1, *An Intellectual Biography* (Cambridge: Cambridge University Press, 1993), 45.

25. Comte, *Positive Philosophy*, 804–5.

26. Quoted in Comte, *Positive Philosophy*, 441.

27. Mabel V. Wilson, "Auguste Comte's Conception of Humanity," *International Journal of Ethics*, 38 (1927), 93.

28. Comte to Georges Audiffrent, January 14, 1855, in John K. Ingram, *Passages from the Letters of Auguste Comte Selected and Translated* (London: Adam and Charles Black, 1901), 204.

29. Frederic Harrison, *On Society* (London: Macmillan, 1918), 16.

30. Read Charles de Rouvre, *L'amoureuse histoire d'Auguste Comte et de Clotilde de Vaux* (Paris: Calmann-Lévy, 1917).

31. Martha Nussbaum, "Reinventing the Civil Religion: Comte, Mill, Tagore," *Victorian Studies*, 54 (2011), 8–9.

32. Comte, *General View of Positivism*, 94, 100.

33. Comte, *Positive Philosophy*, 645–46.

34. Comte, *Positive Philosophy*, 642.

35. Comte, *General View of Positivism*, 152–53, 372–74.

36. Richard Vernon, "Auguste Comte and the Withering-Away of the State," *Journal of the History of Ideas*, 45 (1984), 549–66.

37. See Henri de Saint-Simon, *Social Organization, the Science of Man, and Other Writings* (New York: Harper and Row, 1964), 72–75; Frank E. Manuel, *The Prophets of Paris: Turgot, Condorcet, Saint-Simon, Fourier and Comte* (New York: Harper and Row, 1965), 251–60.

38. Comte, *General View of Positivism*, 125. In 1851 Comte lent his support to the coup d'état by Napoleon III, a decision he hoped would bring a quick end to the nation's anarchic forces. Although he eventually regretted his decision, it nevertheless marked his turning away from Europe and hoping instead to convince the Russian czar and the grand vizier of the Ottoman Empire on the merits of positivism. According to historian Mary Pickering, Comte concluded that positivism would make a greater impact on leaders in the East than on those in the West, whom he considered too reactionary. "Positivism could show them the road to progress that was best adapted to their national characteristics so that their development could be systematic, rapid and trouble-free." Unfortunately, "Comte was ignorant of Nicholas's autocratic nature and his politically stagnant regime." Mary Pickering, *Auguste Comte: An Intellectual Biography* (Cambridge: Cambridge University Press, 2009), 2:78.

39. Comte, *General View of Positivism*, 340–58.

40. Comte, *General View of Positivism*, 213–14, 395–96.

41. Comte, *General View of Positivism*, 3, 6.

42. Comte to John Metcalf, February 28, 1856, in John K. Ingram, *Passages from the Letters of Auguste Comte Selected and Translated* (London: Adam and Charles Black, 1901), 173, 175; Comte, *Positive Philosophy*, 649–51, 652.

43. Comte, *General View of Positivism*, 222–29, 243, 278, 377; Auguste Comte, *The Catechism of Positive Religion*, trans. Richard Congreve (London: John Chapman, 1858), 137.

44. Comte's favorite book was Thomas à Kempis's *The Imitation of Christ*, first published in 1486. Comte, *Catechism of Positive Religion*, 7–19, 21, 26, 39–43, 64.

45. See Auguste Comte, *Calendrier positiviste, ou Système général de commémoration publique* (Paris: A La Librairie Scientifique-Industrielle, 1852).

46. George Sarton, "Auguste Comte, Historian of Science: With a Short Digression on Clotilde de Vaux and Harriet Taylor," *Osiris*, 10 (1952), 332, 353–54. The Americans in the calendar were Benjamin Franklin, George Washington, Robert Fulton, Thomas Jefferson, James Madison, and James Fennimore Cooper. According to George Sarton, while Comte was a teacher of mathematics, he was never a "real man of science . . . and less and less so as he grew older." Nor was he a true historian, as he had no idea of historical methods. Although well-educated and with a fair knowledge of the history of science, he was the type of person to whom "halfwits" were always drawn.

47. Nussbaum, "Reinventing the Civil Religion," 11.

48. In France there were Taine, Ribot, and de Roberty; in Germany, Duhring and Avenarius; in Sweden, A. Nystrom; in Brazil and Chile, Benjamin Constant and Miguel Lemos.

49. John Stuart Mill, *Utilitarianism* (New York: Liberal Arts Press, 1957 [1861]).

50. Nussbaum, "Reinventing the Civil Religion," 14.

51. G. W. F. Meyor, "Auguste Comte: An Intellectual Biography," *Contemporary Sociology*, 40 (2011), 612.

52. Thomas H. Huxley, "On the Physical Basis of Life," *Fortnightly Review*, 5 (1869), 141.

53. According to C. D. Cashdollar, Comtean positivism was a popular topic in the writings of Lyman Atwater, Albert Barnes, John Bascom, Horace Bushnell, Robert Lewis Dabney, George P. Fisher, Samuel Harris, Laurens P. Hickok, Archibald A. Hodge, Charles Hodge, Noah Porter, Charles W. Shields, Henry Boynton Smith, Newman Smyth, and Ransom B. Welch. See Charles D. Cashdollar, "Auguste Comte and the American Reformed Theologians," *Journal of the History of Ideas*, 39 (1978), 62. Read also Richmond L. Hawkins, *Auguste Comte and the United States, 1816–1853* (Cambridge: Harvard University Press, 1936); and Richmond L. Hawkins, *Positivism in the United States, 1853–1861* (Cambridge: Harvard University Press, 1938). Unitarians such as John Fiske, Francis Ellingwood Abbot, and Octavius Brooks were known advocates of positivism. Read C. D. Cashdollar, "European Positivism and the American Unitarians," *Church History*, 45 (1976), 490–506.

54. Cashdollar, "Auguste Comte and the American Reformed Theologians," 66.

55. Read James McCosh, *The Method of Divine Government, Physical and Moral* (New York: R. Carter, 1855); James McCosh, *Christianity and Positivism* (New York: R. Carter, 1871).

56. James McCosh, *Boston Lectures, 1870: Christianity and Skepticism* (Boston,

1870); James McCosh, et. al., *Questions of Modern Thought* (Philadelphia: Ziegler and McCurdy, 1871).

57. O. B. Frothingham, "The Religion of Humanity," *Radical*, 10 (1872), 251.

58. Cashdollar, "European Positivism and the American Unitarians," 491.

59. O. B. Frothingham, *The Religion of Humanity* (New York: D. G. Francis, 1873), 33. Although Comte denied only the comprehensibility of God and was not technically an atheist, Reformed writers and lecturers chose not to make a distinction between the two. It was the skepticism in positivism and its inductive method that served as the brush with which critics painted it as a dangerous form of materialism and infidelity.

60. Gillis J. Harp, "'The Church of Humanity': New York's Worshipping Positivists," *Church History*, 60 (1991), 512–14.

61. George Sarton, "Auguste Comte, Historian of Science," *Osiris*, 10 (1952), 328–57.

## Chapter 2

1. John Henry Newman, *Apologia pro Vita Sua* (London: Longman, Green, Longman, Roberts, and Green, 1864), 288.

2. Read Ian T. Ker, *John Henry Newman: A Biography* (Oxford: Clarendon Press, 1989), 311–12; Ian T. Ker, *The Achievement of John Henry Newman* (Notre Dame, IN: University of Notre Dame Press, 1990); John Kent, "The Victorian Resistance: Comments on Religious Life and Culture, 1840–80," *Victorian Studies*, 12 (1968), 145–54.

3. John Henry Newman, *An Essay in Aid of a Grammar of Assent* (London: Burns, Oates, 1870), 177, 499; John Henry Newman, *Discourses Addressed to Mixed Congregations* (London: James Duffy, 1862), 260.

4. Quoted in P. J. FitzPatrick, "Newman and Kingsley," in David Nicholls and Fergus Kerr (eds.), *John Henry Newman: Reason, Rhetoric and Romanticism* (Carbondale: Southern Illinois University Press, 1991), 88.

5. In *The Idea of a University*, Newman set out the qualities of a great author: "He writes passionately, because he feels keenly; forcibly, because he conceives vividly; he sees too clearly to be vague; he is too serious to be otiose; he can analyze his subject, and therefore he is rich; he embraces it as a whole and in its parts, and therefore he is consistent; he has a firm hold of it, and therefore, he is luminous." John Henry Newman, *The Idea of a University* (London: Longmans, Green, 1891), 184.

6. Newman, *Apologia pro Vita Sua*, 72.

7. Newman, *Apologia pro Vita Sua*, 56, 59; William Samuel Lill, *Characteristics from the Writings of John Henry Newman* (London: Henry S. King, 1874), B-2.

8. Newman, *Apologia pro Vita Sua*, 385.

9. John J. O'Meara, "Augustine and Newman: Comparison in Conversion," *University Review*, 1 (1954), 27–36.

10. Newman, *Apologia pro Vita Sua*, 59–61, 63.

11. Newman, *Apologia pro Vita Sua*, 63.

12. John Henry Newman, "Poetry, with Reference to Aristotle's *Politics*," *London Review*, 1 (1829), reprinted in John Henry Newman, *Essays Critical and Historical* (London: Basil Montagu Pickering, 1871), 1–29. See also Newman, *Apologia pro Vita Sua*, 68–70.

13. Newman, *Apologia pro Vita Sua*, 65.

14. Newman, *Apologia pro Vita Sua*, 72.

15. Newman, *Apologia pro Vita Sua*, 95.

16. John Henry Newman, *Letters and Correspondence of John Henry Newman during His Life in the English Church*, 2 vols. (London: Longmans, Green, 1891), 1:390.

17. Newman, *Apologia pro Vita Sua*, 85–86.

18. *Tracts for the Times*, 6 vols. (Oxford: J. G. and F. Rivington and J. H. Parker, 1834–1841), 1:iii, v. The motto of the tracts: "If the trumpets give an uncertain sound, who shall prepare himself to the battle?"

19. This continued to be Newman's position until 1845, when he wrote Bishop Nicholas Wiseman to announce his conversion. "I could find nothing better to say to him, than that I would obey the Pope as I had obeyed my own Bishop in the Anglican Church." See Newman, *Apologia pro Vita Sua*, 113, 121, 123.

20. Newman had difficulty making Pusey understand his differences and died before the two men could work through their issues. Newman felt distraught over the situation and blamed himself for the impediments that had entangled their relationship. See Newman, *Apologia pro Vita Sua*, 106–7, 136–39, 140, 358–59.

21. Newman, *Apologia pro Vita Sua*, 155.

22. Wilfred Ward, *The Life of John Henry Cardinal Newman* (London: Longmans, Green, 1912), 2:114–15, 393–95.

23. *Tracts 41, Via Media* (London: J. G. and F. Rivington, and J. H. Parker, Oxford, 1839), 1:2–3; Newman, *Apologia pro Vita Sua*, 159.

24. Newman, *Apologia pro Vita Sua*, 142, 147, 150, 180.

25. *Tract XC on Certain Passages in the XXXIX Articles by the Rev. J. H. Newman, B.D., 1841, with A Historical Preface by the Rev. E. B. Pusey, D. D. and Catholic Subscription to the XXXIX Articles Considered in Reference to Tract XC by the Rev. John Keble, M.A., 1841* (London: John Henry and James Parker, Oxford, and Rivingtons, 1865), 4–5.

26. Peter Nockles, "Oxford, Tract 90 and the Bishops," in David Nicholls and Fergus Kerr (eds.), *John Henry Newman: Reason, Rhetoric and Romanticism* (Carbondale: Southern Illinois University Press, 1991), 28–87.

27. Newman, *Apologia pro Vita Sua*, 175, 329.

28. Newman, *Apologia pro Vita Sua*, 175.

29. Newman, *Apologia Pro Vita Sua*, 349–50.

30. Newman, *Apologia pro Vita Sua*, 176, 257–58.

31. Aubrey de Vere, "Some Recollections of Cardinal Newman," *Living Age*, 211 (1896), 151.

32. Vehemently anti-Catholic (e.g., *The Water Babies*, 1853), Kingsley engaged in heated debates with Newman. Sympathetic with Chartism and one of the co-founders of Christian Socialism, he wrote many articles in support of humanitarian reform. P. J. FitzPatrick, "Newman and Kingsley," David Nicholls and Fergus Kerr (eds.), *John Henry Newman: Reason, Rhetoric and Romanticism*, 88–108. Probably the most lasting outcome from their protracted exchange was Newman's introduction of the phrase "poisoning the well," which he explained in his *Apologia pro Vita Sua*: "[Charles Kingsley attempted] to cut the ground from under my feet;—to poison by anticipation the public mind against me . . . and to infuse into the imaginations of my readers, suspicion and mistrust of everything that I may say in reply to him. This I call poisoning the wells. . . . Controversies should be decided by reason; is it legitimate warfare to appeal to the misgivings of the public mind and to its dislikings?"

33. Newman, *Idea of a University* (London: Basil Montagu Pickering, 1873), 58. See also "Louvain Newman Society," https://newmansociety.wordpress.com/2011/01/26/the-newman-louvain-leuven-connection, accessed October 5, 2015.

34. Newman, *Idea of a University*, 332.

35. Newman, *Idea of a University*, xviii, 10–13, 57, 122–24.

36. Newman, *Idea of a University*, 10–11.

37. Read Russell Kirk, "The Conservative Mind of Newman," *Sewanee Review*, 60 (1952), 675.

38. Gilbert Clive Binyon, *The Christian Socialist Movement in England* (London: Society for Promoting Christian Knowledge, 1931), 74–143; William George Peck, *The Social Implications of the Oxford Movement* (New York: C. Scribner's Sons, 1933), 53.

39. Ian T. Ker, *John Henry Newman*, 384, 551–52.

40. Marvin R. O'Connell, "Newman: The Limits of Certitude," *Review of Politics*, 35 (1973), 158–59.

41. Newman, *Idea of a University*, 322–336.

42. Quoted in Peter E. Hodgson, "Newman and Science," *Sapientia*, 54 (1999), 405.

43. Read Eric Steinberg, "Newman's Distinction between Inference and Assent," *Religious Studies*, 23 (1987), 351–65; M. Jamie Ferreira, *Doubt and Religious Commitment: The Role of the Will in Newman's Thought* (Oxford: Clarendon Press, 1980); David A. Pailin, *The Way to Faith: An Examination of Newman's "Grammar of Assent" as a Response to the Search for Certainty in Faith* (London: Epworth Press, 1969).

44. John Henry Newman, "Faith and Private Judgment," in *Discourses to Mixed Congregations* (Denville, NJ: Dimension Books, 1984), 194.

45. Read John R. T. Lamont, "Newman on Faith and Rationality," *International Journal for Philosophy of Religion*, 40 (1996), 63–84.

46. John Henry Newman, *Discourses Addressed to Mixed Congregations* (London: Longman, Brown, Green, and Longmans, 1849), 282.

47. Newman, *Grammar of Assent*, 201, 145–46.

48. Jay Newman, "Cardinal Newman's Phenomenology of Religious Belief," *Religious Studies*, 10 (1974), 130–31.

49. Ian T. Ker, "Recent Critics of Newman's 'A Grammar of Assent,'" *Religious Studies*, 13 (1977), 66.

50. Read Karl Barth, *The Epistle to the Romans* (London: Oxford University Press, 1953), 45.

51. Newman, *Grammar of Assent*, 98.

52. Ironically, in utilizing Butler's *Analogy of Religion*, which discusses the role of probability to shore up man's imperfect knowledge, Newman borrowed the very instrument used by Darwin to build a case for his theory of natural selection.

53. Read Thomas J. Norris, *Newman and His Theological Method: A Guide for the Theologian Today* (Leiden: E. J. Brill, 1977).

54. W. E. Gladstone (ed.), *The Works of Joseph Butler, D.C.L., Sometime Lord Bishop of Durham*, 2 vols. (Oxford: Clarendon Press, 1897), 1:5. Read also Ian Hacking, *The Emergence of Probability* (Cambridge: Cambridge University Press, 1975); and Lorraine Daston, *Classical Probability in the Enlightenment* (Princeton: Princeton University Press, 1988); Theodore M. Porter, *The Rise of Statistical Thinking, 1820–1900* (Princeton: Princeton University Press, 1986).

55. Newman, *Apologia pro Vita Sua*, 29.

56. Jonathan Smith, Lawrence I. Berkove, and Gerald A. Baker, "A Grammar of Dissent: 'Flatland,' Newman, and the Theology of Probability," *Victorian Studies*, 39 (1996), 129–50; Edwin A. Abbott, *The Anglican Career of Cardinal Newman*, 2 vols. (London: Macmillan, 1892); Edwin A. Abbott, *Flatland*, 2nd ed. (Princeton: Princeton University Press, 1991 [1884]); Edwin A. Abbott, *The Kernel and the Husk* (Boston: Roberts, 1887).

57. Read Frederick D. Aquino, *Communities of Informed Judgment: Newman's Illative Sense and Accounts of Rationality* (Washington, DC: Catholic University of America Press, 2004).

58. Kirk, "Conservative Mind of Newman," 664, 666.

59. Newman, *Grammar of Assent*, 320, 340, 346.

60. Compare the meta-analysis with Newman's *Grammar of Assent*, 288–327.

61. John Henry Newman, *Sermons Preached before the University of Oxford between 1826 and 1843* (London: Rivingtons, 1887), 257.

62. William James, "Clifford's 'Lectures and Essays,'" *Collected Essays and Reviews* (London: Longmans, Green, 1920), 140; William James, *The Will to Believe, and Other Essays on Popular Philosophy* (London: Longmans, Green, 1897), 61–62.

63. D. H. Meyer, "American Intellectuals and the Victorian Crisis of Faith," *American Quarterly*, 27 (1975), 590. See also James, *Will to Believe*, 1–31.

64. Read John S. Haller Jr., *Shadow Medicine: The Placebo in Conventional and Alternative Therapies* (New York: Columbia University Press, 2014), 61–88.

65. Read John Henry Newman, *Two Essays on Scriptural Miracles and on Ecclesiastical*, 2nd ed. (London: Pickering, 1870).

66. Abbott, *Philomythus: An Antidote against Credulity*, 2nd ed. (London: Macmillan, 1891), lxvii, 32–33, 136. Read also Smith, Berkove, and Baker, "Grammar of Dissent," 129–50.

67. Newman, *Grammar of Assent*, 91–92.

68. Otto Karrer, Frederick C. Ellert, and Alvan S. Ryan, "Newman and the Spiritual Crisis of the Occident," *Review of Politics*, 9 (1947), 238. See *Apologia pro Vita Sua*, 24, 53, 148, 194.

69. Newman, *Apologia pro Vita Sua*, 243–45; Newman, *Oxford University Sermons*, 54.

70. Kirk, "Conservative Mind of Newman," 659.

71. John Henry Newman, "The Tamworth Reading Room," in *Discussion and Arguments* (London: Longmans, Green, 1891), 272.

72. Patrick Allitt, *Catholic Converts: British and American Intellectuals Turn to Rome* (New York: Cornell University Press, 1997), ix, 77.

73. Gordon K. Lewis, "From Faith to Skepticism: A Note on Three Apologetics," *Journal of Politics*, 13 (1951), 175–76.

## Chapter 3

1. Arthur J. Taylor, "The Originality of Herbert Spencer," *University of Texas Studies in English*, 34 (1955), 101–6.

2. Charles Darwin to E. Ray Lankester, March 15, 1870, in Francis Darwin (ed.), *Life and Letters of Charles Darwin* (New York: D. Appleton, 1891), 2:301.

3. His initial subscribers included John Stuart Mill, Charles Darwin, Thomas Huxley, Charles Lyell, Thomas Hooker, Sir John Lubbock, William Herschel, Augustus De Morgan, George Henry Lewes, Hugh Elliot, George Grote, Alexander Bain, Henry Buckle, Jules Simon, E. L. Youmans, and Andrew Carnegie. The American editions of *First Principles* and *Social Statics* appeared in 1864, entering an intellectual climate that was preponderantly religious in tone. Despite this, the books resonated with readers, offering faith in the order of divine purpose and in the moral laws of the universe. Having only recently subscribed to numerous perfectionist theories and the enactment of dozens of perfectionist communities, Spencer's books resonated with the nation's idea of individualism, suspicion of government, and belief in progress, the nation's exceptionalism, and human perfectibility.

4. E. L. Youmans, the founder of *Popular Science Monthly*, arguably did more to advance Spencer's popularity than any other in England or America. A loyal and lifelong friend, he regarded him as "the foremost intellect in our civilization [and a] man beyond all men of his age to control the thought of the future." Youmans alone raised some $7,000 from American donors to support the publication costs of *Synthetic Philosophy*. Throughout his life, Youmans promoted Spencer's system of thought, rendering him a place beside Emerson and Carlyle as among the brightest men of the century. D. Duncan (ed.), *Life and Letters of Herbert Spencer* (London: Williams and Norgate, 1911), 75.

5. George Sarton, *The Life of Science: Essays in the History of Civilization* (Bloomington: Indiana University Press, 1960), 116.

6. Herbert Spencer, *An Autobiography of Herbert Spencer*, 2 vols. (New York: D. Appleton, 1904), 1:52, 80.

7. Paul Elliott, "Erasmus Darwin, Herbert Spencer, and the Origins of the Evolutionary Worldview in British Provincial Scientific Culture, 1770–1850," *Isis*, 94 (2003), 1–29.

8. Spencer, *Autobiography*, 1:100–101.

9. Spencer, *Autobiography*, 1:150, 162, 344.

10. Spencer, *Autobiography*, 1:261.

11. J. D. Y. Peel, *Herbert Spencer: The Evolution of a Sociologist* (New York: Basic Books, 1971), 70, 78, 193.

12. Herbert Spencer, *Social Statics; or, The Conditions Essential to Human Happiness Specified, and the First of Them Developed* (London: John Chapman, 1851), 59, 63, 65.

13. Herbert Spencer, *The Classification of the Sciences to which are added Reasons for Dissenting from the Philosophy of M. Comte* (New York: Herbert, 1864), 37–41, 51. An initial disagreement regarding alleged borrowing from Comte stemmed from a series of articles on sociology that he wrote for the *Pilot*. See Spencer, *Autobiography*, 1:292–93.

14. Spencer, *Autobiography*, 1:517–18.

15. Spencer, *Social Statics*, 1–16, 38, 50.

16. Spencer, *Social Statics*, 68, 103. Read also F. W. Maitland, "Mr. Herbert Spencer's Theory of Society," *Mind*, 8 (1883), 506–24.

17. Spencer, *Social Statics*, 338.

18. Spencer, *Social Statics*, 269, 283, 330–32, 380, 381.

19. Spencer, *Social Statics*, 322, 324.

20. William James, "Herbert Spencer," in Gustav Pollak, *Fifty Years of American Idealism* (Boston: Houghton Mifflin, 1915), 377.

21. Spencer, *Autobiography*, 2:7.

22. Duncan, *Life and Letters of Herbert Spencer*, 75.

23. "The Development Hypothesis," *Leader*, in Herbert Spencer, *Essays Scientific, Political and Speculative*, 3 vols. (London: Williams and Norgate, 1891), 1:1–7; "A Theory of Population Deduced from the General Law of Animal Fertility," *Westminster Review*, 57 (1852), 468–501; "Art of Education," *North British Review*, 21 (1854), 137–71.

24. Herbert Spencer, "Progress: Its Law and Cause," *Westminster Review*, 67 (1857), 445–85.

25. Count Goblet d'Alviella, *The Contemporary Evolution of Religious Thought in England, America and India* (London: Williams and Norgate, 1885), 41.

26. Marvin Harris, *The Rise of Anthropological Theory* (London: Routledge and Kegan Paul, 1968), 107.

27. Spencer, *First Principles*, 343.

28. Werner Stark, "Herbert Spencer's Three Sociologies," *American Sociological Review*, 26 (1961), 515, 519.

29. While Wallace urged Darwin to replace his term "natural selection" with Spencer's "survival of the fittest," Darwin demurred, choosing instead to include Spencer's expression in his 1869 and 1872 editions of the *Origin*. Herbert Spencer, *Principles of Biology*, 2 vols. (New York: D. Appleton, 1866), 2: 53; *Social Statics*, 288–89, 349–50; *Study of Sociology* (New York: D. Appleton, 1874), 318, 322–23; *Principles of Sociology* (New York: D. Appleton, 1874), 2:240–42, 608, 610, 720–21; Robert J. Richards, "The Relation of Spencer's Evolutionary Theory to Darwin's," in Greta Jones and Robert Peel, *Herbert Spencer: The Intellectual Legacy* (London: Galton Institute, 2004), 12.

30. Peter J. Bowler, *The Eclipse of Darwinism: Anti-Darwinian Evolution Theories in the Decades around 1900* (Baltimore: Johns Hopkins University Press, 1883), 70.

31. Herbert Spencer, *First Principles* (New York: D. Appleton, 1898 [1864]), 17, 48, 70, 101.

32. Spencer, *First Principles*, 17, 48, 70, 101.

33. Spencer, *First Principles*, 105–6, 108–9.

34. Spencer, *First Principles*, 24, 26, 62, Read Elijah Jordan, "The Unknowable of Herbert Spencer," *Philosophical Review*, 20 (1911), 291–309; Timothy Fitzgerald, "Herbert Spencer's Agnosticism," *Religious Studies*, 23 (1987), 477–91.

35. William S. Bishop, "The Philosophy of Herbert Spencer," *Sewanee Review*, 13 (1905), 48–49.

36. James, "Herbert Spencer," in Pollak, *Fifty Years of American Idealism*, 376–77.

37. Derek Freeman, "The Evolutionary Theories of Charles Darwin and Herbert Spencer," *Current Anthropology*, 15 (1974), 215.

38. Francis Darwin (ed.), *The Life and Letters of Charles Darwin*, 3 vols. (London: John Murray, 1888), 3:55–56.

39. Charles H. Cooley, "Reflections upon the Sociology of Herbert Spencer," *American Journal of Sociology*, 26 (1920), 143.

40. Read Walter M. Simon, "Herbert Spencer and the 'Social Organism,'" *Journal of the History of Ideas*, 21 (1960), 294–99.

41. Quoted in Casper Sylvest, *British Liberal Internationalism, 1880–1930: Making Progress?* (Manchester: Manchester University Press, 2009), 112.

42. Vernon Louis Parrington, *The Beginnings of Critical Realism in American: 1860–1920* (New York: Harcourt, Brace, and World, 1958 [1930]), 201.

43. Quoted in Robert A. Heineman, *Authority and the Liberal Tradition: From Hobbes to Rorty* (Durham, NC: Carolina Academic Press, 1984), 81; Arthur Mann, "British Social Thought and American Reformers of the Progressive Era," *Mississippi Valley Historical Review*, 42 (1956), 672–92.

44. Charles Elwood, "The Theory of Imitation in Social Psychology," *American Journal of Sociology*, 6 (1901), 731–36.

45. Andrew Carnegie, *The Gospel of Wealth, and Other Essays* (Cambridge: Belknap Press, 1962), 16, 26–27.

46. A. H. Lloyd, "The Philosophy of Herbert Spencer," *Scientific Monthly*, 11 (1920), 111.

47. Franklin H. Giddings, quoted from *Independent*, December 17, 1903, in Walter J. Marvin, "Appreciation of Herbert Spencer," *Journal of Philosophy, Psychology and Scientific Methods*, 1 (1904), 52.

48. Cooley, "Reflections upon the Sociology of Herbert Spencer," 129.

49. William Henry Hudson, "Herbert Spencer: A Character Study," *North American Review*, 178 (1904), 9.

50. Frederic Harrison, "Agnostic Metaphysics," *Nineteenth Century*, 16 (1884), 363–64.

51. Quoted in Spencer, *Autobiography*, 1:421.

52. George Sarton, "Herbert Spencer 1820–1903," *Isis*, 3 (1921), 384. Derek Freeman, "The Evolutionary Theories of Charles Darwin and Herbert Spencer," *Current Anthropology*, 15 (1974), 220.

53. James, "Herbert Spencer," in Pollak, *Fifty Years of American Idealism*, 379.

54. Quoted in William Henry Hudson, *An Introduction to the Philosophy of Herbert Spencer* (London: Watts and Co., 1904), 52.

55. Richards, "Relation of Spencer's Evolutionary Theory to Darwin's," 7.

56. Hudson, "Herbert Spencer," 1–9.

57. H. Wildon Carr, "Critical Notices," *Mind*, 26 (1917), 366.

58. George Kimball Plochmann, "Darwin or Spencer?" *Science*, 130 (1959), 1452.

59. Talcott Parson, *The Structure of Social Action* (New York: Free Press, 1968 [1937]), 3. Read also C. Crane Brinton, *English Political Thought in the Nineteenth Century* (London: Benn, 1933).

## Chapter 4

1. Read Ross A. Slotten, *The Heretic in Darwin's Court: The Life of Alfred Russel Wallace* (New York: Columbia University Press, 2004); Michael Shermer, *In Darwin's Shadow: The Life and Science of Alfred Russel Wallace* (Oxford: Oxford University Press, 2002); Peter Raby, *Alfred Russel Wallace: A Life* (Princeton: Princeton University Press, 2001); Michael Flannery, *Nature's Prophet: Alfred Russel Wallace and His Evolution from Natural Selection to Natural Theology* (Tuscaloosa: University of Alabama Press, 2018); Martin Fichman, *An Elusive Victorian: The Evolution of Alfred Russel Wallace* (Chicago: University of Chicago Press, 2004); Roger Smith, "Alfred Russel Wallace: Philosophy of Nature and Man," *British Journal for the History of Science*, 6 (1972), 177–78; Jim Endersby, "Escaping Darwin's Shadow," *Journal of the History of Biology*, 36 (2003), 385–403.

2. Alfred Russel Wallace, *My Life; A Record of Events and Opinions*, 2 vols. (New York: Dodd, Mead, 1905), 1:1, 5–14, 17.

3. Wallace, *My Life*, 1:64–72, 78.

4. Wallace, *My Life*, 1:55.

5. Wallace, *My Life*, 1:58, 61–62.

6. Alfred Russel Wallace, *On Miracles and Modern Spiritualism* (London: James Burns, 1875), vi.

7. Over the years, Wallace came to appreciate Henry George's *Progress and Poverty* (1879) and Edward Bellamy's *Looking Backward* (1888) and *Equality* (1897) as further evidence of this destructive action. Wallace joined the General Committee of the Land Tenure Reform Association and, like George, insisted on equality of opportunity for all, which, because of the act, had done much to turn him into a socialist. "I am a Socialist," he admitted, "because I believe that the highest law for mankind is justice. . . . That is absolute social justice; that is ideal Socialism. It is, therefore, the guiding star for all true social reform." Wallace, *My Life*, 1:151, 155, 157; James Marchant (ed.), *Alfred Russel Wallace: Letters and Reminiscences* (New York: Harper, 1916), 2:143, 152–53; Wendy McElroy, "The Enclosure Acts and the Industrial Revolution," http://fff.org/explore-freedom/article/enclosure-acts-industrial-revolution/, accessed October 16, 2015.

8. Wallace, *My Life*, 1:87–88; Greta Jones, "Alfred Russel Wallace, Robert Owen and the Theory of Natural Selection," *British Journal for the History of Science*, 35 (2002), 73–96.

9. Marchant, *Alfred Russel Wallace: Letters and Reminiscences*, 2:209.

10. Wallace, "The Origin of the Human Races and the Antiquity of Man Deduced from the Theory of Natural Selection," *Journal of the Anthropological Society of London*, 2 (1864), clxxxvi; Alfred Russel Wallace, *Contributions to the Theory of Natural Selection* (London: Macmillan, 1870), 302–31.

11. Bernard J. Stern, "Letters of Alfred Russel Wallace to Lester F. Ward," *Scientific Monthly*, 40 (1935), 375–79.

12. Ross A. Slotten, *The Heretic in Darwin's Court: The Life of Alfred Russel Wallace* (New York: Columbia University Press, 2004), 444–46.

13. Wallace, *My Life*, 1:89–90, 104; Greta Jones, "Alfred Wallace, Robert Owen and the Theory of Natural Selection," *British Journal for the History of Science*, 35 (2002), 75.

14. Wallace, *My Life*, 1:80.

15. Wallace, *My Life*, 1:190–93.

16. Wallace, *My Life*, 1:205–22, 233–35, 257–62, 275–76.

17. Wallace, *My Life*, 1:264–89.

18. Wallace, *My Life*, 1:336.

19. Wallace, *My Life*, 1:338.

20. Wallace, *My Life*, 1:355.

21. Darwin ignored the subject in *Origin of Species*, expressing to Wallace his preference to avoid the matter as it was "so surrounded with prejudices." Even after publication of the *Origin*, Darwin continued to stand apart from the issue while urging Wallace to write on man's origination, something which Wallace did with his paper on "The Origin of Human Races and the Antiquity of Man Deduced from the Theory of Natural Selection" which he read before the

Anthropological Society of London in March 1864. See Marchant, *Alfred Russel Wallace: Letters and Reminiscences*, 1:126.

22. Quoted in Charles Darwin, *The Autobiography of Charles Darwin* (New York: Norton, 1958) 130–31.

23. Ian McCalman, *Darwin's Armada: Four Voyages and the Battle for the Theory of Evolution* (New York: W. W. Norton, 2009), 266.

24. Read R. M. Young, "Malthus and the Evolutionists: The Common Context of Biological and Social Theory," *Past and Present*, 43 (1969), 109–45; Sandra Herbert, "Darwin, Malthus and Selection," *Journal of the History of Biology*, 4 (1971), 209–217; Peter J. Bowler, "Malthus, Darwin and the Concept of Struggle," *Journal of the History of Ideas*, 37 (1976), 631–50; Dov Ospovat, "Darwin After Malthus," *Journal of the History of Biology*, 12 (1979), 211–30. Wallace remarked in his autobiography that the problem of the origin of species had already been formulated in his mind by the mid to late 1840s. "I believed the conception of evolution through natural law so clearly formulated in the "Vestiges," to be, so far as it went, a true one." See Wallace, *My Life*, 1:257.

25. Wallace, *My Life*, 1:361–62.

26. The Frenchman Lamarck's *Zoological Philosophy* (1809) conceived of evolution as a more or less rapid process whose catalyst was the animal's "will" to change. If organs were not used, they regressed; but when used, they were perfected into more useful purposes.

27. Charles Darwin to Charles Lyell, June 18, 1858, http://www.darwinproject .ac.uk/letter/entry-2285, accessed November 2, 2015.

28. A number of scholars have found differences between Darwin and Wallace including the argument that Wallace's emphasis on competition between varieties differed substantially from Darwin's competition between individuals. Read Michael Bulmer, "The Theory of Natural Selection of Alfred Russel Wallace FRS," *Notes and Records of the Royal Society of London*, 59 (2005), 125–36; M. J. Kotter, "Charles Darwin and Alfred Russel Wallace: Two Decades of Debate over Natural Selection," in D. Kohn (ed.), *The Darwinian Heritage* (Princeton: Princeton University Press, 1985), 367–432; P. J. Bowler, "Alfred Russel Wallace's Concepts of Variation," *Journal of the History of Medicine*, 31 (1976), 17–29.

29. Wallace, *My Life*, 1:374.

30. Read Jeremy Vetter, "The Unmaking of an Anthropologist: Wallace Returns from the Field, 1862–70," *Notes and Records of the Royal Society of London*, 64 (2010), 25–42.

31. Charles Darwin, *The Variation of Animals and Plants under Domestication* (New York: D. Appleton, 1868), 236.

32. Alfred Russel Wallace, *Natural Selection and Tropical Nature: Essays on Descriptive and Theoretical Biology* (London: Macmillan, 1895), 182.

33. Wallace, "The Origin of Human Races," clxx; John R. Durant, "Scientific Naturalism and Social Reform in the Thought of Alfred Russel Wallace," *British Journal for the History of Science*, 12 (1979), 41.

34. Wallace, "Origin of the Human Races," clxix.

35. Alfred Russel Wallace, "Sir Charles Lyell on Geological Climates and the Origin of Species," *Quarterly Review*, 126 (1869), 393.

36. Alfred Russel Wallace, *Contributions to the Theory of Natural Selection* (London: Macmillan, 1891), 186–214; Alfred Russel Wallace, *Man's Place in the Universe* (New York: McClure, Phillips, 1903); Alfred Russel Wallace, *The World of Life—A Manifestation of Creative Power, Directive Mind and Ultimate Purpose* (London: Chapman and Hall, 1911). In the appendix to his *Contributions*, Wallace opined that intelligences other than "God" could have been an agent in the development of the human species. See Wallace, *Contributions to the Theory of Natural Selection*, 372.

37. Alfred Russel Wallace, *Natural Selection and Tropical Nature, Essays on Descriptive and Theoretical Biology* (London: Macmillan, 1891), 204.

38. P. J. Vorzimmer, *Charles Darwin: The Years of Controversy* (Philadelphia: Temple University, 1970), 190; Wallace, *My Life*, 1:418, 2:17.

39. Marchant, *Alfred Russel Wallace: Letters and Reminiscences*, 1:241, 250–51; Flannery, *Nature's Prophet*, 52–67.

40. Marchant, *Alfred Russel Wallace: Letters and Reminiscences*, 1:244.

41. Marchant, *Alfred Russel Wallace: Letters and Reminiscences*, 2:187.

42. Francis Darwin (ed.), *The Life and Letters of Charles Darwin, Including an Autobiographical Chapter*, 3 vols. (London: John Murray, 1888), 3:116.

43. Wallace, *Contributions to the Theory of Natural Selection*, 186–88.

44. Wallace, *Contributions to the Theory of Natural Selection*, 340–43, 351–54, 359–60.

45. Wallace, *Contributions to the Theory of Natural Selection*, 370.

46. Wallace, *Contributions to the Theory of Natural Selection*, 476.

47. Wallace, "Sir Charles Lyell on Geological Climates and the Origin of Species," *Quarterly Review*, 126 (1869), 359–94.

48. Charles Lyell, *Life, Letters, and Journals of Sir Charles Lyell*, 2 vols. (London: John Murray, 1881), 2:442; Martin Fichman, *An Elusive Victorian* (Chicago: University of Chicago Press, 2004), 81–84; Michael Ruse, *The Darwinian Revolution* (Chicago: University of Chicago Press, 1979), 247.

49. Ronald L. Numbers, *Darwinism Comes to America* (Cambridge: Harvard University Press, 1998), 40.

50. Marchant, *Alfred Russel Wallace: Letters and Reminiscences*, 2:17.

51. G. J. Romanes, "Darwin's Latest Critics," *Nineteenth Century*, 27 (1890), 831.

52. John R. Durant, "Scientific Naturalism and Social Reform in the Thought of Alfred Russel Wallace," *British Journal for the History of Science*, 12 (1979), 31.

53. Fichman, *Elusive Victorian: The Evolution of Alfred Russel Wallace*, 188–89; Flannery, 99–121.

54. Jennifer Bann, "Ghostly Hands and Ghostly Agency: The Changing Figure of the Nineteenth-Century Specter," *Victorian Studies*, 51 (2009), 663–85; Lyons, *Species, Serpents, Spirits, and Skulls*, 111–46.

55. Read E. C. Rogers, *Philosophy of Mysterious Agents, Human and Mundane* (Boston: John P. Jewett, 1853).

56. Alfred Russel Wallace, *A Defense of Modern Spiritualism* (Boston: Colby and Rich, 1874), 13. The events were reminiscent of those that had disturbed the Wesley families in the seventeenth and eighteenth centuries.

57. Alfred Russel Wallace, *On Miracles and Modern Spiritualism* (London: James Burnes, 1875), 125.

58. Wallace, *My Life*, 2:275–76; Wallace, *On Miracles and Modern Spiritualism*, 124–25.

59. Wallace, *On Miracles and Modern Spiritualism*, 125.

60. Wallace, *On Miracles and Modern Spiritualism*, 126–27.

61. Wallace, *A Defense of Modern Spiritualism*, 14; Wallace, *On Miracles*, 133–34, 162–63; Martin Fichman, *An Elusive Victorian: The Evolution of Alfred Russel Wallace*, 168.

62. Wallace, *On Miracles and Modern Spiritualism*, 52–53.

63. Wallace, *On Miracles and Modern Spiritualism*, 212.

64. Wallace, *On Miracles and Modern Spiritualism*, 213–14. Alfred Russel Wallace, *A Defense of Modern Spiritualism*, iii–iv. The book was one of several published around the same time, including Judge Edmond's *Spiritual Tracts* (1858–1860); Robert Dale Owen's *Footfalls on the Boundary of Another World* (1861) and *Debatable Land between This World and the Next* (1871); E. Hardinge's *Modern American Spiritualism* (1870), *Report on Spiritualism of the Committee of the London Dialectical Society* (1871), *Year-Book of Spiritualism* (1871), Hudson Tuttle's *Arcana of Spiritualism* (1871), *Spiritual Magazine* (1861–1874), *Spiritualist Newspaper* (1872–1874), and *The Medium and Daybreak* (1869–1874).

65. Wallace, *On Miracles and Modern Spiritualism*, 108.

66. Wallace, *Defense of Modern Spiritualism*, 7, 10, 33.

67. Malcolm Jay Kottler, "Alfred Russel Wallace, the Origin of Man, and Spiritualism," *Isis*, 65 (1974), 171; F. Darwin (ed.), *Life of Darwin*, 3:186–88; Tim M. Berra, *Darwin and His Children; His Other Legacy* (Oxford: Oxford University Press, 2013).

68. George Eliot and her partner George Henry Lewes, a disciple of Comte and one of Britain's more vocal positivists, attended numerous séances and included within their circle Annie Besant of the Theosophical Society, as well as Helena Blavatsky and Wilkie Collins. Their penchant for the occult turned to both native roots and Eastern religions. Marchant, *Alfred Russel Wallace: Letters and Reminiscences*, 2:212.

69. Marchant, *Alfred Russel Wallace: Letters and Reminiscences*, 2:187. Numerous Victorians took part in séances, some as believers and many as skeptics. They included Huxley, Lewes, Augustus De Morgan, Francis Galton, George Eliot, W. B. Carpenter, Tyndall, William Crookes, and even Charles Darwin, who attended a séance in 1874 at the home of his son. Francis Darwin (ed.), *Life of Darwin*, 2:186–88.

70. Wallace, *On Miracles and Modern Spiritualism*, 214.

71. Wallace, *Defense of Modern Spiritualism*, 58, 62.

72. Michael Flannery, *Alfred Russel Wallace's Theory of Intelligent Evolution: How Wallace's World of Life Challenged Darwinism*, rev. ed. (Riesel, TX: Erasmus Press, 2008), 22.

73. Wallace, *On Miracles and Modern Spiritualism*, 222.

74. Martin Fichman, "Science in Theistic Contexts: A Case Study of Alfred Russel Wallace on Human Evolution," *Osiris*, 16 (2001), 237.

75. Alfred Russel Wallace, *The World of Life: A Manifestation of Creative Power, Directive Mind and Ultimate Purpose* (London: Chapman and Hall, 1914), 396.

76. Wallace, *World of Life*, 395.

77. Wallace, *World of Life*, 399.

78. Wallace, *World of Life*, 400.

79. Wallace, *On Miracles and Modern Spiritualism*, vii.

80. Fichman, "Science in Theistic Contexts," 234–35.

81. Wallace, *World of Life*, 400.

## Chapter 5

1. Read Sherrie Lyons, *Thomas Henry Huxley: The Evolution of a Scientist* (Amherst, NY: Prometheus Books, 1999); Adrian Desmond, *Huxley: From Devil's Disciple to Evolution's High Priest* (Reading, MA: Addison-Wesley, 1997); Alan P. Barr (ed.), *Thomas Henry Huxley's Place in Science and Letters: Centenary Essays* (Athens: University of Georgia Press, 1997).

2. P. Chalmers Mitchell, *Thomas Henry Huxley; A Sketch of His Life and Work* (New York: G. P. Putnam's Sons, 1900), 10; J. R. Ainsworth Davis, *Thomas H. Huxley* (New York: E. P. Dutton, 1907), 3–4.

3. Theo. Gill, "Huxley and His Work," *Science*, 3 (1896), 254.

4. Mitchell, *Thomas Henry Huxley*, 33; Desmond, *Huxley*, 323, 486; Frank M. Turner, "The Victorian Conflict between Science and Religion: A Professional Dimension," *Isis*, 69 (1978), 364–65.

5. Read Frank M. Turner, *Contesting Cultural Authority: Essays in Victorian Intellectual Life* (Cambridge: Cambridge University Press, 1993); Desmond, *Huxley*.

6. With his income assured, he married Henrietta ("Nettie") Anne Heathorn, whom he met in Sydney in 1847. Together, they had five daughters and three sons.

7. Lyons, *Huxley*, 231–54.

8. Quoted in Mitchell, *Thomas Henry Huxley*, 101.

9. Francis Darwin (ed.), *The Life and Letters of Charles Darwin, Including an Autobiographical Chapter* (London: John Murray, 1887), 2:197.

10. Owen's archetypes were the same as those of Louis Agassiz, both depending on a Supreme Mover for their existence.

11. Quoted in Gill, "Huxley and His Work," 256. See also James Moore, "Deconstructing Darwinism: The Politics of Evolution in the 1860s," *Journal of the History of Biology*, 24 (1991), 353–408; William Irvine, *Apes, Angels, and Victorians:*

*The Story of Darwin, Huxley, and Evolution* (New York: McGraw-Hill, 1955); J. R. Lucas, "Wilberforce and Huxley: A Legendary Encounter," *Historical Journal*, 22 (1979), 313–30; Sheridan Gilley, "The Huxley-Wilberforce Debate: A Reconstruction," in Keith Robbins (ed.), *Religion and Humanism* (Oxford: Basil Blackwell, 1981), 325–40; J. Vernon Jensen, "Return to the Wilberforce–Huxley Debate," *British Journal of the History of Science*, 21 (1988), 161–79; A. R. Ashwell and Reginald G. Wilberforce, *Life of the Right Reverend Samuel Wilberforce*, 3 vols. (London: John Murray, 1880–1882); Cyril Bibby, "The Huxley–Wilberforce Debate: A Postscript," *Nature*, 176 (1955), 363; Charles S. Blinderman, "The Oxford Debate and After," *Notes and Queries*, 202 (1957), 126–28.

12. Peter J. Bowler, *Evolution: The History of an Idea* (Berkeley: University of California Press, 1984), 184.

13. Thomas Huxley, *Life and Letters of Thomas Huxley*, 3 vols. (London: Macmillan, 1913), 3:124.

14. Huxley, *Life and Letters of Thomas Huxley*, 3:124.

15. Quoted in Ronald W. Clark, *The Survival of Charles Darwin: A Biography of a Man and an Idea* (New York: Random House, 1984), 124.

16. Mitchell, *Thomas Henry Huxley*, 121.

17. Peter J. Bowler, *Charles Darwin: The Man and His Influence* (Cambridge: Cambridge University Press, 1990), 144.

18. Writers including J. M. Robertson, J. B. Bury, Bertrand Russell, and Arthur Balfour were strong believers in this assumed conflict. See Bertrand Russell, *Religion and Science* (New York: Holt, 1935); Arthur Balfour, "Introduction," in Joseph Needham (ed.), *Science, Religion, and Reality* (New York: Macmillan, 1928), 1–18.

19. Sydney Eisen, "Huxley and the Positivists," *Victorian Studies*, 7 (1964), 337–58; "Mr. Huxley on M. Comte," *Fortnightly*, 5 (1869), 407–18; Herbert Spencer, *The Classification of the Sciences: To Which Are Added Reasons for Dissenting from the Philosophy of M. Comte* (London: Williams and Norgate, 1871); John Stuart Mill, *Auguste Comte and Positivism* (Boston: William V. Spencer, 1866); Walter M. Simon, *European Positivism in the Nineteenth Century: An Essay in Intellectual History* (Port Washington, NY: Kennikat Press, 1972).

20. Thomas Huxley, "On the Physical Basis of Life," *Fortnightly*, 5 (1869), 141.

21. Sheridan Gilley and Ann Loades, "Thomas Henry Huxley: The War between Science and Religion," *Journal of Religion*, 61 (1981), 285–86. Read John R. Lucas, "Wilberforce and Huxley: A Legendary Encounter," *Historical Journal*, 22 (1979), 313–20. The Higher Criticism, which began in Germany, made significant inroads into belief in the inspiration of the Bible, a conclusion that Darwin had come to in the 1830s: "I [came] to see," explained Darwin, "that the Old Testament from its manifestly false history of the world and from its attributing to God the feelings of a revengeful tyrant, was no more to be trusted than the sacred books of the Hindoos, or the beliefs of any barbarian." Charles Darwin, *The Autobiography of Charles Darwin 1809–1882: With Original Omissions Restored* (New York: Harcourt, Brace, 1959), 85.

22. Read J. W. Colenso, *The Pentateuch and Book of Joshua Critically Examined*

(London: Longman, Green, Longman, Roberts and Green, 1862); Lyons, *Thomas Henry Huxley*, 189–230.

23. Read John Brooke and Geoffrey Cantor, *Reconstructing Nature: The Engagement of Science and Religion* (Edinburgh: Clark, 1998); David B. Wilson, "Victorian Science and Religion," *History of Science*, 15 (1977), 52–67.

24. Thomas H. Huxley, *Man's Place in Nature, and Other Anthropological Essays* (New York: D. Appleton, 1894), 54.

25. Huxley, *Man's Place in Nature, and Other Anthropological Essays*, 77–78, 149.

26. Huxley quoted in *Alfred R. Wallace, Darwinism: An Exposition of the Theory of Natural Selection, with Some of Its Applications* (London: Macmillan, 1889), 449. Read John S. Haller Jr., *Outcasts from Evolution: Scientific Attitudes of Racial Inferiority, 1859–1900* (Urbana: University of Illinois Press, 1971), 78–79, 132.

27. Janet Browne, *Charles Darwin: The Power of Place* (Princeton: Princeton University Press, 2003), 26–62; Sherrie Lyons, *Species, Serpents, Spirits and Skulls: Science at the Margins in the Victorian Age* (New York: SUNY Press, 2009), 147–70; Ronald W. Clark, *The Survival of Charles Darwin: A Biography of a Man and an Idea* (New York: Random House, 1984), 130.

28. Thomas H. Huxley, "Darwin on the Origin of Species," *Westminster Review*, 17 (1860), 541–70.

29. Mivart, "Difficulties of the Theory of Natural Selection," *Month*, 11 (1869), 35–53 134–53, 274–89; Mivart, "Some Reminiscences of Thomas Henry Huxley," *Nineteenth Century*, 42 (1897), 988–93; Jacob W. Gruber, *A Conscience in Conflict: The Life of St. George Jackson Mivart* (New York: Columbia University Press, 1960), chapters 1 and 2; John D. Root, "Catholicism and Science in Victorian England," *Clergy Review*, 88 (1981), 138–47, 162–70.

30. David L. Hull, "Darwinism and Historiography," in Thomas F. Glick (ed.), *The Comparative Reception of Darwinism* (Austin: University of Texas Press, 1974), 388.

31. Bowler, *Charles Darwin*, 140.

32. Quoted in Clark, *The Survival of Charles Darwin*, 154.

33. Huxley, "A Critical Examination of the Position of Mr. Darwin's Work, 'On the Origin of Species,' in Relation to the Complete Theory of the Causes of the Phenomena of Organic Nature," *Westminster Review* (1860), in Thomas H. Huxley, *Man's Place in Nature, and Other Essays* (New York: E. P. Dutton, 1910), 333.

34. Quoted in Mitchell, *Thomas Henry Huxley*, 108. See also Desmond, *Huxley*, 119–22.

35. Thomas H. Huxley, "Mr. Darwin's Critics," *Contemporary Review*, 18 (1871), 443–76.

36. John C. Greene, "Darwin and Religion," *Proceedings of the American Philosophical Society*, 103 (1959), 720.

37. Huxley, "A Critical Examination of the Position of Mr. Darwin's Work," 258.

38. Frank M. Turner, "The Victorian Conflict between Science and Religion: A Professional Dimension," *Isis*, 69 (1978), 356–76.

39. Huxley's choice of title derived from the blastoderm, a layer of cells formed

at one pole of the bird egg and from which the embryo develops. It was perceived as the germinal seat of the development of all parts of the organism. Among the more prominent members of the Club were John Tyndall, William Spottiswoode, Joseph Dalton Hooker, Thomas Henry Huxley, George Busk, Edward Frankland, Herbert Spencer, Richard Holt Hutton, Sir John Lubbock, and Bishop John William Colenso. Read Richard J. Helmstadter and Bernard Lightman (eds.), *Victorian Faith in Crisis: Essays on Continuity and Change in Nineteenth-Century Religious Belief* (Houndmills, Hampshire: Macmillan, 1990); Ruth Barton, "Huxley, Lubbock, and Half a Dozen Others: Professionals and Gentlemen in the Formation of the X Club," *Isis*, 89 (1998), 410–44; J. Vernon Jensen, "Interrelationships within the Victorian 'X Club,'" *Dalhousie Review*, 51 (1972), 539–52; Roy M. MacLeod, "The X-Club: A Social Network of Science in Late-Victorian England," *Notes and Records of the Royal Society of London*, 24 (1970), 305–22. Read Sydney Eisen, "Huxley and the Positivists," *Victorian Studies*, 7 (1964), 337–58; A. W. Benn, *The History of English Rationalism in the Nineteenth Century*, 2 vols. (London: Longmans, Green, 1906); A. J. Balfour, *The Religion of Humanity* (Edinburgh: David Douglas, 1888); J. Vernon Jensen, "The X Club: Fraternity of Victorian Scientists," *British Journal of the History of Science*, 5 (1970), 63–72; Desmond, *Huxley*, 625.

40. Bernard Lightman, "Huxley and Scientific Agnosticism: The Strange History of a Failed Rhetorical Strategy," *British Journal for the History of Science*, 35 (2002), 273–74.

41. Quoted in A. G. N. Flew, "Agnosticism," *Encyclopedia Britannica*, 15th ed. (Chicago: University of Chicago Press), 312. Robert Flint, *Agnosticism* (New York: Charles Scribner's Sons, 1903).

42. Quoted in George W. Hallam, "Source of the Word 'Agnostic,'" *Modern Language Notes*, 70 (1955), 267.

43. Nora Barlow (ed.), *The Autobiography of Charles Darwin* (New York: Norton, 1958 [1887]), 87.

44. Piers Benn, "Some Uncertainties about Agnosticism," *International Journal for Philosophy of Religion*, 46 (1999), 172; J. H. Clapperton, "The Agnostic at Church," *Nineteenth Century* 11 (1882), 653–54.

45. Bernard Lightman, *The Origins of Agnosticism: Victorian Unbelief and the Limits of Knowledge* (Baltimore: Johns Hopkins University Press, 1987), 132.

46. Some, like F. E. Abbot, attempted to connect agnosticism to liberal theology, arguing that as religion became more enlightened—meaning more adaptive of scientific findings—it would acquire a larger vision of man's purpose in the world. Read F. E. Abbot, *The Way Out of Agnosticism, or the Philosophy of Free Religion* (London: Macmillan, 1890).

47. Spencer, "Religion: A Retrospect and Prospect," *Nineteenth Century*, 15 (1884), 1–12; Herbert Spencer, *First Principles* (New York: Appleton, 1896 [1862]), 3–126.

48. Bernard Lightman, *The Origins of Agnosticism: Victorian Unbelief and the Limits of Knowledge* (Baltimore: Johns Hopkins University Press, 1987), 29, 92.

49. Bernard Lightman, "Huxley and Scientific Agnosticism: The Strange

History of a Failed Rhetorical Strategy," *British Journal for the History of Science*, 35 (2002), 283. See S. Eisen, "Frederic Harrison and Herbert Spencer," *Victorian Studies*, 12 (1968), 33–56.

50. Huxley, "Agnosticism," *Nineteenth Century*, 25 (1889), 169–94, 183–84.

51. Thomas H. Huxley, "Agnosticism in Its Relation to Modern Unitarianism," *Westminster Review*, 153 (1900), 49.

52. Thomas H. Huxley, "Agnosticism and Christianity," in *Science and Christian Tradition: Essays* (New York: D. Appleton, 1896), 310; Jack Goody, "A Kernel of Doubt," *Journal of the Royal Anthropological Institute*, 2 (1996), 667–81; Emile J. Dillon, *The Sceptics of the Old Testament: Job, Koheleth, Agur* (London: Isbister, 1895); Karen Armstrong, *A History of God: From Abraham to the Present: The 4000-Year Quest of Judaism, Christianity, and Islam* (London: Heinemann, 1993); Peter Laslett, *The World We Have Lost* (London: Methuen, 1965); Richard H. Popkin, *The History of Scepticism from Erasmus to Descartes* (New York: Humanities Press, 1964); James Thrower, *A Short History of Western Atheism* (London: Pemberton, 1971).

53. Thomas H. Huxley, *Science and Christian Tradition* (New York: D. Appleton, 1895), 239.

54. Albert Stratford G. Canning, *Thoughts on Religious History* (London: Edin, Remington, 1891), 100–102.

55. Thomas Huxley, "The Scientific Aspects of Positivism," *Fortnightly*, 5 (1869), 654.

56. Matthew Day, "Reading the Fossils of Faith: Thomas Henry Huxley and the Evolutionary Subtext of the Synoptic Problem," *Church History*, 74 (2005), 534–56. This is the same individual who also explained: "Extinguished theologians lie about the cradle of every science as the strangled snakes beside that of Hercules." See Thomas H. Huxley, "Origin of Species," in *Darwiniana* (New York: D. Appleton, 1896), 52.

57. Thomas H. Huxley, "Mr. Darwin's Critics," in *Darwiniana, Essays* (New York: D. Appleton, 1893), 148.

58. James McCosh, president of Princeton University, one of the early critics of Huxley, compared him to the materialist school of Hartley, Hume, and Mill, accusing him of undermining "all belief in the supernatural. . . . The creed destroys the foundation of all religions, even the rationalistic, not only supernatural but natural theism, not only Christianity but every form of deism." James McCosh, "Agnosticism as Developed in Huxley's Hume," *Popular Science Monthly*, 15 (1879), 486–87. Even Lenin answered Huxley's disclaimer of being a materialist, remarking that "in Huxley agnosticism serves as a fig leaf for materialism." Vladimir Lenin, *Materialism and Empirio-Criticism* (New York, 1927–32), 13:172.

59. Quoted in Mitchell, *Thomas Henry Huxley*, 222.

60. Quoted in Mitchell, *Thomas Henry Huxley*, 231.

61. Christopher Clausen, "Agnosticism, Religion, and Science: Some Unexamined Implications," *Rocky Mountain Review of Language and Literature*, 30 (1976), 80–81. Read A. O. J. Cockshut, *The Unbelievers* (London: Collins, 1964).

62. Bernard Lightman, "Huxley and Scientific Agnosticism: The Strange History of a Failed Rhetorical Strategy," *British Journal for the History of Science*, 35 (2002), 271–89.

63. Thomas H. Huxley, "On the Physical Basis of Life," *Fortnightly*, 5 (1869), 141; Lyons, *Thomas Henry Huxley*, 255–78.

64. Thomas H. Huxley, "Science and Morals," in *Evolution and Ethics, and Other Essays* (New York: D. Appleton, 1894), 128.

65. Quoted in Mitchell, *Thomas Henry Huxley*, 265. Jacques Barzun suggests that "Huxley, like almost every other scientific philosopher of the period, had been inwardly divided. Had the public followed him attentively, they would have heard him assail the Bible but insist on its use in the schools; scorn the believers, but declare no man should be unreligious; remind himself of a Hebrew prophet, but worship the calm austerity of the scientist. He peppered the journals with a gunfire of new directions—of science, education, faith, truth. He asked workmen to lend him their ear, assuring them that they only needed common sense to understand science. Then he would denounce the 'spurious metaphysics of vulgar common sense.' All this because his philosophic culture was inadequate to his needs." Barzun, *Darwin, Marx, Wagner*, 102–103.

66. Thomas H. Huxley, *Evolution and Ethic, and Other Essays* (New York: D. Appleton, 1897), 52; [Paul Carus], "Ethics and the Cosmic Order: A Criticism of Professor Thomas H. Huxley's Position," *Monist*, 4 (1894), 405.

67. Huxley, *Evolution and Ethics, and Other Essays*, 80–81, 82.

68. Huxley, *Evolution and Ethics, and Other Essays*, 50–53, 59, 83, 85.

69. Quoted in Mitchell, *Thomas Henry Huxley*, 260.

70. Caroline A. F. Rhys Davids, *Buddhism: A Study of the Buddhist Norm* (London: T. Butterworth, 1928); T. W. Rhys Davids, *Buddhism: Its History and Literature* (New York: G. P. Putnam's Sons, 1896); Vijitha Rajapakse, "Buddhism in Huxley's 'Evolution and Ethics': A Note on a Victorian Evaluation and Its Comparativist Dimension," *Philosophy East and West*, 35 (1985), 295–304; Christopher Clausen, "Victorian Buddhism and the Origins of Comparative Religion," *Journal of Religion and Religions*, 5 (1975), 1–15.

71. Thomas H. Huxley, "Evolution and Ethics," in *Evolution and Ethics, and Other Essays* (New York: D. Appleton, 1894), 85.

72. Huxley, "Evolution and Ethics," 83.

73. Quoted in Mitchell, *Thomas Henry Huxley*, 168, 180.

74. Joel S. Schwartz, "Robert Chambers and Thomas Henry Huxley, Science Correspondents: The Popularization and Dissemination of 19th Century Natural Science," *Journal of the History of Biology*, 32 (1999), 344. See also William Chambers, *Memoir of Robert Chambers with Autobiographical Reminiscences of William Chambers* (New York: Scribner, Armstrong, 1872).

75. These efforts, however, paled before the large number of Anglican ministers and women authors outside professional science whose allegiance to Christianity resulted in a heavy dose of natural theology, revealing an orderly and

divinely designed universe. Bernard Lightman, "The Voices of Nature: Popularizing Victorian Science," in Bernard Lightman (ed.), *Victorian Science in Context* (Chicago: University of Chicago Press, 1997), 187–211. An example of this was Agnes Clerke, a devout Catholic whose *A Popular History of Astronomy during the Nineteenth Century* (Edinburgh: Adam and Charles Black, 1885) provided a visual testament to the glory of God and His heavens. See Desmond, *Huxley*, 625.

76. Read Peter Bowler, *The Non-Darwinian Revolution* (Baltimore: Johns Hopkins University Press, 1988); George Levine, "Huxley, the Most Powerful Sage of Them All," *Victorian Studies*, 42 (1998), 117.

77. Jacques Barzun, *Darwin, Marx, Wagner: Critique of a Heritage* (Garden City, NY: Doubleday, 1958), 63.

78. Bowler, *Charles Darwin*, 142.

## Chapter 6

1. Robert G. Ingersoll, *Works of Robert G. Ingersoll*, 13 vols. (New York: Dresden, 1909–15), 4:463.

2. Donald Harvey Meyer, "American Intellectuals and the Victorian Crisis of Faith," *American Quarterly*, 27 (1975), 589.

3. John Spencer Clark, *The Life and Letters of John Fiske*, 2 vols. (Boston: Houghton Mifflin, 1917), 1:21–22.

4. Clark, *Life and Letters of John Fiske*, 1:24–26, 8.

5. Clark, *Life and Letters of John Fiske*, 1:59.

6. Clark, *Life and Letters of John Fiske*, 1:30, 66–68, 85.

7. Clark, *Life and Letters of John Fiske*, 1:69–70.

8. Clark, *Life and Letters of John Fiske*, 1:88–111.

9. Clark, *Life and Letters of John Fiske*, 1:115.

10. Clark, *Life and Letters of John Fiske*, 1:103.

11. Clark, *Life and Letters of John Fiske*, 1:390.

12. Clark, *Life and Letters of John Fiske*, 1:118, 123, 127–28. Forty years later Fiske returned to Middletown as orator for the town's 250th anniversary.

13. Fiske, *Outlines of Cosmic Philosophy, Based on the Doctrine of Evolution, with Criticisms on the Positive Philosophy*, 4 vols. (Boston: Houghton, Mifflin, 1902), 1:241.

14. Fiske, *Outlines of Cosmic Philosophy*, 1:241.

15. Vernon Louis Parrington, *Main Currents in American Thought*, vol. 3, *The Beginnings of Critical Realism in America: 1860–1920* (New York: Harcourt, Brace and World, 1958 [1930]), 205.

16. Clark, *Life and Letters of John Fiske*, 1:232–34.

17. Clark, *Life and Letters of John Fiske*, 1:217, 294.

18. Quoted in Clark, *Life and Letters of John Fiske*, 1:294–95.

19. Clark, *Life and Letters of John Fiske*, 1:260.

20. Clark, *Life and Letters of John Fiske*, 1:287, 307.

21. Clark, *Life and Letters of John Fiske*, 1:311, 361.

22. Andrew McFarland Davis, "John Fiske," *Proceedings of the American Academy of Arts and Sciences*, 37 (1902), 671.

23. Albert B. Hart, "The Historical Service of John Fiske," *Connecticut Magazine*, 7 (1901), 612.

24. At the time the library's collection amounted to 160,000 volumes. See Clark, *Life and Letters of John Fiske*, 1:403.

25. Vernon Louis Parrington, *The Beginnings of Critical Realism in America: 1860–1920* (New York: Harcourt, Brace and World, 1958 [1930]), 206.

26. Henry Holt, *Garrulities of an Octogenarian Editor, with Other Essays Somewhat Biographical and Autobiographical* (Boston: Henry Holt, 1923), 328.

27. Clark, *Life and Letters of John Fiske*, 1:349. He, along with Ralph Waldo Emerson and philosopher J. Elliot Cabot, was invited by Eliot to offer lectures for the academic year.

28. Clark, *Life and Letters of John Fiske*, 2:3–48.

29. In the introduction in the 1902 edition, Harvard philosopher Josiah Royce wrote that Fiske's polemic against Comte had been unnecessary and that more space could have been devoted to the evolutionary literature. He felt, however, that above all else, Fiske had distinguished himself from being simply a disciple and expositor of Spencer. As he explained, Fiske admired Darwin as a naturalist, but he followed Spencer as his master. But besides agreeing with Spencer's opinions, he freely rearranged and introduced new materials into the discussion, restating the case as he would have preferred. Royce described Fiske as having "the child's love of the unseen and mysterious with the modern skeptical student's scorn for superstition." Fiske, *Outlines of Cosmic Philosophy*, 1:xxxvi. See also Davis, "John Fiske," 676.

30. Fiske, *Outlines of Cosmic Philosophy*, 9:68; see also William Norman Guthrie, "Fiske's 'Through Nature to God,'" *Sewanee Review*, 8 (1900), 15–16.

31. Fiske, *Outlines of Cosmic Philosophy*, 4:3–4.

32. Fiske, *Outlines of Cosmic Philosophy*, 4:8–9; Alfred Russel Wallace, *Contributions to the Theory of Natural Selection* (New York: Macmillan, 1870), 312.

33. John Fiske, *Excursions of an Evolutionist* (Boston: Houghton, Mifflin, 1884), 316.

34. Fiske, *Outlines of Cosmic Philosophy*, 9:207–8. There is a stark similarity between Fiske's theory and that of the unknown author ("V.F.") who wrote the essay "On the Helpless State of Infancy" in an odd volume titled *The Friend's Annual; or, Aurora Borealis*, prepared by Members of the Society of Friends in 1834. It suggests a much prior recognition of the helpless condition of the child and its meaning. "This helpless condition, then, in which it hath pleased our Maker that we should be introduced in the present state, exhibits many marks of benevolent and wise design," wrote the unknown author. "It ought to be regarded with thankfulness, as necessary to the formation of that strong and durable affection between parent and child, which is one distinguishing feature of the human race, and a mark of its superior character." According to Wesley Raymond Wells, who discovered the similarity between the two men, "the obvious similarity of thought

and expression simply shows how hard it is to be wholly original in the sense of thinking and saying what no one ever thought or said before." Wesley Raymond Wells, "An Historical Anticipation of John Fiske's Theory regarding the Value of Infancy," *Journal of Philosophy*, 19 (1922), 208–10.

35. John Fiske, *The Meaning of Infancy* (Boston: Houghton, Mifflin, 1883), 11.

36. Fiske, *Outlines of Cosmic Philosophy*, 4:93.

37. Quoted in Fiske, *Outlines of Cosmic Philosophy*, 4:50.

38. Read John S. Haller Jr., *Outcasts from Evolution: Scientific Attitudes of Racial Inferiority, 1859–1900* (Urbana: University of Illinois Press, 1971), 132–38.

39. Parrington, *Main Currents in American Thought*, vol. 2, *The Beginnings of Critical Realism in America: 1860–1920*, 210–11.

40. Fiske, *Outlines of Cosmic Philosophy*, 9:14, 19, 20.

41. James Moore, *The Post-Darwinian Controversies* (Cambridge: Cambridge University Press, 1979), 332–33, 344–45; Richard England, "Natural Selection, Teleology, and the Logos: From Darwin to the Oxford Neo-Darwinists, 1859–1909," *Osiris*, 16 (2001), 271.

42. Dov Ospovat, *The Development of Darwin's Theory* (Cambridge: Cambridge University Press, 1981); Dov Ospovat, "God and Natural Selection: The Darwinian Idea of Design," *Journal of the History of Biology*, 13 (1980), 169–94; John Brooke, "The Relations between Darwin's Science and His Religion," in John Durant (ed.), *Darwinism and Divinity* (Oxford: Blackwell, 1985), 40–75; David Kohn, "Darwin's Ambiguity: The Secularization of Biological Meaning," *British Journal of the History of Science*, 22 (1989), 215–39; Charles Darwin, *On the Origin of Species* (London: Murray, 1859), 201; Charles Darwin, *The Descent of Man and Selection in Relation to Sex* (London: Murray, 1871), 153; Asa Gray, "Natural Selection and Natural Theology," *Nature*, 28 (1883), 78.

43. Read Henry Ward Beecher, *Evolution and Religion* (New York: Fords, Howard and Hulbert, 1885).

44. Quoted in Ronald W. Clark, *The Survival of Charles Darwin: A Biography of a Man and an Idea* (New York: Random House, 1984), 161.

45. Read Lyman Abbott, *The Evolution of Christianity* (Boston: Houghton, Mifflin, 1892); Lyman Abbott, *Theology of an Evolutionist* (Boston: Houghton, Mifflin, 1898).

46. Quoted in A. Dwight Culler, *The Imperial Intellect: A Study of Newman's Educational Ideal* (New Haven: Yale University Press, 1958), 267.

47. Fiske, *Outlines of Cosmic Philosophy*, 1:20–21, 9:93–94, 98, 102.

48. Fiske, *Outlines of Cosmic Philosophy*, 2:209, 223–24; Fiske, *The Destiny of Man Viewed in the Light of His Origin* (Boston: Houghton, Mifflin, 1884), 118–19.

49. David W. Marcell, "John Fiske, Chauncey Wright, and William James: A Dialogue on Progress," *Journal of American History*, 56 (1970), 808.

50. Fiske, *Outlines of Cosmic Philosophy*, 6:96, Read also Milton Berman, *John Fiske: The Evolution of a Popularizer* (Cambridge: Harvard University Press, 1961). See also Lester D. Stephens, *Joseph LeConte: Gentle Prophet of Evolution* (Baton

Rouge: Louisiana State University Press, 1982); Ira V. Brown, *Lyman Abbott: Christian Evolutionist: A Study in Religious Liberalism* (Cambridge: Harvard University Press, 1953); William G. McLoughlin, *The Meaning of Henry Ward Beecher: An Essay on the Shifting Values of Mid-Victorian America, 1840–1870* (New York: Knopf, 1970); Clifford E. Clark Jr., *Henry Ward Beecher: Spokesman for a Middle-Class America* (Urbana: University of Illinois Press, 1978).

51. Quoted in Clark, *Life and Letters of John Fiske,* 2:51–52.

52. Fiske, *Outlines of Cosmic Philosophy,* 9:78–79.

53. Fiske, *Outlines of Cosmic Philosophy,* 4:238.

54. Fiske, *Outlines of Cosmic Philosophy,* 4:232.

55. Fiske, *Outlines of Cosmic Philosophy,* 4:78–79, 207–37, 244, 247.

56. Quoted in Andrew McFarland Davis, "John Fiske," *Proceedings of the American Academy of Arts and Sciences,* 37 (1902), 671.

57. John Fiske, *Life Everlasting* (Boston: Houghton, Mifflin, 1901), 53, 60.

58. Fiske, *Life Everlasting,* 63, 85, 86–87.

59. Clark, *Life and Letters of John Fiske,* 1:xvii.

60. Hart, "Historical Service of John Fiske," 614.

61. Hart, "Historical Service of John Fiske," 613.

62. Henry Steele Commager, "John Fiske: An Interpretation," *Proceedings of the Massachusetts Historical Society,* 66 (1941), 339.

63. Andrew McFarland Davis, "John Fiske," *Proceedings of the American Academy of Arts and Sciences,* 37 (1902), 675.

64. Commager, "John Fiske," 337.

65. J. B. Sanders, "John Fiske," *Mississippi Valley Historical Review,* 17 (1930), 275.

66. Albert Bushnell Hart, "The Historical Services of Fiske," *International Monthly,* 4 (1901), 566–68.

67. Commager, "John Fiske," 333–34.

68. Commager, "John Fiske," 332.

## Chapter 7

1. Arthur O. Lovejoy, "William James as Philosopher," *International Journal of Ethics,* 21 (1911), 145.

2. Read Frederic I. Carpenter, "William James and Emerson," *American Literature,* 11 (1939), 42–44.

3. It was Emerson's vagueness that James, the proverbial moralist, found most objectionable. As an example, it was sometimes difficult to separate the abstractness of Emerson's transcendentalism from the practical consequences that fed the popular mind. Emerson's description of "The Young American," read before the Mercantile Library Association of Boston in 1844, was not recognition of the "gritty" struggles of the poor and laboring classes overcoming the challenges of life, but recognition of an idea that tallied with his abstract conviction that Nature was guiding the nation toward some mystical concept of justice and humanity.

While the eloquence of his words spoke of action and most certainly resonated with his audience, his words were used to empower American imperialism and destiny, something that James could not approve. While Emerson suggests that citizens had a responsibility to lead, others took his idealism and transformed it into schemes of greed. "The Young American exists both as a literary construct and a real world phenomenon," wrote Brady Harrison, but it was used in ways Emerson had not anticipated, with "other truly young Americans . . . stepping forward to lead the nation in the construction of empires." Ralph Waldo Emerson, "The Young American," in *Ralph Waldo Emerson: Essays and Lectures* (New York: Library of America, 1983), 217; Brady Harrison, "The Young Americans: Emerson, Walker, and the Early Literature of American Empire," *American Studies*, 40 (1999), 75–97.

4. Read Richard M. Gale, *The Divided Self of William James* (Cambridge: Cambridge University Press, 1999). Others, like James O. Pawelski, viewed James as steering a course ("Integration Theory") between a rationalistic system not sufficiently empirical and an empirical system too materialistic to account for ethics, and settling on a pluralistic moralism based on a spiritualistic but nonprovidential faith in the democratic man. Read James O. Pawelski, "William James's Divided Self and the Process of Its Unification: A Reply to Richard Gale," *Transactions of the Charles S. Peirce Society*, 39 (2003), 645; James O. Pawelski, "William James and the Journey toward Unification," *Transactions of the Charles S. Peirce Society*, 40 (2004): 795; David Baggett, "On a Reductionist Analysis of William James's Philosophy of Religion," *Journal of Religious Ethics*, 28 (2000), 423–48.

5. Ralph Barton Perry, *The Thought and Character of William James*, 2 vols. (Boston: Little, Brown, 1935), 1:105.

6. Read L. Menand, *The Metaphysical Club: A Story of Ideas in America* (Boston: Houghton Mifflin, 2006).

7. Cushing Strout, "William James and the Twice-Born Sick Soul," *Daedalus*, 97 (1968), 1062–82. Read Charles Renouvier, *Essais de critique générale* (Paris: Librairie Philosophique de Ladrange, 1864). William James simply asserted that his will was free. As his first act of freedom, he said, he chose to believe his will was free. He was encouraged to do this by reading Charles Renouvier. In his diary entry of April 30, 1870, he wrote, "I think that yesterday was a crisis in my life. I finished the first part of Renouvier's second *Essais* and see no reason why his definition of free will—'the sustaining of a thought *because I choose to* when I might have other thoughts'—need be the definition of an illusion. At any rate, I will assume for the present—until next year—that it is no illusion. My first act of free will shall be to believe in free will." See Perry, *Thought and Character of William James*, 1:323.

8. Howard V. Knox, "William James and His Philosophy," *Mind*, 86 (1913), 231.

9. William James, *Essays in Radical Empiricism* (Cambridge: Harvard University Press, 1976), 86.

10. William James, "Lectures on the Elements of Comparative Anatomy,"

*North American Review*, 100 (1865), 290–98; William James, "The Origin of the Human Races," *North American Review*, 101 (1865), 261–63.

11. William James, "Remarks on Spencer's Definition of Mind as Correspondence," *Journal of Speculative Philosophy* 12 (1878), 1–18.

12. Matthew Crippen, "William James on Belief: Turning Darwinism against Empiricistic Skepticism," *Transactions of the Charles S. Peirce Society*, 46 (2010), 482.

13. Ralph Barton Perry, "The Philosophy of William James," *Philosophical Review*, 20 (1911), 3.

14. James Campbell, "One Hundred Years of Pragmatism," *Transactions of the Charles S. Peirce Society*, 43 (2007), 1–15; James Mark Baldwin, "The Limits of Pragmatism," *Psychological Review*, 11 (1904), 30–60; Charles Hartshorne, Paul Weiss and Arthur W. Burks (eds.), *Collected Papers of Charles Sanders Peirce*, 8 vols. (Cambridge: Harvard University Press, 1931–1958), 5:414. The book, an effort to bring some level of unity to his writings, was based on lectures delivered at the Lowell Institute in Boston and at Columbia University. The effort proved unsatisfying to critics like Lovejoy, whose "The Thirteen Pragmatisms" (1908) indicated his less-than-enthusiastic view of James's effort. Read Arthur O. Lovejoy, *The Thirteen Pragmatisms, and Other Essays* (Baltimore: Johns Hopkins Press, 1963).

15. Gary Alexander, "The Hypothesized God of C. S. Peirce and William James," *Journal of Religion*, 67 (1987), 304–21.

16. Henry James (ed.), *The Letters of William James* (Boston: Atlantic Monthly Press, 1920), 2:203.

17. William James, *Pragmatism and the Meaning of Truth* (Cambridge: Harvard University Press, 1975), 273, 283–84.

18. William James, *Pragmatism, A New Name for Some Old Ways of Thinking* (New York: Longman Green, 1907), 4–5.

19. H. S. Thayer, "On William James on Truth," *Transactions of the Charles S. Peirce Society*, 13 (1977), 3–19.

20. William James, *Some Problems of Philosophy* (Cambridge: Harvard University Press, 1979), 113.

21. William James, *Will to Believe, and Other Essays in Popular Philosophy* (New York: Dover, 1956), 90.

22. G. L. Doore, "William James and the Ethics of Belief," *Philosophy*, 58 (1983), 353–64.

23. James, *Will to Believe, and Other Essays in Popular Philosophy*, 90.

24. Michael R. Slater, *William James on Ethics and Faith* (Cambridge: Cambridge University Press, 2009), 32; H. S. Thayer, "The Right to Believe: William James's Reinterpretation of the Function of Religious Belief," *Kenyon Review*, 5 (1983), 89–105.

25. James, *Will to Believe, and Other Essays in Popular Philosophy*, 22.

26. James, *A Pluralistic Universe* (New York: Longmans, Green, 1909), 329.

27. James, *Pragmatism* (Cambridge: Harvard University Press, 1975), 107.

28. Phil Cox, "William James's Epistemological 'Gamble,'" *Transactions of the Charles S. Peirce Society*, 36 (2000), 284–96; James, *The Will to Believe, and Other Essays in Popular Philosophy*, 11. See also Blaise Pascal, *Pensées de Pascal: Précédés de sa vie* (Paris: Librairie de Firmin Didot Frères, 1855).

29. John Hick, *Philosophy of Religion* (Englewood Cliffs, NJ: Prentice-Hall, 1990), 59. For an opposite position, read Ludwig F. Schlecht, "Re-reading 'The Will to Believe,'" *Religious Studies*, 33 (1997), 217–25.

30. James, *Pragmatism, and Other Writings* (New York: Penguin Books, 2000), 119, 228–29.

31. James, *Pragmatism, and Other Writings*, 240.

32. Bertrand Russell, *A History of Western Philosophy* (New York: Simon and Schuster, 1945), 814; W. Richard Comstock, "William James and the Logic of Religious Belief," *Journal of Religion*, 47 (1967), 187–209.

33. James, *Varieties of Religious Experience; A Study in Human Nature; Being the Gifford Lectures on Natural Religion Delivered at Edinburgh in 1901–1902.* (New York: Modern Library, 1902), 457.

34. William James, "Rationality, Activity, and Faith," *Princeton Review*, 2 (1882), 74–75.

35. James, *Will to Believe, and Other Essays*, 91, 99.

36. James, *Pragmatism*, title page. Read also Arthur O. Lovejoy, "William James as Philosopher," *International Journal of Ethics*, 21 (1911), 143.

37. Read D. Capps, *Men, Religion, and Melancholia: James, Otto, Jung, and Erickson* (New Haven: Yale University Press, 1997); Anne Harrington, *The Cure Within: A History of Mind-Body Medicine* (New York: Norton, 2008); R. W. B. Lewis, *The Jameses: A Family Narrative* (New York: Farrar, Straus and Giroux, 1991).

38. James, *Varieties of Religious Experience*, 425, 515.

39. Gary Alexander, "The Hypothesized God of C. S. Peirce and William James," *Journal of Religion*, 67 (1987), 312.

40. A. Eustace Haydon, *Biography of the Gods* (New York: Macmillan, 1945), 329.

41. Quoted in Perry, *Thought and Character of William James*, 318.

42. James, *Will to Believe, and Other Essays*, 69, 86. Sam Harris, Richard Dawkins, Victor Stenger, and Christopher Hitchens took strident exception to religious fundamentalism but were also critical of agnosticism, treating it as an untenable alternative to religious faith. Read Richard Dawkins, *The God Delusion* (Boston: Houghton Mifflin, 2008); Sam Harris, *The End of Faith: Religion, Terror, and the Future of Reason* (New York: W. W. Norton, 2004); Christopher Hitchens, *God Is Not Great: How Religion Poisons Everything* (New York: Twelve, 2007); Victor J. Stenger, *The New Atheism: Taking a Stand for Science and Reason* (New York: Prometheus Books, 2009); Scot D. Yoder, "Making Space for Agnosticism: A Response to Dawkins and James," *American Journal of Theology and Philosophy*, 34 (2013), 135–53.

43. Andrew Fiala, "Militant Atheism, Pragmatism, and the God-Shaped Hole," *International Journal for Philosophy of Religion*, 65 (2009), 147. Read also John Dewey, *A Common Faith* (New Haven: Yale University Press, 1934); S. Harris, *The*

*End of Faith* (New York: Norton, 2004); Hitchens, *God Is Not Great*; Richard Rorty, *Philosophy and Social Hope* (New York: Penguin, 1999).

44. David Paulsen, "The God of Abraham, Isaac, and (William) James," *Journal of Speculative Philosophy*, 13 (1999), 125.

45. Henry James (ed.), *The Letters of William James*, 2 vols. (Boston: Atlantic Monthly Press, 1920), 2:211.

46. Read John K. Roth, "William James, John Dewey, and the 'Death-of-God,'" *Religious Studies*, 7 (1971), 53–61.

47. James, *Varieties of Religious Experience*, 129.

48. James, *Varieties of Religious Experience*, 130.

49. Richard A. S. Hall, "The Polytheism of William James," *Pluralist*, 4 (2009), 21.

50. Michael R. Slater, "Pragmatism, Realism, and Religion," *Journal of Religious Ethics*, 36 (2008), 653–81.

51. Michael R. Slater, "William James's Pluralism," *Review of Metaphysics*, 65 (2011), 63.

52. James, *Will to Believe, and Other Popular Essays in Philosophy*, 263–98.

53. James, *Varieties of Religious Experience*, 514–15.

54. James, *Varieties of Religious Experience*, 514.

55. Ralph Barton Perry, *The Thought and Character of William James: Briefer Version* (New York: Harper and Row, 1947 1935), 164–68.

56. Roger Martin Du Gard, *Jean Barois* (New York: Bobbs-Merrill, 1969 [1913]), 252.

57. William James, *Human Immortality: Two Supposed Objections to the Doctrine* (London: Archibald Constable, 1906), 9.

58. James, *Human Immortality*, 11, 24–25, 26, 32, 39, 47–48.

59. James, *Human Immortality*, 57.

60. James, *Human Immortality*, 64, 70, 71, 75, 83, 87.

61. Sami Pihlström, "William James on Death, Mortality, and Immortality," *Transactions of the Charles S. Peirce Society*, 38 (2002), 612.

62. William James, *Pluralistic Universe* (New York: Longmans, Green, 1909), 310; William James, *Memories and Studies* (New York: Longmans, Green, 1911), 204; James, *Varieties of Religious Experience*, 389.

63. William James, *Writings, 1902–1910* (New York: Library of America, 1987), 1263. See also James H. Leuba, "William James and Immortality," *Journal of Philosophy, Psychology and Scientific Methods*, 12 (1915), 409–16.

64. William James, "Leonora Piper," https://en.wikipedia.org/wiki/Leonora_Piper, accessed August 23, 2018.

65. Deborah J. Coon, "One Moment in the World's Salvation: Anarchism and the Radicalization of William James," *Journal of American History*, 83 (1996), 70–99.

66. William James to William Dean Howells, Nov. 16, 1900, quoted from the William Dean Howells Papers at Harvard University in Deborah J. Coon, "'One

Moment in the World's Salvation': Anarchism and the Radicalization of William James," *Journal of American History*, 83 (1996), 71.

67. Scott R. Stroud, "William James on Meliorism, Moral Ideals, and Business Ethics," *Transactions of the Charles S. Peirce Society*, 45 (2009), 379.

68. Wayne Proudfoot, "William James on an Unseen Order," *Harvard Theological Review*, 93 (2000), 60.

69. Theodore Roosevelt, "The Strenuous Life," http://www.bartleby.com/58/1.html, accessed January 7, 2016.

70. Ralph Barton Perry, *In the Spirit of William James* (Bloomington: Indiana University Press, 1958), 147. Read also Andrew F. Smith, "William James and the Politics of Moral Conflict," *Transactions of the Charles S. Peirce Society*, 40 (2004), 135–51.

71. James Livingston, *Pragmatism and the Political Economy of Cultural Revolution, 1850–1940* (Chapel Hill: University of North Carolina Press, 1994); Robert L. Beisner, *Twelve against Empire: The Anti-Imperialists, 1898–1900* (New York: McGraw-Hill, 1968). See Daniel W. Bjork, *The Compromised Scientist: William James in the Development of American Psychology* (New York: Columbia University Press, 1983); Howard Feinstein, *Becoming William James* (Ithaca: Cornell University Press, 1984); Bruce Kuklick, *The Rise of American Philosophy, Cambridge, Massachusetts, 1860–1930* (New Haven: Yale University Press, 1977); James Kloppenberg, *Uncertain Victory: Social Democracy and Progressivism in European and American Thought, 1870–1920* (New York: Oxford University Press, 1986); Frank Lentricchia, *Ariel and the Police: Michel Foucault, William James, Wallace Stevens* (Madison: University of Wisconsin Press, 1988); James Livingston, *Pragmatism and the Political Economy of Cultural Revolution, 1850–1940* (Chapel Hill: University of North Carolina Press, 1994); Cornel West, *The American Evasion of Philosophy: A Genealogy of Pragmatism* (Madison: University of Wisconsin Press, 1989).

72. Perry, *Thought and Character of William James*, 2:383.

73. Alfred North Whitehead, *Modes of Thought* (New York: Free Press, 1938), 3; Jane Mayhall paraphrasing Van Wyck Brooks in "William James and the Modern World," *Antioch Review*, 8 (1948), 292.

74. Andrew J. Reck, "The Influence of William James on John Dewey in Psychology," *Transactions of the Charles S. Peirce Society*, 20 (1984), 87–117.

75. William James, *Psychology, Briefer Course* (New York: Henry Holt and Co., 1913), 262.

## Chapter 8

1. Impressed with Ward's brilliant career, Edward A. Ross of the University of Wisconsin commented: "One feels that if Aristotle had by chance been born in Illinois about the middle of the nineteenth century, his career would have resembled that of Lester F. Ward more than that of any other American of our times." Quoted in Samuel Chugerman, *Lester F. Ward, the American Aristotle: A Summary and Interpretation of His Sociology* (Durham: University of North Carolina

Press, 1939), 14. The name Nestor came from the wise and elderly counselor to the Greeks at Troy. See John C. Burnham, "Lester Frank Ward as Natural Scientist," *American Quarterly*, 6 (1954), 259, 262; James Q. Dealey et al., "Lester Frank Ward," *American Journal of Sociology*, 19 (1913), 64. For the full extent of Ward's thought, see Harry Elmer Barnes, *An Introduction to the History of Sociology* (Chicago: University of Chicago Press, 1948); Charles A. Ellwood, *The Story of Social Philosophy* (New York: Prentice-Hall, 1938); Ernest Becker, *The Structure of Evil: An Essay on the Unification of the Science of Man* (New York: Free Press, 1968); and J. R. Wilson, *Darwinism and the American Intellectual* (Homewood, IL: Dorsey Press, 1967).

2. During his lifetime, his works were translated into French, German, Italian, Spanish, Russian, and even Japanese. Read Alvin F. Nelson, *The Development of Lester Ward's World View* (Ft. Worth, TX: Branch-Smith, 1968).

3. Andrew A. Sorensen, "Lester Frank Ward, 'The American Aristotle,' in Illinois," *Journal of the Illinois State Historical Society*, 63 (1970), 164–65. Ward spoke little of his family or his ancestry, agreeing with Robert G. Ingersoll "that those who are most proud of their ancestors usually have nothing but ancestors to be proud of." See Emily Palmer Cape, *Lester F. Ward: A Personal Sketch* (New York: G. P. Putnam's Sons, 1922), 20.

4. Lester Ward, "Letter to Mr. W. H. Thompson," *Glimpses of the Cosmos*, 6 vols. (New York: G. P. Putnam's Sons, 1913), 1:31–32. At the time he entered the war, he fell in love with Elizabeth Carolyn Vought, whom he married quickly before he left for war. She bore him a son, who died within a year, and she died a decade later in Washington, DC.

5. Lester Ward, "The Punishment of Traitors," *Glimpses of the Cosmos*, 1:37.

6. See *Annual Report of the United States Geological Survey*, 1881–1904 (Washington, DC: Government Printing Office, 1883–1904).

7. Lester F. Ward, *Dynamic Sociology, or Applied Social Science, as Based upon Statical Sociology and the Less Complex Sciences* (New York: D. Appleton, 1883), 139.

8. Steven L. Piott, *American Reformers, 1870–1920: Progressives in Word and Deed* (Lanham, MD: Rowman and Littlefield, 2006), 16.

9. Lester Ward, "The Situation," in *Glimpses of the Cosmos*, 1:44.

10. Lester Ward, "The Present Age," in *Glimpses of the Cosmos*, 1:49.

11. Ward, *Dynamic Sociology*, 1:19–20.

12. Lester Ward, "Revealed Religion," in *Glimpses of the Cosmos*, 1:91–95.

13. Lester Ward, "Religion and Progress," in *Glimpses of the Cosmos*, 1:86.

14. Lester Ward, "Science vs. Theology," in *Glimpses of the Cosmos*, 1:87.

15. Lester Ward, *Pure Sociology, A Treatise on the Origin and Spontaneous Development of Society* (New York: Macmillan, 1903), 136.

16. Quoted in Cape, *Lester F. Ward*, 82–83, 88.

17. Lester Ward, "F," in *Glimpses of the Cosmos*, 1:52.

18. Lester Ward, "The Gospel of Action," in *Glimpses of the Cosmos*, 6:63.

19. Lester Ward, "Science vs. Theology," in *Glimpses of the Cosmos*, 1:53.

20. Quoted in Cape, *Lester F. Ward: A Personal Sketch*, 186, 194.

21. Lester Ward, "Beecher's Belief in Immortality," in *Glimpses of the Cosmos*, 1:123.

22. Lester Ward, "The Natural Storage of Energy," *Monist*, 5 (1895), 247.

23. Quoted in James Quayle Dealey, "Masters of Social Science, Lester Frank Ward," *Social Forces*, 4 (1925), 264.

24. Ward, *Dynamic Sociology*, 1:90–91.

25. Lester Ward, "Herbert Spencer's Sociology," *Glimpses of the Cosmos*, 6:172, 177. Edmund Burke thought hard and deep on the role of the state. To him the question turned on "what the state ought to take upon itself to direct by public wisdom, and what it ought to leave, with as little interference as possible, to individual freedom" (quoted in Library of Economics and Liberty, http://www.econlib .org/library/LFBooks/Burke/brkSWv1c2.html, accessed March 17, 2016). It seems odd that individuals would accept Spencer's extreme point of view. What, one wonders, was the mind-set that gave credence to his interpretation of evolution, let alone society's indulgence in its acceptance? Nothing seemed to justify improving the standard of living if, perchance, it infringed on the freedom of an individual. Anything less was perceived as a step in the direction of socialism or other form of deviant social behavior. American reformers were quick to point out that Spencer had built his philosophy under the banner of inductive thinking when, in fact, its basic elements were largely deductive. Instead of laissez-faire serving the interests of the many, it had become an assault on the working classes. Classical economics was neither classical nor fair; rather, it was unequal and punitive, prophesying where it had no basis to prophesy, and indifferent to the human lives left in its wake. An ethically insensitive philosophy, it abetted the cruelest forms of capitalism, justifying the economic individualism of the few at the expense of the many.

26. Lester Ward, "Herbert Spencer's Autobiography," in *Glimpses of the Cosmos*, 6:186; Lester Ward, "The Career of Herbert Spencer," in *Glimpses of the Cosmos*, 6:308.

27. Lester Ward, "Mind as a Social Factor," *Mind*, 9 (1884), 563–64, 565.

28. Ward, "Mind as a Social Factor," 567, 568–70.

29. Ward, *Dynamic Sociology*, 5–10.

30. Ward, *Pure Sociology*, 15.

31. Ward, "Mind as a Social Factor," 572–73.

32. Ward, "Mind as a Social Factor," 563.

33. Ward, *Dynamic Sociology*, 1:16, 71, 81.

34. Ward, *Dynamic Sociology*, 1:15–16.

35. Cape, *Lester F. Ward*, 143.

36. Ward, *Dynamic Sociology*, 1:29.

37. Bernhard J. Stern, "Letters of Alfred Russel Wallace to Lester F. Ward," *Scientific Monthly*, 40 (1935), 375–79.

38. William A. Dunning, *The History of Political Theories from Rousseau to Spencer* (New York: Macmillan, 1920), 398.

39. Joseph L. Blau, "The Cooperative Commonwealth as Secular Apocalypse," *Transactions of the Charles S. Peirce Society*, 12 (1976), 209–22; Arthur Mann, "British Social Thought and American Reformers of the Progressive Era," *Mississippi Valley Historical Review*, 42 (1956), 672–92.

40. J. B. Lamarck, *Zoological Philosophy: An Exposition with Regard to the Natural History of Animals* (Chicago: University of Chicago Press, 1984 [1809]), 11.

41. Read Richard Hofstadter, *Social Darwinism in American Thought* (Boston: Beacon Press, 1955); George W. Stocking Jr., "Lamarckianism in American Social Science: 1890–1915," *Journal of the History of Ideas*, 23 (1962), 239–56.

42. See John C. Greene's "Biology and Social Theory in the Nineteenth Century: Auguste Comte and Herbert Spencer," in *Critical Problems in the History of Science*, ed. Marshall Clagett (Madison: University of Wisconsin Press, 1959), 419–46.

43. Ward, *Outlines of Sociology*, 21, 25–26.

44. Ward, *Outlines of Sociology*, 30, 36.

45. Lester Ward, "Neo-Darwinism and Neo-Lamarckism," in *Glimpses of the Cosmos*, (1891), 290–95.

46. William Graham Sumner, *Folkways: A Study of the Sociological Importance of Uses, Manners, Customs, Mores and Morals* (Boston: Ginn, 1906); William Graham Sumner, *What the Social Classes Owe to Each Other* (New York: Harper and Brothers, 1883).

47. Ward, *Dynamic Sociology*, 2:40, 227–28.

48. Ward, *Dynamic Sociology*, 35, 36.

49. https://people.wku.edu/charles.smith/wallace/S418.htm, accessed September 3, 2018.

50. Bernhard J. Stern, "Letters of Alfred Russel Wallace to Lester Ward," *Scientific Monthly*, 40 (1935), 375–78.

51. Ward, *Pure Sociology*, 571–72.

52. Lester Ward, *Outlines of Sociology* (New York: Macmillan, 1898), 293.

53. Ward, *Psychic Factors of Civilization* (Boston: Ginn, 1893), 330.

54. James E. Fleming, "The Role of Government in a Free Society: The Conception of Lester Frank Ward," *Social Forces*, 24 (1946), 265.

55. Ward, *Psychic Factors of Civilization*, 327.

56. Ward, *Dynamic Sociology*, 2:250.

57. Lester Ward, "1906 Presidential Address, American Sociological Society," http://www.asanet.org/lester-ward-1906-presidential-address, accessed September 3, 2018.

58. Quoted in Sorensen, "Lester Frank Ward, 'The American Aristotle' in Illinois," 165.

59. James Q. Dealey et al., "Lester Frank Ward," *American Journal of Sociology*, 19 (1913), 63.

60. Quoted in Dealey, "Lester Frank Ward," 76.

61. Dealey, "Masters of Social Science, Lester Frank Ward," 262.

62. Don Martindale, "American Sociology before World War II," *Annual Review of Sociology*, 2 (1976), 138–39; Robert A. Jones, "John Bascom 1827–1911: Anti Positivism and Intuitionism in American Sociology," *American Quarterly* 24 (1972), 501–22.

63. Martindale, "American Sociology before World War II," 121–43.

64. Read Henry Steele Commager (ed.), *Lester Ward and the Welfare State* (Indianapolis: Bobbs-Merrill, 1967).

65. Ward, *Pure Sociology*, 555; Ward, *Outlines of Sociology*, 107–9; Ward, *Psychic Factors of Civilization*, 297.

66. Lester F. Ward, "The Sociology of Political Parties," *American Journal of Sociology*, 14 (1908), 440–41.

67. Quoted in Harry Elmer Barnes, "Two Representative Contributions of Sociology to Political Theory: The Doctrines of William Graham Sumner and Lester Frank Ward," *American Journal of Sociology*, 25 (1919), 155.

68. Alvin F. Nelson, "Lester Ward's Conception of the Nature of Science," *Journal of the History of Ideas*, 33 (1972), 636.

## Chapter 9

1. Paul Carus, "Professor Haeckel's Monism," *Monist*, 2 (1891–92), 598–60.

2. Julius Goebel, "Paul Carus," *Open Court*, 33 (1919), 513–21; Paul Carus, *The Idea of God* (Chicago: Open Court, 1896), 4.

3. Harold Henderson, *Catalyst for Controversy: Paul Carus of Open Court* (Carbondale: Southern Illinois University Press, 1993), 10–11.

4. Paul Carus, *Monism and Meliorism* (New York: Cherouny, 1885), 5; Paul Carus, *Primer of Philosophy* (Chicago: Open Court 1893), 1, 2, 4.

5. Paul Carus, *Kant and Spencer: A Study of the Fallacies of Agnosticism* (Chicago: Open Court, 1904), 2.

6. Carus, *Monism and Meliorism*, 9.

7. Carus, *Monism and Meliorism*, 15.

8. Carus, *Monism and Meliorism*, i, 15, 23.

9. Carus, *Monism and Meliorism*, 7, 10, 15, 30–31; Carus, *Primer of Philosophy*, 1, 2, 4. By no means shy, Carus remarked: "If Kant compared his work to that of Copernicus, I may fairly liken mine to that of Kepler who filled out the Copernican system and reduced the law of motion of planets to simple mathematical formulae." See Carus, *Monism and Meliorism*, 13.

10. Carus, *Monism and Meliorism*, 54.

11. Donald Harvey Meyer, "Paul Carus and the Religion of Science," *American Quarterly*, 14 (1962), 599–602.

12. Carus, *Monism and Meliorism*, 15–16, 62.

13. Carus, *Fundamental Problems* (Chicago: Open Court, 1889), 21.

14. Carus, *Fundamental Problems*, title page.

15. Carus, *Idea of God*, 27, 29.

16. Paul Carus, *Homilies of Science* (Chicago: Open Court, 1892), 98.

17. Carus, *Monism and Meliorism*, 71, 76.

18. Carus, *Monism and Meliorism*, 72–73.

19. Hegeler and Matthiessen immigrated to the United States in 1857 with the idea of building a zinc-smelting plant. After investigating possibility in Bethlehem, Pennsylvania, they selected La Salle, Illinois, as the ideal location due to its proximity to zinc and coal deposits. By the late 1880s, the company employed upwards of three hundred workers and produced eight million pounds of zinc annually.

20. William H. Hay, "Paul Carus: A Case-Study of Philosophy on the Frontier," *Journal of the History of Ideas*, 17 (1956), 503–5. Read also B. F. and A. S. Underwood, *A Statement by the Editors of the Open Court to Their Connection with That Journal and Their Reasons for Resigning* (n.p., 1887).

21. Henderson, *Catalyst for Controversy*, 323–34, 41.

22. B. F. Underwood, *The Influence of Christianity on Civilization* (New York: Truth Seeker, 1889), 97.

23. Mary Hegeler, the oldest of Hegeler's ten children, majored in mathematics and chemistry at the University of Michigan and, following her graduation in 1882, attended lectures on metallurgy at Freiberg before returning to La Salle to work in the plant of her father. At the time of her death, she was holding senior management positions of the Matthiessen and Hegeler Zinc Company as well as associate editor to the Open Court Publishing Company, where she provided editorial assistance to both *Open Court* and *Monist*. Read David Eugene Smith, "Mary Hegeler Carus, 1861–1936," *American Mathematical Monthly*, 44 (1937), 280–83.

24. Paul Carus, "The Work of the Open Court," in Paul Carus, *The Dawn of a New Religious Era, and Other Essays* (Chicago: Open Court, 1899), 114.

25. Carl T. Jackson, "The Meeting of East and West: The Case of Paul Carus," *Journal of the History of Ideas*, 29 (1968), 75.

26. See N. W. Ayer, *American Newspaper Annual* (Philadelphia: N. W. Ayer and Son, 1909), 158–59; Henderson, *Catalyst for Controversy*, 41. *Open Court* had an eclectic look, mixing religion with biology, mathematics, and metaphysics, while *Monist*, begun in 1890, was devoted to the philosophy of science.

27. Paul Carus, *The Religion of Science*, 2nd ed. (Chicago: Open Court, 1896), iv–v.

28. "The Work of the Open Court," in Carus, *Dawn of a New Religious Era, and Other Essays*.

29. Carus, *Religion of Science*, 79–81.

30. Carus, *Religion of Science*, 79–81, 197.

31. Carus, *Homilies of Science*, 5.

32. Carus, *Religion of Science*, 87–90, 95–96.

33. Carus, "The Revision of a Creed," in Carus, *The Dawn of a New Religious Era, and Other Essays*, 74.

34. Paul Carus, *Homilies of Science*, 12, 16, 17.

35. Carus, *Religion of Science*, 7, 8, 11.

36. Carus, *Religion of Science*, 20–22.

37. Carus, *Idea of God*, 14.

38. Carus, *The Philosophy of Form* (New York: AMS Press, 1980 [1911]), 36.

39. Paul Carus, "Science as a Religious Revelation," *Open Court*, 7 (1893), 3810; Paul Carus, "God-Nature," *Open Court*, 28 (1914), 402; Meyer, "Paul Carus and the Religion of Science," 601–2.

40. Carus, *Religion of Science*, 59, 60–62.

41. Carus, *Religion of Science*, 47–48, 51–53, 55–56.

42. Read Sir Travers Twiss, *Religion and Science, the Reconciliation Mania of Dr. Paul Carus of Open Court* (Chicago: H. Green, 19??); Henry Collin Minton, "A Review of Dr. Carus' 'Fundamental Problems' and 'The Surd of Metaphysics,'" *Monist*, 14 (1904), 452–58.

43. Carus, *Religion of Science*, 106, 110, 112–15.

44. Carus, *Idea of God*, 20, 23, 25–27, 29.

45. Carus, *Primer of Philosophy*, 196.

46. Carus, *Dawn of a New Era, and Other Essays*, 26.

47. His three speeches included "The Philosophy of the Tool," "Our Need of Philosophy," and "Religion in Its Relation to the Natural Sciences." See John Henry Barrows, *The World's Parliament of Religions: An Illustrated and Popular Story of the World's First Parliament of Religions, Held in Chicago in Connection with the Columbian Exposition of 1893*, 2 vols. (Chicago: Parliament, 1893); Carus, *Dawn of a New Religious Era, and Other Essays*, 24–25.

48. Carus, *Dawn of a New Religious Era, and Other Essays*, 37.

49. Carus, *Dawn of a New Religious Era, and Other Essays*, 10, 17. To be sure, some of the sessions degenerated into exercises in name-calling, due largely to the growing hostility of Eastern delegates to the dogmatic stance and aggressive behavior of Christian missionaries. Overall, however, the parliament engendered lively discussion and an ecumenical spirit toward all faiths and philosophies. For his part, Carus served as secretary of the Religious Parliament Extension, whose role was to have articles published and disseminated to dignitaries in the sovereign authorities in all countries for promoting a peace and goodwill. See Paul Carus, *The World's Parliament of Religions and the Religious Parliament Extension* (LaSalle, IL: Open Court, 1896).

50. Carus, "The World's Religious Parliament Extension," in *The World's Parliament of Religions and the Religious Parliament Extension*, 36, 38.

51. Carus, "The Progress of the Movement," 41–45.

52. Carus no doubt had been acquainted with the thought and culture of the East from his early studies under Hermann Grassmann as well as from the works of Joseph Wolff, Johann Gottfried Herder, John Wolfgang Goethe, Paul Deussen, Arthur Schopenhauer, Kant, Grassmann, Max Müller, and Friedrich and August Wilhelm Schlegel. See Friedrich Wilhelm, "The German Response to

Indian Culture," *Journal of the American Oriental Society*, 31 (1961), 395–405; Henderson, *Catalyst for Controversy*, 89.

53. Martin J. Verhoeven, "Introduction," in Paul Carus, *The Gospel of Buddha According to Old Records* (Chicago: Open Court, 2004), 7.

54. Max Müller, *Chips from a German Workshop* (New York: Scribner, Armstrong, 1874), 1:243, 247.

55. Thomas A. Tweed, *The American Encounter with Buddhism 1844–1912: Victorian Culture and the Limits of Dissent* (Bloomington: Indiana University Press, 1992), 65.

56. Jackson, "Meeting of East and West," 85.

57. Verhoeven, "Introduction," 3.

58. Paul Carus, "Buddhism and Christianity," *Monist*, 5 (1894), 67, 83–85, 86–87.

59. Read Paul Carus, *Karma: A Story of Buddhist Ethics* (Chicago: Open Court, 1917).

60. Carus, "Buddhism and Christianity," 65–103.

61. Paul Carus, "Brahmanism and Buddhism, or, the Religion of Postulates and the Religion of Facts," *Open Court*, 10 (1896), 4853.

62. Quoted in Jackson, "Meeting of East and West," 82.

63. Carus, "Buddhism and the Religion of Science," 4845.

64. Paul Carus, *Buddhism and Its Christian Critics* (Chicago: Open Court, 1897), 8.

65. Paul Carus, "Words and Their Meaning," *Open Court*, 8 (1894), 42.

66. Paul Carus, "Buddhism and Christianity," 89, 93.

67. Carus, *Buddhism and Its Christian Critics*, 10–11.

68. Carus, *Dawn of a New Religious Era, and Other Essays*, 22, 25, 26.

69. Paul Carus, *The Surd of Metaphysics* (Chicago: Open Court, 1908), 165; Paul Carus, "Truth," *Monist*, 20 (1910), 507.

70. Donald H. Bishop, "The Carus-James Controversy," *Journal of the History of Ideas*, 35 (1974), 510–11; William James, *Pragmatism* (New York: Longmans, Green, 1907), 76.

71. James, *Pragmatism*, 201.

72. Paul Carus, "Pragmatism," *Monist*, 18 (1908), 329, 345–46.

73. Read Paul Carus, *Truth on Trial: An Exposition of the Nature of Truth* (Chicago: Open Court, 1911), 46, 51.

74. Carus, *Fundamental Problems*, 5–6.

75. Paul Carus, *The Ethical Problem* (Chicago: Open Court, 1910), xii.

76. Carus, *Religion of Science*, 8.

77. Paul Carus, *Philosophy as a Science* (Chicago: Open Court Publishing Co., 1909), 5.

78. Carus, *The Philosophy of Form*, 1–3, 5, 13.

79. Meyer, "Paul Carus and the Religion of Science," 601.

80. Carus, *Philosophy of Form*, 19, 25, 28.

81. Carus, *Philosophy of Form*, 34.

82. Henderson, *Catalyst for Controversy*, 144.

83. Martin Verhoeven, "The Dharma through Carus's Lens," in Carus, *The Gospel of Buddha*, 56.

84. Meyer, "Carus and the Religion of Science," 606.

85. Paul Carus, "Scholaromania," *Open Court*, 9 (1895), 4435.

86. Jackson, "Meeting of East and West," 92.

## Chapter 10

1. F. O. Matthiessen, *American Renaissance: Art and Expression in the Age of Emerson and Whitman* (New York: Oxford University Press, 1941), viii. Supporters of Swedenborg's beliefs were best represented in the remarkable writings of Henry James Sr., who interpreted evolution as a process of creation that included both the growth of consciousness in humanity and a process of redemption with God reuniting Himself with humanity. Read Henry James, *Society the Redeemed Form of Man* (Boston: Houghton, Osgood, 1879); Henry James, *Christianity the Logic of Creation* (London: William White, 1857); and Henry James *Substance and Shadow* (Boston: Ticknor and Fields, 1863).

2. Henry David Thoreau, "Walking," in Henry David Thoreau, *The Writings of Henry David Thoreau: Excursions, Translations, and Poems* (Boston: Houghton Mifflin, 1906), 217. Darrel Abel, *Democratic Voices and Vistas: American Literature from Emerson to Lanier* (Bloomington, IN: iUniverse, 2002), 80.

3. https://newtopiamagazine.wordpress.com/2013/01/15/the-platonist-on-sunset-blvd/, accessed March 31, 2017.

4. Read Ethan Allen Hitchcock, *Remarks upon Alchemy and the Alchemists* (Boston: Crosby, Nichols, 1857), Ethan Allen Hitchcock, *Swedenborg, a Hermetic Philosopher* (New York: D. Appleton, 1858). See also http://sueyounghistories.com/archives/2013/11/30/alexander-wilder-1823-1908/, accessed March 30, 2017.

5. Hitchcock, *Remarks upon Alchemy and the Alchemists*, iv–ix, 45, 146, 225; I. Bernard Cohen, "Ethan Allen Hitchcock: Soldier—Humanitarian—Scholar, Discoverer of the "True Subject" of Hermetic Art," *Proceedings of the American Antiquarian Society* 61 (1951), 29–136.

6. "The Platonist," *Platonist*, 2 (1884), front matter. According to proponents of psychometry, every object receives and retains impressions of all that happens to it. Those impressions are indelible and can be reproduced in the mind as clearly as a picture.

7. "Salutatory," *Platonist*, 2 (1884), 1.

8. "Books and Periodicals," *Platonist*, 1 (1881), 111. See also G. Wyld, *Theosophy and the Higher Life* (London: Trübner, 1881).

9. https://newtopiamagazine.wordpress.com/2013/01/15/the-platonist-on-sunset-blvd/, accessed April 1, 2017.

10. As a teaching camp for Sunday-school teachers, it quickly expanded into concerts, theatre and lecture series that attracted middle-class families and

imparted an appreciation for education, religion, and the arts. Read Andrew C. Riser, *The Chautauqua Movement: Protestants, Progressives, and the Culture of Modern Liberalism* (New York: Columbia University Press, 2003).

11. Austin Warren, "The Concord School of Philosophy," *New England Quarterly*, 2 (1929), 202.

12. A. Bronson Alcott, H. K. Jones, W. T. Harris, S. H. Emery Jr., and F. B. Sanborn, "The Concord Summer School of Philosophy," *Journal of Speculative Philosophy*, 14 (1880), 138.

13. Bruce Ronda, "The Concord School of Philosophy and the Legacy of Transcendentalism," *New England Quarterly*, 82 (2009), 581, 588; Ednah Dow Cheney (ed.), *Louisa May Alcott: Her Life, Letters and Journals* (Boston: Roberts, 1889), 68.

14. "The American Akadêmê," *Platonist*, 2 (1884), 16.

15. https://newtopiamagazine.wordpress.com/2013/01/15/the-platonist-on-sunset-blvd/, accessed April 1, 2017.

16. "Constitution: The American Akadêmê," *The Platonist*, 2 (1884), front piece.

17. "American Akadêmê," 80.

18. Stephen Prothero, "From Spiritualism to Theosophy: 'Uplifting' a Democratic Tradition," *Religion and American Culture: A Journal of Interpretation*, 3 (1993), 197–216.

19. Olcott became the society's president, Blavatsky corresponding secretary, George Felt and Seth Pancoast vice presidents, and William Q. Judge general counsel.

20. http://sueyounghistories.com/archives/2013/11/30/alexander-wilder-1823-1908/, accessed March 31, 2017. As early as 1857, the faculty at Harvard University announced its opinion that "any connection with spiritualistic circles, so called, corrupts the morals, and degrades the intellect." A few years later Thomas Henry Huxley wrote the London Dialectical Society that he had neither the time nor the interest to participate in any investigation of the subject. Quoted from Henry S. Olcott, *People from the Other Side* (Hartford, CT: American, 1875), v.

21. H. S. Olcott, "Spiritualism and Theosophy: Their Agreements and Disagreements," *Theosophist*, 19 (1897), 101–5.

22. Howard Murphet, *When Daylight Comes: A Biography of Helena Petrovna Blavatsky* (Wheaton, IL: Theosophical, 1975), 66.

23. George M. Beard, "Chittendon Phenomena," *New York Daily Graphic*, October 27, 1874; Helena P. Blavatsky, "Dr. Beard Criticized," *New York Daily Graphic*, November 10, 1874, p. 3.

24. Emerson once described New York's genteel society as the "best class, who shall be masters instructed in all the great arts of life . . . wise, temperate, brave public men, adorned with dignity and accomplishments." Quoted in Bender, *New York Intellect*, 172.

25. H. P. Blavatsky, *Isis Unveiled: A Master-Key to the Mysteries of Ancient and Modern Science and Theology*, 2 vols. (New York: J. W. Bouton, 1892), 1:ix–x.

26. Helena P. Blavatsky, *Collected Writings* (Wheaton, IL: Theosophical, 1977), 1:101–2, 137.

27. Blavatsky, *Isis Unveiled*, 2:588.

28. Mark Bevir, "The West Turns Eastward: Madame Blavatsky and the Transformation of the Occult Tradition," *Journal of the American Academy of Religion*, 62 (1994), 747–67. Also read John Michael Andrick, "A Modern Mecca of Psychic Forces: The Psychical Science Congress and the Culture of Progressive Occultism in Fin-de-Siècle Chicago, 1885–1900," PhD dissertation, History, University of Illinois at Urbana-Champaign, 2016.

29. See Marchant, *Alfred Russel Wallace: Letters and Reminiscence*, 2:205.

30. Prothero, "Henry Steel Olcott and 'Protestant Buddhism,'" 286.

31. Prothero, "Henry Steel Olcott and 'Protestant Buddhism,'" 295.

32. Henry Steel Olcott, *The Buddhist Catechism* (Madras: The Theosophist Office, Adyar), 53, 95–97.

33. Olcott, *Buddhist Catechism*, 1–3, #363.

34. David L. McMahan, "Modernity and the Early Discourse of Scientific Buddhism," *Journal of the American Academy of Religion*, 72 (2004), 898.

35. John Lukacs, *At the End of an Age* (New Haven: Yale University Press, 2002), 113.

36. Read Stephen Hawkins, Daniel Yudkin, Miriam Juan-Torres, and Tim Dixon, *Hidden Tribes: A Study of America's Polarized Landscape* (New York: More in Common, 2018).

# Selected Bibliography

Abbot, Francis Ellingwood. *The Way out of Agnosticism, or the Philosophy of Free Religion.* London: Macmillan, 1890.

Abbott, Edwin A. *The Anglican Career of Cardinal Newman.* 2 vols. London: Macmillan, 1892.

———. *Flatland.* 2nd ed. Princeton: Princeton University Press, 1991 [1884].

———. *The Kernel and the Husk.* Boston: Roberts, 1887.

———. *Philomythus: An Antidote against Credulity.* 2nd ed. London: Macmillan, 1891.

Abbott, Lyman. *The Evolution of Christianity.* Boston: Houghton, Mifflin, 1892.

———. *Theology of an Evolutionist.* Boston: Houghton, Mifflin, 1898.

Abel, Darrel. *Democratic Voices and Vistas: American Literature from Emerson to Lanier.* Bloomington, IN: iUniverse, 2002.

Ahlstrom, Sidney (ed.). *Theology in America: The Major Protestant Voices from Puritanism to Neo-Orthodoxy.* Indianapolis: Bobbs-Merrill, 1967.

Allitt, Patrick. *Catholic Converts: British and American Intellectual Turn to Rome.* New York: Cornell University Press, 1997.

Aquino, Frederick D. *Communities of Informed Judgment: Newman's Illative Sense and Accounts of Rationality.* Washington, DC: Catholic University of America Press, 2004.

Armstrong, Karen. *A History of God: The 4000-Year Quest of Judaism, Christianity, and Islam.* London: Heinemann, 1993.

Arnold, Harvey. *Near the Edge of Battle: A Short History of the Divinity School and the "Chicago School of Theology" 1866–1966.* Chicago: Divinity School Association, 1966.

Ashwell, A. R., and Reginald G. Wilberforce. *Life of the Right Reverend Samuel Wilberforce.* 3 vols. London: John Murray, 1880–1882.

Aveling, Edward. *The Creed of an Atheist.* London: Free Thought, 1881.

———. *The Student's Darwin.* London: Free Thought, 1881.

Ayer, N. W. *American Newspaper Annual.* Philadelphia: N. W. Ayer and Son, 1909.

Balfour, Arthur James. *The Religion of Humanity.* Edinburgh: David Douglas, 1888.

Barlow, Nora (ed.). *The Autobiography of Charles Darwin, 1809–1882.* New York: Harcourt, Brace, 1958.

Barnes, Harry Elmer. *An Introduction to the History of Sociology.* Chicago: University of Chicago Press, 1948.

Barr, Alan P. (ed.). *Thomas Henry Huxley's Place in Science and Letters: Centenary Essays* Athens: University of Georgia Press, 1997.

Barrett, Paul H. (ed.). *The Collected Papers of Charles Darwin*. 2 vols. Chicago: University of Chicago Press, 1977.

Barrow, Logie. *Independent Spirits: Spiritualism and English Plebeians*. New York: Methuen, 1986.

Barrows, John Henry. *The World's Parliament of Religions, an Illustrated and Popular Story of the World's First Parliament of Religions, Held in Chicago in Connection with the Columbian Exposition of 1893*. Chicago: Parliament, 1893.

Barth, Karl. *The Epistle to the Romans*. London: Oxford University Press, 1953.

———. *The Word of God and the Word of Man*. New York: Harper and Row, 1957 [1828].

Barzun, Jacques. *Darwin-Marx-Wagner: Critique of a Tradition*. 2nd ed. Chicago: University of Chicago Press, 1981.

———. *A Stroll with William James*. New York: Harper and Row, 1983.

Becker, Ernest. *The Structure of Evil: An Essay on the Unification of the Science of Man*. New York: Free Press, 1968.

Beecher, Henry Ward. *Evolution and Religion*. New York: Fords, Howard and Hulbert, 1885.

Beisner, Robert L. *Twelve against Empire: The Anti-Imperialists, 1898–1900*. New York: McGraw-Hill, 1968.

Bellamy, Edward. *Equality*. New York: Cosimo Classics, 2007 [1897].

———. *Looking Backward*. Cleveland: World, 1945.

Benn, Alfred William. *The History of English Rationalism in the Nineteenth Century*. 2 vols. London: Longmans, Green, 1906.

Berman, Milton. *John Fiske: The Evolution of a Popularizer*. Cambridge: Harvard University Press, 1961.

Binyon, Gilbert Clive. *The Christian Socialist Movement in England*. London: Society for Promoting Christian Knowledge, 1931.

Bischof, Gunter. *Auguste Comte and Positivism: The Essential Writings*. London: Taylor and Francis, 2017.

Bjork, Daniel W. *The Compromised Scientist: William James in the Development of American Psychology*. New York: Columbia University Press, 1983.

Blavatsky, Helena P. *Collected Writings*. Vol. 1. Wheaton, IL: Theosophical, 1977.

———. *Isis Unveiled: A Master-Key to the Mysteries of Ancient and Modern Science and Theology*. 2 vols. New York: J. W. Bouton, 1892.

Blum, Deborah. *Ghost Hunters: William James and the Search for Scientific Proof of Life after Death*. New York: Penguin Press, 2006.

Boddice, Rob. *The Science of Sympathy: Morality, Evolution, and Victorian Civilization*. Urbana: University of Illinois Press, 2016.

Boodin, John E. *Cosmic Evolution: Outlines of Cosmic Idealism*. New York: Macmillan, 1925.

Booth, Arthur John. *Saint-Simon and Saint-Simonism: A Chapter in the History of Socialism in France*. London: Longmans, Green, Reader and Dyer, 1871.

Bordogna, Francesca. *William James at the Boundaries: Philosophy, Science, and the Geography of Knowledge*. Chicago: University of Chicago Press, 2008.

Bowlby, John. *Charles Darwin: A New Life*. New York: W. W. Norton, 1990.

Bowler, Peter J. *Charles Darwin: The Man and His Influence*. Cambridge: Cambridge University Press, 1990.

———. *The Eclipse of Darwinism: Anti-Darwinian Evolution Theories in the Decades around 1900*. London: Galton Institute, 2004.

———. *Evolution: The History of an Idea*. Berkeley: University of California Press, 1984.

———. *The Non-Darwinian Revolution*. Baltimore: Johns Hopkins University Press, 1988.

———. *Reconciling Science and Religion: The Debate in Early-Twentieth-Century Britain*. Chicago: University of Chicago Press, 2001.

Brinton, C. Crane. *English Political Thought in the Nineteenth Century*. London: Benn, 1933.

Brooke, John H. *Science and Religion: Some Historical Perspectives*. Cambridge: Cambridge University Press, 1991.

Brooke, John H., and Geoffrey Cantor. *Reconstructing Nature: The Engagement of Science and Religion*. Edinburgh: Clark, 1998.

Brown, Ira V. *Lyman Abbott: Christian Evolutionist: A Study in Religious Liberalism*. Cambridge: Harvard University Press, 1953.

Browne, Janet. *Charles Darwin: The Power of Place*. Princeton: Princeton University Press, 2002.

———. *Charles Darwin: Voyaging*. Princeton: Princeton University Press, 1995.

Burnham, John C. *Lester Frank Ward in American Thought*. Washington, DC: Public Affairs Press, 1956.

Butler, Joseph. *The Analogy of Religion, Natural and Revealed*. New York: E. P. Dutton, 1906.

Butler, Lance St. John. *Victorian Doubt: Literary and Cultural Discourses*. New York: Harvester Wheatsheaf, 1990.

Canning, Albert Stratford. *Thoughts on Religious History*. London: Edin, Remington, 1891.

Cape, Emily Palmer. *Lester F. Ward: A Personal Sketch*. New York: G. P. Putnam's Sons, 1922.

Capps, Donald. *Men, Religion, and Melancholia: James, Otto, Jung, and Erikson*. New Haven: Yale University Press, 1997.

Carnegie, Andrew. *The Gospel of Wealth, and Other Essays*. Cambridge: Belknap Press, 1962.

Carroll, Thomas (ed.). *An Annotated Calendar of the Letters of Charles Darwin in the Library of the American Philosophical Society*. Wilmington: Scholarly Resources, 1976.

Carus, Paul. *Buddhism and Its Christian Critics*. Chicago: Open Court, 1897.

———. *The Dawn of a New Religious Era, and Other Essays*. Chicago: Open Court, 1916.

———. *The Ethical Problem*. Chicago: Open Court, 1910.

———. *Fundamental Problems*. Chicago: Open Court, 1889.

————. *God; An Enquiry into the Nature of Man's Highest Ideal and a Solution of the Problem from the Standpoint of Science*. Chicago: Open Court, 1908.

————. *Homilies of Science*. Chicago: Open Court, 1892.

————. *The Idea of God*. Chicago: Open Court, 1896.

————. *Kant and Spencer: A Study of the Fallacies of Agnosticism*. Chicago: Open Court, 1904.

————. *Karma: A Story of Buddhist Ethics*. Chicago: Open Court, 1917.

————. *Monism and Meliorism*. New York: Cherouny, 1885.

————. *Philosophy as a Science*. Chicago: Open Court, 1909.

————. *The Philosophy of Form*. New York: AMS Press, 1980 [1911].

————. *Primer of Philosophy*. Chicago: Open Court, 1893.

————. *The Religion of Science*. Chicago: Open Court, 1893.

————. *The Soul of Man: An Investigation of the Facts of Physiological and Experimental Psychology*. Chicago: Open Court, 1892.

————. *The Surd of Metaphysics*. Chicago: Open Court, 1908.

————. *Truth on Trial: An Exposition of the Nature of Truth*. Chicago: Open Court, 1911.

————. *The World's Parliament of Religions and the Religious Parliament Extension*. LaSalle, IL: Open Court, 1896.

Cauthen, Kenneth. *The Impact of American Religious Liberalism*. Washington, DC: University Press of America, 1983.

Chambers, Robert. *Vestiges of the Natural History of Creation*. London: W. and R. Chambers, 1884.

Chambers, William. *Memoir of Robert Chambers with Autobiographical Reminiscences of William Chambers*. New York: Scribner, Armstrong, 1872.

Cheny, Edna Dow (ed.). *Louisa May Alcott: Her Life, Letters and Journals*. Boston: Roberts, 1889.

Chugerman, Samuel. *Lester F. Ward, the American Aristotle: A Summary and Interpretation of His Sociology*. Durham: University of North Carolina Press, 1939.

Clagett, Marshall (ed.). *Critical Problems in the History of Science*. Madison: University of Wisconsin Press, 1959.

Clark, Clifford E. *Henry Ward Beecher: Spokesman for a Middle-Class America*. Urbana: University of Illinois Press, 1978.

Clark, John Spencer. *The Life and Letters of John Fiske*. 2 vols. Boston: Houghton Mifflin, 1917.

Clark, Ronald W. *The Survival of Charles Darwin: A Biography of a Man and an Idea*. New York: Random House, 1984.

Clendening, John. *The Life and Thought of Josiah Royce*. Nashville, TN: Vanderbilt University Press, 1999.

Clerke, Agnes. *A Popular History of Astronomy during the Nineteenth Century*. Edinburgh: Adam and Charles Black, 1885.

Cockshut, A. O. J. *The Unbelievers*. London: Collins, 1964.

Colenso, John William. *The Pentateuch and Book of Joshua Critically Examined*. London: Longman, Green, Longman, Roberts and Green, 1862.

Collins, Randall. *Conflict Sociology*. New York: Academic Press, 1977.

Commager, Henry Steele (ed.). *Lester Ward and the Welfare State*. Indianapolis: Bobbs-Merrill, 1967.

Comte, Auguste. *Appeal to Conservatives*. London: Trübner, 1889.

———. *Calendrier positiviste, ou, Système général de commémoration publique*. Paris: A. La Librairie Scientifique-Industrielle, 1852.

———. *The Catechism of Positive Religion*. London: John Chapman, 1858.

———. *The Catechism of Positive Religion*. London: Trübner, 1891.

———. *Cours de philosophie positive*. Paris: Bachelier, 1841.

———. *A Discourse on the Positive Spirit*. London: Reeves, 1903.

———. *A General View of Positivism*. London: Trübner, 1865.

———. *The Positive Philosophy*. 2 vols. New York: Calvin Blanchard, 1858.

———. *Social Physics: From the Positive Philosophy*. New York: Calvin Blanchard, 1856.

———. *Subjective Synthesis*. London: Kegan Paul, 1891.

———. *System of Positive Polity*. London: Longmans, Green, 1875–1877.

Cormier, Harvey. *The Truth Is What Works: William James, Pragmatism, and the Seed of Death*. Lanham, MD: Rowman and Littlefield, 2001.

Costa, James. T. *Wallace, Darwin, and the Origin of Species*. Cambridge: Harvard University Press, 2014.

Croce, Paul J. *Young William James Thinking*. Baltimore: Johns Hopkins University Press, 2018.

Crosby, John F. *The Personalism of John Henry Newman*. Washington, DC: Catholic University of America Press, 2014.

Culler, A. Dwight. *The Imperial Intellect: A Study of Newman's Educational Ideal*. New Haven: Yale University Press, 1958.

d'Alviella, Count Goblet. *The Contemporary Evolution of Religious Thought in England, America and India*. London: Williams and Norgate, 1885.

Darwin, Charles. *The Autobiography of Charles Darwin*. New York: Norton, 1958.

———. *The Autobiography of Charles Darwin 1809–1882: With Original Omissions Restored*. New York: Harcourt, Brace, 1959.

———. *The Descent of Man and Selection in Relation to Sex*. London: Murray, 1871.

———. *On the Origin of Species*. London: Murray, 1859.

———. *The Variation of Animals and Plants under Domestication*. New York: D. Appleton, 1868.

Darwin, Francis (ed.). *The Life and Letters of Charles Darwin*. 2 vols. New York: D. Appleton, 1896.

———. *The Life and Letters of Charles Darwin, Including an Autobiographical Chapter*. 3 vols. London: John Murray, 1888.

———. *The Life and Letters of Charles Darwin, Including an Autobiographical Chapter*. 2 vols. New York: Appleton, 1898.

Daston, Lorraine. *Classical Probability in the Enlightenment*. Princeton: Princeton University Press, 1988.

Davids, Caroline A. F. Rhys. *Buddhism: A Study of the Buddhist Norm*. London: T. Butterworth, 1928.

Davids, T. W. *Buddhism: Its History and Literature*. New York: G. P. Putnam's Sons, 1896.

Davis, J. R. Ainsworth. *Thomas H. Huxley*. New York: E. P. Dutton, 1907.

Davis, Roy. *The Darwin Conspiracy: Origins of a Scientific Crime*. London: Golden Square Books, 2008.

Dawkins, Richard. *The God Delusion*. Boston: Houghton Mifflin, 2008.

Dawson, Gowan, and Bernard Lightman. *Victorian Scientific Naturalism: Community, Identity, Continuity*. Chicago: University of Chicago Press, 2014.

Dennett, Daniel C. *Darwin's Dangerous Idea: Evolution and the Meanings of Life*. London: Allen Lane, 1995.

Denton, Michael. *Evolution: A Theory in Crisis*. Bethesda, MD: Adler and Adler, 1989.

Desmond, Adrian. *Huxley: From Devil's Disciple to Evolution's High Priest*. Reading, MA: Addison-Wesley, 1997.

———. *Richard Owen: Victorian Naturalist*. New Haven: Yale University Press, 1994.

Desmond, Adrian, and James Moore. *Darwin: The Life of a Tormented Evolutionist*. London: Michael Joseph, 1991.

Dewey, John. *A Common Faith*. New Haven: Yale University Press, 1934.

Dillon, E. J. *The Sceptics of the Old Testament: Job, Koheleth, Agur*. London: Isbister, 1895.

Dorrien, Gary. *The Making of American Liberal Theology: Idealism, Realism, and Modernity, 1900–1950*. Louisville: Westminster John Knox Press, 2003.

Doyle, Arthur Conan. *The History of Spiritualism*. 2 vols. Cambridge: Cambridge University Press, 2011 [1926].

Drey, Sylvan. *Herbert Spencer's Theory of Religion and Morality*. London: Williams and Norgate, 1887.

Du Gard, Roger Martin. *Jean Barois*. New York: Bobbs-Merrill, 1969 [1913].

Duncan, D. (ed.). *Life and Letters of Herbert Spencer*. London: Williams and Norgate, 1911.

Dunning, William A. *The Political Theories from Rousseau to Spencer*. New York: Macmillan, 1920.

Durant, John (ed.). *Darwinism and Divinity*. Oxford: Blackwell, 1985.

Eisley, Loren. *Darwin's Century: Evolution and the Men Who Discovered It*. New York: Barnes and Noble, 2009 [1958].

Ellwood, Charles A. *The Story of Social Philosophy*. New York: Prentice-Hall, 1938.

Emerson, Ralph Waldo. *Ralph Waldo Emerson: Essays and Lectures*. New York: Library of America, 1983.

Feinstein, Howard. *Becoming William James*. Ithaca: Cornell University Press, 1984.

Ferguson, Kennan. *William James: Politics in the Pluriverse*. Lanham, MD: Rowman and Littlefield, 2007.

Fern, Vergilius (ed.). *Contemporary American Theology: Theological Autobiographies*. 2 vols. New York: Round Table Press, 1932–1933.

Ferreira, M. Jamie. *Doubt and Religious Commitment: The Role of the Will in New-man's Thought.* Oxford: Clarendon Press, 1980.

Fetzer. James H. *Scientific Knowledge.* Dordrecht: D. Reidel, 1981.

Fichman, Martin. *Alfred Russel Wallace.* Boston: Twayne, 1981.

———. *An Elusive Victorian: The Evolution of Alfred Russel Wallace.* Chicago: University of Chicago Press, 2004.

———. *Evolutionary Theory and Victorian Culture.* Amherst, NY: Humanity Books, 2002.

Fiske, John. *The Destiny of Man Viewed in the Light of His Origin.* Boston: Houghton, Mifflin 1884.

———. *Excursions of an Evolutionist.* Boston: Houghton, Mifflin, 1884.

———. *Life Everlasting.* Boston: Houghton, Mifflin, 1901.

———. *The Meaning of Infancy.* Boston: Houghton Mifflin, 1883.

———. *Outlines of Cosmic Philosophy, Based on the Doctrine of Evolution, with Criticisms on the Positive Philosophy.* 4 vols. Boston: Houghton, Mifflin, 1902.

Flannery, Michael. *Alfred Russel Wallace: A Rediscovered Life.* Seattle Discovery Institute, 2011.

———. *Alfred Russel Wallace's Theory of Intelligent Evolution: How Wallace's World of Life Challenged Darwinism.* Riesel, TX: Erasmus Press, 2011.

———. *Nature's Prophet: Alfred Russel Wallace and His Evolution from Natural Selection to Natural Theology.* Tuscaloosa: University of Alabama Press, 2018.

Fleming, Donald. *John William Draper and the Religion of Science.* Philadelphia: University of Pennsylvania Press, 1950.

Flint, Robert. *Agnosticism.* New York: Charles Scribner's Sons, 1903.

Foster, George Burman. *The Finality of the Christian Religion.* Chicago: University of Chicago Press, 1906.

Francis, Mark. *Herbert Spencer and the Invention of Modern Life.* Ithaca: Cornell University Press, 2007.

Frankenberry, Nancy. *Religion and Radical Empiricism.* Albany: SUNY Press, 1987.

Franklin, J. Jeffrey. *Spirit Matters: Occult Beliefs, Alternative Religions, and the Crisis of Faith in Victorian Britain.* Ithaca: Cornell University Press, 2018.

Frothingham, O. B. *The Religion of Humanity.* New York: D. G. Francis, 1873.

Fuller, Steve. *Science vs. Religion.* Cambridge: Polity Press, 2007.

Gane, Mike. *Auguste Comte.* London: Routledge, 2006.

Gardner, Howard. *Creating Minds: An Anatomy of Creativity Seen through the Lives of Freud, Einstein, Picasso, Stravinsky, Eliot, Graham, and Gandhi.* New York: Basic Books, 2011 [1993].

Gayon, Jean. *Darwinism's Struggle for Survival: Heredity and the Hypothesis of Natural Selection.* Cambridge: Cambridge University Press, 1998.

George, Henry. *Progress and Poverty.* New York: Modern Library, 1938.

Gillespie, Neal C. *Charles Darwin and the Problem of Creation.* Chicago: University of Chicago Press, 1979.

Gillies, Donald. *Philosophical Theories of Probability.* London: Routledge, 2000.

Gladstone, W. E. (ed.). *The Works of Joseph Butler, D.C.L., Sometime Lord Bishop of Durham.* 2 vols. Oxford: Clarendon Press, 1897.

Glick, Thomas F. (ed.). *The Comparative Reception of Darwinism.* Austin: University of Texas Press, 1974.

Gray, Asa. *Darwiniana: Essays and Reviews Pertaining to Darwinism.* New York: D. Appleton, 1986.

———. *Natural Science and Religion: Two Lectures.* New York: Scribner's, 1880.

Gruber, Jacob W. *A Conscience in Conflict: The Life of St. George Jackson Mivart.* New York: Columbia University Press, 1960.

Hacking, Ian. *The Logic of Statistical Inference.* New York: Cambridge University Press, 1965.

———. *The Taming of Chance.* New York: Cambridge University Press, 1990.

Haeckel, Ernst. *Riddle of the Universe at the Close of the Nineteenth Century.* New York: Harper and Brothers, 1900.

Haller, John S. *Outcasts from Evolution: Scientific Attitudes of Racial Inferiority, 1859–1900.* Urbana: University of Illinois Press, 1971.

———. *Shadow Medicine: The Placebo in Conventional and Alternative Therapies.* New York: Columbia University Press, 2014.

Hardinge, Emma Britten. *Modern American Spiritualism: A Twenty Years' Record of the Communion between Earth and the World of Spirits.* New York: the Author, 1870.

Harnack, Adolf. *The Mission and Expansion of Christianity in the First Three Centuries.* Grand Rapids, MI: Christian Classics Ethereal Library, 2005.

Harp, Gillis J. *Positivist Republic: Auguste Comte and the Reconstruction of American Liberalism, 1865–1920.* University Park: Pennsylvania State University Press, 1995.

Harrington, Anne. *The Cure Within: A History of Mind-Body Medicine.* New York: Norton, 2008.

Harris, Marvin. *The Rise of Anthropological Theory.* London: Routledge and Kegan Paul, 1968.

Harris, Sam. *The End of Faith: Religion, Terror, and the Future of Reason.* New York: W. W. Norton, 2004.

Harrison, Frederic. *On Society.* London: Macmillan, 1918.

Hartshorne, Charles, Paul Weiss, and Arthur W. Burks (eds.). *Collected Papers of Charles Sanders Peirce.* 8 vols. Cambridge: Harvard University Press, 1931–58.

Harvey, Van A. *The Historian and the Believer.* New York: Macmillan, 1965.

Hawkins, Mike. *Social Darwinism in European and American Thought, 1860–1945: Nature as Model and Nature as Threat.* New York: Palgrave, 1997.

Hawkins, Richmond L. *Auguste Comte and the United States, 1816–1853.* Cambridge: Harvard University Press, 1938.

Hawkins, Stephen, Daniel Yudkin, Miriam Juan-Torres, and Tim Dixon. *Hidden Tribes: A Study of America's Polarized Landscape.* New York: More in Common, 2018.

Haydon, A. Eustace. *Biography of the Gods*. New York: Macmillan, 1945.

Heineman, Robert A. *Authority and the Liberal Tradition: From Hobbes to Rorty*. Durham, NC: Carolina Academic Press, 1984.

Helmstadter, Richard J., and Bernard Lightman (eds.). *Victorian Faith in Crisis: Essays on Continuity and Change in Nineteenth-Century Religious Belief*. Houndmills, Hampshire: Macmillan, 1990.

Henderson, Harold. *Catalyst for Controversy: Paul Carus of Open Court*. Carbondale: Southern Illinois University Press, 1993.

Herbert, Sandra (ed.). *The Red Notebook of Charles Darwin*. Ithaca: Cornell University Press, 1980.

Hick, John. *Philosophy of Religion*. Englewood Cliffs, NJ: Prentice-Hall, 1990.

Hitchcock, Ethan Allen. *Remarks upon Alchemy and the Alchemists*. Boston: Crosby, Nichols, 1857.

———. *Swedenborg, a Hermetic Philosopher*. New York: D. Appleton, 1858.

Hitchens, Christopher. *God Is Not Great: How Religion Poisons Everything*. New York: Twelve, 2007.

Hodge, Charles. *What Is Darwinism?* N.p.: BiblioBazaar, 2007 [1874].

Hofstadter, Richard. *Social Darwinism in American Thought*. Boston: Beacon Press, 1955.

Holifield, E. Brooks. *Theology in America: Christian Thought from the Age of the Puritans to the Civil War*. New Haven: Yale University Press, 2003.

Holt, Henry. *Garrulities of an Octogenarian Editor, with Other Essays Somewhat Biographical and Autobiographical*. Boston: Henry Holt, 1923.

Howarth, O. J. R. *The British Association for the Advancement of Science: A Retrospect, 1831–1921*. London: The Association, 1922.

Hudson, William Henry. *An Introduction to the Philosophy of Herbert Spencer*. London: Watts, 1904.

Hunter, James Davison. *Culture Wars: The Struggle to Define America*. New York: Basic Books, 1991.

Huxley, Thomas H. *Darwiniana: Essays*. New York: D. Appleton, 1896.

———. *Evolution and Ethics, and Other Essays*. New York: D. Appleton, 1894.

———. *Lay Sermons, Addresses, and Reviews*. London: Macmillan, 1887.

———. *Life and Letters of Thomas Huxley*. 3 vols. London: Macmillan, 1913.

———. *Man's Place in Nature, and Other Anthropological Essays*. New York: D. Appleton 1894.

———. *Man's Place in Nature, and Other Essays*. New York: E. P. Dutton, 1910.

———. *Science and Christian Tradition*. New York: D. Appleton, 1896.

Ingersoll, Robert G. *Works of Robert G. Ingersoll*. 13 vols. New York: Dresden, 1909–1915.

Ingram, John K. *Passages from the Letters of Auguste Comte Selected and Translated*. London: Adam and Charles Black, 1901.

Irvine, William. *Apes, Angels and Victorians: The Story of Darwin, Huxley, and Evolution*. New York: McGraw-Hill, 1955.

James, Henry (ed.). *The Letters of William James.* 2 vols. Boston: Atlantic Monthly Press, 1920.

James, William. *Collected Essays and Reviews.* London: Longmans, Green, 1920.

————. *Essays in Radical Empiricism.* Cambridge: Harvard University Press, 1986.

————. *Human Immortality: Two Supposed Objections to the Doctrine.* London: Archibald Constable, 1906.

————. *Memories and Studies.* New York: Longmans, Green, 1911.

————. *A Pluralistic Universe.* New York: Longmans, Green, 1909.

————. *Pragmatism.* Cambridge: Harvard University Press, 1975.

————. *Pragmatism, a New Name for Some Old Ways of Thinking.* New York: Longman, Green, 1907.

————. *Pragmatism, and Other Writings.* New York: Penguin Books, 2000.

————. *Pragmatism and the Meaning of Truth.* Cambridge: Harvard University Press, 1975.

————. *Psychology, Briefer Course.* New York: Henry Holt, 1913.

————. *Some Problems of Philosophy.* Cambridge: Harvard University Press, 1979.

————. *The Varieties of Religious Experience: A Study in Human Nature: Being the Gifford Lectures on Natural Religion Delivered at Edinburgh in 1901–1902.* New York: Modern Library, 1902.

————. *The Will to Believe, and Other Essays on Popular Philosophy.* London: Longmans, Green, 1897.

————. *Writings, 1902–1910.* New York: Library of America, 1987.

Jensen, John Vernon. *Thomas Henry Huxley: Communicating for Science.* Newark: University of Delaware Press, 1991.

Johnson, Curtis. *Darwin's Dice: The Idea of Chance in the Thought of Charles Darwin.* New York: Oxford University Press, 2015.

Jones, Greta, and Robert Peel. *Herbert Spencer: The Intellectual Legacy.* London: Galton Institute, 2004.

Kaufman, Walter (ed.). *Religion from Tolstoy to Camus.* New York: Harper and Row, 1961.

Kellogg, Vernon L. *Darwinism To-Day: A Discussion of Present-Day Scientific Criticism of the Darwinian Selection Theories, Together with a Brief Account of the Principal Other Auxiliary and Alternative Theories of Species-Forming.* London: Bell, 1889.

Kennedy, James Gettier. *Herbert Spencer.* Boston: Twayne, 1978.

Ker, Ian. *The Cambridge Companion to John Henry Newman.* Cambridge: Cambridge University Press, 2009.

————. *John Henry Newman: A Biography.* New York: Oxford University Press, 2009.

Kloppenberg, James. *Uncertain Victory: Social Democracy and Progressivism in European and American Thought, 1870–1920.* New York: Oxford University Press, 1986.

Kohn, D. (ed.). *The Darwinian Heritage.* Princeton: Princeton University Press, 1985.

Krumbine, Miles H. (ed.). *Essays in Honor of Dean Shailer Mathews*. New York: Macmillan, 1933.

Kuklick, Bruce. *The Rise of American Philosophy, Cambridge, Massachusetts, 1860–1930*. New Haven: Yale University Press, 1977.

Lamarck, J. B. *Zoological Philosophy: An Exposition with Regard to the Natural History of Animals*. Chicago: University of Chicago Press, 1984 [1809].

Lamont, Peter. *Extraordinary Beliefs: A Historical Approach to a Psychological Problem*. Cambridge: Cambridge University Press, 2013.

Lane, Christopher. *The Age of Doubt: Tracing the Roots of Our Religious Uncertainty*. New Haven: Yale University Press, 2011.

Larsen, Timothy. *Crisis of Doubt: Honest Faith in Nineteenth-Century England*. Oxford: Oxford University Press, 2006.

Larson, Edward J. *Evolution: The Remarkable History of a Scientific Theory*. New York: Modern Library, 2004.

Laslett, Peter. *The World We Have Lost*. London: Methuen, 1965.

Lenin, Vladimir. *Materialism and Empirio-Criticism*. New York: International, 1927–1932.

Lentricchia, Frank. *Ariel and the Police: Michel Foucault, William James, Wallace Stevens*. Madison: University of Wisconsin Press, 1988.

Lewis, R. W. B. *The Jameses: A Family Narrative*. New York: Farrar, Straus and Giroux, 1991.

Lightman, Bernard. *The Age of Scientific Naturalism: Tyndall and His Contemporaries*. London: Pickering and Chatto, 2014.

———. *Evolutionary Naturalism in Victorian Britain: The "Darwinians" and Their Critics*. Farnham, England: Ashgate/Variorum, 2009.

———. *The Origins of Agnosticism: Victorian Unbelief and the Limits of Knowledge*. Baltimore: Johns Hopkins University Press, 1987.

———. *Victorian Science in Context*. Chicago: University of Chicago Press, 1997.

———. *Victorian Scientific Naturalism: Community, Identity, Continuity*. Chicago: University of Chicago Press, 2014.

Lill, William Samuel. *Characteristics from the Writings of John Henry Newman*. London: Henry S. King, 1874.

Lillie, Arthur. *The Influence of Buddhism on Primitive Christianity*. London: Swan Sonnenschein, 1893.

Lindsey, William D. *Shailer Mathews' Lives of Jesus—The Search for a Theological Foundation for the Social Gospel*. Albany: SUNY Press, 1997.

Livingston, James. *Pragmatism and the Political Economy of Cultural Revolution, 1850–1940*. Chapel Hill: University of North Carolina Press, 1994.

Loetscher, Lefferts A. (ed.). *Twentieth-Century Theology at Chicago*. Grand Rapids, MI: Baker, 1955.

Lovejoy, Arthur O. *The Great Chain of Being: A Study of the History of an Idea*. New York: Harper and Row, 1965.

———. *The Thirteen Pragmatisms, and Other Essays*. Baltimore: Johns Hopkins Press, 1963.

Lukacs, John. *At the End of an Age*. New Haven: Yale University Press, 2002.

Lyons, Sherrie L. *Species, Serpents, Spirits, and Skulls: Science at the Margins in the Victorian Age*. New York: State University of New York Press, 2009.

————. *Thomas Henry Huxley: The Evolution of a Scientist*. Amherst, NY: Prometheus Books, 1999.

Mackie, John L. *Truth, Probability, and Paradox*. Oxford: Clarendon Press, 1973.

Manier, Edward. *The Young Darwin and His Cultural Circle*. Dordrecht, Holland, D. Reidel, 1978.

Manuel, Frank Edward. *The New World of Henri Saint-Simon*. Cambridge: Harvard University Press, 1956.

————. *The Prophets of Paris: Turgot, Condorcet, Saint-Simon, Fourier and Comte*. New York: Harper and Row, 1965.

Marchant, James (ed.). *Alfred Russel Wallace: Letters and Reminiscences*. 2 vols. New York: Harper, 1916.

Martin, Brian. *John Henry Newman: His Life and Work*. London: Continuum, 2000.

Matthiessen, F. O. *American Renaissance: Art and Expression in the Age of Emerson and Whitman*. New York: Oxford University Press, 1941.

McCalman, Iain. *Darwin's Armada: Four Voyages and the Battle for the Theory of Evolution*. New York: W. W. Norton, 2009.

McCosh, James. *Boston Lectures, 1870: Christianity and Skepticism*. Boston, 1870.

————. *Christianity and Positivism*. New York: R. Carter, 1871.

————. *The Method of Divine Government, Physical and Moral*. New York: R. Carter, 1855.

————. *Questions of Modern Thought*. Philadelphia: Ziegler and McCrudy, 1871.

McGrath, Alister. *The Twilight of Atheism: The Rise and Fall of Disbelief in the Modern World*. New York: Doubleday, 2006.

McLoughlin, William G. *The Meaning of Henry Ward Beecher: An Essay on the Shifting Values of Mid-Victorian America, 1840–1870*. New York: Knopf, 1970.

Mead, Sidney. *The Lively Experiment*. New York: Harper and Row, 1963.

Menand, Louis. *The Metaphysical Club: A Story of Ideas in America*. Boston: Houghton Mifflin, 2006.

Mill, John Stuart. *Auguste Comte and Positivism*. London: N. Trübner, 1866.

————. *Utilitarianism*. New York: Liberal Arts Press, 1957.

Mitchell, P. Chalmers. *Thomas Henry Huxley: A Sketch of His Life and Work*. New York: G. P. Putnam's Sons, 1900.

Monod, Jacques. *Chance and Necessity*. New York: Knopf, 1971.

Moore, James. *The Post-Darwinian Controversies: A Study of the Protestant Struggle to Come to Terms with Darwin in Great Britain and America, 1870–1900*. Cambridge: Cambridge University Press, 1979.

Müller, Max. *Chips from a German Workshop*. Vol. I. New York: Scribner, Armstrong, 1874.

Murphet, Howard. *When Daylight Come: A Biography of Helena Petrovna Blavatsky*. Wheaton, IL: Theosophical, 1975.

Myers, Gerald Eugene. *William James: His Life and Thought.* New Haven: Yale
  University Press, 1986.

Nelson, Alvin F. *The Development of Lester Ward's World View.* Ft. Worth, TX:
  Branch-Smith, 1968.

Newman, Jay. *The Mental Philosophy of John Henry Newman.* Waterloo, ON: Wil-
  frid Laurier University Press, 1986.

Newman, John Henry. *Apologia pro Vita Sua.* London: Longman, Green, Longman, Roberts and Green, 1864.

———. *Discourses Addressed to Mixed Congregations.* London: Longman, Brown,
  Green, and Longmans, 1849.

———. *Discourses Addressed to Mixed Congregations.* London: James Duffy, 1862.

———. *Discourses Addressed to Mixed Congregations.* Denville, NJ: Dimension
  Books, 1984.

———. *Discussion and Arguments.* London: Longmans, Green, 1891.

———. *An Essay in Aid of a Grammar of Assent.* London: Burns, Oates, 1870.

———. *Essays Critical and Historical.* London: Basil Montagu Pickering, 1871.

———. *The Idea of a University.* London: Basil Montagu Pickering, 1873.

———. *Letters and Correspondence of John Henry Newman during his Life in the English Church.* 2 vols. London: Longmans, Green, 1891.

———. *Sermons Preached before the University of Oxford between 1826 and 1843.*
  London: Rivingtons, 1887.

———. *Two Essays on Scriptural Miracles and on Ecclesiastical.* 2nd ed. London:
  Pickering, 1870.

Nicholls, David, and Fergus Kerr (eds.). *John Henry Newman: Reason, Rhetoric,
  and Romanticism.* Carbondale: Southern Illinois University Press, 1991.

Niebuhr, H. Richard. *The Kingdom of God in America.* Hamden, CT: Shoe String
  Press, 1956.

Noll, Mark. *America's God: From Jonathan Edwards to Abraham Lincoln.* Oxford:
  Oxford University Press, 2002.

Norris, Thomas J. *Newman and His Theological Method: A Guide for the Theologian
  Today.* Leiden: E. J. Brill, 1977.

Numbers, Ronald L. *Darwinism Comes to America.* Cambridge: Harvard University Press, 1998.

Olcott, Henry S. *People from the Other Side.* Hartford, CT: American, 1875.

Oldroyd, D. R. *Darwinian Impacts: An Introduction to the Darwinian Revolution.*
  Atlantic Highlands, NJ: Humanities Press, 1980.

Ospovat, Dov. *The Development of Darwin's Theory.* Cambridge: Cambridge University Press, 1981.

Owen, Robert Dale. *Debatable Land between This World and the Next.* New York:
  G. W. Carleton, 1872.

———. *Footfalls on the Boundary of Another World.* Philadelphia: J. B. Lippincott,
  1860.

Pailin, David A. *The Way to Faith: An Examination of Newman's "Grammar of*

Assent" as a Response to the Search for Certainty in Faith. London: Epworth Press, 1969.

Parrington, Vernon Louis. *The Beginnings of Critical Realism in America: 1860–1920*. New York: Harcourt, Brace, and World, 1958 [1930].

Parson, Talcott. *The Structure of Social Action*. New York: Free Press, 1968 [1937].

Pascal, Blaise. *Pensées de Pascal: Précédés de sa vie*. Paris: Librairie de Firmin Didot Frères, 1855.

Peck, William George. *The Social Implications of the Oxford Movement*. New York: C. Scribner's Sons, 1933.

Peel, J. D. Y. *Herbert Spencer: The Evolution of a Sociologist*. New York: Basic Books, 1971.

Perry, Ralph Barton. *In the Spirit of William James*. Bloomington: Indiana University Press, 1958.

———. *The Thought and Character of William James*. 2 vols. Boston: Little, Brown, 1935.

———. *The Thought and Character of William James: Briefer Version*. New York: Harper and Row, 1935.

Pickering, Mary. *August Comte*. Vol. 1, *An Intellectual Biography*. Cambridge: Cambridge University Press, 1993.

Piott, Steven L. *American Reformers, 1870–1920: Progressives in Word and Deed*. Lanham, MD: Rowman and Littlefield, 2006.

Plantinga, Alvin. *Where the Conflict Really Lies: Science, Religion, and Naturalism*. New York: Oxford University Press, 2011.

Pollak, Gustav. *Fifty Years of American Idealism*. Boston: Houghton Mifflin, 1915.

Popkin, Richard H. *The History of Skepticism from Erasmus to Descartes*. New York: Humanities Press, 1964.

Porter, Theodore M. *The Rise of Statistical Thinking, 1820–1900*. Princeton: Princeton University Press, 1986.

Raby, Peter. *Alfred Russel Wallace: A Life*. Princeton: Princeton University Press, 2001.

Rafferty, Edward C. *Apostle of Human Progress: Lester Frank Ward and American Political Thought, 1841–1913*. Lanham, MD: Rowman and Littlefield, 2003.

Rauschenbusch, Walter. *Christianity and the Social Crisis*. New York: Macmillan, 1907.

———. *Christianizing the Social Order*. New York: Macmillan Co., 1914.

Reichenbach, H. *The Theory of Probability: An Inquiry into the Logical and Mathematical Foundation of the Calculus of Probability*. Berkeley: University of California Press, 1949.

Renouvier, Charles. *Essais de critique générale*. Paris: Librairie Philosophique de Ladrange, 1864.

Richardson, Robert D. *William James: In the Maelstrom of American Modernism: A Biography*. Boston: Houghton Mifflin, 2006.

Riser, Andrew C. *The Chautauqua Movement: Protestants, Progressives, and the*

*Culture of Modern Liberalism*. New York: Columbia University Press, 2003.

Robbins, Keith (ed.). *Religion and Humanism*. Oxford: Basil Blackwell, 1981.

Rogers, E. C. *Philosophy of Mysterious Agents, Human and Mundane*. Boston: John P. Jewett, 1853.

Rorty, Richard. *Philosophy and Social Hope*. New York: Penguin, 1999.

Rouvre, Charles de. *L'amoureuse histoire d'Auguste Comte et de Clotilde de Vaux*. Paris: Calmann-Levy, 1917.

Rucker, Darnell. *The Chicago Pragmatists*. Minneapolis: University of Minnesota Press, 1969.

Ruse, Michael. *The Darwinian Revolution: Science Red in Tooth and Claw*. Chicago: University of Chicago Press, 1979.

Russell, Bertrand. *A History of Western Philosophy*. New York: Simon and Schuster, 1945.

Saint-Simon, Henri de. *The New Christianity*. London: B. D. Cousins and P. Wilson, 1834.

———. *Social Organization, the Science of Man, and Other Writings*. New York: Harper and Row, 1964.

Sargent, Epes. *The Scientific Basis of Spiritualism*. Boston: Colby and Rich, 1881.

Sarton, George. *The Life of Science: Essays in the History of Civilization*. Bloomington: Indiana University Press, 1960.

Schlesinger, Arthur M., and Morton White (eds.). *Paths of American Thought*. Boston: Houghton Mifflin, 1970.

Schlossberg, Herbert. *Conflict and Crisis in the Religious Life of Late Victorian England*. New Brunswick, NJ: Transaction, 2009.

Seydel, Rudolf. *Die Buddha-Legende und das Leben Jesu nach den Evangeli*. Leipzig: Otto Schulze, 1884.

Shermer, Michael. *In Darwin's Shadow: The Life and Science of Alfred Russel Wallace*. Oxford: Oxford University Press, 2002.

Simon, Walter Michael. *European Positivism in the Nineteenth Century: An Essay in Intellectual History*. Ithaca: Cornell University Press, 1972.

Sklar, Lawrence. *Physics and Chance: Philosophical Issues in the Foundations of Statistical Mechanics*. Cambridge: Cambridge University Press, 1993.

Slater, Michael R. *William James on Ethics and Faith*. Cambridge: Cambridge University Press, 2009.

Slotten, Ross A. *The Heretic in Darwin's Court: The Life of Alfred Russel Wallace*. New York: Columbia University Press, 2004.

Smith, Charles Hyde, and George Beccaloni (eds.). *Natural Selection and Beyond: The Intellectual Legacy of Alfred Russel Wallace*. Oxford: Oxford University Press, 2008.

Smith, Gerald B. *Current Christian Thinking*. Chicago: University of Chicago Press, 1928.

Smith, James W., and A. L. Jamieson (eds.). *Religion in American Life*. Vol. 1, *The Shaping of American Religion*. Princeton: Princeton University Press, 1961.

Smith, Kenneth L. *Shailer Mathews: Theologian of Social Process.* PhD diss. Duke University, 1959.

Sober, Elliott. *The Nature of Selection: Evolutionary Theory in Philosophical Focus.* Cambridge: MIT Press, 1984.

Spencer, Herbert. *An Autobiography of Herbert Spencer.* 2 vols. New York: D. Appleton, 1904.

———. *The Classification of the Sciences to Which Are Added Reasons for Dissenting from the Philosophy of M. Comte.* New York: D. Appleton, 1864.

———. *Essays Scientific, Political and Speculative.* 3 vols. London: Williams and Norgate, 1891.

———. *First Principles.* New York: D. Appleton, 1898.

———. *Principles of Biology.* 2 vols. New York: D. Appleton, 1866.

———. *Principles of Psychology.* 2nd ed. London: Williams and Norgate, 1870.

———. *Principles of Sociology.* New York: Appleton, 1897.

———. *Social Statics; or, The Conditions Essential to Human Happiness Specified, and the First of Them Developed.* London: John Chapman, 1851.

———. *Study of Sociology.* New York: D. Appleton, 1874.

St. Aubyn, Giles. *Souls in Torment: Victorian Faith in Crisis.* London: Sinclair-Stevenson, 2011.

Stenger, Victor J. *The New Atheism: Taking a Stand for Science and Reason.* New York: Prometheus Books, 2009.

Stephens, Lester D. *Joseph LeConte: Gentle Prophet of Evolution.* Baton Rouge: Louisiana State University Press, 1982.

Strange, Roderick. *John Henry Newman: A Mind Alive.* London: Darton Longman and Todd, 2008.

Sugg, Joyce. *John Henry Newman: Snapdragon in the Wall.* Huntington, IN: Our Sunday Visitor, 1982.

Sumner, William Graham. *Folkways: A Study of the Sociological Importance of Uses, Manners, Customs, Mores and Morals.* Boston: Ginn, 1906.

———. *What the Social Classes Owe to Each Other.* New York: Harper and Brothers, 1883.

Sylvest, Casper. *British Liberal Internationalism, 1880–1930: Making Progress?* Manchester: Manchester University Press, 2009.

Taylor, Michael. *The Philosophy of Herbert Spencer.* London: Continuum, 2007.

Therborn, G. *The Ideology of Power and the Power of Ideology.* London: Verso, 1980.

Thomas, à Kempis. *The Imitation of Christ.* New York: E. P. Dutton, 1910.

Thompson, Kenneth. *Auguste Comte: The Foundation of Sociology.* London: Nelson, 1976.

Thomson, Keith. *The Young Charles Darwin.* New Haven: Yale University Press, 2009.

Thoreau, Henry David. *The Writings of Henry David Thoreau: Excursions, Translations, and Poems.* Boston: Houghton Mifflin, 1906.

Thrower, James. *A Short History of Western Atheism.* London: Pemberton, 1971.

*Tracts for the Times.* 6 vols. Oxford: J. G. and F. Rivington and J. H. Parker, 1834–41.

Turner, Frank M. *Between Science and Religion: The Reaction to Scientific Naturalism in Late Victorian England.* New Haven: Yale University Press, 1974.

———. *Contesting Cultural Authority: Essays in Victorian Intellectual Life.* Cambridge: Cambridge University Press, 1993.

———. *John Henry Newman: The Challenge to Evangelical Religion.* New Haven: Yale University Press, 2002.

Turner, Jonathan H. *Herbert Spencer: A Renewed Appreciation.* Beverly Hills: Sage, 1985.

Tuttle, Hudson. *Arcana of Spiritualism.* Chicago: J. R. Francis, 1904.

Tweed, Thomas A. *The American Encounter with Buddhism 1844–1912: Victorian Culture and the Limits of Dissent.* Bloomington: Indiana University Press, 1992.

Twiss, Sir Travers. *Religion and Science, the Reconciliation Mania of Dr. Paul Carus of Open Court.* Chicago: H. Green, 19??.

Underwood, B. F. *The Influence of Christianity on Civilization.* New York: Truth Seeker Co., 1889.

Underwood, B. F., and S. A. *A Statement by the Editors of the Open Court to Their Connection with That Journal and Their Reasons for Resigning.* N.p., 1887.

United States Geological Survey. *Annual Report of the United States Geological Survey, 1881–1904.* Washington, DC: Government Printing Office, 1883–1904.

Vorzimmer, Peter J. *Charles Darwin: The Years of Controversy.* Philadelphia: Temple University, 1970.

Wallace, Alfred Russel. *Contributions to the Theory of Natural Selection.* London: Macmillan, 1870.

———. *Darwinism: An Exposition of the Theory of Natural Selection, with Some of Its Applications.* London: Macmillan, 1889.

———. *A Defense of Modern Spiritualism.* Boston: Colby and Rich, 1874.

———. *Man's Place in the Universe.* New York: McClure, Phillips, 1903.

———. *My Life: A Record of Events and Opinions.* 2 vols. New York: Dodd, Mead, 1905.

———. *Natural Selection and Tropical Nature: Essays on Descriptive and Theoretical Biology.* London: Macmillan, 1895.

———. *On Miracles and Modern Spiritualism.* London: James Burns, 1875.

———. *Social Environment and Moral Progress.* New York: Cassell, 1913.

———. *The Wonderful Century.* New York: Dodd, Mead, 1898.

———. *The World of Life—a Manifestation of Creative Power, Directive Mind and Ultimate Purpose.* London: Chapman and Hall, 1911.

Ward, Lester. *Dynamic Sociology, or Applied Social Science, as Based upon Statical Sociology and the Less Complex Sciences.* New York: D. Appleton, 1883.

———. *Glimpses of the Cosmos.* 6 vols. New York: G. P. Putnam's Sons, 1913.

———. *Outlines of Sociology.* New York: Macmillan, 1898.

———. *Psychic Factors of Civilization.* Boston: Ginn, 1893.

————. *Pure Sociology, A Treatise on the Origin and Spontaneous Development of Society*. New York: Macmillan, 1903.

Ward, Wilfred. *The Life of John Henry Newman*. London: Longmans, Green, 1912.

Weir, Todd H. *Monism: Science, Philosophy, Religion, and the History of a Worldview*. New York: Palgrave Macmillan, 2012.

Wernick, Andrew. *Auguste Comte and the Religion of Humanity: The Post-Theistic Program of French Social Theory*. Cambridge: Cambridge University Press, 2001.

West, Cornel. *The American Evasion of Philosophy: A Genealogy of Pragmatism*. Madison: University of Wisconsin Press, 1989.

Whitehead, Alfred North. *Modes of Thought*. New York: Free Press, 1938.

Wilson, J. R. *Darwinism and the American Intellectual*. Homewood, IL: Dorsey Press, 1967.

Wright, Terrence R. *John Henry Newman, a Man for Our Time?* Newcastle upon Tyne: Grevatt and Grevatt, 1983.

Wyld, G. *Theosophy and the Higher Life*. London: Trübner, 1881.

# Index